—

EARLY MUSIC HISTORY 6

EDITORIAL BOARD

EARLY MUSIC HISTORY 6

STUDIES IN MEDIEVAL
AND
EARLY MODERN MUSIC

Edited by

IAIN FENLON
Fellow of King's College, Cambridge

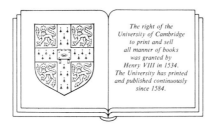

The right of the
University of Cambridge
to print and sell
all manner of books
was granted by
Henry VIII in 1534.
The University has printed
and published continuously
since 1584.

CAMBRIDGE UNIVERSITY PRESS

Cambridge

London   New York   New Rochelle

Melbourne   Sydney

Published by the Press Syndicate of the University of Cambridge
The Pitt Building, Trumpington Street, Cambridge CB2 1RP
32 East 57th Street, New York, NY 10022, USA
10 Stamford Road, Oakleigh, Melbourne 3166, Australia

First published 1986

Printed in Great Britain at the University Press, Cambridge

ISSN 0261–1279
ISBN 0 521 33463 2

CONTENTS

Contents

NOTES FOR CONTRIBUTORS

PRESENTATION

Contributors should write in English, or be willing to have their articles translated. All typescripts must be double spaced with margins of at least 2.5 cm (1″). Footnotes, bibliographies, appendixes, tables and displayed quotations must also be double spaced. The 'top' (ribbon) copy of the typescript must be supplied. Scripts submitted for consideration will not normally be returned unless specifically requested.

Tables, graphs, diagrams and music examples must be supplied on separate sheets from the text of the article. Illustrations should be in the form of black and white prints, measuring 20.3 × 15.2 cm (8″ × 6″). All illustrative material should carry the contributor's name and should be numbered and carefully keyed into the typescript. Captions should be separately typed, double spaced.

SPELLING

English spelling, idiom and terminology should be used, e.g. bar (not measure), note (not tone), quaver (not eighth note). Where there is an option, '-ise' endings should be preferred to '-ize'.

PUNCTUATION

English punctuation practice should be followed: (1) single quotation marks, except for 'a "quote" within a quote'; (2) punctuation outside quotation marks, unless a complete sentence is quoted; (3) no comma before 'and' in a series; (4) footnote indicators follow punctuation; (5) square brackets [ ] only for interpolation in quoted matter; (6) no stop after abbreviations that include the last letter of a word, e.g. Dr, St (but Prof.).

QUOTATIONS

A quotation of no more than 60 words of prose or one line of verse should be continuous within the text and enclosed in single quotation marks. Longer quotations should be displayed and quotation marks should not be used. For quotations from foreign languages, the English translation should be given in the text, the foreign-language original in the footnote.

NUMBERS

Numbers below 100 should be spelled out, except page, bar, folio numbers etc., sums of money and specific quantities, e.g. 20 ducats, 45 mm. Pairs of numbers should be elided as follows: 190–1, 198–9, 198–201, 212–13. Dates should be given in the following forms: 10 January 1983, the 1980s, sixteenth century (16th century in tables and lists), sixteenth-century polyphony.

CAPITALISATION

Incipits in all language (motets, songs, etc.), and titles except in English, should be capitalised as in running prose; titles in English should have all important words capitalised, e.g. *The Pavin of Delight*. Most offices should have a lower-case initial except in official titles, e.g. 'the Lord Chancellor entered the cathedral', 'Bishop Fisher entered the cathedral' (but 'the bishop entered the cathedral'). Names of institutions should have full (not prose-style) capitalisation, e.g. Liceo Musicale.

ITALICS

Titles and incipits of musical works in italic, but not genre titles or sections of the Mass/English Service, e.g. Kyrie, Magnificat. Italics for foreign words should be kept to a minimum; in general they should be used only for unusual words or if a word might be mistaken for English if not italicised. Titles of manuscripts should be roman in quotes, e.g. 'Rules How to Compose'. Names of institutions should be roman.

Notes for Contributors

Authors' and editors' forenames should not be given, only initials; where possible, editors should be given for Festschriften, conference proceedings, symposia, etc. In titles, all important words in English should be capitalised; all other languages should follow prose-style capitalisation, except for journal and series titles which should follow English capitalisation. Titles of series should be included, in roman, where relevant. Journal and series volume numbers should be given in arabic, volumes of a set in roman ('vol.' will not be used). Places and dates of publication should be included but not publishers' names. Dissertation titles should be given in roman and enclosed in quotation marks. Page numbers should be preceded by 'p.' or 'pp.' in all contexts. The first citation of a bibliographical reference should include full details; subsequent citations may use the author's surname, short title and relevant page numbers only. *Ibid.* and *op. cit.* may be used, but not *loc. cit.*

ABBREVIATIONS

Abbreviations for manuscript citations, libraries, periodicals, series, etc. should not be used without explanation; after the first full citation an abbreviation may be used throughout text and notes. Standard abbreviations may be used without explanation. In the text, 'Example', 'Figure' and 'bars' should be used (not 'Ex.', 'Fig.', 'bb.'). In references to manuscripts, 'fols.' should be used (not 'ff.') and 'v' (verso) and 'r' (recto) should be typed superscript where appropriate. The word for 'saint' should be spelled out or abbreviated according to language, e.g. San Andrea, SS. Pietro e Paolo, St Paul, St Agnes, St Denis, Ste Clothilde.

NOTE NAMES

Flats, sharps and naturals should be indicated by the conventional signs, not words. Note names should be roman and capitalised where general, e.g. C major, but should be italic and follow the Helmholtz code where specific ($C_{,,}$ $C_{,}$ C c c' c'' c'''; c' = middle C). A simpler system may be used in discussions of repertories (e.g. chant) where different conventions are followed.

Substantial changes in wording, other than corrections of printing errors, may be subject to a charge.

LAWRENCE F. BERNSTEIN

A FLORENTINE CHANSONNIER OF THE EARLY SIXTEENTH CENTURY: FLORENCE, BIBLIOTECA NAZIONALE CENTRALE, MS MAGLIABECHI XIX 117*

The legacy of Pierre Attaingnant, Royal Printer of Music, has done much to clarify our knowledge of the French polyphonic chanson during the first half of the sixteenth century. The great Parisian printer's invention and introduction of music printing with movable type in 1528 contributed to an increasing coalescence in the style of the chansons composed in France between 1530 and 1550. By mid-century, composers at the French royal court and throughout the provinces, too, routinely composed what came to be known as Parisian chansons, the genre most clearly exemplified in the works of Claudin de Sermisy.[1]

Many problems, however, becloud our view of the sixteenth-century chanson before the ascendancy of the Parisian variety. The

* A shorter version of this paper was read at a colloquium on Renaissance music in honour of Prof. Alvin H. Johnson held at the University of Pennsylvania on 16 April 1982. Other versions were read at the celebration of the fiftieth anniversary of the Isham Memorial Library at Harvard University, on 4 May 1984; and at the Twelfth Annual Conference on Medieval and Renaissance Music, held at Canterbury, 3–6 August 1984.

A generous grant from the American Philosophical Society made it possible for me to examine at length the manuscript treated in this study, along with a significant number of related sources in various Italian libraries. I am also indebted to Profs. Herbert Kellman and Joshua Rifkin for discussing various aspects of *Florence 117* with me.

The sigla used to identify manuscripts and early prints throughout the present study are explicated at the beginning of the Appendix (pp. 88–94).

[1]   On Attaingnant's impact both as inventor and as 'arbiter of taste', see D. Heartz, *Pierre Attaingnant, Royal Printer of Music: A Historical Study and Bibliographical Catalogue* (Berkeley and Los Angeles, 1969), chap. 3. For a study of the stylistic diversity of the French chanson before Attaingnant's influence was fully felt, see L. F. Bernstein, 'The "Parisian Chanson": Problems of Style and Terminology', *Journal of the American Musicological Society*, 31 (1978), pp. 193–240.

repertorial transmission reflected in the important Petrucci chansonniers, for example, needs to be traced more definitively.[2] The very origin of the Parisian chanson is the subject of markedly different interpretations.[3] And, despite recent strides in assigning a number of manuscript chansonniers of the period to French provenance, we still face a dearth of northern sources for the sixteenth-century chanson before the rise of music printing in France.[4]

Such lacunae in our knowledge as these suggest that the relatively few manuscript chansonniers from the early sixteenth century deserve our most scrupulous attention. We need to determine their provenance and chronology – a task already accomplished for many of the sources – and to assess the style of the chansons they contain. Equally great is the need to understand the role these compositions may have played in the dramatic transformations of style that the polyphonic chanson was undergoing at this decisive moment in its history.

One of the most important – and most nettlesome – chansonniers of the early sixteenth century may be found at the Biblioteca

---

[2] An important methodological approach to this question is set forth in S. Boorman, 'Petrucci's Type-Setters and the Process of Stemmatics', *Quellenstudien zur Musik der Renaissance*, I, ed. L. Finscher, Wolfenbütteler Forschungen 6 (Munich, 1981), pp. 245–80.

[3] For a survey of different views of the nascency of the Parisian chanson and a new interpretation, see L. F. Bernstein, 'Notes on the Origin of the Parisian Chanson', *The Journal of Musicology*, 1 (1982), pp. 275–323.

[4] On the chansonniers of the French royal court, see L. Litterick, 'The Manuscript Royal 20.A.XVI of the British Library' (Ph.D. diss., New York University, 1976), pp. 39–82; J. Rifkin, 'Scribal Concordances for Some Renaissance Manuscripts in Florentine Libraries', *Journal of the American Musicological Society*, 26 (1973), pp. 318–26; *idem*, 'Pietrequin Bonnel and Ms. 2794 of the Biblioteca Riccardiana', *ibid.*, 29 (1976), pp. 284–96; and I. Fenlon, 'La diffusion de la chanson continentale dans les manuscrits anglais entre 1509–1570', *La chanson à la renaissance*, ed. J.-M. Vaccaro, Actes du XXe Colloque d'Études Humanistes du Centre d'Études Supérieures de la Renaissance de l'Université de Tours, juillet 1977 (Tours, 1981), pp. 172–81.

Two chansonniers prepared at the court of Marguerite of Austria are provided with scholarly editions and ample commentary in M. Picker, ed., *The Chanson Albums of Marguerite of Austria* (Berkeley and Los Angeles, 1965). And the chansons written down in Paris by a Swiss humanist in 1510 are discussed and edited in *Das Liederbuch des Johannes Heer von Glarus*, ed. A. Geering and H. Trümpy, Schweizerische Musikdenkmäler 5 (Basel, 1967).

An extremely important chansonnier from provincial France in the collection of the University Library at Uppsala was recently introduced by H. M. Brown in his paper, 'A New French Chansonnier of the Early Sixteenth Century', read at the forty-sixth annual meeting of the American Musicological Society, held at Denver in 1980, and to be published in *Musica Disciplina*. I am grateful to Prof. Brown for sending me the typescript of this article prior to its publication.

Nazionale Centrale in Florence: the manuscript Magliabechi XIX 117.[5]

Physical description. The manuscript is written in choirbook format on paper that measures 162×244 mm. The paper is of a grainy quality and has grown brown with age; it contains no watermarks. Fragments of what is presumably the original leather binding are pasted on the new boards into which the manuscript has been bound. The tooling on these leather fragments includes alternating rows of floral swirls and diamond-shaped grids which contain a pattern resembling a sunburst. These particular designs appear often on Italian bookbindings of the late fifteenth and early sixteenth centuries, but they are insufficiently confined to a specific region to bear upon the provenance of our manuscript.[6] Sixty-four folios survive, but there were at one time many more, for the original foliation runs to 87. Leaves have been torn out at various places in the manuscript, and several entire gatherings are missing. Inked calligraphic initials of no more than competent quality appear at intervals, invariably in conjunction with the work of the principal scribe.

Contents. Fifty-one compositions are preserved in what remains of *Florence 117*. Included are 41 chansons (24 for three voices and 17 *a 4*), 3 motets, 4 Italian secular pieces and 8 textless compositions (of which five have been identified and included among the genres just enumerated). The manuscript contains a number of additional unidentified textless fragments. These were copied by a variety of extremely sloppy hands, and they appear in the midst of what seem to be exercises in calligraphy and counterpoint. Only a few ascriptions may be found within the folios of our manuscript: the names of Baccio Fiorentino (= Bartolomeo degli Organi), Izagha (= Isaac?),

---

[5] For a brief description of the manuscript and a somewhat faulty list of its contents, see B. Becherini, *Catalogo dei manoscritti musicali della Biblioteca Nazionale di Firenze* (Kassel, 1959), pp. 51–2.

[6] See, for example, the reproductions of Italian Renaissance bindings from Naples, Urbino and Venice in T. De Marinis, *La legatura artistica in Italia nei secoli XV e XVI* (Florence, 1960), I, pls. XI and C5; II, pl. C15, respectively.

La Fage, Layolle and Mouton appear over seven pieces. But concordances enable us to identify an additional twenty-one compositions as the work of Compère (4 pieces), Antoine de Févin (7), Hayne van Ghizeghem (2), Clément Janequin (1), Thomas Janequin (1), Josquin des Prez (1), Moulu (1), Mouton (2), Prioris (1) and Richafort (1).[7]

Conflicting views of the manuscript's provenance. At first, *Florence 117* was thought to have been of Medicean provenance,[8] for the manuscript bears the stamp (fol. 2^r) of the Biblioteca Mediceo Palatino, a collection that was incorporated within that of the Biblioteca Nazionale Centrale in 1861. The stamp of the latter library was added to *Florence 117* in 1883. That a secular Italian work by Bartolomeo degli Organi can be found within the manuscript has been seen as entirely compatible with a view of the choirbook's Florentine provenance, for the secular music of this composer was generally written for specific occasions in Florence and is otherwise preserved solely in Florentine sources.[9] The manuscript was surely in Italy not long after it was compiled, for, as we have seen, it was bound into leather covers of the sort crafted in Italy around the turn of the sixteenth century. Moreover, the sundry jottings added to the source on various folios include, in several sixteenth-century hands, snippets of what appear to be madrigal texts. They also include – again, in sixteenth-century hands – two names: D[omi]no Ant[oni]o di Jaccopo and D[omi]no Nicc[ol]o d'Alexandro.[10] We shall have occasion to return to the first of these names below.

More recent views of the choirbook's provenance set greater store by an assessment of its physical characteristics and bibliographical ties, and they suggest that the source is a composite manuscript. Several strands of evidence are given in support of this proposition. First, although the Italian secular works contained in the manu-

---

[7] Not every one of these attributions is absolutely secure, however; see below p. 76 and esp. n. 91.

[8] See Becherini, *Catalogo*, p. 51; and D. Heartz, 'Les goûts réunis: Or the Worlds of the Madrigal and the Chanson Confronted', *Chanson & Madrigal, 1480–1530: Studies in Comparison and Contrast*, ed. J. Haar (Cambridge, Mass., 1964), p. 113.

[9] F. D'Accone, 'Alessandro Coppini and Bartolomeo degli Organi: Two Florentine Composers of the Renaissance', *Analecta Musicologica*, 4 (1967), pp. 55–6.

[10] The excerpts from the madrigal texts appear on fols. (22^r), (33^r), (46^v) and (62^v); the names on fol. (32^v) and on the end paper. (Here and throughout this study parentheses are used to designate folio numbers not present in the manuscript; square brackets denote missing folios.)

4

script are seen as having been copied in Florence, the handwriting of the main scribe, among the various hands found in the source, shows unequivocally that he was a northerner. Second, segments of the French repertory included in *Florence 117* are, for the most part, concordant with French sources and foreign to Italian manuscripts. And, finally, the choirbook is not consistently gathered in quinternions, the fascicle structure most often found in Florentine music manuscripts.[11] Two interpretations of the manuscript's provenance have been drawn from this evidence: (1) that the various layers of this manuscript were all compiled in Florence, albeit by different scribes and in a manner very uncharacteristic of Florentine manuscripts of Renaissance polyphony;[12] and (2) that the earliest layer of the manuscript may have been copied in the north, the rest in Florence.[13]

Establishing the provenance of this manuscript is crucial for gaining an understanding of the transmission of its repertory – some of it a unique repertory. And determining the provenance of this source necessitates making a choice between these two conflicting assessments in the literature of our manuscript's place of origin. The evidence upon which these assessments are based is in need of some refinement, which we shall attempt now, turning our attention first to the original foliation of the manuscript.

Foliation. Two systems of foliation may be found in the manuscript: the original one (in ink, in the upper right corners of many – but not all – recto folios) and a modern one (in pencil, near the bottom of the gutter margin of the rectos). The old foliation has many gaps, owing to the excision of numerous leaves as well as to the scribe's failure to number some of the folios. The modern foliation, on the other hand, is consecutive throughout the manuscript and obviously was added after the missing leaves were torn out. References throughout this article will be to the original foliation, which I have attempted to reconstruct.[14] However, to facilitate comparison with other

---

[11] A. Atlas, *The Cappella Giulia Chansonnier (Rome, Biblioteca Apostolica Vaticana, C.G. XIII.27)*, Musicological Studies 27 (Brooklyn, 1975–6), I, p. 244. More detailed information on the fascicle structure of the manuscript is given below (pp. 32–5).

[12] Atlas, *The Cappella Giulia Chansonnier*, I, p. 244.

[13] C. Hamm and H. Kellman, eds., *Census-Catalogue of Manuscript Sources of Polyphonic Music, 1400–1550*, Renaissance Manuscript Studies 1 (Neuhausen-Stuttgart, 1979–), I, p. 226.

[14] The fascicle structure of the manuscript serves as the basis for this reconstruction. See below, pp. 32–5 and Figure 10.

references to our manuscript in the literature, the reconstructed original foliation is matched to the modern series in Table 1. (Parentheses designate folio numbers not present in the manuscript; square brackets denote missing folios. We shall adhere to this convention throughout the present study.)

The original foliation was written in a uniform hand and in a light brown ink, very similar to the ink used by the principal scribe of the manuscript. (All of the other copyists who contributed to the manuscript wrote with dark brown ink.) It is inconceivable, however, that the principal scribe of *Florence 117* provided the original foliation. As we see in Figure 1, the folio numbers were written in the same hand as were those of a related source, *Florence 178*, a chansonnier compiled in Florence in the 1490s.[15] In the latter choirbook the scribe who numbered the folios also provided the tabula that was appended to the manuscript, and the handwriting in which the incipits are written in the tabula is unquestionably a more hurried version of the same hand that provided the incipits and

Table 1 *The original and modern foliation of Florence 117*

Old	Modern	Old	Modern	Old	Modern	Old	Modern
[0]	—	19	(19)	38	32	71	48
(1)	(1)	20	20	39	33	72	49
2	(2)	21	21	40	34	73	50
3	3	(22)	22	41	35	74	51
4	4	(23)	23	42	36	75	52
5	5	24	24	[43]	—	76	53
6	6	(25)	25	[44]	—	77	54
7	7	(26)	26	(45)	37	78	55
8	8	(27)	27	(46)	38	79	56
9	9	[28]	—	[47–61]	—	80	57
10	10	[29]	—	(62)	39	81	58
11	11	[30]	—	(63)	40	82	59
12	12	[31]	—	64	41	83	60
13	13	(32)	28	65	42	[84]	—
14	14	(33)	29	66	43	(85)	(61)
15	15	34	30	67	44	86	(62)
16	16	[35]	—	68	(45)	87	63
17	17	[36]	—	69	46	(88)	64
18	18	37	31	70	47	[89]	—

[15] On the provenance and chronology of *Florence 178*, see Atlas, *The Cappella Giulia Chansonnier*, I, p. 247.

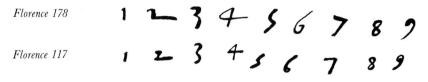

Figure 1   Comparison of the foliation in *Florence 178* and
Florence 117 (diplomatic facsimile)

attributions throughout the manuscript.[16] Indeed, this particular
artisan can be shown to have played an even greater role in the
compilation of *Florence 178*: undoubtedly, he is the first of the two
scribes who copied all of the music. We can ascertain this from the
colours of the inks used. Invariably, whenever we find evidence of a
change in the ink the first music scribe used, the attributions and
incipits on the same folio change accordingly. Significantly,
however, no such correlation occurs where the character of the ink
changes in folios copied by the second music scribe.

Now, the first music scribe of *Florence 178* was an Italian, as we can
easily determine by his corruptions of French texts (e.g. [*J*]*Am pris
amors*, [*E*]*Na tendant*, [*E*]*t quilla dira*, [*A*]*Diu mens amors*, etc.). It is for
this reason that we can tell he could not have been the main scribe of
Florence 117, for the latter artisan, as we have already suggested, was
a northerner, and we shall see presently that he copied French texts
with impeccable accuracy.

We may conclude, then, that an Italian scribe numbered the folios
of *Florence 117*. The manner in which he did so, moreover, tells us
something about the sequence in which various compositions were
entered within the manuscript. Some leaves lack foliation, and the
character of their contents suggests that, as a general rule, numbers
were not provided for blank folios. Thus, for example, eight complete
openings contain scribbling of one sort or another, generally
exercises in calligraphy or counterpoint. These are afterthoughts of
the most casual character, and they demand to be considered the
latest additions to the manuscript.[17] Not a single one of these leaves

---

16   Compare, for example, the capital *J*s of the tabula with the initial of Josquin's name (fol.
      39ᵛ), or the *G* of 'Gentil galans' in the tabula with the initial of Gaspart (fol. 72ᵛ). Similarly,
      note in the incipit 'Sempre giro piangendo per aspre selve forte' (fol. 21ᵛ) the juncture of
      the letters *asp* in the fifth word, and compare it to their appearance in 'Ma*sp*enses' in the
      tabula. Numerous additional examples could be cited.
17   The eight 'openings' are fols. (22ᵛ–23ʳ), (26ᵛ–27ʳ), (27ᵛ–32ʳ), (32ᵛ–33ʳ), 42ᵛ/(45ʳ), (45ᵛ–
      46ʳ), (46ᵛ/62ʳ) and (62ᵛ–63ʳ).

bears foliation, suggesting that the scribbling was, indeed, a very late supplement – one that postdated the addition of folio numbers by the principal scribe of *Florence 178*.[18] We shall return to the matter of foliation as we discuss the contributions of various scribes to the manuscript and attempt to approximate the order in which they made their entries. It is to the general issue of scribal hands that we turn our attention next.

Handwriting: main scribe. The principal scribe of *Florence 117* copied thirty-three of the surviving compositions in the source. As we see from the sample of his handwriting in Figure 2, he writes in a smooth bâtarde text hand, maintains impeccable French orthography, and avoids cursive elements in his music script. (It is evident from the colour of the ink that the main scribe wrote both the music and the text in his portion of the manuscript. Indeed, it is equally evident that he provided the calligraphic initials, too.) It would seem that *Florence 117* was organised around a plan originally conceived by the main scribe, for he appears to have arranged his contributions to the source quite systematically in three layers. Table 2 shows that he begins the manuscript with eleven three-voice chansons, five of which may be attributed to composers of the French royal court during the reign of Louis XII. The work of several different scribes intervenes, after which the main scribe introduces a second set of seven chansons *a 3*. Most of these come from an older repertory and consist chiefly of settings by Compère and Hayne van Ghizeghem of poems with the word 'regret' in the first line. A motley group of French-, Italian- and Latin-texted pieces in sundry hands follows, and it includes one piece copied by the main scribe (fols. 65^v–66^r). After another work in a different hand, the main scribe commences his third layer: a group of thirteen four-voice chansons and one incomplete untexted work. Many of these are unique in our manuscript.

Not surprisingly, for sections of this manuscript that must figure

[18] A folio number does appear over the work of one of the scribblers in the one instance in which the scribbling shares an opening with a 'formal' copy of a piece of music (fols. 66^v–67^r). It is clear, however, that the main scribe added the number here because of the presence of the formal copying (fol. 66^v). Prioris's brief *Consumo la mia vita* appears in its entirety on this verso. It is the only place in the manuscript where a full composition occupies only one side of an opening. Although the music appears on the verso, and the scribbling on the facing recto, the appropriate place for the folio number is, of course, the recto, which probably was blank when the folio number was written.

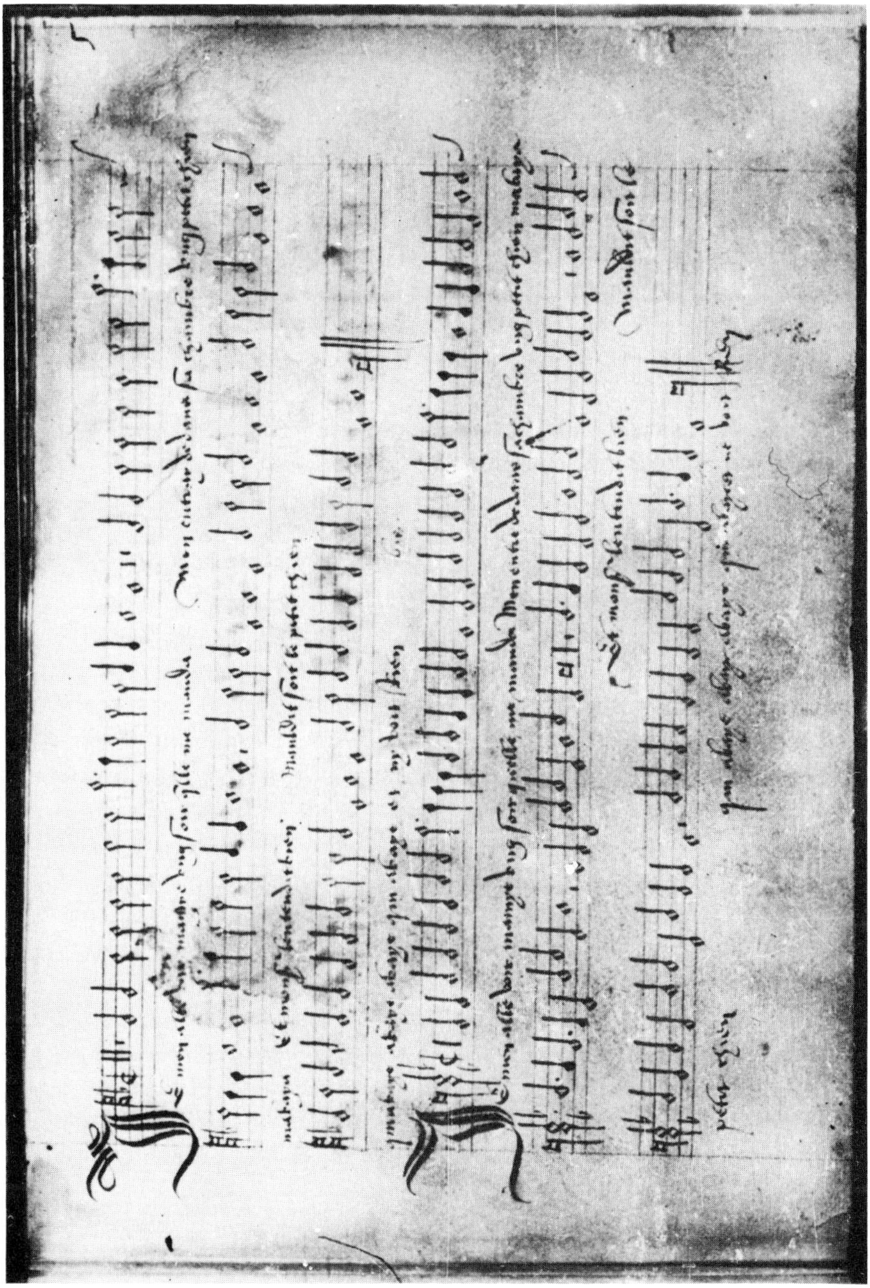

Figure 2　The handwriting of the main scribe (*Florence 117*, fol. 5r)

Table 2 *The entries of the main scribe*

Incipit	Composer	Folio	No. of voices
Souvent je m'esbatz et mon cueur est marry	—	[0ᵛ]–(1ʳ)	3
Hélas, j'en suis marry	[Févin]	(1ᵛ)–2ʳ	3
Chescun mauldit ses jaleux	[Févin]	2ᵛ–4ʳ	3
Je m'en allé voir m'amye ung soir	—	4ᵛ–5ʳ	3
Pleust a la vierge Marie	—	5ᵛ–6ʳ	3
Je le levray puis qu'il m'y bat	[Févin]	6ᵛ–7ʳ	3
On a mal dit de mon amy	[Févin]	7ᵛ–8ʳ	3
Orsus, orsus, vous dormez trop	[Janequin]	8ᵛ–10ʳ	3
Mais que ce fust le plaisir d'elle	[Mouton]	10ᵛ–11ʳ	3
Monseigneur le grant maistre	—	11ᵛ–12ʳ	3
Qui vous vouldroit entretenir	—	12ᵛ–13ʳ	3
Et mirelaridaine Regnauldin	—	(33ᵛ)–34ʳ	3
Triste et pensif suis sans mot dire	—	34ᵛ	3
Sourdez regretz, avironnez mon cueur	[Compère]	37ᵛ	3
Venez regretz, venez, il est en heure	[Compère]	37ᵛ–38ʳ	3
Allés regretz, vuidez de ma plaisance	[Hayne]	38ᵛ–39ʳ	3
Va t'en regretz, celluy qui me convoye	[Compère]	39ᵛ–40ʳ	3
Les grans regretz qui sans cesser je porte	[Hayne]	40ᵛ–41ʳ	3
L'aultre jour parmy ces champs	—	65ᵛ–66ʳ	4
Fortune la diverse m'est bien assaillir	—	67ᵛ–68ʳ	4
Si j'ayme mon amy trop plus que mon mary	—	68ᵛ–70ʳ	4
[La jeusne dame va au molin]	—	70ᵛ–71ʳ	4
Chantons dançons ceste saison nouvelle	—	71ᵛ–72ʳ	4
En attendant la bergerotte	—	72ᵛ–73ʳ	4
Noz bergers et noz bergeres	[T. Janequin?]	73ᵛ–74ʳ	4
Sire Dondieu, tant y sont aisés noz bergeres	—	74ᵛ–75ʳ	4
L'aultre jour fu chenilée si doulcement	—	75ᵛ–76ʳ	4
La guille des luron lureau, triboulle marteau	—	76ᵛ–77ʳ	4
Trut trut trut, avant, il fault boire	—	77ᵛ–78ʳ	4
N'emez jamais une villaine	[Févin]	78ᵛ–79ʳ	4
M'y levay par ung matin	La Fage	79ᵛ–80ʳ	4
Hélas, hélas, madame, tant my donnez de peyne	[Moulu]	80ᵛ–81ʳ	4
Two voices of what would appear to have been a multi-voice composition. All that is supplied by way of text is an inked calligraphic initial 'I'.	—	81ᵛ–82ʳ	?

among the very earliest, virtually all of the main scribe's entries bear folio numbers. Only one lacks them: folio 1. Although ultraviolet light revealed no trace of a number in the appropriate corner of this folio, it is evident that the upper right-hand corner of folio (1ʳ) has been repaired. Evidently, a folio number once appeared there, but the leaf became dog-eared with use and ultimately lost the corner bearing its folio number. (Folio 2 appears to be lacking a number in the original series, too, but faint traces of light brown ink are visible beneath a modern, pencilled '2' when the upper right-hand corner of this leaf is viewed under magnification.)

Excluding the calligraphic exercises of the scribblers, we can identify the hands of five additional scribes in *Florence 117*. None of these appears with the frequency or regularity with which the main hand does. Nor do any of these subsidiary scribes seem to have shared with the main scribe responsibility for the master repertorial design of the whole manuscript. We shall now survey briefly the role each of the subsidiary scribes played in the compilation of our manuscript.

Second northern scribe. Figure 3 shows the work of the scribe whose first entries immediately follow the main scribe's first layer. He too seems to be a northerner, to judge from the accuracy of his French orthography and the clarity of his bâtarde text hand. His contributions to *Florence 117*, as we see in Table 3, include three chansons *a 3*, one *a 4*, and the three-voice version of Prioris's *Consumo la mia vita*. Joshua Rifkin has shown that the handwriting of this scribe can be found in another manuscript: he is the man who added a little group of five compositions (four with Spanish texts, one on an Italian poem) to the concluding folios of another manuscript at the Biblioteca Nazionale Centrale, MS Magliabechi xɪx 107bis.[19] These works include pieces by Juan del Encina and Pedro Escobar – compositions far more likely to have been copied in Italy than in the north; undoubtedly, therefore, the scribe under consideration made his contribution to *Florence 107bis* in the place where the main portion of that manuscript was compiled, namely Florence.[20] It is likely that

[19] Rifkin, 'Scribal Concordances', pp. 309–12. For the four Spanish pieces, see G. Haberkamp, *Die weltliche Vokalmusik in Spanien um 1500*, Münchner Veröffentlichungen zur Musikgeschichte 12 (Tutzing, 1968), pp. 335–9. The anonymous Italian composition seems to be unique in *Florence 107bis*.
[20] For evidence in support of the Florentine provenance of *Florence 107bis*, see Atlas, *The*

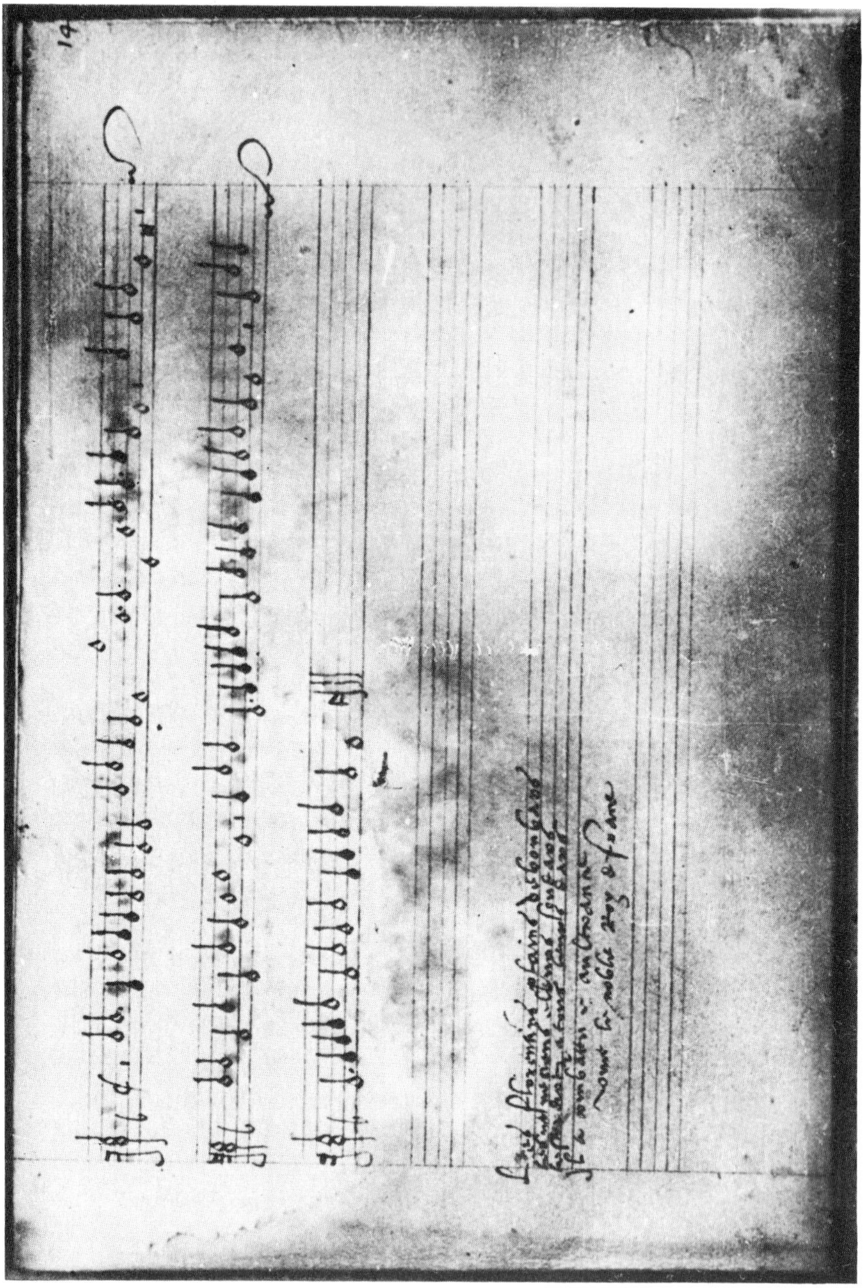

Figure 3   The handwriting of the second northern scribe (*Florence 117*, fol. 14ᶠ)

Table 3 *The entries of the second northern scribe*

Incipit	Composer	Folio	No. of voices
Vive le noble roy de France	[Compère]	13ᵛ–14ʳ	3
Adyeu soullas, tout playsir et liesse	[Févin]	14ᵛ–15ʳ	3
D'amour je suis desheritée	—	15ᵛ–16ʳ	3
[N'a] tu point veu la viscontine	[Richafort?]	(23ᵛ)–24ʳ	4
Rejuissés vous borgeses, belles filles de Lion (incipit and attribution)	Jo. mouton	(63ᵛ)–65ʳ	4
Consumo la mia vita	[Prioris]	66ᵛ	3

he worked on *Florence 117* in the Tuscan city, too. First, Rifkin has also demonstrated that this scribe added the textual incipit and attribution to a chanson in our manuscript, for which the music was copied by another artisan, and, as we shall see presently, the latter man definitely worked in Florence.[21] Second, the version of *Consumo la mia vita* in the second northern scribe's hand often differs significantly in the readings it presents from what is preserved in all the northern sources of the piece (see Example 1). Clearly, our scribe had recourse to a transmission of Prioris's composition strikingly different from that preserved in virtually all northern sources of the work, and the unique readings of the piece in *Florence 117* may, perhaps, be best explained by suggesting that they are derived from an Italian, as opposed to a northern, transmission. Finally, to argue that the second northern scribe worked on our manuscript outside Florence forces us to presume that a scribe known to have copied music in Florence worked elsewhere on a manuscript that was itself in Florence before it was completed.[22]

Nonetheless, the latter scenario, complicated as it seems, is not wholly implausible. Conceivably, for example, it might have been the second northern scribe who brought our manuscript to Florence from a northern centre where both he and the main scribe worked

Cappella Giulia Chansonnier, I, p. 243. His convincing proof rests upon filiation of the musical readings, watermarks and repertorial considerations.

[21] For the identification of the incipit and attribution, see Rifkin, 'Scribal Concordances', pp. 309–12 and n. 24. The music to which the incipit and attribution were added was copied by the scribe designated the 'Layolle' scribe below.

[22] It will be demonstrated presently that several of the other scribes made their contributions to our manuscript in Florence.

Lawrence F. Bernstein

Example 1. Selected variants from *Consumo la mia vita*

together. One cannot ascertain beyond a doubt, therefore, the locus of the second northern scribe's contributions to *Florence 117*. Wherever he worked on our manuscript, the second northern scribe evidently did so before the latest additions were made to the choirbook, for every one of the folios he copied bears foliation.

'Layolle' scribe. The scribe whose hands appears in Figure 4 copied two works by Francesco de Layolle into our manuscript. As is shown in Table 4, he also executed Isaac's *Palle palle*, and his association with all three of these works links him firmly to Florence. In addition, he is responsible for three French works: Févin's widely disseminated *Sancta trinitas*, Josquin's equally famous *Plus nulz regretz* and Mouton's *Rejuissés vous borgeses*.[23] Strikingly, however, he leaves these three works entirely untexted, in a manner not unusual in Italian sources of French polyphony. (It is Mouton's chanson for which the textual incipit and attribution were added by the second northern scribe.) The Layolle scribe writes his text in a cursive

---

[23] The identification of Josquin's *Plus nulz regretz* appears in Rifkin, 'Scribal Concordances', pp. 309–12, n. 24.

14

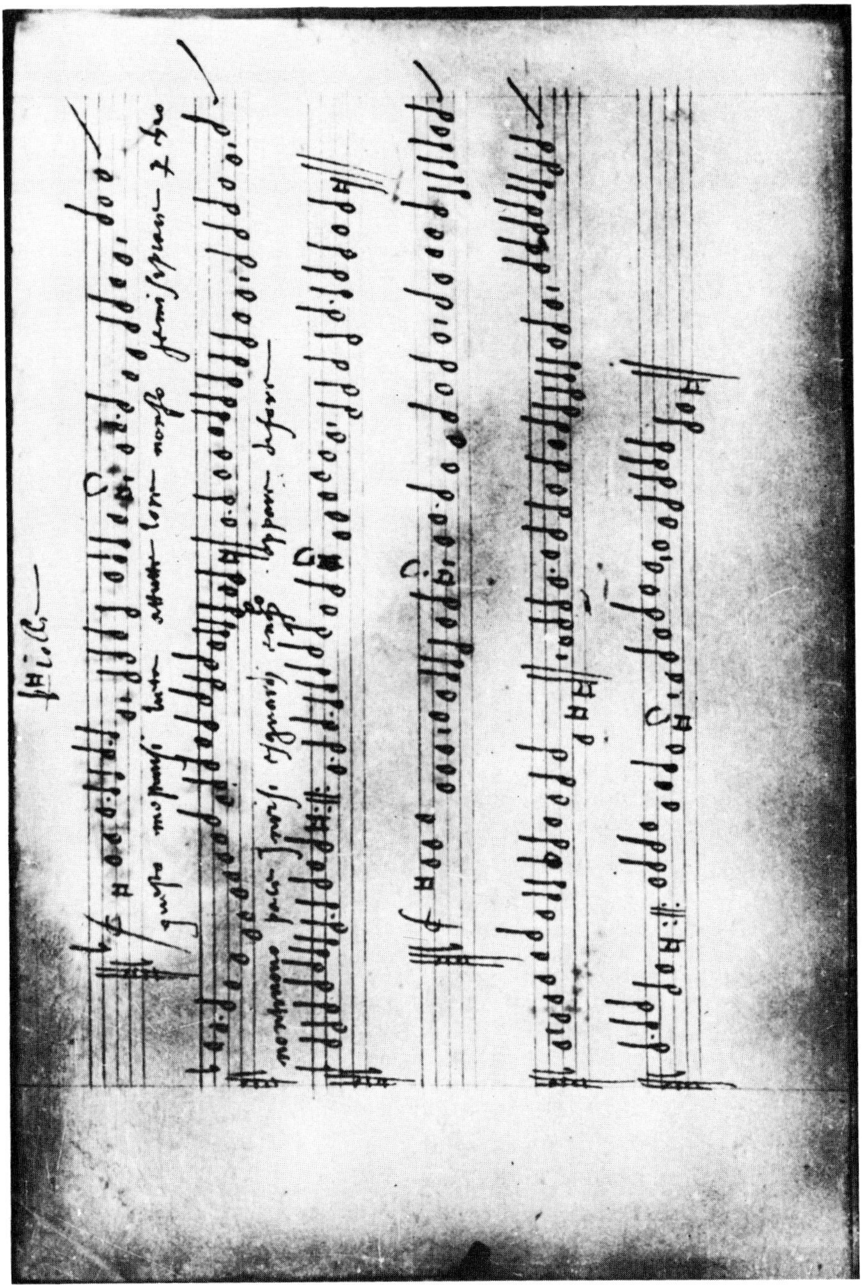

Figure 4a   The handwriting of the Layolle scribe (*Florence 117*, fol. 16ᵛ)

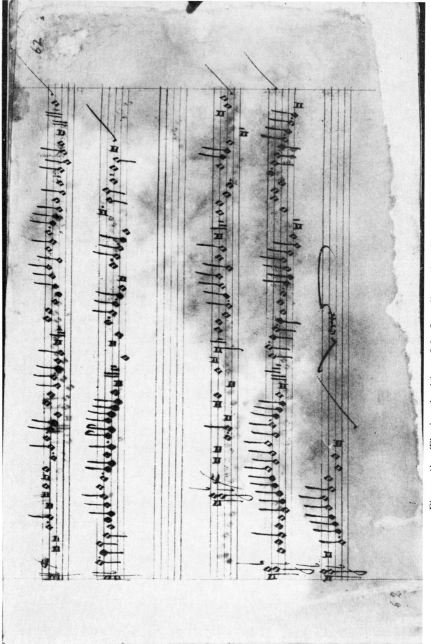

Figure 4b The handwriting of the Layolle scribe (*Florence 117*, fol. 86ᵛ)

16

Table 4 *The entries of the Layolle scribe*

Incipit	Composer	Folio	No. of voices
Questo mostrarsi lieta	♭ iolla	16ᵛ–17ʳ	3
Laudate Dominum, omnes gentes	♭ iolla	41ᵛ–42ʳ	4
Rejuissés vous borgeses, belles filles de Lion (music; attribution and incipit written by the second northern scribe)	Jo. mouton	(63ᵛ)–65ʳ	4
Palle palle	Yzac	82ᵛ–83ᵛ	4
[Plus nulz regretz]	[Josquin]	(85ʳ)	4
[Sancta trinitas unus Deus]	[Févin]	(85ᵛ)–87ʳ	4

humanist script and generally uses a rounded style for his note heads, too (see Figure 4a). Yet, interestingly, in the works by Févin and Mouton – the ones most likely to have been copied from French exemplars – he resorts to diamond-shaped notes (see Figure 4b). The clefs, mensuration signs, custodes and distinctive slant that appear throughout these pieces are all idiosyncratic traits of the Layolle scribe and show clearly that he copied the works by Févin and Mouton, too, despite his use in them of angular note heads. Undoubtedly, we may account for the differences in this scribe's handwriting on the basis of his susceptibility to the calligraphic style of his exemplars.

The Layolle scribe, like 'Northern 2', worked on *Florence 117* before the very latest additions were made within its folios, for each of his contributions appears on a numbered folio.[24]

'Baccio' scribe. In Figure 5 we see the work of a scribe who added only one piece to *Florence 117*, the composition ascribed to Baccio Fiorentino (= Bartolomeo degli Organi). The attribution and incipit are written in a clear sixteenth-century Italian book hand. When we consider this along with the fact that Baccio's secular works never appear outside Florence, we are led to regard it as very

---

[24] Fols. 17 and 85 are among those bearing works executed by the Layolle scribe, and neither appears to carry a folio number. Inspection of the manuscript under ultraviolet light, however, shows that the first of these once did clearly show the number '17' in the same hand as the rest of the folio numbers. Either the number was erased, or it wore out. Fol. 85 is damaged, and the corner where the folio number would appear is torn off. All surrounding folios are numbered, however, and we can presume that this one was, too.

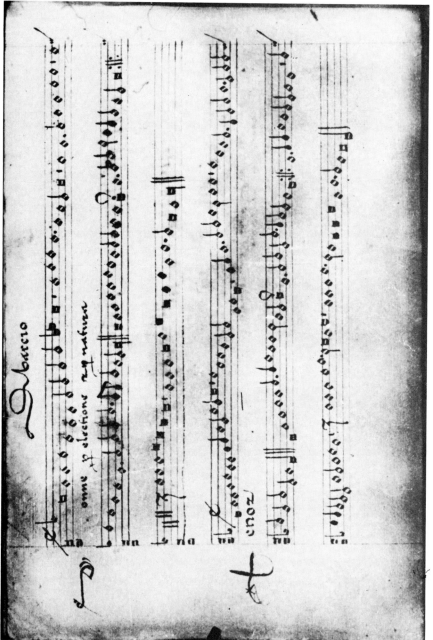

Figure 5   The handwriting of the Baccio scribe (*Florence 117*, fol. 17ᵛ)

18

likely that the single piece by him in our manuscript was copied there, too. The one composition in the hand of the Baccio scribe appears on a folio that bears a number, suggesting that his work on the source antedates its latest additions.[25]

'Izagha' scribe. Immediately after the work by Bartolomeo degli Organi, there begins a series of four compositions copied in yet another hand, the one represented in Figure 6.[26] As we see in Table 5, only the first of these works bears a text; it is the well-known *Amy, soufré que je vous aime*. The text hand resembles a bâtarde, but it is so shaky a specimen of that script that one could aptly characterise it as an attempt at that style of handwriting by a scribe not accustomed to writing in it. The orthography, moreover, suggests that the scribe who copied the poetry was not a native of a French-speaking land. For example, in various parts he writes '*se* vous aime' instead of '*je* vous aime', 'nemetene' as a single word instead of 'ne me tené', 'leri gueur' instead of 'la rigueur', etc. From this we might conclude that the present scribe, like several of his colleagues, worked in Italy. The evidence is not clear-cut, however, for the music of this piece, on the one hand, and its text and incipit, on the other, were written in inks of different colours and could well have been copied by different scribes.

What seems to be an attribution appears over the verso folio of this redaction of *Amy, soufré*; it reads 'Do[mino] Izagha', which has been interpreted as a reference to Heinrich Isaac. Again, the evidence points to Florence, but again it is less than unequivocal, for although Isaac's name is spelled in many different ways, never, to my knowledge, does it appear elsewhere spelled *Izagha*.[27] We simply cannot be certain, therefore, that the name over this chanson is that of Heinrich Isaac. Indeed, we cannot even be sure it is meant to refer

25 Fol. 18, which contains the piece in the hand of the Baccio scribe, also seems at first to lack a folio number, but the foliation can be seen under ultraviolet light.

26 The first three pieces executed by this scribe are for three voices; the fourth, on fols. 24v–(26r), is *a 4*. A first attempt at copying the latter piece on fols. 21v–(22r) was abandoned by the scribe before it was completed. For the reasons why this first attempt was aborted, see below, pp. 25–6.

27 Johannes Wolf included *Amy, soufré* in the supplement to his edition of the secular works of Isaac. See *Nachtrag zu den weltlichen Werken von Heinrich Isaac*, Denkmäler der Tonkunst in Österreich 32, Jg. XVI, 1 (Vienna, 1909; repr. Graz, 1959), pp. 204–5. Cf. Bernstein, 'Notes on the Origin of the Parisian Chanson', pp. 318–22. Most often in Florentine music manuscripts Isaac's name is spelled *Yzac* (as it appears later in *Florence 117*) or *Yçac* (the form used in *Florence 229*, among other sources).

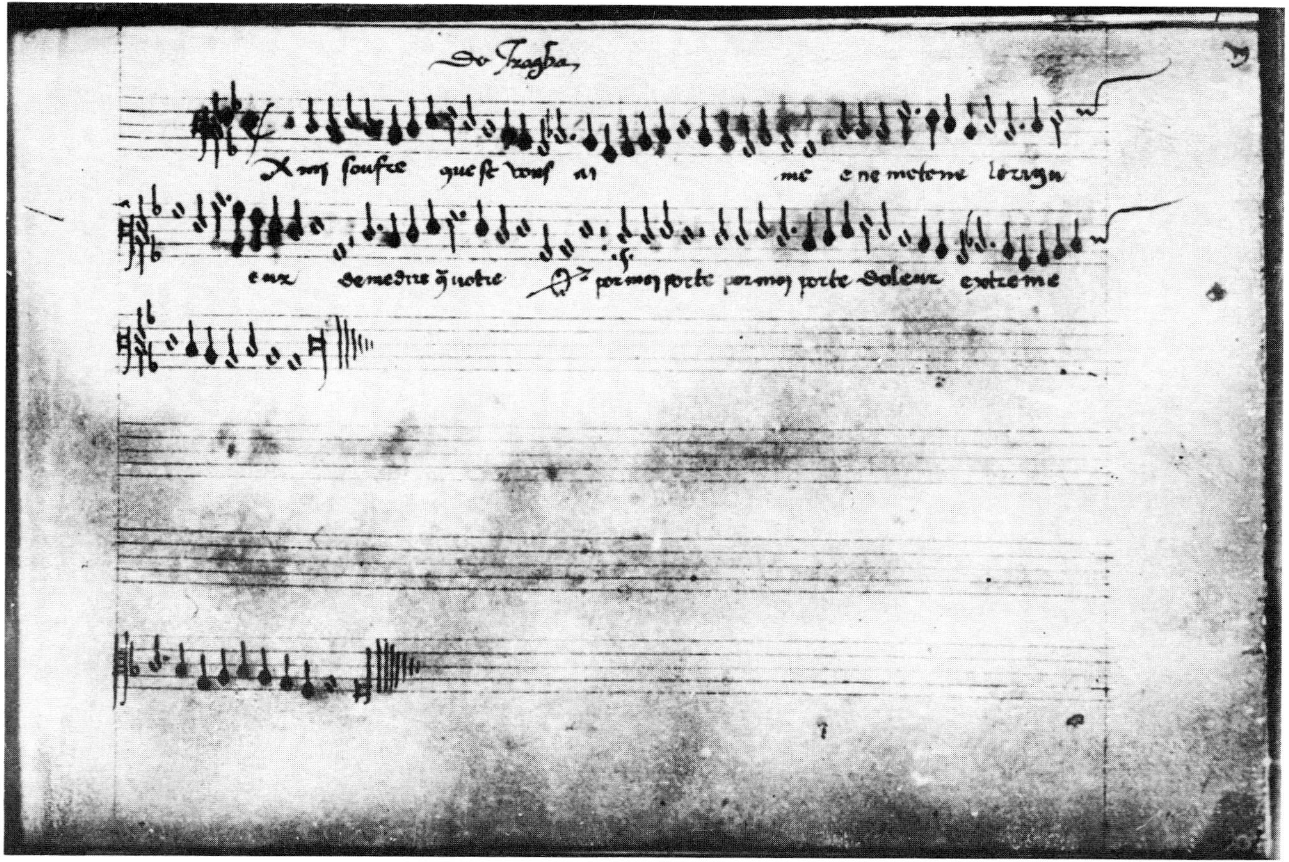

Figure 6   The handwriting of the Izagha scribe (*Florence 117*, fol. 19ʳ)

Table 5 *The entries of the Izagha scribe*

Incipit	Composer	Folio	No. of voices
Amy, soufré que je vous aime	Isaac, Le Heurteur, Moulu or Sermisy	18ᵛ–19ʳ	3
[J'ay mis mon cueur en ung lieu seulement]	—	19ᵛ–20ʳ	3
[Ces facheux sotz qui mesdisent d'aymer]	—	20ᵛ–21ʳ	3
An incomplete attempt at copying the composition listed next	—	21ᵛ–(22ʳ)	3 of 4
Unidentified textless composition	—	24ᵛ–(26ʳ)	4

to the composer of the music, for another name, 'Madame Lanydin', appears over the music on the facing recto.[28]

In the next three pieces, the Izagha scribe supplies no texts, incipits or ascriptions; two of the three compositions, however, can be identified as chansons. The second piece in the series of four is a setting *a 3* of *J'ay mis mon cueur en ung lieu seulement,* and the third is the well-known *Ces facheux sotz* for three voices.[29] The appearance of the latter in our manuscript calls to mind a Florentine connection, for among the many polyphonic works based on this chanson is a parody Mass by Francesco de Layolle, one of the major Florentine composers and one whose music is represented in our choirbook. Noteworthy, too, in this light is Layolle's setting *a 5* of *J'ay mis mon cueur,* which shares its head motif and poem with the companion piece to *Ces facheux sotz* in *Florence 117.*

Frank D'Accone believes both the Mass and five-voice chanson to be late works of Layolle, written long after the composer left Florence

---

[28] I have been unsuccessful in my attempts to identify Madame Lanydin.

[29] Of the many settings of *J'ay mis mon cueur,* most of which descend from the monophonic tune preserved in the Bayeux chansonnier, the one closest to the unique version in *Florence 117* is the three-voice chanson in Attaingnant's *Quarante et deux chansons* of 1529. A modern edition of the latter piece appears in *Thirty Chansons (1529) for Three Instruments or Voices,* ed. B. Thomas, The Parisian Chanson 10 (London, 1977), p. 21. For the monophonic tune, see T. Gérold, ed., *Le manuscrit de Bayeux: texte et musique d'un recueil de chansons du XVᵉ siècle* (Strasbourg, 1921), p. 24.

The identification of *Ces facheux sotz* appears in C. Adams, 'The Three-part Chanson during the Sixteenth Century: Changes in its Style and Importance' (Ph.D. diss., University of Pennsylvania, 1974), p. 367. For a modern edition of this work, see *Thirty Chansons (1529),* p. 18.

in 1518 to settle in Lyons a few years later. D'Accone suggests that the Mass was composed between 1532 and 1540, presumably because the work did not appear in the 1532 edition of Jacques Moderne's *Liber decem missarum*, but only in the expanded reprint of 1540. He maintains, furthermore, that the Mass is based on the two-voice *Ces facheux sotz* by Antonio Gardane, a work printed in 1539 by Layolle's Lyonnaise collaborator, Moderne.[30] We must bear in mind, however, that Moderne published a great deal of Layolle's music in 1540, much of it in collections devoted exclusively to his works. Obviously, much of the music published in this way stands a reasonable chance, at least, of having been published retrospectively. Moreover, as we see from the evidence of parody in Example 2, there can be no doubt that Layolle based his Mass on the three-voice *Cex facheux sotz* – the one in *Florence 117*, that is to say – and not on Gardane's duo.

As for *J'ay mis mon cueur*, D'Accone believes it to have been composed in Lyons because its cantus firmus is a French melody. The book that contains this chanson, moreover, Moderne's *Venti-cinque canzoni di M. Franciesco Layolle* (1540), consists mainly of five-voice madrigals, none of which were printed in the Venetian madrigal books of 1538–44. D'Accone alludes to the dearth of five-voice madrigals at this time and suggests that if Layolle had left such pieces in Florence they would have been likely to have been printed in Italy. This speaks for the contemporaneity of the repertory in the book that contains Layolle's *J'ay mis mon cueur*.[31] However, we must recall that many chansons composed in Italy made recourse to French melodies for their cantus firmi, and the evidence for the chronology of the madrigals need not apply to the few chansons in this book. The style of Layolle's chanson, furthermore, is anomalous among chansons composed in Lyons about 1540. The piece combines a strict cantus firmus in the tenor with free counterpoint in the other voices. This technique has more in common with such chansons as, say, Isaac's *Et qui la dira* than it does with the works Moderne printed in his chansonniers.[32] I would see more compelling reasons,

---

[30] F. D'Accone, 'Francesco de Layolle', *The New Grove Dictionary of Music and Musicians*, ed. S. Sadie, 20 vols. (London, 1980), x, p. 568.

[31] *Francesco de Layolle: Collected Secular Works for 2, 3, 4, and 5 Voices*, vol. III of *Music of the Florentine Renaissance*, ed. F. D'Accone, Corpus Mensurabilis Musicae 32 (1969), pp. xii–xiii.

[32] For a modern edition of Isaac's chanson, see H. Hewitt, ed., *Harmonice musices odhecaton A*,

Example 2. The model for Francesco de Layolle's *Missa Ces facheux sotz*: (a) excerpts from the Kyrie of Layolle's Mass (after the *Opera omnia*, ed. F. D'Accone); (b) the chanson *a3* (*Florence 117*); (c) Gardane's duo (*Moderne 1539*[19])

Mediaeval Academy of America: Studies and Documents 5 (Cambridge, Mass., 1942; repr. New York, 1978), pp. 242–3.

23

therefore, to associate Layolle's chanson with his Florentine period than with the days of his Lyonnaise sojourn.

It is tempting, thus, to regard these two chansons as having been part of a Florentine repertory when Francesco de Layolle drew upon one of them directly for a parody Mass and upon the melody of the other for the head motif of a cantus-firmus chanson. And this in turn suggests that the Izagha scribe could well have had access to these compositions had he made his contributions to our manuscript in Florence. Once more, however, the evidence that points to the Tuscan city is controvertible, for the two works that are suggestive of connections with a Florentine repertory are French and obviously would have been just as readily accessible in the north as in Italy.

Perhaps the location of the Izagha scribe's entries in *Florence 117* may provide firmer evidence of where he carried out his work. His contributions to the choirbook occur in the third and fourth fascicles (see Figure 7). The first appearance of the Izagha scribe's work comes in mid-fascicle, just after two compositions copied by scribes unequivocally identified as Florentines ('Layolle' and 'Baccio'). Surely we may assume that the Izagha scribe would have begun his series of pieces on the first available blank folio of the gathering. This suggests that he must have worked after the Italian scribes did and hence that he too worked in Florence.

Although this seems the most plausible and likely conclusion, one question does come to mind. Could not the Izagha scribe have found fascicle C with nothing written in it save for the opening and closing entries made by the second northern scribe? He might then have ascertained the number of folios he needed for his entries in this fascicle, counted back from the existing work on the last folio, and begun his entries there, leaving fols. 16^v–18^r blank, to be filled in later by the Italian scribes. Speaking for this scenario is the fact that the work the Izagha scribe began on fol. 21^v is a composition for four voices, and he may have wanted to place this piece in immediate proximity to the last composition in the gathering, the first texted chanson *a 4* in the manuscript.[33] Actually, additional evidence allows

[33] Fols. (22^v–23^r), however, separate the work of the Izagha scribe from that of the concluding folio of the fascicle in the hand of 'Northern 2', and these leaves bear the jottings of one of the very late scribblers. Obviously, the Izagha scribe left these folios blank. It might be argued, therefore, that he never intended to extend his entries right up to the work of the second northern scribe on fols. (23^v)–24^r. We shall see presently, however, that this was indeed the intention of the Izagha scribe until a copying error prevented him from carrying it out.

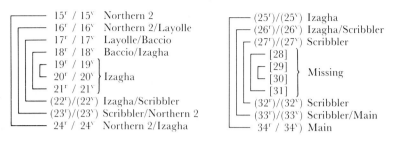

Figure 7   Fascicles C and D of *Florence 117*, showing the position of the Izagha scribe's entries

us to argue against the latter scenario and thereby enhance the case for the Izagha scribe's having worked after his Florentine colleagues. To set forth this evidence, however, we need to retrace the order in which the Izagha scribe made his entries.

As we have seen, the Izagha scribe copied four works into our manuscript – three chansons *a 3* and one piece for four voices. He began with the three-voice works, each of which occupies a single opening (fols. 18ᵛ–19ʳ, 19ᵛ–20ʳ and 20ᵛ–21ʳ). Then he started to copy the composition *a 4* on fol. 21ᵛ. In the course of copying this composition, however, he committed a gross and irremediable error. Fol. 21ᵛ contains the superius and tenor parts of the beginning of the piece. The facing recto, however, contains a third part – but of what is quite clearly the end of a work. We might never have been able to determine that this concluding section belongs to the piece begun on fol. 21ᵛ were it not for the music the Izagha scribe copied in the next fascicle on fols. 24ᵛ–(26ʳ). This textless work spans two spreads. The first opening of its superius and tenor parts (fol. 24ᵛ) is identical with the music on fol. 21ᵛ, while the second opening of the contratenor part on fol. (26ʳ) matches precisely the third voice copied opposite fol. 21ᵛ. Clearly, the Izagha scribe began by copying the superius and tenor parts of this work on fol. 21ᵛ. Then he went on to copy the contratenor and bassus parts on the facing page, but at this point he mistakenly turned, in his exemplar, to the residual folio of the piece. He realised his error after completing the contratenor part, as we may see in his failure to supply this part with his characteristic sign of conclusion (a series of short lines of decreasing length).

Now, there are only two ways he could have rectified this error within the confines of fascicle C. He could have inserted a rogue leaf between fols. 21^v and (22^r), or he could have inserted a new bifolio at the same juncture. As we have seen, however, he rejected both of these options, preferring instead to copy the entire piece afresh in the next fascicle. We can readily understand why he would not resort to the insertion of a rogue leaf, which could easily fall out of the fascicle. But surely it would have been easier for him to transfer to fascicle C a blank bifolio from another fascicle (say, the one that became fols. 27/ 32) than to re-copy two entire pages of his four-voice piece. What would the effect of making such a transfer have been on the continuity of fascicle C? From Figure 8 we can see that the insertion of a blank bifolio between fols. 21^v and (22^r) would have introduced a blank leaf between fols. 17^v and 18^r. There would, of course, have been no obstacle to the introduction of such a new blank leaf between the two latter folios had they themselves been blank at the time. Only had fols. 17^v–18^r been filled can we understand the Izagha scribe's willingness to correct his error by re-copying two full pages of his four-voice composition. Fols. 17^v–18^r, in fact, contain the work of the Baccio scribe, and it would appear likely, in light of this, that the entries made in our manuscript by this Florentine copyist preceded those of the Izagha scribe.

Again, the evidence points to Florence as the site of the Izagha scribe's contributions to our manuscript, although again the evidence is circumstantial, depending as it does upon our acceptance of three presuppositions: (1) that the manuscript was not yet bound at the time the Izagha scribe worked on it; (2) that the Izagha scribe would have been willing to disturb the sequence of any foliation that might already have been added to the manuscript at the time he worked on it; and (3) that he had the ingenuity to think of the option of inserting an additional blank folio within fascicle C (even if he was only to reject it!). We can neither prove nor disprove any of these presuppositions. As a result, the manner in which the Izagha scribe corrected his copying error can be used to support the argument for his having worked in Florence only with the utmost caution.

Nonetheless, another factor strengthens the case for Florence as the site of the Izagha scribe's activity. He must have made his entries in our manuscript at least partly at a very late stage in the compilation of the source. We know this because some of his contributions were made after the foliation was added. Thus, the

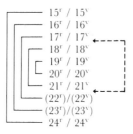

Figure 8   Fascicle C of *Florence 117*, showing the effect of the hypothetical
insertion of a blank bifolio between fols. 21^v and (22^r)

three chansons *a3* in the hand of the Izagha scribe bear folio
numbers, but the composition *a4* – both the aborted attempt at it
and the corrected version in fascicle D – lacks foliation. The Izagha
scribe added the four-voice work, then, at some point after a
Florentine artisan numbered the folios of our manuscript.

To summarise, various features of one or more of the four
compositions in the music hand with which we are at present
concerned suggest that their scribe is more likely to have worked in
Florence than anywhere else. These include his Italianate manner of
leaving several chansons untexted, what appears to be an attribution
over one of his works that may denote Heinrich Isaac, several ties
linking his pieces with a Florentine repertory, and the apparent
placement of his work directly after the initial entries of two
Florentine scribes. To these elements of circumstantial evidence
may be added the more concrete fact that the Izagha scribe carried
out at least part of his work after the manuscript was foliated in
Florence.

The last scribe. The last of the six main scribes who contributed to
Florence 117 is represented in Figure 9. His hand appears only once in
the manuscript, in the last piece that remains in the choirbook:
Mouton's *Ave sanctissima Maria*, on fols. 87^v–(88^v).[34] This scribe
seems to have added Mouton's work to a manuscript already in a
state of completion because the original foliation stops on the leaf
just prior to our scribe's entry (fol. 87^r). This suggests that he was the
last scribe to work on the manuscript. If he worked after the scribes
known to have contributed to the source in Florence, which city was

---

[34]   The motet is incomplete in *Florence 117*: the contratenor and bassus parts of the end of the
piece are missing.

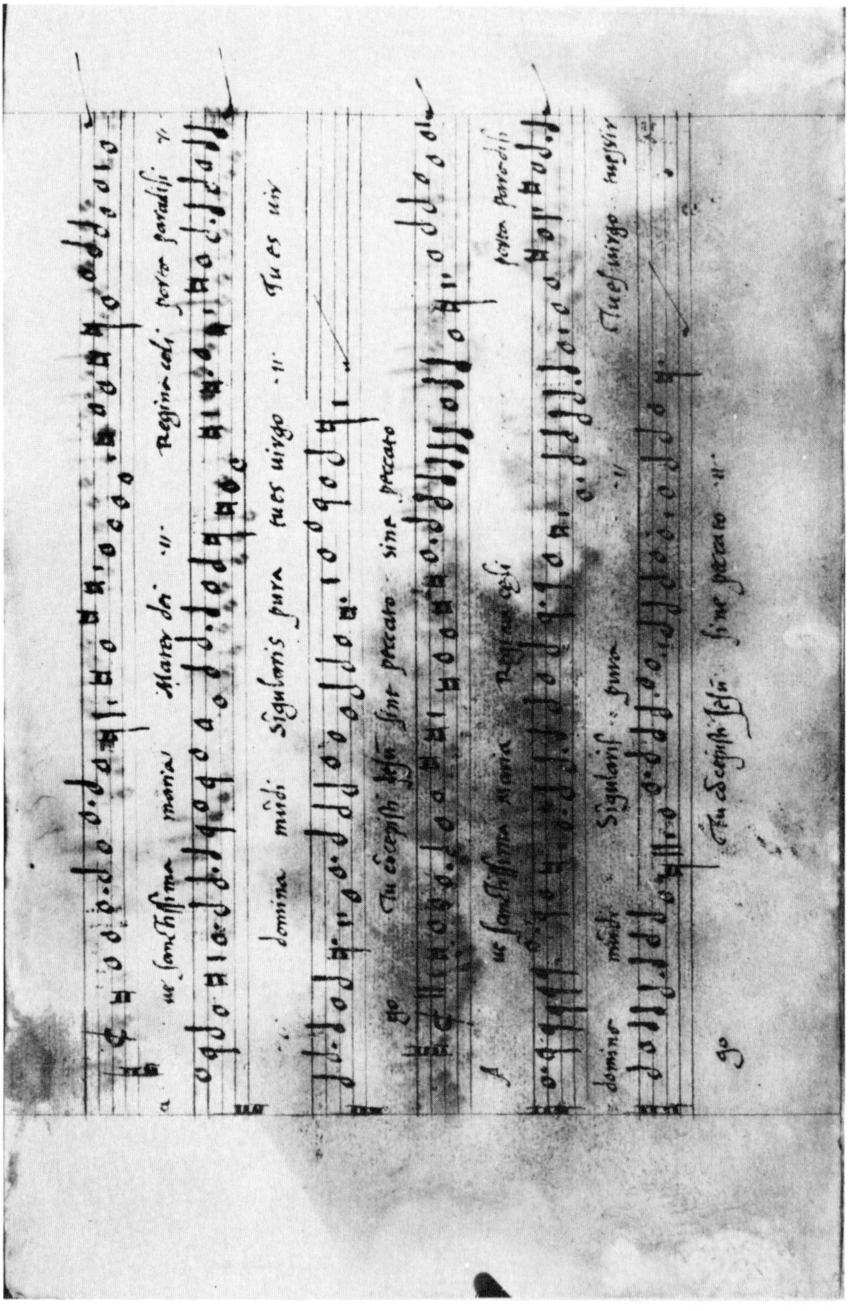

Figure 9 The handwriting of the last scribe (*Florence 117*, fol. 87ᵛ)

Table 6 *The scribes of Florence 117*

Scribe	Nationality	Place of work on *Florence 117*
Main	northerner	?
Northern 2	northerner	Florence (at least in part)
Layolle	Italian	Florence
Baccio	Italian	Florence
Izagha	?	Florence
Last	Italian	Florence

to become the repository of the manuscript, it would appear safe to conclude that he made his addition to the manuscript there, too. His cursive music hand and cultivated, humanist text hand support this thesis.

What we have learned about the six principal scribes of *Florence 117* is summarised in Table 6. Two of the scribes are northerners, three are Italian, and one is of uncertain nationality. Of the five subsidiary scribes, three (Baccio, Layolle and the last) definitely worked on our manuscript in Florence; a fourth (Izagha) surely did, too (at least when he made his last contribution to it); and the fifth (Northern 2) made some (and possibly all) of his additions to the manuscript in the Tuscan city. Where the main scribe did his work, however, remains a mystery. And for our purposes that is a critical question, because by far the greatest number and the greatest variety of chansons in the source were copied by him.

Format of the paper. Let us now examine the paper on which our choirbook was copied. To begin, the paper was cut and folded to produce an oblong format (162 × 244 mm), the one almost invariably found in Florentine music manuscripts of the early sixteenth century.[35] Indeed, a few Florentine manuscripts closely approximate the dimensions of ours: *Florence 107bis* (165 × 235 mm), *Florence 111* (170 × 235 mm) and *Florence 112* (170 × 238 mm). By way of contrast, French music manuscripts from the 1480s to the early sixteenth century appear nearly always to have been copied in upright

---

[35] See, for example, *Florence 99–102, Florence 107bis, Florence 111, Florence 112, Florence 121, Florence 122–5, Florence 125bis, Florence 164–7* and *Florence 178.*

format.[36] It would be tempting to conclude from these relatively uniform practices that our manuscript, like the many other Florentine manuscripts in oblong format, was copied in Florence, too. Caution is in order, however, for we have evidence of music manuscripts from various northern centres that were copied in oblong format. Some of these boast text hands that match the skill of our main scribe in the fluency of their French orthography. These sources include *Florence 2439*, a product of the Netherlands court (168 × 240 mm); *Brussels IV 90/Tournai 94*, copied in Bruges about 1511 (78 × 110 mm); *The Hague 74/h/7*, a mid-century Flemish source (98 × 143 mm); and *St Gall 462*, copied mainly in Paris by Johannes Heer (183 × 250 mm).[37]

Unfortunately, as we suggested earlier, *Florence 117* contains no watermark, but the manner in which it was ruled is of some interest. Each page contains six staves, drawn with a rastrum of the type that produces one stave at a time.[38] This can be ascertained by measuring the height of the staves and the distance between them. The staves are uniformly 10.5 mm high, while the spaces between them vary from folio to folio in amounts up to about 3 mm.[39] Could this have significance for the provenance of the manuscript? One might think so, considering some patterns I have observed in the use of rastra in sixteenth-century chansonniers. Table 7 shows that Florentine music manuscripts were generally ruled with multi-stave rastra, whereas northern manuscripts were ruled one line at a time. *Florence 117* thus conforms with the type of ruling generally found in northern sources. The evidence is not conclusive, though, as one might suspect upon noting in Table 7 the anomalous entry for *Florence 112* — a little chansonnier lined with a single-stave rastrum, but copied on

[36] Examples are *Cambridge 1760, Copenhagen 1848, Florence 2794, London 1070, London 5242, London 20.A.XVI, Paris 1596, Paris 1597, Paris 2245, Uppsala 76a* and *Uppsala 76b*.

[37] Further on these manuscripts and their dimensions, see Hamm and Kellman, eds., *Census-Catalogue, passim*.

[38] A detailed and sophisticated study of the use of rastra appears in J. and E. Wolf, 'Rastrology and its Use in Eighteenth-Century Manuscript Studies', *Studies in Musical Sources and Style: Essays in Honor of Jan LaRue*, ed. E. Roesner and E. Wolf (Madison, 1987), forthcoming. I am very grateful to the authors of this study for making it available to me prior to its publication.

[39] Samples of the variation in distance between the second and third staves, for example, may be reported as follows: fol. (1r) (10.5 mm), fol. 4r (11.7 mm), fol. 15r (10 mm), fol. (25r) (11.2 mm), fol. 37r (10.1 mm), fol. 67r (9.3 mm). (These measurements were taken with a comparator, a lens that provides six-power magnification through a transparent template (called a reticle), onto which are etched measurements calibrated in tenths of millimetres.)

Table 7 *Types of rastra used in selected music manuscripts of the period c. 1490–c. 1535*

Manuscript	Provenance	Date[a]	Type of rastrum used
London 20.A.XVI	French royal court	1483–*c.* 1490	single-stave
Florence 2794	French royal court	before 1488	single-stave
Paris 2245	French royal court	1496–8	single-stave
Paris 1596	French royal court	*c.* 1500	single-stave
Paris 1597	Lorraine?	*c.* 1500–10	single-stave
Cambridge 1760	French royal court	1509–14	single-stave
London 5242	French royal court	1509–14	single-stave
Copenhagen 1848	Lyons	*c.* 1525	single-stave
Florence 178	Florence	1492–4	6-stave
Florence 121	Florence	*c.* 1500–10	4-stave
Florence 107bis	Florence	before 1513	6-stave
Florence 2440	Florence	*c.* 1515–20	4- and 6-stave
Florence 164–7	Florence	*c.* 1515–*c.* 1522	3-stave
Bologna Q 21	Florence	1523–7	several 4-stave rastra
Florence 111	Florence	after 1528	6-stave
→*Florence 112*	Florence	after 1528	single-stave←
Florence 122–5	Florence	1532–7	5-stave
Florence 99–102	Florence	*c.* 1535	5-stave

Note:

   [a] On the chronology of these manuscripts, see Hamm and Kellman, eds., *Census-Catalogue, passim.* For the date of *Florence 121* particularly, see the article by Bonnie Blackburn cited in n. 44, below.

paper that is unquestionably Florentine.[40] Significantly, though, the scribe of *Florence 112* (to judge from his hand) is a northerner. It would appear that he ruled his paper in the northern manner – that is, using a single-stave rastrum – even when working in Florence, and that is what could have been done in the case of *Florence 117*, too.

   The minute fluctuations in the distances between staves in *Florence 117* are significant enough to demonstrate the use of a single-stave rastrum, but the spaces are, at the same time, uniform enough (within 3 mm) to make it inescapable that the folios of our manuscript were ruled by a single artisan – irrespective of whether a given

[40] On the Florentine provenance of this manuscript, see Hamm and Kellman, eds., *Census-Catalogue*, I, pp. 224–5.

folio contains the work of a northern or an Italian scribe. This gives rise to two strikingly different possible scenarios regarding the provenance of the manuscript. (1) All the scribes drew their ruled paper from a common source, which would suggest that they worked in the same place. That would have to be Florence, given the demonstrable presence there of most of the copyists. Or (2) the main scribe – the only one who seems to have had a plan for the manuscript – worked independently of the others. His place of activity is most likely to have been in the north, given the character of his hand and the nature of his repertory. From there, the manuscript was dispatched to Florence, along with enough blank folios to accommodate the additions by the five other scribes. The place of the main scribe's work on the manuscript thus seems to hinge on what we can learn about the manner of his interaction with the other copyists. In the hope of shedding some light on this matter, therefore, we turn to a consideration of the fascicle structure of our manuscript.

Fascicle structure. Figure 10 correlates our analysis of the fascicles in *Florence 117* with the disposition of the various scribal hands found therein. Gatherings of different sizes can be found in the manuscript. In some cases (fascicle groups F and I), the present form of the gatherings cannot be what it was originally, for the original structure has been grossly distorted by the excision of many folios and by the resultant shifts of position during the modern reconstruction of the manuscript. Of the remaining gatherings, however, two (fascicles B and H) consist of three bifolia each, and five (fascicles A, C, D, E and G) are quinternions. Regional predilections for the size of gatherings in music manuscripts of the Renaissance are now well known. Chansonniers of the French royal court, for example, are generally gathered in quaternions, while the Florentine sources are usually made up of quinternions.[41] Indeed, at least one Florentine stationer in the late fifteenth century normally divided his stock into quinterns

---

[41]   The characteristic use of quinternions in Florentine music manuscripts from about 1500 was first pointed out by K. Jeppesen, 'The Manuscript Florence, Biblioteca Nazionale Centrale, Banco Rari 230: An Attempt at a Diplomatic Reconstruction', *Aspects of Medieval and Renaissance Music: A Birthday Offering to Gustave Reese*, ed. J. LaRue *et al.* (New York, 1966), p. 446. On the use of quaternions in northern chansonniers, see *idem*, *Der Kopenhagener Chansonnier* (Copenhagen and Leipzig, 1927), pp. xxiv–xxv; and Litterick, 'The Manuscript Royal 20.A.xvi of the British Library', chap. 2, *passim*.

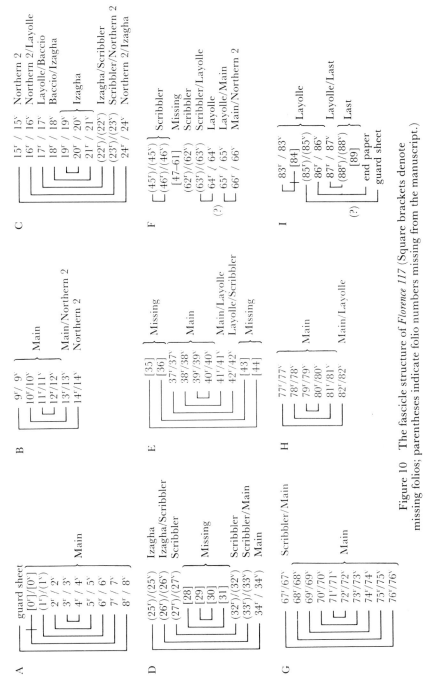

Figure 10 The fascicle structure of *Florence 117* (Square brackets denote missing folios; parentheses indicate folio numbers missing from the manuscript.)

33

and sold it in such units.[42] Obviously, however, it is dangerous to project the provenance of a manuscript on the basis of such predilections, for the scribe who assembles his own gatherings can easily be guided by the regional conventions associated with his normal place of activity irrespective of where he worked on a given manuscript (for example, a northern scribe may just as readily gather in fours in Florence as in Paris).[43] Moreover, there is no guarantee that the normal conventions of a particular region were adhered to inviolately. Even in Florence, for example, where gathering in quinternions was routine, inexpensive bound books of blank music paper were sold by the stationers Gherardo and Monte di Giovanni, and these were made up in gatherings of four folded sheets.[44] Nonetheless, it is noteworthy that *Florence 117*, whose principal scribe is a northerner who might be expected to assemble gatherings of four folded sheets, contains five quinterns and not a single quaternion.[45]

The gathering structure of *Florentine 117* could be very useful in our search for information about the interaction of the main scribe with his colleagues. Were his work to follow that of the other scribes within respective gatherings, we should have strong evidence that he worked in consort with them. As we see in Figure 10, however, the work of the main scribe generally either fills a gathering (completely, or up to the final recto – as in fascicles A, G and H) or precedes the

[42] G. Martini, *La bottega di un cartolaio fiorentino della seconda metà del quatrocento*, suppl. to *La Bibliofilia*, 58 (1956), pp. 45–50; 75, n. 4; 77, n. 21; quoted in H. M. Brown, *A Florentine Chansonnier from the Time of Lorenzo the Magnificent*, Monuments of Renaissance Music 7 (Chicago, 1983), text vol., p. 6 and n. 7.

[43] The so-called 'Strozzi chansonnier' (*Florence 2442*), for example, is the work of a northern scribe, and that manuscript, which was gathered in quaternions, was surely written in Florence. On this important source of chansons, see H. M. Brown, 'Chansons for the Pleasure of a Florentine Patrician: Florence, Biblioteca del Conservatorio di Musica, MS Basevi 2442', *Aspects of Medieval and Renaissance Music*, pp. 56–66; and *idem*, 'The Music of the Strozzi Chansonnier (Florence, Biblioteca del Conservatorio de Musica, MS Basevi 2442)', *Acta Musicologica*, 40 (1968), pp. 115–29.

 Joshua Rifkin has taken issue with the suggested Florentine provenance of this manuscript (in the discussion following H. M. Brown, 'Words and Music in Early 16th-Century Chansons: Text Underlay in Florence, Biblioteca del Conservatorio, Ms Basevi 2442', *Quellenstudien zur Musik der Renaissance*, I, p. 122), but cf. Bernstein, 'Notes on the Origin of the Parisian Chanson', pp. 286–7 and n. 28.

[44] See Brown, *A Florentine Chansonnier*, text vol., p. 6, n. 7, and the data quoted there from Martini, *La bottega*. Further on inconsistencies in scribal practice with respect to the size of gatherings, see B. Blackburn, 'Two "Carnival Songs" Unmasked: A Commentary on MS Florence Magl. XIX. 121', *Musica Disciplina*, 35 (1981), pp. 121–2, n. 2.

[45] Even the mixture of quinternions with gatherings of other sizes that we encounter in *Florence 117* is not unknown in other manuscripts of unquestioned Florentine provenance. Cf., for example, *Florence 99–102* (gatherings of 3, 4 and 5 folded sheets), *Florence 107bis* (4 and 5 folded sheets), and *Florence 164–7* (4, 5 and 6 folded sheets).

work of the subsidiary scribes (as in fascicles B and E). His work does follow that of the Izagha scribe in fascicle D, but he could easily have decided to fill the last two folios of this gathering before anyone else worked on it. Normally, a scribe will take up the last verso of one gathering to make a complete spread with the opening recto of the next fascicle. At issue in fascicle D is the fact that the main scribe began to copy within this gathering on the penultimate, as opposed to the last, verso. This can be explained, however. Fascicle E contains the main scribe's group of *regret* settings. Although the first two folios of the gathering are missing, the last chanson from fascicle D – the one that would have made a full spread with the missing opening folio of fascicle E – is the anonymous *Triste et pensif suis*, a composition clearly related in sentiment to the subsequent *regret* chansons. To this series of compositions the main scribe then seems to have added the one chanson that is entirely out of character with the sorrowful cast of the rest of the group, *Et mirelaridaine*. It would have been logical for him to place this piece on some blank folios that remained near the end of fascicle D.

We must bear in mind, moreover, that the jottings of scribblers occupy fols. (26^v–27^v) and (32^r–33^r), separating the work of the main scribe from that of the Izagha copyist in fascicle D. Presumably, these folios were blank when the main scribe took the gathering in hand, and it seems just as likely that the Izagha scribe had not made his entry yet either. Indeed, the absence of foliation from the latter artisan's contribution to this gathering, as we have seen, suggests strongly that he wrote within this fascicle at a very late stage (i.e. after the main scribe, whose entry on fol. 34 carries foliation).

Thus, the fascicle structure of *Florence 117* offers inconclusive evidence of the main scribe's interaction with his subsidiary colleagues. The lack of quaternions and distinct presence of quinternions, even in gatherings devoted entirely to the work of the main scribe, faintly hints at Florentine provenance. But the self-containment of the main scribe's entries speaks for his isolation from the other copyists. Obviously, we are in need of additional evidence, and, in its pursuit, we turn to other criteria, beginning with the texting policies of the various scribes.

Texting. Table 8 lists all the chansons of the manuscript that were copied by the subsidiary scribes; it also shows in what manner they

Table 8 *Chansons copied by the subsidiary scribes and the manner of their texting*

Scribe	Incipit	Texting
Northern 2	Vive le noble roy de France	superius only
Northern 2	Adyeu soullas, tout playsir et liesse	superius only
Northern 2	D'amour je suis desheritée	superius only
Northern 2	[N']a tu point veu la viscontine	superius only
Izagha	Amy, soufré que je vous aime	all parts
Izagha	[J'ay mis mon cueur en ung lieu seulement]	textless
Izagha	[Ces facheux sotz qui mesdisent d'aymer]	textless
Izagha	Unidentified work *a4* (possibly a chanson)	textless
Layolle	Rejuissés vous borgeses, belles filles de Lion	textless (incipit provided by Northern 2)
Layolle	[Plus nulz regretz]	textless

are provided with text. It is plain to see that for only one of these pieces is full text provided in all parts. In the other nine pieces, either the superius alone is texted or no text at all is underlaid. This is not surprising, given that most of the subsidiary scribes seem to have worked in Florence, for chansons were customarily left textless or partially texted in Italian chansonniers both before and after the turn of the century. In northern chansonniers, by way of contrast, texts are provided for all voices, beginning as early as the 1490s.[46]

Now, the main scribe provides full texts for all parts throughout each of his first two groups of chansons. In his third layer of compositions, however, he departs from this practice more than once. We find him texting only the superius and tenor in one piece (fols. 75^v–76^r) and the superius alone in two others (fols. 76^v–78^r). For yet another composition (fols. 70^v–71^r) he provides no text at all – not even an incipit. These departures from the main scribe's general policy of meticulously texting all parts raise the possibility either that he might have intended these pieces for performance in Italy or that he copied them from Italian exemplars. Here, too, however, we must be careful to consider alternative explanations for

---

[46] On texting practices in both northern and Italian chansonniers, see L. Litterick, 'Performing Franco-Netherlandish Secular Music of the Late 15th Century: Texted and Untexted Parts in the Sources', *Early Music*, 8 (1980), pp. 474–85.

the main scribe's inconsistency in texting practice. Indeed, one is suggested by another of his four-voice chansons, *Si j'ayme mon amy* (fols. 68^v–70^r). In this piece, which spans two openings, all parts are fully texted on the first spread; none are on the second. The omission is clearly the result of haste, and it may not be coincidental that the composition which follows in the manuscript is the one piece in the main scribe's hand that bears no text at all.

There are other signs of haste within this segment of the manuscript. The main scribe did not complete the last composition that appears in his hand (fols. 81^v–82^r). This piece seems to be a duo, but the two voices do not result in a self-sufficient contrapuntal structure. There is space for additional voices on the opening; obviously, one or more of them simply was not copied. In addition, the two voices provided are not complete. The abbreviation for 'verte' appears at the end of each of them, but the following folio contains a separate piece, copied by the Layolle scribe. Finally, in the three compositions for which the main scribe supplied poetry for only one or two voices we find that he provided the textless parts with calligraphic initials nonetheless. Perhaps he intended to supply poetry for these voices but neglected to for one reason or another.

It is clear, then, that the subsidiary scribes systematically texted their chansons in *Florence 117* in the Italian manner, and it is possible that the main scribe did so, too, in a number of instances. But we cannot claim this uncategorically in the case of the main scribe, because his omissions may have resulted from the haste with which he appears to have been working on this final portion of the manuscript.

Given the highly circumstantial character of nearly all of the codicological evidence presented thus far, it is not difficult to understand why the literature is divided in its assessment of the provenance of *Florence 117*. For in an almost devilish manner all of the evidence is susceptible to strikingly different interpretations – interpretations that lead, respectively, to views of the manuscript's having been written mainly in the north, or entirely in Florence. Let us summarise briefly the pattern of ambiguity.

First, the nationality of the scribes and the site of their activity: three are clearly Italians; two are definitely northerners; the nationality of one cannot be ascertained. The three Italians unquestionably worked in Florence; the one of uncertain nationality surely worked there, too. The second northern scribe is known to have worked in Florence, and some of his work on our manuscript was definitely carried out there. All of this speaks for the Florentine provenance of the choirbook. However, we have not presented evidence that precludes the second northern scribe's having begun work on the manuscript in the north. More significantly, we have offered no evidence of the main scribe's activity south of the Alps.

As to paper, the oblong format of *Florence 117* is characteristic of Florentine sources, some of which are of dimensions virtually indentical with those of our manuscript. But we have taken note of a good number of northern sources also written in the oblong configuration.

The layout of the staves on the page is invariable throughout the manuscript, which suggests that all the scribes took their paper from the same supply. That would have them all working together in Florence, the demonstrable site of activity for most of them. But it is also possible that the main scribe planned and executed the earliest layer of the manuscript – which amounts to most of it – in the north, whence it was sent to Florence with enough ruled but unwritten folios to accommodate the additions of the subsidiary scribes.

The staves were ruled with a single-stave rastrum, which is the conventional way in which the music paper for northern manuscripts was prepared. But nothing prevents a northern scribe from using his single-stave rastrum wherever he may happen to be. Indeed, we have shown evidence of the use of such a device by a northern scribe who copied French chansons on paper that is clearly Florentine.

Several of the gatherings in our choirbook are quinternions, the fascicle form most commonly found in Florentine music manuscripts. And we detect no quaternions, the preferred form of gathering in northern musical sources of this period. But a scribe putting together a manuscript like ours may assemble gatherings according to his own regional conventions wherever he happens to be. He may also have purchased blank paper already folded and gathered by the stationer, and we have seen evidence of both quaternions and quinternions being sold by a Florentine stationer. In short, we cannot tell very much about the provenance of a manuscript from the size of its gatherings alone.

The disposition of the handwriting within the fascicle structure supplies no evidence of the main scribe's interaction with the subsidiary copyists. It suggests, rather, that the master plan for the manuscript was his and that the subsidiary scribes essentially worked around this plan, adding their entries to the pre-existent work of the main craftsman. But, although this may tell us how the main scribe worked with respect to the subsidiary copyists, it does not tell us where he worked.

Finally, the secondary scribes all text their chansons in the Italian manner: that is, they supply partial texting, incipits alone, or no text at all. That the main scribe occasionally follows such practices, too, suggests that he may have done so in Italy. Nonetheless, we cannot ignore an alternative explanation for the main scribe's failure to text some of his chansons fully: the haste with which he copied certain portions of the manuscript.

Obviously, we need to transcend the limitations of the circumstantial codicological evidence in attempting to determine the provenance of this source. We turn, therefore, to another body of evidence: the source tradition whereby the music in our manuscript was transmitted.

Source traditions. In assessing the possible interactions of the main scribe and the subsidiary copyists, it is important to focus on such repertorial agreement as may be found among their respective contributions to *Florence 117*. Many of the compositions executed by the subsidiary scribes – particularly the Italian repertory – have no relationship at all to the systematic groups of different types of chansons the main scribe set out to provide. But a good number of the pieces added by the secondary copyists seem to complement his repertory nicely. For example, the folios immediately after the main scribe's first section – the group of three-part arrangements – incorporate similar works in the hand of the second northern scribe, the copyist who also worked on *Florence 107bis*.[47] That artisan and the Layolle scribe, moreover, also contributed four-part chansons similar in style to those in the hand of the main scribe.

Also suggestive of interaction between the main scribe and at least

---

[47]   The three chansons *a 3* in the hand of the second northern scribe are Compère's *Vive le noble roy de France* (fols. 13ᵛ–14ʳ), Févin's *Adyeu soullas* (fols. 14ᵛ–15ʳ), and an anonymous *D'amour je suis desheritée* (fols. 15ᵛ–16ʳ).

one of the subsidiary scribes is the source tradition reflected in the music copied into the first layer of *Florence 117*. As we have just suggested, the second northern scribe added a group of chansons *a 3* to the main scribe's first layer in the manuscript. All three of these compositions also appear in the chansonnier recently discovered at Uppsala by Howard Mayer Brown.[48] The readings of these compositions in the two sources are extremely close, and often they join in contradicting the readings of the same pieces preserved in the central chanson sources of the French royal court. Thus, for example, in Févin's *Adyeu soullas*, *Florence 117* contains a number of significant variants from the readings of *Cambridge 1760* and *London 5242* (both manuscripts that were written at the royal court), and, in each case, the same variants appear in *Uppsala 76a* (Example 3).[49] Similarly, the musical readings of *D'amour je suis desheritée* in *Florence 117* are identical with those in *Uppsala 76a* (and very close, too, to those in *Copenhagen 1848*, a Lyonnaise chansonnier copied in the 1520s). They include a rather asperous dissonance that is ameliorated in a later edition printed by Pierre Attaingnant (see the leap into a minor seventh followed by an unsuspended diminished fifth in Example 4a).[50] Except for one example of insignificant rhythmic ornamentation, moreover, the versions of Compère's *Vive le noble roy de France* in the two manuscripts are also identical musically. And, finally, the settings of *Adyeu soullas* and *Vive le noble roy de France* in *Florence 117* include additional lines of poetry beneath the music. These appear in only one other source, *Uppsala 76a*. In orthography and placement on the page, the appearance of the additional verse in the two sources is so similar that we are tempted to suggest that one might have influenced the writing of the other indirectly (or, perhaps, even directly). Thus, the second northern scribe, in adding these chansons to our manuscript, seems to have worked from exemplars that show signs of a source tradition that emanated from provincial

---

[48] For a study of this manuscript, see the paper by H. M. Brown cited in n. 4, above.

[49] Other variants could be cited in which *Cambridge 1760* is jointly contradicted by *Florence 117* and *Uppsala 76a*. The close affinity between the readings in the latter two manuscripts was first suggested by Louise Litterick in her response to Howard Brown's paper on the Uppsala chansonnier, read at the forty-sixth annual meeting of the American Musicological Society, held at Denver in 1980.

[50] It should be noted, however, that the poetry of *D'amour je suis desheritée* is transmitted rather differently in *Florence 117* and *Uppsala 76a*. In the former manuscript the music is provided with no more text than that which fits beneath the music, whereas the latter source contains additional lines of poetry. In fact, *Uppsala 76a* presents the chanson as a rondeau, as Howard Brown points out in his study of this manuscript.

Example 3. Selected variants from *Adyeu soullas*

Cambridge 1760, London 5242, London 35087

Florence 117, Uppsala 76a

Example 4. Variant readings in *D'amour je suis desheritée*

Florence 117, Uppsala 76a

Attaingnant 1529[4]

France, for the Uppsala chansonnier appears to have been copied in Gascony.[51]

Interestingly, there is evidence that at least some of the arrangements copied by the main scribe in the first layer of *Florence 117* stem from the same source tradition. Five of this group of eleven chansons also appear in *Uppsala 76a*, and the musical readings of these compositions in our manuscript are sometimes closer to those of the newly discovered Gascon source than they are to those of the central chansonniers of the French royal court.

Consider, for example, Févin's *Chescun mauldit*, which appears in

---

[51] Brown ('A New French Chansonnier') cites the use of Gascon dialect in the poetic section of *Uppsala 76a*, the presence in its paper of watermarks found in papers used at Toulouse, and a reference to Bordeaux in one of its poems. He concludes that the manuscript seems to have been compiled in south-western France.

Florence 117, Uppsala 76a and *Cambridge 1760*. The poem is a virelai,[52] and three of its quatrains are set to the music preserved by all the sources of Févin's polyphony. In all three of these manuscripts, moreover, the chanson is spread over two openings, with the division occurring after the traditional medial longa. But the division of the form and the change of folio do not occur in the same place in all of the sources. As we see in Table 9, the scribe of the Cambridge manuscript places the corona at the end of the first quatrain (which corresponds to the end of the first folio). The next quatrain is set to two phrases of new music repeated, and the last four lines of poetry are set to a repeat of the music of the first opening. If the first opening itself were then repeated in its entirety, the chanson would have the form of a perfect virelai (*AbbaA*). The main scribe of *Florence 117*, however, divides the chanson at the end of the sixth line of poetry (i.e. in the middle of the second quatrain). He does so by using a longa for the cadence at the end of this line (where the Cambridge scribe had supplied shorter note values) and by extending the first opening to this point. This is a significant error: it obscures the rhyme scheme of the poem and makes it less likely that the work would be performed as a proper virelai, for, in returning to the first opening, the singer would not necessarily know where to conclude the chanson. Tellingly, the reading of the chanson in *Uppsala 76a* mishandles the relationship between the poetic and musical forms in precisely the same way. The musical readings of these two sources, furthermore, are virtually identical,[53] down to the sharing of several alterations in the repeat of the opening music, none of which occur in the Cambridge manuscript.[54] And the two former manuscripts

---

[52] Cf. G. Paris and A. Gevaert, eds., *Chansons du XVᵉ siècle* (Paris, 1875), pp. 18–19, and music section, p. 9; and Gérold, ed., *Le manuscrit de Bayeux*, p. 39.

[53] Only two variants separate the readings of this piece in the two manuscripts: the version in Uppsala divides the breve in the superius just before the return of the opening polyphony and mistakenly provides a semibreve instead of a minim for the *g* eight notes earlier. Otherwise, the musical readings in *Florence 117* and *Uppsala 76a* are precisely the same.

[54] The alterations in the repeat of the opening passage may be listed as follows:

Location	Cambridge 1760	Florence 117, Uppsala 76a
superius, bar 19/2	semibreve	2 minims
tenor, bar 14/1	semibreve	2 minims
bassus, bars 4/5–5/2	minim, 2 semiminims	semibreve
bassus, bar 11/2	*d*	*c*

For a modern edition of this chanson, see E. Clinkscale, 'The Complete Works of Antoine de Févin' (Ph.D. diss., New York University, 1965), ii, pp. 451–4.

Table 9 *Variants in the formal structure and poetry of 'Chescun mauldit ses jaleux'*

Form	Poem	Cambridge 1760	Division of piece and change of folio Uppsala 76a and Florence 117
A	Chescun mauldit ces jaleux Mais je ne les maulditz mye Car il n'est par vray amoureux Qui n'est jaleux de s'amye. ⟶ ⌢		
b	L'aultre jour jouer maloye ⟶ verso Tout a l'entour d'ung vert buisson ⟶ ⊐⌐		
b	Je trouvay[a] la miene amye ⟶ verso Qui parloit a ung compaignon.		
a	Mais je ne scay que luy soit Le jeune me plaisoit mye Don jeu le cueur triste et mary Et entré en ta jalousie[b]		

Notes:
[a] 'viz' in *Uppsala 76a* and *Florence 117*.
[b] 'fantasie' in *Uppsala 76a* and *Florence 117*.

contain textual variants in their respective readings of *Chescun mauldit* that jointly contradict the version transmitted in *Cambridge 1760*.[55] There can be little doubt that the main scribe of our manuscript derived his reading of *Chescun mauldit* not from the branch of its transmission that may be identified with the French royal court but, rather, from another one, very closely related to the provincial tradition reflected in *Uppsala 76a*.

Another chanson by Févin, *Hélas, j'en suis marry*, also shows the proximity of our main scribe's readings with those of the newly discovered chansonnier from Uppsala. In the repeat of the concluding phrase, four alterations are introduced in *Florence 117* (see Example 5). All four also appear in *Uppsala 76a* – none of them in *Cambridge 1760* or *London 5242*. There are, moreover, some twenty-five instances in which the musical readings of this chanson in *Florence 117* and *Uppsala 76a* jointly contradict those in *Cambridge 1760*.

[55] See the textual variants noted at the bottom of Table 9.

43

Example 5. Variants in the concluding phrase of Févin's *Hélas, j'en suis marry* (The passages within boxes show, by direction of the stems, alterations in the repeat of the phrase.)

Admittedly, not one of these variants is an error, and theoretically either scribe could have supplied any one of them strictly by conjecture. Nonetheless, even where relatively insignificant variants are involved, it seems all but impossible that two scribes copying so short a work could replicate twenty-five readings that jointly contradict those of the central transmission unless their own exemplars were more closely related to each other than to the central sources.

The remaining three chansons copied by the main scribe of *Florence 117* that also appear in the Uppsala chansonnier – Mouton's *Mais que ce fust le plaisir d'elle* and Févin's *Je le levray puis qu'il m'y bat* and *On a mal dit* – offer less striking evidence of a relationship between those two sources. In all cases, the reading in *Florence 117* is closer to that in *Uppsala 76a* than to that of any of the French court manuscripts, but the variants that establish this proximity are relatively insignificant and their numbers less impressive than those cited for *Hélas, j'en suis suis marry*. Still, even if the evidence for linking the transmission of these three chansons in our manuscript to that of *Uppsala 76a* is relatively weak, it is stronger than any case that might

44

be advanced for joining the main scribe's work to the transmission we identify with the French royal court.

That the main scribe derived at least some of his readings of the Févin repertory from the same provincial tradition that was drawn upon by the second northern scribe of *Florence 117* argues most persuasively for their interaction in the compilation of the manuscript. Unfortunately, however, it cannot help us to ascertain where the main scribe worked on the choirbook. For, although the second northern scribe is known to have copied music in Florence and, indeed, to have added the incipit and ascription to a piece of music copied by the Florentine Layolle scribe, he is, after all, a native of the north. As we have suggested, it is at least conceivable, therefore, that the second northern scribe worked on our manuscript together with the main scribe somewhere in the north, brought it thence to Florence, and there added the incipit and ascription to the work of the Layolle scribe. The latter scenario is complicated – perhaps even a bit tortuous – but its possibility has to be conceded. We must therefore continue our pursuit of evidence that may help us to establish where the main scribe planned and executed his contributions to *Florence 117*.

The main scribe's second layer in *Florence 117*, it will be recalled, includes a group of well-known *chansons de regret* by Compère and Hayne van Ghizeghem. These chansons were widely disseminated and therefore afford the opportunity to compare the readings of them in *Florence 117* with those in both northern and Italian manuscripts. Hayne's *Allés regretz* provides a case in point. When a venerable 'Burgundian' chanson is disseminated throughout Europe over a period of forty years and survives in some twenty-six sources, its variant readings will themselves be spread far and wide. Thus, although the sources of this chanson preserve literally scores of variants, it is difficult to find significant ones that do not cross over the respective groups of northern and Italian manuscripts. One variant, however, is particularly fascinating; it occurs at one of those moments of syncopation for which many a scribe seems to have provided his own solution (see Example 6). The various sources preserve twelve different readings of this passage. The disparities consist largely in ornamental detail, but certain broad structural patterns suggest that the various readings may be grouped into two basic families, labelled *A* and *B* in the example. In the first of these,

Example 6. A significant variant in Hayne's *Allés regretz*

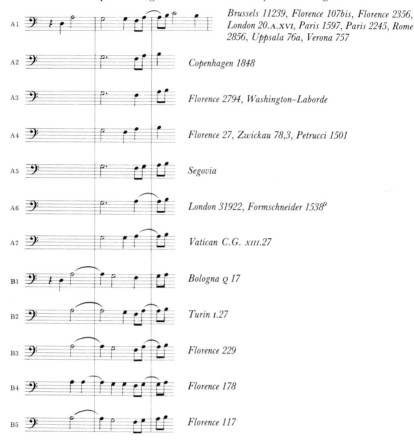

A1 — Brussels 11239, Florence 107bis, Florence 2356, London 20.A.XVI, Paris 1597, Paris 2245, Rome 2856, Uppsala 76a, Verona 757

A2 — Copenhagen 1848

A3 — Florence 2794, Washington–Laborde

A4 — Florence 27, Zwickau 78,3, Petrucci 1501

A5 — Segovia

A6 — London 31922, Formschneider 1538⁹

A7 — Vatican C.G. XIII.27

B1 — Bologna Q 17

B2 — Turin I.27

B3 — Florence 229

B4 — Florence 178

B5 — Florence 117

the initial downward step to *g* occurs immediately and on the tactus; in the second, it is delayed and generally falls after the tactus. Interestingly, every northern source preserves one of the readings from the first group, and the only ones to transmit the second type are Italian, chiefly Florentine, manuscripts. The reading in *Florence 117* belongs to the latter group, and it seems reasonable to suggest, therefore, that our main scribe may have made recourse to an Italian reading of Hayne's chanson. This suggestion is offered with a measure of temerity, however, because by the time the main scribe had copied *Allés regretz* into *Florence 117* the work had already circulated widely for about thirty years.[56] Such longevity and

---

[56] On the chronology of *Florence 117*, see below, pp. 52–4.

breadth of dissemination make it rather precarious to link particular variant readings from the later redactions to specific regional traditions. The danger arises because the exemplars from the later stages in the transmission may embody a redaction that was already 'international' – the product of syntheses of different local traditions made years, or even decades, earlier. We must, therefore, seek better evidence of the influence of an Italian source tradition on our main scribe. It is to be found in his reading of a work by Loyset Compère.

Compère's *Va t'en regretz* is transmitted in eight sources besides *Florence 117* (see Table 10). Using the reading of this chanson in *Paris 2245*, the so-called 'Compère chansonnier', as a point of departure and comparing the readings of other sources with it, we discover a clear distinction between the northern and Italian transmissions of this chanson. None of the French sources contains more than four musical variants from the readings preserved in *Paris 2245*, and all of these variants are relatively insignificant. Much the same applies to the versions from Bruges, Savoy and the Netherlands court, which contain four, four and six variants, respectively. The Florentine source of this chanson (*Florence 107bis*) offers a significantly different version of the composition. It departs from the reading of *Va t'en regretz* in *Paris 2245* twenty-six times, and seventeen of these variants cannot be found in any northern source. Not all of these are truly separative variants, but, as we might expect of a reading that preserves no text, the version of *Va t'en regretz* in *Florence 107bis* changes the rhythms in ways that leave the composition less directly wedded to the rhythmic implications of the poem for which it was composed. Consider Example 7, in which the variants from the Florentine source appear as dotted ties or small notes. In each excerpt, the readings from *Florence 107bis* alter the conventional use of initial repeated notes to anticipate the customary division of the decasyllabic line after the fourth syllable. The variant preserved in Example 7b is especially far removed from the rhythm of the poetic line, for it would force the line to be divided clumsily after the third syllable ('Car ou tu / es ne peult estre ma joye').

Significantly, the reading of *Va t'en regretz* preserved in *Florence 117* reveals a profile not unlike that of *Florence 107bis*. When compared with the version in *Paris 2245*, it yields seventeen variants, of which twelve cannot be found in any northern source. Eight of these variants can also be found in *Florence 107bis*, which suggests that the

Table 10 *The source tradition for Compère's 'Va t'en regretz, celluy qui me convoye'*

Northern manuscripts	Italian manuscripts	Provenance	Number of variants in conflict with *Paris 2245* (the 'Compère chansonnier')
Paris 1596		French royal court	4
Paris 1597		Lorraine?	4
Paris 2245		French royal court	0
Copenhagen 1848		Lyons	4
Brussels 228		Netherlands court	6
Brussels IV 90/ Tournai 94		Bruges	4
Brussels 11239		Savoy	4
	Florence 107bis	Florence	26
	Florence 117[a]	?	17

Note:

[a] *Florence 117* has been grouped with the Italian manuscripts here simply for convenience.

two versions might belong to the same branch of the chanson's transmission.[57] More importantly, the character of the variants in *Florence 117* resembles precisely that of the unique readings in *Florence 107bis*. That is, the discrepancies from the northern tradition often depart from the implications of the poetry exactly as they did in the Florentine source. An illustration appears in Example 8. Here the doubling of the initial note value leaves the phrase one note short of accommodating the first hemistich of the poetic line ('soupessonant' in the northern sources, 'Par toy je crains' in *Florence 117*).[58] A

[57] These eight variants are reported below. For the reading in *Paris 2245*, see *Loyset Compère: Opera omnia*, ed. L. Finscher, Corpus Mensurabilis Musicae 15 (1958–72), v, p. 58. A number of these variants (those marked with an asterisk) appear only in *Florence 107bis* and *Florence 117*; a few others (those marked with a dagger) can be found elsewhere only in the Savoyard manuscript, *Brussels 11239*, a source that was compiled in a region rather closer to Italy than were the French or Netherlandish sources of this chanson:

tenor:	*bar 10/2–3: breve	bassus:	bar 3/2–3: breve
	†bar 15/4–6: semibreve (*e*)		*bar 10/2–3: breve
	†bars 16/5–17/2: longa		*bar 14/3–4: dotted minim
	*bar 18/1: dotted minim		bar 32: no flat

[58] This unique poetic variant in *Florence 117* is also noteworthy for further distinguishing the reading of *Va t'en regretz* in the latter manuscript from those in the northern sources.

Example 7. Excerpts from Compère's *Va t'en regretz*: the readings of *Paris 2245* and *Florence 107bis* compared (The example follows *Paris 2245*, after the *Opera omnia*, ed. L. Finscher. Variants from *Florence 107bis* are shown by dotted ties and small notes.)

Example 8. Readings from the superius of Compère's *Va t'en regretz* in *Paris 2245* (after the *Opera omnia*) and *Florence 117*

reading such as this one could be expected to appear in a source like *Florence 107bis*, where, as we have seen, *Va t'en regretz* was copied without poetry. But the chanson appears fully texted in *Florence 117*,

49

which makes it all the more significant that the musical reading of Compère's chanson in the latter manuscript preserves the freer, 'instrumental' attitude towards rhythm of an Italian chansonnier. It is also important to note that variants of this sort are not limited to the bassus part of this reading; they appear, too, in the cantus and tenor parts – the ones most likely to have been sung and, consequently, the ones we would expect to have been texted properly. In short, it is difficult to resist the conclusion that the main scribe copied Compère's *Va t'en regretz* into *Florence 117* from an exemplar that belonged to the same Italian branch of the transmission as does the reading in *Florence 107bis*.

The important question for us, of course, is where the main scribe availed himself of this Italian transmission. The character of the dissemination of *Va t'en regretz* and, most significantly, the manner in which it differs from that of, say, Hayne's *Allés regretz* are telling with respect to this issue. Compère's piece appears to have had a rather more limited history than Hayne's chanson. It is preserved in nine sources, all but the very latest of which were written between 1496 and 1515.[59] The transmission involves northern manuscripts almost exclusively, and the work appears in two manuscripts of the French royal court. Conspicuously absent are concordances in Italian sources of the 1480s and 1490s. Presumably, therefore, *Va t'en regretz* may be regarded as a product of Compère's tenure at the French royal court, and it would appear to have been composed between 1486 and 1496, the respective dates of his first recorded presence at the court of Charles VIII and the earliest source of the chanson.[60] Thus, a scribe copying this piece in the north about 1510–15 would have been working at a relatively early stage in the work's transmission, and he would have been close to both the site of its composition and the centre of its dissemination. He would have had no obvious need to turn to a 'foreign' exemplar. That the main scribe of *Florence 117* did, indeed, base his reading of *Va t'en regretz* upon the Italian transmission of the chanson argues compellingly, therefore, for his presence in Italy.[61]

[59] Cf. Table 10 on p. 48.

[60] Ludwig Finscher includes *Va t'en regretz* among a group of 'perfect examples of the Burgundian song idiom' and assigns the work to the period of Compère's 'larger Burgundian works', *c.* 1485–90. L. Finscher, *Loyset Compère (c 1450–1518): Life and Works*, Musicological Studies and Documents 12 (1964), p. 235.

[61] On the chronology of *Florence 117*, see below, pp. 52–4.

For the sake of completeness, one might wish to entertain the possibility that, for some

Provenance: conclusions. I suggest that the evidence from the source tradition permits us to break the log jam that resulted from the circumstantial character of the codicological evidence. Indeed, it puts the circumstantial evidence into a clearer perspective, enabling us to draw lines of congruence among its various facets.

Surely, the main scribe must have carried out his work on our

unknown reason, the main scribe, although working in the north, copied *Va t'en regretz* from an exemplar that embodied the Italian transmission of the work. Indeed, Allan Atlas has recently initiated the investigation of the possible influence of Italian redactions upon manuscripts copied in the north. He alludes to significant concordances that link *Copenhagen 1848* – a Lyonnaise chansonnier of the 1520s – to several manuscripts of the central Florentine tradition of the late fifteenth century (*Florence 229* and *Vatican City C.G. XIII.27*). And he suggests that in the transmission of Robert Morton's *Le souvenir de vous me tue* two late, French provincial chansonniers (*Uppsala 76a* and *Copenhagen 1848*) follow a number of earlier Italian manuscripts (*Bologna Q 16, Florence 176* and *Paris 15123*) in contradicting the readings of various Franco-Burgundian sources of this composition.

The evidence Atlas cites is necessarily of a preliminary nature, and it gives rise to a number of questions. *Copenhagen 1848* does, indeed, share unique concordances with two Florentine chansonniers, but, as Atlas himself points out, the readings of the French source lack significant agreement with those of its Florentine counterparts. Which evidence ought to weigh more heavily upon our consideration of this matter, that of significant concordances or that of significant disagreement among the respective readings?

The redaction of Morton's *Le souvenir* in the two French chansonniers is analogous in some ways to the transmission of Hayne's *Allés regretz*, to which we referred earlier, and it raises problems similar to those we cited in connection with that composition. That is, the late French sources preserve readings that were introduced near the end of a transmission that continued for about half a century. How can we be certain that the reading in these sources that seems to reflect the influence of an Italian tradition is not, in reality, the result of an 'internationalisation' of a redaction of Morton's chanson made much earlier in the history of its transmission?

Finally, Atlas's case for Italian influence on the transmission of Morton's *Le souvenir* in the two French chansonniers rests principally upon the evidence of a single significant variant. The difference that distinguishes the older Franco-Burgundian reading of this passage from that of the later French chansonniers together with their putative Italian models consists essentially in the manner in which the contratenor approaches the final cadence of the chanson. The two readings, however, are equally conventional among the various cadential formulas of the day, and their location but a few tacti before the end of the piece is one that is highly amenable to the introduction of scribal improvisation. Can we ignore altogether the possibility that this particular variant may conceivably be the result of scribal conjecture?

These questions notwithstanding, Prof. Atlas has raised a serious methodological issue concerning the regional character of the redaction of musical sources. It is a subject most worthy of further investigation. As far as *Va t'en regretz* is concerned, however, we still lack any serious reason to assume that its Italian redaction would have had an impact within French musical circles.

On the significant concordances between *Copenhagen 1848* and the Florentine manuscripts, cf. A. Atlas, 'Conflicting Attributions in Italian Sources of the Franco-Netherlandish Chanson, C. 1465–C. 1505: A Progress Report on a New Hypothesis', *Music in Medieval and Early Modern Europe: Patronage, Sources and Texts*, ed. I. Fenlon (Cambridge, 1981), pp. 251–2, esp. n. 7; and *idem, The Cappella Giulia Chansonnier*, I, pp. 221–2, 228. The case for Italian influence on late French readings of Morton's chanson appears in *Robert Morton: The Collected Works*, ed. A. Atlas, Masters and Monuments of the Renaissance 2 (New York, 1981), pp. xxx, 71–2.

51

manuscript in Florence. To suggest otherwise is to require a scenario so convoluted as to strain the imagination. That would be as follows:

The main scribe copies French music according to the readings of a demonstrably Italian source tradition. He writes on paper cut to oblong format and gathered largely in quinternions – paper that conforms precisely, that is, to the manner in which it is most commonly sold and used in Florence. And he texts a number of chansons as they would be texted in an Italian chansonnier. All of this he does in France! He works in his northern centre with a colleague, the second northern scribe, with whom he shares readings that can be associated with south-western France. The latter scribe then takes the manuscript, along with a great quantity of blank, ruled paper, to Florence, where he and four Italian scribes make numerous additions to it.

Clearly, the simpler explanation – and the one that may be defended on the strength of both codicological and textual evidence – cries out for acceptance: the main scribe also worked in Florence. Establishing the site of the main scribe's activity in Florence, at any rate, clarifies greatly our view of the provenance of *Florence 117*. I believe that we may safely conclude that, in its entirety, it was copied and compiled in the great Tuscan city.

Chronology. The dating of *Florence 117* is almost as elusive as its provenance. Our most secure anchor is the presence in it of Josquin's *Plus nulz regretz*, which was composed between 1508 and 1511.[62] From this we may ascertain that the Layolle scribe, in whose hand Josquin's chanson was copied, worked on *Florence 117* no earlier than the same span of years (1508–11). The second northern scribe seems to have made some entries before the Layolle scribe, for his characteristically northern hand precedes that of his Florentine colleague at the beginning of fascicle C.[63] But there is also evidence that the second northern scribe wrote after the Layolle scribe: as we have

---

[62] On the date of this chanson, see M. Picker, 'Josquin and Jean Lemaire: Four Chansons Re-examined', *Essays Presented to Myron P. Gilmore*, ed. S. Bertelli and G. Ramakus (Florence, 1978), ii, pp. 448 and 453, n. 5; and H. Kellman, 'Josquin and the Courts of the Netherlands and France: The Evidence of the Sources', *Josquin des Prez: Proceedings of the International Josquin Festival-Conference*, ed. E. E. Lowinsky in collaboration with B. J. Blackburn (London, 1976), pp. 182–3.

[63] See Figure 10 on p. 33.

seen, it was this northern copyist who added the attribution and incipit to another chanson for which the Layolle scribe provided the music, Mouton's *Rejuissés vous borgeses*.[64] That these two copyists seem both to have preceded and followed each other in making their respective entries in *Florence 117* speaks for their having worked on the manuscript at about the same time. From our consideration of source traditions, moreover, we have learned of the especially close relationship between the second northern scribe and the main scribe. Thus, the principal copyist of *Florence 117* would seem to have been occupied with the manuscript at about the same time as the two subsidiary scribes just noted (i.e. Northern 2 and 'Layolle').

Of course, the main scribe, as architect of the manuscript's original plan, obviously wrote first and, theoretically, could have prepared much of the manuscript well before any of the other scribes touched it. Actually, though, he is unlikely to have copied his various layers much before the *terminus post quem* of 1508–11 we established for the interaction of Northern 2 and 'Layolle'. Had the main scribe made his entries even five years before this range of dates, we would have to explain the anomalous appearance in a Florentine source of a group of chansons by members of the Févin circle some five to ten years before these compositions first appeared in French sources.[65] To repeat, the *terminus post quem* for most of *Florence 117* would seem to be *c.* 1508–11.

The *terminus ante quem* for the compilation of the manuscript is even harder to determine. It is most unlikely, however, that the great majority of the work on the choirbook would have been done any later than 1520. That is the latest we find any significant signs in Italian manuscripts of the repertories represented in *Florence 117*. The Florentine sources concordant with our manuscript are particularly telling. Table 11 lists, in approximate chronological order, all of the Florentine manuscripts that contain music in common with our chansonnier. Not surprisingly, these manuscripts include a substantial portion of our repertory; some nineteen concordances can be cited. Significantly, none of these sources can be dated later than

---

[64] See above, p. 13.
[65] The principal French sources of this repertory of chansons are *Cambridge 1760* and *London 5242*, both of which can be dated *c.* 1509–14. On the dating of these two manuscripts, see Litterick, 'The Manuscript Royal 20.A.XVI of the British Library', pp. 54–5 and 45, respectively.

Table 11 *Florentine manuscripts concordant with Florence 117*

Manuscript	Date[a]	Number of Concordances
Florence 2356	*c.* 1480–5	1
Florence 229	1491	1
Florence 178	1492–4	1
Florence 230	1492–4	1
Vatican C.G. XIII.27	1492–4	3
London 3051/Washington M6	*c.* 1495	1
Bologna Q 17	after 1500	2
Florence 2442	1508–*c.* 1515	1
Florence 107bis	before 1513	4
Cortona 95–6/Paris 1817	*c.* 1515–16	1
Florence 164–7	*c.* 1515–*c.* 1552	1
Florence 2440	*c.* 1515–20	1
Florence 337	*c.* 1520	1

Note:

[a] On the chronology of these manuscripts, see Hamm and Kellman, eds., *Census-Catalogue, passim.* For the date of *Bologna Q 17* particularly, see C. Wright, 'Antoine Brumel and Patronage at Paris', *Music in Medieval and Early Modern Europe*, ed. I. Fenlon (Cambridge, 1981), p. 52.

1520, and the concentration of concordances (15 of the 19) appears in manuscripts that can be dated 1515 or earlier.[66]

It is perhaps not unreasonable, on the basis of this information, to date the compilation of *Florence 117* at *c.* 1515.[67]

THE CHANSONS OF *FLORENCE 117*

Chansons for three voices. Twenty-four chansons for three voices may be found in *Florence 117*. Most of these (eighteen) are in the hand

[66] Noteworthy, too, is the fact, alluded to earlier, that the scribe who added the foliation to our manuscript was the Florentine copyist who served as the principal scribe of *Florence 178*, a manuscript that can be dated *c.* 1492–4 on the basis of its paper and repertorial ties. Admittedly, it is possible that this artisan remained active in Florence for, say, thirty years, in which case he could have foliated *Florence 117* as late as *c.* 1524. A tenure that long would have been most unusual, however, particularly in the light of the vicissitudes of Florentine politics about the turn of the century. A maximum of twenty years seems a more realistic estimate of the scribe's tenure at Florence, and this would place the *terminus ante quem* for his involvement with *Florence 117* at *c.* 1515, a date more or less the same as that suggested by the range of concordances for the music in our manuscript.

[67] If the foliation was added to our manuscript no later than *c.* 1515, then almost all of the music in the source would have been in place by that time. Only the entry of the last scribe, the work *a 4* of the Izagha scribe, and the jottings of the scribblers appear without foliation and would seem, therefore, to have been later additions.

of the main scribe. The second northern scribe and the Izagha scribe each contributed three additional chansons *a3*. Those in the main hand are grouped in two layers. The second layer (fols. 33^v–41^r), as we have seen, consists largely, but not exclusively, of a 'cycle' of works by Compère and Hayne van Ghizeghem that treat the theme of *regret* in their poems. It is not surprising to find the group of five *regret* chansons in our manuscript. These compositions were widely disseminated and appear in numerous manuscripts from various centres, both northern and Italian. Nearly all of them may be found in other Florentine sources, too. However, the presence in *Florence 117* of the other three-voice chansons – those relegated mainly to the main scribe's first layer – requires further explanation.

The first group of chansons *a3* in the hand of the main scribe consists of eleven pieces. Five of these bear attributions elsewhere either to Antoine de Févin or to Jean Mouton and, as one might expect of three-voice chansons by these composers, they conform to the rubrics of what Howard Brown has called the 'three-part arrangement'.[68] That is, they are simple, imitative pieces, in which a pre-existent melody appears in the tenor and is made the subject, in the two other voices, of prior imitation and contrapuntal continuation. Often, as we see in Table 12, the borrowed melody may also be found as an independent monophonic tune. But even when a pre-existent source for the melody is lacking, its existence may be posited on the basis of the lengthier rests, simpler rhythms and melodies, and more frequent internal repetition that are characteristically found in the tenor parts of these chansons. The main scribe included another composition of this type in *Florence 117*, outside the perimeters of his first layer: the second composition within his second layer of chansons may be aptly characterised as a three-part arrangement.

The remaining chansons *a3* in the main hand depart from the conventions of the Févin-like arrangements. One of these, the anonymous setting of *Pleust a la vierge Marie*, appears in Example 9. This piece differs from the three-part arrangements in a number of ways. It is more concise. None of its parts can be identified as pre-existent material, and none behaves as if it were. The typically

---

[68] H. M. Brown, 'The *Chanson rustique*: Popular Elements in the 15th- and 16th-Century Chanson', *Journal of the American Musicological Society*, 12 (1959), pp. 16–26; idem, 'The Genesis of a Style: The Parisian Chanson, 1500–1530', *Chanson & Madrigal, 1480–1530*, pp. 21–5.

Table 12 *Three-part arrangements in the hand of the main scribe*

No.	Incipit	Composer	Source of the monophonic tune	Does tenor behave like pre-existent material?
1	Souvent je m'esbatz et mon cueur est marry	—	*Paris 9346* *Paris 12744*	yes
2	Hélas, j'en suis marry	[Févin]	—	yes
3	Chescun mauldit ses jaleux	[Févin]	*Paris 9346* *Paris 12744*	yes
4	Je m'en allé voir m'amye ung soir	—	[a] *Chansons nouvelles en langaige provensal*	yes
6	Je le levray puis qu'il m'y bat	[Févin]	*Paris 9346*	yes
7	On a mal dit de mon amy	[Févin]	*Paris 9346* *Paris 12744*	yes
9	Mais que ce fust le plaisir d'elle	[Mouton]	*Paris 9346*	yes
10	Monseigneur le grant maistre	—	—	yes
11	Qui vous vouldroit entretenir	—	—	yes
24	Triste et pensif suis sans mot dire	—	*Paris 9346*	yes

Note:

[a] The presence of the monophonic tune in this printed source is reported by H. M. Brown, *Music in the French Secular Theater* (Cambridge, Mass., 1963), p. 238.

Example 9. Anonymous, *Pleust a la vierge Marie* (*Florence 117*, fols. 5ᵛ–6ʳ)

Example 9 – continued

58

widely spaced imitative entries of the three-part arrangement give way to an onomatopoeic refrain, in which a diminutive and highly syllabic motif is bandied about the texture in imitation and part exchange.

How may we account for the differences in style that set off this composition from other three-voice chansons in our manuscript? Its poem provides a clue:

Pleust a la vierge Marie	I would pray to the virgin Mary
Et a tous les sainctz qui sont	and to all the saints there are
Que mon mari fust a Naples;	that my husband might be at Naples;
Nous fussions de ça les montz.	that the Alps might separate him
Tirelirelire,	from us.
Mon joly cueur luy respond,	Tirelirelire,
Tirelirelire.	my gay heart replies to him,
	Tirelirelire.

The text contains the ironic prayer of the wife of a French soldier. She wishes that her husband might be dispatched to Naples, that the Alps might separate him from her and from her lover. The references to Naples and to the Alps make clear the context to which this poem belongs: Charles VIII's Neapolitan campaign of 1494–5.[69] Let us recall that members of the French king's musical entourage accompanied him to Italy in 1494,[70] which suggests at least the possibility that this particular chanson was composed in Italy. Indeed, Compère, who was one of the musicians in Italy with Charles, composed his *Vive le noble roy de France* to celebrate the outcome of the battle of Fornovo, which was touted by some as a French victory in the Neapolitan campaign, and its style is as far-removed from that of the three-part arrangement as is that of *Pleust a la vierge Marie*.[71] Interestingly, Compère's chanson also appears in

---

[69] For a detailed account of Charles's futile military adventures in Italy, see F. Guicciardini, *La historia d'Italia* (Venice, 1567), pp. 35–113; trans. S. Alexander (London, 1969), pp. 43–109.

[70] See the letter published in L. Lockwood, 'Music at Ferrara in the Period of Ercole I d'Este', *Studi Musicali*, 1 (1972), pp. 115–16, 129–30.

[71] Compère's chanson is brief, essentially homorhythmic, and largely syllabic. See the modern edition in *Loyset Compère: Opera omnia*, v, p. 60. Further on the historical occasion for which this chanson was composed, see M. B. Winn, 'Some Texts for Chansons by Loyset Compere', *Musica Disciplina*, 33 (1979), pp. 48–50. Dr Winn offers convincing evidence that this text is explicitly linked to the battle of Fornovo, despite its anomalous inclusion of the Florentines, who were Charles's allies, among those reportedly vanquished by the French king. The battle of Fornovo, itself, is characterised by Dr Winn as a decisive victory for France, in line with the views of such French chroniclers as Phillipe

our manuscript, but in the hand of the second northern scribe. It is not surprising that the pair of compositions was preserved in a Florentine source for, despite numerous enticements to do so, Florence refused to join the Italian League, which brought together, in alliance against Charles VIII, Pope Alexander VI, Emperor Maximilian I, Ferdinand King of Spain, Ludovico il Moro (Duke of Milan) and the Venetians. Florence, that is, would have been one of the few regions in Italy in which works sympathetic to Charles are likely to have been preserved.

Another chanson in the hand of the main scribe is a stylistic twin of *Pleust a la vierge Marie*. *Et mirelaridaine*, excerpts of which appear in Example 10, opens the principal scribe's second layer of chansons.[72] Like *Pleust a la vierge Marie*, it lacks pre-existent material, is extremely concise, and incorporates a refrain on what might appear to be nonsense syllables.[73] The refrain is set to a tightly knit motif of rapid repeated notes that is subjected to light imitation. Thus it is very much like the refrain of *Pleust a la vierge Marie*. Refrains on collections of syllables like these appear in a small corpus of chansons that, for the most part, seem to be associated with traditions other than those of the central chanson repertory of the French royal court. Table 13 lists a number of these compositions. It shows that many of them either mention in their poems a specific region of provincial France or were set by composers who lived and worked somewhere outside the orbit of the royal court.

The specific refrain 'Et mirelaridaine' may be found not only in the chanson at present under consideration, but in two others as well. One is by Ninot Le Petit, who worked at the papal chapel between 1488 and 1501. It appears in a Florentine chansonnier written about the same time as our manuscript (*Florence 2442*).[74] The other, presumably a later work, is by Guillaume Le Heurteur, who served as preceptor of the choirboys at St Martin of Tours.[75] The

---

de Commynes. A different perspective on the outcome of the battle may be read in Guicciardini's account of it (see the citation in n. 69, above).

[72] On the likelihood that the main scribe added this piece to a blank opening that preceded the 'real' beginning of his second layer, see above, p. 35.

[73] Rabelais, however, uses 'mirelaridaine' to denote imaginary articles of food. See E. Huguet, *Dictionnaire de la langue française du seizième siècle* (Paris, 1925–67), v, p. 281.

[74] On Ninot's biography, see *Ninot Le Petit: Collected Works*, ed. B. Hudson, Corpus Mensurabilis Musicae 87 (Neuhausen–Stuttgart, 1979), pp. xi–xiii. The chanson in question, *En chevauchant pres d'ung molin*, appears *ibid.*, pp. 1–4. On the date of *Florence 2442*, see my article, 'Notes on the Origin of the Parisian Chanson', pp. 286–7, n. 28.

[75] On Le Heurteur, see L. F. Bernstein, 'Le Heurteur, Guillaume', *The New Grove Dictionary*,

Example 10. The opening of *Et mirelaridaine Regnauldin* (*Florence 117*, fols. 33ᵛ–34ʳ)

x, pp. 622–3. The refrain under consideration opens Le Heurteur's *Mirelaridon don don don daine*, which appeared in *Attaingnant 1533¹*.

Table 13 *Selected chansons with refrains on nonsense syllables*

Refrain	Composer	Place mentioned	Incipit	Source
'bon bon bon bon'	Mouton	Lyons	En venant de Lyon	Attaingnant 1528
'hari bouriquet'	Sermisy	Toulouse	Les dames se sont tailladés	Attaingnant 1531[1]
'la frelin frelorion'	Lupi	Noyon	En revenant de Noyon	Attaingnant 1540[4]
'milorin falin falot'	—	Lorraine	En revenant de Lorayne	Scotto [1535][9]
'myrely myrela bon bas'	Willaert	Arras	Dessus le marche d'Arras	Attaingnant [c. 1528][9]

Refrain	Composer	Location of composer	Incipit	Source
'Et harribourri lasne'	Le Heurteur	Tours	Troys jeunes bourgeoises	Attaingnant 1533[1]
'Mirelaridon don don don daine'	Le Heurteur	Tours	Mirelaridon don don don daine	Attaingnant 1533[1]
'mirelaridaine'	Ninot Le Petit	Rome	En chevauchant pres d'ung molin	Florence 2442
'Va, mirelidrogue'	Passerau	Bourges	Va, mirelidrogue	Attaingnant 1533[1]

Example 11. The refrain 'mirelaridaine' in two settings: (a) Anonymous, *Et mirelaridaine Regnauldin* (*Florence 117*); (b) Ninot Le Petit, *En chevauchant pres d'ung molin* (*Florence 2442*, after the *Opera omnia*, ed. B. Hudson)

refrain in Ninot's piece, as we see in Example 11, is very close to that of the anonymous chanson in our manuscript with respect to both poetry and music. Could this suggest that the anonymous *Et mirelaridaine*, like the related setting by Ninot Le Petit, was composed in Italy? I think so. Like Ninot's piece, the anonymous setting appears exclusively in a Florentine source. Again, like the work by Ninot, the anonymous *Et mirelaridaine* lacks any demonstrable connection with the rich repertory of French monophonic song – the repertory mined so consistently as a source of borrowed melodies by Févin and his colleagues in their chansons for three voices. And the style of the anonymous version is, as we have seen, very close to that of *Pleust a la vierge Marie*, which we have linked to Charles VIII's Italian campaign of 1494–5.

The last three-voice chanson copied by the main scribe that is neither a three-part arrangement nor one of the *regret* settings is the famous *Chant de l'alouette* by Clément Janequin.[76] The three-part

---

[76] The authorship of this chanson has been the subject of a great deal of controversy, which has most recently been summarised in P. Christoffersen, ' "Or sus vous dormez trop": The Singing of the Lark in French Chansons of the Early Sixteenth Century', *Festskrift Henrik Glahn*, ed. M. Müller (Copenhagen, 1979), pp. 35–67.

The controversy arises because none of the five sources that contain the three-voice *Chant de l'alouette* bears an attribution. The suggestion that Janequin composed the work is generally made because Attaingnant printed a four-voice setting of the text that is securely attributed to Janequin; three of its parts are close to, but not identical with, the polyphony contained in the version *a 3*.

Dr Christoffersen believes that Janequin wrote the four-voice setting, but not the one *a 3*. He offers the following evidence: (1) The three-voice *Chant de l'alouette* is not as unique stylistically as has been heretofore maintained. It combines elements of several established techniques of chanson composition: the three-part arrangement and the use of such onomatopoeic devices as may be characteristically found as early as the fourteenth-century virelais. (2) The contratenor part in the four-voice setting seems to have been composed last and tends to produce textural 'friction' with the superius in a manner uncharacteristic of Janequin. (3) A later edition of the version *a 4* substitutes a more felicitous contratenor part. Dr Christoffersen concludes that, in his four-part *Chant de*

chansons copied by the principal scribe thus include music that emanated from provincial France, for Janequin spent the major portion of his career in various provincial posts – at Bordeaux, Auch and Angers.[77] The *Chant de l'alouette* is a product of his *période Bordelaise*.

Apart from the complex of *regret* settings, thus, the three-voice chansons copied by the main scribe consist of two types of composition: three-part arrangements of the Févin variety and pieces in other styles, which can be linked either with Italy or with provincial France. Indeed, as we have seen earlier, even some of the three-part arrangements in the main hand can be connected to south-western France because of readings in common with *Uppsala 76a*, a manuscript of the early sixteenth century now believed to have been compiled in Gascony.[78]

The second northern scribe added three chansons *a 3* to the main scribe's first layer of three-voice chansons. They commence in the folios left blank by the main scribe at the end of the second gathering. As a group, the three pieces provide a microcosm of the principal scribe's first layer of chansons. Two of the compositions are three-part arrangements by Févin and emanate, presumably, from the French royal court. But the third piece is Compère's *Vive le noble roy de France*, written, as we have seen, for the Italian campaign of 1494–5. Evidence of ties to provincial France are strong, too, because all three of these chansons preserve musical readings virtually identical with those in *Uppsala 76a*.

Three chansons *a 3* remain to be considered; all are in the hand we identified as that of the Izagha scribe. This appellative, it will be recalled, is derived from the name ('Do. Izagha') that appears over

---

l'alouette, Janequin 'resorted to making an arrangement of the widely known three-part chanson' (p. 52).

Because no source for the three-voice setting names any composer, however, Christoffersen admits that Janequin *could* be its composer. That seems to me by far the more attractive option. The lengthy onomatopoeic section of the three-voice *Chant de l'alouette* reflects precisely the same highly idiosyncratic style we find in Janequin's other programme chansons. In scope and intensity, it would seem to be without precedent in the chanson literature of the early sixteenth century. Surely, it is more natural to view Janequin as the composer of both versions of the *Chant de l'alouette* than to suggest that his extremely individual style was anticipated in a single work by an unknown composer, to which he then added a new contratenor part. I believe we may safely conclude that Janequin is the likely composer of the *Chant de l'alouette* found in *Florence 117*.

[77] H. M. Brown, 'Janequin, Clément', *The New Grove Dictionary*, ix, pp. 491–2.
[78] See above, pp. 41–5.

the first of the chansons copied by this artisan, the well-known *Amy, soufré que je vous aime*. In this work we find all the basic attributes of a mature Parisian chanson ensconced in a three-voice texture.[79] The authorship of this chanson is beclouded by conflicting attributions. Le Roy & Ballard printed the piece several times many years after the compilation of *Florence 117* (in *Le Roy & Ballard 1553*[22] and *1578*[14]). In those prints they ascribe the work to Moulu over the music, but either to Le Heurteur (1553) or to Claudin de Sermisy (1578) in the tables of contents. Elsewhere, I have argued on behalf of what might be an attribution to Isaac in our manuscript.[80] Despite the reservations expressed above regarding the unusual spelling of this name and whether it is even intended to designate the composer of the chanson over which it appears, the notion that this chanson might be by Isaac seems not altogether implausible for a number of reasons: (1) The attributions to Claudin and Le Heurteur in the tables of contents of Le Roy & Ballard's prints can surely be dismissed as printer's errors, for they consistently conflict with the ascriptions over the music. (2) The attributions to Moulu appear in sources dating from decades after his last known activity. (3) The style of the work is unlike that of any of the other chansons attributed to Moulu. (4) The name Izagha appears in a source we have shown to have been written in the city of Isaac's residence. (5) Another composition incorporates similar elements of Parisian chanson style, and it is unequivocally attributed to Isaac in one of the most reliable of Florentine chansonniers (*Florence 229*).

Thus, tenuous as it may be, the suggestion that Heinrich Isaac could have been the composer of the *Amy, soufré* setting in our manuscript ought not simply be rejected out of hand. Whoever composed the work, its presence in *Florence 117* testifies to that of the Parisian chanson in Tuscany as early as 1515. It may even suggest – if Isaac was indeed its composer – that such chansons were composed in Florence at this time.

[79] For modern editions of this chanson, see *Pierre Attaingnant: Transcriptions of Chansons for Keyboard*, ed. A. Seay, Corpus Mensurabilis Musicae 20 (1961), pp. 155–6 (attributed to Moulu); Bernstein, 'Notes on the Origin of the Parisian Chanson', p. 319 (attributed to Do. Izagha); *Music at the Court of Henry VIII*, ed. J. Stevens, Musica Britannica 18 (London, 1962), pp. 64–5 (anonymous); *Nachtrag zu den weltlichen Werken von Heinrich Isaac*, ed. J. Wolf, pp. 204–5; *Claudin de Sermisy: Opera omnia*, Corpus Mensurabilis Musicae 52/III–IV, *Chansons*, ed. I. Cazeaux (1974), III, p. 14; *Thirty Chansons (1529) for Three Instruments or Voices*, ed. B. Thomas, p. 22 (attributed to Moulu).

[80] Bernstein, 'Notes on the Origin of the Parisian Chanson', pp. 318–22.

Example 12. 'Parisian' traits in two chansons copied by the Izagha scribe: (a) *Ces facheux sotz qui mesdisent d'aymer*; (b) *J'ay mis mon cueur en ung lieu seulement*

66

The next two works in the hand of the Izagha scribe are completely textless, but they have been identified as chansons. And, as
we see in Example 12, both reflect the salient stylistic elements of the
Parisian chanson, just as *Amy, soufré* does. It is hard to tell where
these two chansons were composed, but their presence in *Florence 117*
and the bonds we pointed out earlier that link them with works by
Francesco de Layolle suggest that these compositions were part of a
Florentine repertory before 1520. Thus, the three chansons the
Izagha scribe copied into *Florence 117* demonstrate that the essential
elements of Parisian chanson style were known, if not actually
practised, in Florence a decade or more before the great efflorescence
of the genre at the hands of Pierre Attaingnant.

Reflecting for a moment on the three-voice chansons in *Florence
117*, we find among them a rather diverse amalgam of styles and
source traditions. Included are: (1) a complex of 'Burgundian' *regret*
settings; (2) a group of three-part arrangements from the French
royal court – drawn, however, from a source tradition that can be
traced to south-western France; (3) several pieces in a light patter
style that can be linked to Italy through historical references or the
nature and substance of their refrains; (4) a chanson composed in
Bordeaux; and (5) a group of works that are clearly couched in the
conventions of the Parisian chanson, at least one of which may have
been composed in Florence. The mixture of influences – those of
Italy, provincial France and the royal court – on the compilation of
this repertory is striking, and we shall be alert for the presence of
similar influences while assessing the background of the four-voice
chansons in our manuscript.

Chansons for four voices. Seventeen chansons for four voices
appear in *Florence 117*, all but four of them in the main scribe's third
group of chansons, which comprises most of the penultimate and
antepenultimate gatherings. Another chanson *a 4* in the principal
scribe's hand appears just before the first of these two fascicles (fols.
65v–66r), the second northern scribe provides one composition for
four voices, and the Layolle scribe another two.[81] These chansons

---

[81] Two other works may also be four-voice chansons. The unidentified textless piece *a 4* in the
hand of the Izagha scribe on fols. 24v–(26r) could originally have had a French text, as do
two of the other compositions copied without text by this scribe. The last work copied by

may be divided into several different groups, which parallel strikingly the various stylistic or regional categories into which we placed the three-voice chansons of *Florence 117*.

Three chansons *a 4* are clearly the work of northern masters and are couched in one or another of the musical dialects favoured by northern chanson composers at the beginning of the sixteenth century. Thus, Josquin's *Plus nulz regretz* is through-composed and disposes a great number of different motifs throughout a pervasively imitative texture, one that incorporates a good measure of inexact canonic writing.[82] Imitation is ubiquitous in Févin's *N'emez jamais une villaine*, too (Example 13). But the style of this chanson is more relaxed than that of Josquin's, for it repeats its simple tune in the superius and tenor, while varying the freely imitative counterpoint in the outer voices.[83] Pierre Moulu's *Hélas, hélas madame* (Example 14) offers a mixture of lengthy homorhythmic phrases, slow-moving counterpoint and sequential melodies. Its style is similar to that of the four-voice *chansons de complaint*, of which a number are attributed to Josquin. These three chansons are the only pieces among the works *a 4* in *Florence 117* that may with certainty be regarded as having been composed at one of the major musical establishments of the north.[84]

The next category of four-voice chansons to be discussed is the one most amply represented in our manuscript. Its most prominent stylistic features may be observed in Example 15, which offers excerpts from a chanson copied with no text or incipit in *Florence 117*. Although the polyphony of this setting is unique to our manuscript, its melody is set elsewhere to the poem of a well-known French lyric, *La jeusne dame va au molin*.[85] Here we have a musical texture that is

the main scribe (fols. 81ᵛ–82ʳ), as we have seen, has only two voices, and all that is supplied by way of text is a calligraphic initial 'I'. As we indicated above, however, it is easy to tell that voices are missing from this work. It, too, could have been a chanson for four voices.

[82] A modern edition of Josquin's chanson appears in *Josquin des Prés: Wereldlijke Werken*, ed. A. Smijers, Afl. VIII, Bund. III (Amsterdam, 1925), no. 29, pp. 74–5.

[83] For a modern edition of Févin's chanson, see Clinkscale, 'The Complete Works of Antoine de Févin', II, pp. 470–3.

[84] *Plus nulz regretz* was composed while Josquin was at Condé; Févin, of course, was in the service of Louis XII. The biographical evidence about Moulu is very sparse, but the occasions for which he composed motets and the nature of his music suggest close ties with the royal court of France.

On Josquin at Condé, see the communication by H. Kellman in the *Journal of the American Musicological Society*, 27 (1974), p. 367. On Moulu, see E. Lowinsky, ed., *The Medici Codex of 1518*, Monuments of Renaissance Music 3–5 (Chicago, 1968), III, pp. 68–9, 72–4.

[85] Further on the melody for *La jeusne dame* and the tradition from which the poem descends,

Example 13. Excerpt from Févin's *N'emez jamais une villaine* (*Florence 117*, fols. 78ᵛ–79ʳ)

extremely mercurial. It shifts unpredictably among homorhythm *a 4*, light imitative entries and homorhythmic voice pairing in which the duets lack the smooth overlapping that is so characteristic of, say, Josquin's voice pairing. Changes from binary to ternary rhythm are also characteristic of this style, as are the simple, highly articulated melodic style that abounds with repeated notes and the obvious need for a syllabic setting of the text.

see L. F. Bernstein, ed., *La couronne et fleur des chansons a troys*, Masters and Monuments of the Renaissance 3 (New York, 1984), Part 2, pp. 102–8, 215–16.

Example 14. The opening of Moulu's *Hélas, hélas madame, tant my donnez de peyne* (*Florence 117*, fols. 80ᵛ–81ʳ)

These elements of style were drawn together in various genres of Italian music. They may be found in Milanese motets of the 1470s, in the *canti carnascialeschi*, in examples of Florentine descriptive music of the late fifteenth century, and in settings of the Ordinary of the Mass by such composers as Heinrich Isaac.[86] Various composers who

[86] On the presence of these stylistic traits in Milanese motets, see L. Finscher, 'Zum Verhältnis von Imitationstechnik und Textbehandlung im Zeitalter Josquins', *Renaissance-Studien: Helmuth Osthoff zum 80. Geburtstag*, ed. L. Finscher (Tutzing, 1979), p. 64.

Examples of carnival songs in this style appear in the *Collected Works of Alessandro Coppini, Bartolomeo degli Organi, Giovanni Serragli, and Three Anonymous Works*, vol. II of *Music of the Florentine Renaissance*, ed. F. D'Accone, Corpus Mensurabilis Musicae 32 (1967), pp. 1–3, 8–9, 11–13, 14–16, 42–4, 44–6.

For examples of the application of these techniques to Florentine descriptive music, see M. Brenet, 'Essai sur les origines de la musique descriptive', *Rivista Musicale Italiana*, 14 (1907), pp. 649–51; and *Nachtrag zu den weltlichen Werken von Heinrich Isaac*, ed. J. Wolf, pp. 221–4.

For Isaac's use of the same devices in an isolated Credo, see *Heinrich Isaac: Opera omnia*, ed. E. Lerner, Corpus Mensurabilis Musicae 65 (1974–), v, pp. 112–19.

Example 15. Excerpts from an anonymous, textless chanson on the melody for *La jeusne dame va au molin* (*Florence 117*, fols. 70ᵛ–71ʳ)

Example 15 – *continued*

MS. reads:

worked or travelled in Italy – among them Bruhier, Compère, Isaac and Ninot Le Petit – adapted these elements of style to the polyphonic chanson, and the results of such efforts are amply represented in Petrucci's three great chansonniers and in a good number of Florentine manuscripts from the period 1490–1520. The principal sources are the 'Strozzi chansonnier' (*Florence 2442*) and a somewhat later set of Florentine partbooks, *Florence 164–7*. This variety of chanson, along with several other distinct stylistic types, was designated by Howard Brown the 'four-part arrangement'.[87]

There can be little doubt that this type of chanson originated in Italy. Not only is it stylistically compatible with a wide array of Italian genres of the late fifteenth century (as we have just suggested), but virtually all of its principal composers were in Italy, and, moreover, it was disseminated almost exclusively in Italian sources. Whether the style was transplanted to the north, and the extent of the impression it may have made there, are the subjects of some controversy. The question is an important one, because this particular type of chanson has been specifically advanced as the progenitor of the type of Parisian chanson that is set to a narrative text.[88] Obviously, to project one style as the antecedent of another requires evidence of the dissemination of the earlier style within the orbit of potential contact with the later one. I have suggested elsewhere, largely on the basis of source studies, that the particular type of four-part arrangement now under consideration made but the slightest impression on northern musical circles.[89] Inasmuch as *Florence 117* contains six examples of this type of chanson, what we have learned about the provenance of the manuscript clarifies our view of the dissemination of this style all the more. Of these six chansons, five were copied by the main scribe; the sixth was done by the Florentine Layolle scribe. Had the main scribe copied these pieces in the north, we would have had additional and substantial evidence of the presence of this style north of the Alps. Our knowledge that the main scribe worked in Florence, however, snatches his five chansons in this style from a putative northern orbit

---

[87] Brown, 'The Genesis of a Style', pp. 24–5; *idem*, 'The Transformation of the Chanson at the End of the Fifteenth Century', *International Musicological Society: Report of the Tenth Congress – Ljubljana, 1967*, ed. D. Cvetko (Kassel, 1970), pp. 78–94; *idem*, 'The Music of the Strozzi Chansonnier', pp. 118–29.

[88] Brown, 'The Genesis of a Style', pp. 24–5, 32–4.

[89] Bernstein, 'Notes on the Origin of the Parisian Chanson', pp. 284–301.

and places them in a context that is less surprising – namely, in one of the several Florentine manuscripts that contain chansons of this type.

Of course, it might be argued that the six four-part arrangements in our manuscript were copied in Florence but composed in France. Again, though, various factors concerning the manner in which these compositions were copied into *Florence 117* suggest that this was not the case. Table 14 lists all of the chansons in the style now under consideration. For purposes of comparison, it also includes the three verifiably northern compositions with which we began our discussion of the four-voice chansons in our manuscript. Note that the two types of chanson are, respectively, placed in separate groups within the choirbook. All of the northern pieces appear after the last of the four-part arrangements, and the five pieces of the latter type that were copied by the main scribe occur in a nearly unbroken sequence. Another important consideration is the manner in which the scribes underlay the text beneath the music of these chansons. It is not surprising to find the chansons copied by the Layolle scribe textless. This may be attributed to his ignorance of French. But the main scribe is generally meticulous about texting all parts fully (as he does, for example, with the two northern chansons in his hand that are listed in Table 14). When he texts only one or two voices or leaves out the poetry altogether (as he does in three of the four-part arrangements), we are led to wonder why. Admittedly, the haste with which the main scribe appears to have copied this final portion of the manuscript offers one explanation for his omission of texts in these chansons. As we suggested above, however, another thoroughly plausible explanation is that he copied the pieces so texted from Italian exemplars, in which French chansons are often left partly, or even entirely, textless. It may not be sheer coincidence, that is to say, that the only chansons the main scribe fails to text fully are expressly those whose style and patterns of transmission suggest ties with Italy.[90]

<hr/>

[90] One four-part arrangement in the hand of the Layolle scribe, Mouton's *Rejuissés vous borgeses*, would seem to impair somewhat the case for the Italian provenance of this type of chanson. At the time we believe *Florence 117* was compiled (*c.* 1515), Mouton, of course, was *maître de chapelle* of the French royal court. Indeed, another chanson by this master, *Jamais, jamais, jamais*, is clearly in the style we are considering, and it appeared in the *Odhecaton* – that is, long before there is any record of Mouton's presence in Italy. Mouton's biography, however, is problematical. We lack any traces of the composer from the last record of his service as *maître de chapelle* at Nesle in 1483 to his appointment as *maître des enfans* at Amiens

Table 14 *Four-part arrangements and northern chansons a 4 in* Florence 117

Incipit	Composer	Folio	Scribe	Texting
Réjuissés vous borgeses, belles filles de Lion	Jo. mouton	(63v)–65r	Layolle (music) Northern 2 (incipit and attribution)	incipit only
[La jeusne dame va au molin]	—	70v–71r	Main	none
Noz bergers et noz bergeres	[T. Janequin?]	73v–74r	Main	all
Sire Dondieu, tant y sont aisés noz bergeres	—	74v–75r	Main	all
L'aultre jour fu chenilée si doulcement	—	75v–76r	Main	superius and tenor only
La guille des luron, lureau, triboulle marteau	—	76v–77r	Main	superius only
N'emez jamais une villaine	[Févin]	78v–79r	Main	all
Hélas, hélas madame, tant my donnez de peyne	[Moulu]	80v–81r	Main	all
[Plus nulz regretz]	[Josquin]	(85r)	Layolle	none

A third group of chansons *a 4* in our manuscript consists of five pieces, all but one of them unique in *Florence 117*. One is attributed to La Fage by the main scribe, the single piece with a concordance in another source is attributed there (probably incorrectly) to Richafort, and the other three pieces remain anonymous.[91] In many ways these compositions resemble the type of four-part arrangement we have just considered, as we see in Example 16. Here we find homorhythmic voice pairing, animated rhythms, short phrases and a syllabic setting of the text. The combination of these traits produces a style that changes rapidly in a thoroughly evanescent manner. What distinguishes these five pieces from the four-part arrangements discussed above is their more consistent and systematic reliance upon imitative entries, specifically upon points of imitation that are extremely short. Their heavier reliance on imitation notwithstanding, these five chansons are sufficiently close in style to the four-part arrangements to suggest that they, too, originated and flourished in Italy.

Compositions that reflect this particular amalgam of stylistic traits are not to be found in great numbers. The *Odhecaton*, for example, contains only one chanson of this sort; *Canti B*, another two. Significantly, however, all three of these pieces are by composers who were in Italy just before the turn of the sixteenth century, and their early transmission occurred exclusively in Italian

in 1500. This seventeen-year period may well have provided Mouton with an opportunity to travel to Italy.

  In addition, it is perhaps worth recalling that Mouton was in Italy at just about the time we suggested for the compilation of *Florence 117* (i.e. he visited there in the autumn of 1515) and may thus have been personally responsible for the transmission of *Rejuissés vous*. On Mouton's travels to Italy, see L. Lockwood, 'Jean Mouton and Jean Michel: New Evidence on French Music and Musicians in Italy, 1501–1520', *Journal of the American Musicological Society*, 32 (1979), pp. 204–7, 211–17.

91 *[N']a tu point veu la viscontine* is given to Richafort in *Paris 4599*, but I believe that attribution is wrong. Stylistically, the chanson is unlike any of the other four-voice chansons reliably assigned to this master. In Antico's *La couronne et fleur des chansons a troys* of 1536, moreover, another setting of the same poem was also mistakenly assigned to Richafort in the table of contents, instead of to Willaert, whose name appears over the music in all three partbooks as well as in all subsequent editions of the piece and who surely composed the chanson. *La couronne* contains a genuine work of Richafort the poem of which begins similarly: *N'avés point veu mal assenée*. Undoubtedly, it is this similarity that gave rise to the misattribution in the table of contents of *La couronne*, and I suggest that the same confusion with respect to *[N']a tu point veu la viscontine* may have been perpetuated by Jean Michel, the Ferrarese scribe of *Paris 4599*. Further, on the problem of this misattribution and on possible connections between Jean Michel and the Antico print, see Bernstein, ed., *La couronne et fleur des chansons*, part 2, pp. 101–2.

Example 16. Jean de La Fage, *M'y levay par ung matin*, bars 1–24 (*Florence 117*, fols. 79ᵛ–80ʳ)

Example 16 – *continued*

sources.[92] A few additional examples of the style may be cited from among the chansons of Ninot Le Petit, who, as we pointed out above, served as a singer in the papal chapel at the end of the fifteenth century.[93]

Confirmation for our sense of the Italian provenance of this style is supplied, moreover, by the five chansons that follow its conventions in *Florence 117*. They are listed in Table 15. To begin, four of the five works appear uniquely in our manuscript (i.e. in a source we have shown to be of Florentine provenance). Furthermore, three of the five compositions were copied with their parts incompletely texted – that is, in the Italian manner. The one chanson not copied by the main scribe, [N']a tu point veu la viscontine, belongs to a complex of polyphonic settings that displays a uniformly Italian pedigree. It includes a related setting in Petrucci's *Canti C*, a Mass by Gaspar van Weerbecke, and a chanson by Willaert.[94] And the anonymous *En attendant* is related to the same complex, for its poem has many elements in common with that of the chanson just discussed:

En attendant la bergerotte
Dessoubz une verte esglantine   [N']a tu point veu la viscontine
Une basse dance godine   Tant popine, tant godine
Roneudit fait la vostre espine   Elle a donné la gore a l'espine
Qui ne suis fine fine...   Sus sa mine la plus fine...

[92] The three compositions are Compère's *Alons, ferons barbe* (*Odhecaton, Florence 107bis, Florence 164–7*), the same composer's *Et d'ont revenis vous* (*Canti B*), and Ninot Le Petit's *Hélas, hélas, hélas, hélas* (*Canti B, Florence 2442* and several later German sources).
     For modern editions of these chansons see, respectively, Hewitt, ed., *Odhecaton*, pp. 275–6; and H. Hewitt, ed., *Ottaviano Petrucci: Canti B, Numero cinquanta*, Monuments of Renaissance Music 2 (Chicago, 1967), pp. 171–3, 150–2.

[93] See *Ninot Le Petit: Collected Works*, pp. 1–4, 5–7, 21–2.

[94] Further on this complex of works, see Bernstein, ed., *La couronne et fleur des chansons*, part 2, pp. 99–102, 222–3.

Table 15 *Imitative chansons with elements of four-part arrangement style*

Incipit	Composer	Folio	Scribe	Texting	Connections with Italy
[N°]a tu point veu la viscontine	[Richafort?]	(23ᵛ)–24ʳ	Northern 2	superius only	belongs to complex of Italian polyphonic pieces
L'aultre jour parmy ces champs	—	65ᵛ–66ʳ	Main	superius and tenor: complete altus: incipits bassus: none	—
En attendant la bergerotte	—	72ᵛ–73ʳ	Main	all	poem draws on that of [N°]a tu point veu, which is set exclusively in Italy
Trut trut trut, avant, il fault boire	—	77ᵛ–78ʳ	Main	superius only	only other setting appears in Venice in 1536
M'y levay par ung matin	La Fage	79ᵛ–80ʳ	Main	all	composer in Italy in 1516

Perhaps the most important evidence for the Italian impact on this style, however, concerns Jean de La Fage. He is, of course, the composer of our illustrative example of this style and, in fact, the only composer to whom any of the five pieces from *Florence 117* that conform to it can be reliably assigned. Until very recently, La Fage was thought to have worked exclusively in France – this on the basis of evidence no more concrete than the appearance of his name in the list of musicians from the Prologue to book IV of *Pantagruel*. In his valuable article on the correspondence of Jean Michel, however, Lewis Lockwood prints a letter written in Rome by Enea Pio and dispatched in June 1516 to Cardinal Ippolito I d'Este. The writer quotes Turleron, a singer in the papal chapel, to the effect that La Fage, the best contrabass in Italy, had recently arrived with his patron, the Cardinal of Auch.[95] We shall return presently to the matter of La Fage's presence in Gascony. The reference to his sojourn in Italy, however, explains a lot. It helps us to understand why nearly all the principal sources of his music are Italian.[96] It explains the presence in some of his motets of homorhythmic voice pairing, chordal writing *a 4*, syllabic setting of the text, and extremely short points of imitation – the very elements of style that may be found in some Italian motets of the late fifteenth century.[97] Significantly, as we have seen, the one surviving secular work that bears an attribution to La Fage, the chanson in our manuscript, reflects, on a smaller scale, precisely the same stylistic profile we find in these motets. That La Fage was in Italy in 1516 – at just the time we believe *Florence 117* was compiled – is surely the most plausible explanation for his adapting these Italian techniques to the French chanson.

Our third group of four-voice chansons thus seems inextricably linked to Italy. Some of the pieces belong to indigenously Italian complexes of polyphonic settings. Others appear in our manuscript

---

95 Lockwood, 'Jean Mouton and Jean Michel', p. 222. Conceivably, Jean de La Fage came from Lafarge, a little hamlet not far from St Yrieix, on the road from Limoges to Périgueux. If so, he would not have wandered far from his place of origin to the site of his post in Gascony, for Lafarge is only about ninety miles north-east of Bordeaux.

96 His motets, for example, appear in the Medici Codex, *Casale Monferrato D(F)*, *London 19583*, *Modena IX*, *Padua A 17* and *Verona 760* – all of which are of Italian provenance – as well as in such Italian prints as *Petrucci 1519¹*, *Antico 1520²* and *Antico 1521⁵*.

97 See, for example, La Fage's *Videns Dominus* and *Elizabeth zacharie* in Lowinsky, ed., *The Medici Codex*, IV, pp. 90–4, 100–6, respectively. On the presence of this style in the Milanese motet, see the article by Ludwig Finscher cited in n. 86, above.

only partly texted (i.e. in the Italian manner). What is most unique about the style of the five compositions, moreover – their distinctive synthesis of the style of the four-part arrangement with pervasive but short points of imitation – can be traced to such models as the motets of Jean de La Fage's stay in Italy.

Only three chansons *a 4* from *Florence 117* have yet to be considered. These compositions are unlike any of the other chansons we have discussed thus far, and they are, in many respects, unlike one another, too. What binds them together, however, is their reliance on various techniques we tend to associate with the style of the Parisian chanson. Thus, in *Fortune la diverse* the melody appears in the superius; its opening strain is repeated; and, although the piece begins imitatively, by its mid-section it consists in pure homorhythm. *Si j'ayme mon amy trop plus que mon mary* resembles the Parisian idiom in its brevity, its repetition of the opening and closing strains of the polyphony, and its closed ternary form ($ABAB^1 / CD / AB^1B^1$). It is *Chantons dançons ceste saison nouvelle* (Example 17), however, that comes closest to the Parisian norms. Here we find division of decasyllabic lines after the fourth syllable, homorhythmic texture, chordal anacruses on repeated notes, light imitative touches, concentration of melodic activity in the superius and – to a lesser extent – in the tenor, repeat of the closing polyphony, and a closed form (in the sense that the medial section of the chanson is set off from the rest of the piece by means of both harmonic and textural contrast).

It is difficult to ascertain the provenance of these three compositions. All are fully texted in the main scribe's hand, and they could, like the works by Févin and Moulu he added to the manuscript, have originated in the north. Yet most of the chansons *a 4* in his hand have turned out to have closer ties to Italy, and these three pieces could just as easily have been composed there, too. At the very least, the appearance of *Chantons dançons* in *Florence 117* attests to the presence in Florence about 1515 of a relatively mature early example of what later became known as the Parisian chanson.[98]

---

[98] A similarly mature example of Parisian chanson style, it will be recalled, appears elsewhere in our manuscript with indications of its possible Florentine provenance: the three-voice *Amy, soufré*, apparently attributed to 'Do. Izagha'. For additional early examples of this style in Italy, see Bernstein, 'Notes on the Origin of the Parisian Chanson', pp. 309–18.

Example 17. Anonymous, *Chantons dançons ceste saison nouvelle* (*Florence 117*, fols. 71^v–72^r)

Conclusions. I close with a summary and a brief but highly speculative peroration. *Florence 117* is a complex mélange of scribal hands and musical genres. Its five subsidiary scribes can be shown to have worked in Italy. The main scribe must have worked there, too, for he derived some of his readings of widely disseminated northern works from a demonstrably Italian transmission. He also took some of his French repertory not from exemplars related to the central sources of the French royal court, but from the same provincial transmission to which the second northern scribe made recourse. The manuscript, thus, is of Florentine provenance. Its contents and concordances, and the life-span of its repertory, suggest that it was compiled *c.* 1515.

The choirbook contains a number of motets and Italian-texted pieces, but it is devoted principally to chansons. These form a repertory of a most diverse character. Separate layers are devoted to three- and four-part chansons. In the first category we find three-part arrangements from the French royal court, a cycle of older *chansons de regret*, compositions that emanated from Charles VIII's Italian campaign of 1494–5, music that served as models for Francesco de Layolle, a chanson of Clément Janequin's *période*

Bordelaise, and a few pieces that 'foreshadow' the style of the Parisian chanson. The chansons for four voices include several compositions that definitely originated in the north and many more with a decidedly Italian cast. Among the latter are examples of the animated, homorhythmic-type four-part arrangement and other compositions that attempt a fusion of that style with a simple, imitative texture. A few of the four-voice chansons also 'anticipate' various characteristics of the Parisian chanson.

'Heterogeneous' is thus the key word in describing *Florence 117*. It preserves a mixed repertory, consisting of French-, Italian- and Latin-texted pieces, and it reflects a similarly wide variety of scribal hands. Some are northern, some Italian; most are of a rather amateurish character. The main scribe set out the original plan for the manuscript, and some of his subsidiary colleagues both preceded and followed each other in making their respective entries within it. Every folio not used for a 'formal' piece of music was later filled in with didactic material of one sort or another, ranging from the hexachordal diagram on the front guard sheet to the many contrapuntal and calligraphic exercises that appear throughout the choirbook.

The picture that emerges is not one of a manuscript that was written and compiled in a traditional scriptorium. We must, therefore, search among other institutions for its probable place of origin. One such institution comes most readily to mind: the musical chapel at one of the great churches at Florence. In the cathedral choir of Santa Maria del Fiore, for example, there came together at various times northern and Italian musicians, experienced singers and novices, teachers and students. At the beginning of the sixteenth century, the chapel at Santa Maria del Fiore included sixteen singers: eleven adults, one of whom served as a teacher, and five boys. Often the cathedral shared its musical personnel with the baptistery, so it is useful to know that the Florentine baptistery in 1515 included in its choir thirteen adults and four boys. Among the French musicians who served in the cathedral were Charles de Launoy and Rubinetto Francioso.[99] It seems wholly plausible that a

[99] On the Florentine musical chapels, see F. D'Accone, 'The Musical Chapels at the Florentine Cathedral and Baptistry during the First Half of the 16th Century', *Journal of the American Musicological Society*, 24 (1971), pp. 1–50, esp. pp. 4, 9; idem, 'The Performance of Sacred Music in Italy during Josquin's Time, c. 1475–1525', *Josquin des Prez*, pp. 601–18, esp. pp. 608–9.

choir of this character could have been responsible for the precise amalgam of repertorial and calligraphic features we found in *Florence 117*: the mixture of French and Italian music, the large number of copyists, the mingling of northern and Italian hands, the amateurish style of handwriting, the contrapuntal and calligraphic exercises, the demonstrable interaction among the copyists, and the erratic order in which they made their entries in the manuscript. In this light we are reminded of one of the names that appears among the various jottings to be found in *Florence 117*: Antonio di Jaccopo. The name is enticingly similar to that of Giovanantonio di Jacopo, a singer in the Florentine baptistery as early as 1515.[100] The temptation to see in this name a link between our manuscript and this important musical chapel is thus a great one.

Were *Florence 117* really the product of a group of Florentine singers, it would seem to have been copied for the private delectation of the musicians themselves. That in turn could help us to understand a development that otherwise appears rather inexplicable: the introduction of fully texted chansons in Florentine sources in the early sixteenth century. As is well known, the major Florentine chansonniers of the late fifteenth century generally offer their examples of French secular music in the form of textless compositions. After the turn of the century, French texts begin to appear in Florentine musical sources, in such manuscripts as *Florence 2242* and *Florence 164–7*. Our own manuscript is among the earliest Florentine sources to provide complete texts for all of the voices of a considerable number of chansons. It has always been a mystery for whom such fully texted versions might have been intended. It may just be that the vocal performance of French-texted secular polyphony in Florence, irrespective of whether it was composed in Italy or in the north, owes its origins to the presence in the Florentine musical chapels of a sprinkling of northern singers – musicians and amateur copyists who wished to perform secular music in their native language and to preserve it in unpretentious manuscripts like *Florence 117*.

In the latter quality – that of unpretentiousness – *Florence 117* is not alone. Other Florentine sources at the Biblioteca Nazionale

---

[100] On the appearance of this name in *Florence 117*, see above, p. 4. For documentation of Giovanantonio di Jacopo's presence at the Florentine baptistery, see D'Accone, 'Musical Chapels', p. 15.

Centrale, including the manuscripts Magliabechi XIX 107bis and 178, share various traits with our choirbook: oblong format, paper material, pages ruled with six staves, highly heterogeneous international repertories, a mixture of scribal hands (some of them markedly amateurish), and an array of didactic scribblings and calligraphic exercises (a number of them identical in all three sources). The three manuscripts share scribal concordances, too, as we have seen – and not only among the more formal compositions, but among the casual jottings, too. The hexachordal diagram on the front guard sheet of *Florence 117*, for example, is written in the same hand as is the name *Pieronino*, which appears in the gutter margin at the beginning of the seventh fascicle (fol. 59^r) of *Florence 178*.[101] The same hand scribbled the motto 'al mio quanto fratello Carl^{mo}' on fol. (22^r) of our manuscript. 'Carl^{mo}' reappears on the guard sheet of *Florence 178*, written in a childish attempt at a formal hand adjacent to a group of infantile drawings. The phrase 'Carl^{mo} mio quanto fratello' also appears on the last folio of *Florence 107bis*, with the name penned in the same distinctive manner in which it appears in *Florence 178*. The three sources are clearly related to one another with respect to both the artisans who compiled them and the singers – quite obviously young singers – who used them. Together, they represent the beginnings of a new and decidedly less formal approach to the preservation of the chanson in Florentine sources. It is an approach that is well suited to the needs and skills of the Florentine choirboys who are undoubtedly responsible for the didactic writing in these manuscripts and who, together with their more experienced mentors, may well have provided a good deal of the more formal entries, too.

Thus, our manuscript serves as an important mirror of the status of French secular polyphony in Tuscany in the early sixteenth century. To treat the source solely as a Florentine document, however, would tell but half the story. For, as we have seen, the bonds that tie our source to provincial France – specifically, to southwestern France – are fast and numerous. The manuscript shares nine concordances with *Uppsala 76a*, a source now thought to have been compiled in Gascony, and often the readings of these two manuscripts are closer to each other than to those of other, more

---

[101] Note, in particular, the tendency to keep letters separate; the thin, undotted *i*; and the wide-angled, *y*-like *r*.

central transmissions. Janequin's *Chant de l'alouette* provides another link with Gascony, because it is one of the works he composed at Bordeaux. And La Fage, the composer of one of the chansons in our manuscript, turns out to have worked at Auch and travelled to Italy. Auch, significantly, is a mere stone's throw from Toulouse, the city in south-western France where the paper on which *Uppsala 76a* was written is known to have been used.[102]

It seems evident that *Florence 117* charts a route of transmission that ran between Gascony and Florence. Three-part arrangements of the French royal court made their way to Florence via a source tradition that can be pinpointed in Gascony. On the other hand, the four-part arrangements in our manuscript and the more imitative pieces that are related to them stylistically were cultivated principally in Italy. To the extent that they were exported to France at all, however, they appear to have begun their northward journey in Florence. The transmission between south-western France and Italy, that is to say, roughly parallels the travels of Jean de La Fage, which brings me to my concluding bit of unbridled speculation.

Of the twenty-eight works in *Florence 117* whose composers can be ascertained, only seven have attributions in the manuscript itself. And, of these, six are in the hands of the subsidiary scribes. This leaves only one attribution by the main scribe: the one to La Fage. Why should the main scribe consistently omit attributions but include just one, for the lone surviving secular work of Jean de La Fage? Could it be because the main scribe was La Fage himself? Of this we have no demonstrable evidence whatsoever. Indeed, of La Fage's stay in Italy we know only that he was in Rome in 1516; we cannot place him in Florence on the basis of any secure factual data. In the absence of such evidence, the case for La Fage as the main scribe of our manuscript must obviously be all but dismissed out of hand. The combined data about his presence in Auch and in Italy and the unique ascription to him in the hand of our main scribe may be particularly seductive in the way that they match patterns that pertain to our manuscript. But we cannot prove that the intersection of these facts is anything more than a coincidence. Still, even if we cannot identify the precise messenger in whose hands several genres of French secular polyphony moved between south-western France

---

[102] The information on the provenance of *Uppsala 76a* is drawn from Brown, 'A New French Chansonnier'.

and Florence, what we know of La Fage's itinerary remains useful. It demonstrates that specific lines of musical transmission were open between Gascony and Italy. Through such conduits might have passed the exemplars from which many of the three-voice chansons in *Florence 117* were copied, making of this unique choirbook a critical guide to the transalpine migrations of the Renaissance chanson during the early sixteenth century.[103]

University of Pennsylvania

APPENDIX

An Inventory of *Florence 117*

1. Sigla

A. *Manuscripts*

Augsburg 142a	Augsburg, Staats- und Stadtbibliothek, MS 2⁰ 142a (*olim* Cim. 43)
Barcelona 454	Barcelona, Biblioteca Central, MS 454
Basel F. IX. 59–62	Basel, Öffentliche Bibliothek der Universität, MSS F IX 59–62
Basel F. X. 1–4	Basel, Öffentliche Bibliothek der Universität, MSS F X 1–4
Basel F. X. 17–20	Basel, Öffentliche Bibliothek der Universität, MSS F X 17–20
Basel F. X. 21	Basel, Öffentliche Bibliothek der Universität, MS F X 21
Bologna Q 16	Bologna, Civico Museo Bibliografico Musicale, MS Q 16
Bologna Q 17	Bologna, Civico Museo Bibliografico Musicale, MS Q 17
Bologna Q 21	Bologna, Civico Museo Bibliografico Musicale, MS Q 21
Brussels 228	Brussels, Bibliothèque Royale de Belgique, MS 228
Brussels 11239	Brussels, Bibliothèque Royale de Belgique, MS 11239

---

[103] With pleasure, respect and affection, I acknowledge a debt of thanks to Martin L. Bernstein, my teacher at New York University. His influence remains a potent force in my work and may be traced in the pages of this study, too. Celebremus: 1984. xii. 14.

Brussels IV 90/Tournai 94	Brussels, Bibliothèque Royale de Belgique, MS IV 90 (superius; tenor partbook in *Tournai 94*)
Cambrai 125–8	Cambrai, Bibliothèque Municipale, MSS 125–8 (*olim* 124)
Cambridge 1760	Cambridge, University Library, Magdalene College, MS Pepys 1760
Casale Monferrato D(F)	Casale Monferrato, Archivio e Biblioteca Capitolare, Duomo, MS D(F)
Copenhagen 1848	Copenhagen, Kongelige Bibliotek, MS Ny. Kgl. Samling 1848–2⁰
Cortona 95–6/Paris 1817	Cortona, Biblioteca Comunale, MSS 95–6 (altus, superius; tenor partbook in *Paris 1817*)
Florence 27	Florence, Biblioteca Nazionale Centrale, MS Panciatichi 27
Florence 99–102	Florence, Biblioteca Nazionale Centrale, MSS Magl. XIX 99–102
Florence 107bis	Florence, Biblioteca Nazionale Centrale, MS Magl. XIX 107bis
Florence 111	Florence, Biblioteca Nazionale Centrale, MS Magl. XIX 111
Florence 112	Florence, Biblioteca Nazionale Centrale, MS Magl. XIX 112
Florence 117	Florence, Biblioteca Nazionale Centrale, MS Magl. XIX 117
Florence 121	Florence, Biblioteca Nazionale Centrale, MS Magl. XIX 121
Florence 122–5	Florence, Biblioteca Nazionale Centrale, MSS Magl. XIX 122–5
Florence 125bis	Florence, Biblioteca Nazionale Centrale, MS Magl. XIX 125bis
Florence 164–7	Florence, Biblioteca Nazionale Centrale, MSS Magl. XIX 164–7
Florence 176	Florence, Biblioteca Nazionale Centrale, MS Magl. XIX 176
Florence 178	Florence, Biblioteca Nazionale Centrale, MS Magl. XIX 178
Florence 229	Florence, Biblioteca Nazionale Centrale, MS Banco Rari 229 (*olim* Magl. XIX 59)
Florence 230	Florence, Biblioteca Nazionale Centrale, MS Banco Rari 230 (*olim* Magl. XIX 141)

Florence 337	Florence, Biblioteca Nazionale Centrale, MS Banco Rari 337 (*olim* Palatino 1178)
Florence 2356	Florence, Biblioteca Riccardiana, MS 2356
Florence 2439	Florence, Biblioteca del Conservatorio di Musica Luigi Cherubini, MS Basevi 2439
Florence 2440	Florence, Biblioteca del Conservatorio di Musica Luigi Cherubini, MS Basevi 2440
Florence 2442	Florence, Biblioteca del Conservatorio di Musica Luigi Cherubini, MS Basevi 2442
Florence 2794	Florence, Biblioteca Riccardiana, MS 2794
The Hague 74/h/7	The Hague, Koninklijke Bibliotheek, MS 74/h/7 (*olim* Utrecht, Bibliotheek der Rijks-universiteit, MS 202; tenor partbook only)
London 20.A.XVI	London, British Library, MS Royal 20.A.XVI
London 42–4	London, British Library, MSS Royal App. 41–4
London 1070	London, Royal College of Music, MS 1070
London 3051/Washington M6	London, British Library, MS Egerton 3051 (additional section in *Washington M6*)
London 5043	London, British Library, Add. MS 5043
London 5242	London, British Library, MS Harley 5242
London 19583	London, British Library, Add. MS 19583
London 31922	London, British Library, Add. MS 31922
London 35087	London, British Library, Add. MS 35087
Modena IX	Modena, Duomo, Biblioteca e Archivio Capitolare, MS Mus. IX
Munich 1503a	Munich, Bayerische Staatsbibliothek, Mus. Ms. 1503a
Munich 1508	Munich, Bayerische Staatsbibliothek, Mus. Ms. 1508
Munich 1516	Munich, Bayerische Staatsbibliothek, Mus. Ms. 1516
Padua A 17	Padua, Biblioteca Capitolare, MS A 17
Paris 1596	Paris, Bibliothèque Nationale, MS f. fr. 1596
Paris 1597	Paris, Bibliothèque Nationale, MS f. fr. 1597
Paris 1817/Cortona 95–6	Paris, Bibliothèque Nationale, nouv. acq. fr. MS 1817 (tenor; altus and superius partbooks in *Cortona 95–6*)
Paris 2245	Paris, Bibliothèque Nationale, MS f. fr. 2245
Paris 4599	Paris, Bibliothèque Nationale, nouv. acq. fr. MS 4599

Paris 9346	Paris, Bibliothèque Nationale, MS f. fr. 9346 (Manuscrit de Bayeux)
Paris 12744	Paris, Bibliothèque Nationale, MS f. fr. 12744
Paris 15123	Paris, Bibliothèque Nationale, MS f. fr. 15123 (Pixérécourt Chansonnier)
Regensburg 3/I	Regensburg, Fürst Thurn und Taxis Hofbibliothek, MS Freie Künste Musik 3/I
Regensburg 120	Regensburg, Proske-Bibliothek, MS C. 120 (Pernner Codex)
Regensburg 940/941	Regensburg, Proske-Bibliothek, MS A.R. 940/941
Rome 2856	Rome, Biblioteca Casanatense, Cod. 2856
St Gall 462	St Gall, Stiftsbibliothek, Cod. 462 (Johannes Heers Liederbuch)
St Gall 463	St Gall, Stiftsbibliothek, Cod. 463 (Aegidius Tschudis Liederbuch; superius and altus partbooks only)
Segovia	Segovia, Catedral, Codex without number
Tournai 94/Brussels IV 90	Tournai, Bibliothèque de la Ville, MS 94 (tenor; superius partbook in *Brussels IV 90*)
Turin I.27	Turin, Biblioteca Nazionale, Riserva musicale MS I.27 (*olim* qm. III. 59)
Ulm 236	Ulm, Münster Bibliothek, Von Schermar'sche Familienstiftung, MSS 236a–d
Ulm 237	Ulm, Münster Bibliothek, Von Schermar'sche Familienstiftung, MSS 237a–d
Uppsala 76a	Uppsala, Universitetsbiblioteket, MS 76a
Uppsala 76b	Uppsala, Universitetsbiblioteket, MS 76b
Uppsala 76c	Uppsala, Universitetsbiblioteket, MS 76c
Vatican 11953	Vatican City, Biblioteca Apostolica Vaticana, Cod. Vat. lat. 11953 (bassus partbook only)
Vatican C.G. XIII.27	Vatican City, Biblioteca Apostolica Vaticana, Cappella Giulia, MS XIII.27 (Cappella Giulia Chansonnier)
Verona 757	Verona, Biblioteca Capitolare, Cod. DCCLVII
Verona 760	Verona, Biblioteca Capitolare, Cod. DCCLX
Vienna 18810	Vienna, Österreichische Nationalbibliothek, Cod. 18810
Washington M6/London 3051	Washington, Library of Congress, MS M2.1 M6 Case (additional section in *London 3051*)

Washington–Laborde	Washington, Library of Congress, MS M2.1 L252 Case (Laborde Chansonnier)
Zwickau 78,3	Zwickau, Ratsschulbibliothek, MS LXXVIII,3 (*olim* 12)

B. *Early prints*

Antico 1520²	*Motetti novi libro tertio.* Venice: A. Antico & L. A. Giunta, 15 October 1520
Antico 1520⁶	*Chansons a troys.* Venice: A. Antico & L. A. Giunta, 15 October 1520 (lacking tenor partbook)
Antico 1521⁵	*Motetti libro quarto.* Venice: A. Antico, August 1521
Attaingnant 1528	[*Chansons et motets en canon a quatre parties sur deux.* Paris: P. Attaingnant, 1528]
Attaingnant [c. 1528]⁹	*Six gaillardes et six pavanes avec treze chansons musicales a quatre parties....* Paris: P. Attaingnant, 1529 (= 1530 n.s.)
Attaingnant 1529⁴	*Quarante et deux chansons musicales a troys parties....* Paris: P. Attaingnant, 22 April 1529
Attaingnant 1531¹	*Vingt et huit chansons nouvelles en musique a quatre parties....* Paris: P. Attaingnant, February 1531 (= 1532 n.s.)
Attaingnant 1533¹	*Vingt et sept chansons musicales a quatre parties....* Paris: P. Attaingnant, April 1533
Attaingnant 1534³	*Liber primus quinque et viginti musicales quatuor vocum motetos complectitur....* Paris: P. Attaingnant, April 1534
Attaingnant 1540¹⁴	*Neufviesme livre contenant xxvii. chansons nouvelles a quatre parties....* Paris: P. Attaingnant & H. Jullet, 1540
Berg & Neuber [1560]¹	*Selectissimorum tricinorum.* Nuremberg: J. von Berg & U. Neuber, n.d.
Egenolff [c. 1535]¹⁴	[*Lieder zu 3 & 4 Stimmen*]. Frankfurt am Main: C. Egenolff, n.d.
Formschneider 1538⁹	*Trium vocum carmina a diversis musicis composita.* Nuremberg: H. Formschneider, 1538

Gardane 1541[13]	*Di Constantio Festa il primo libro de madrigali a tre voci, con la gionta de quaranta madrigali di Ihan Gero, novamente ristampato . . . aggiuntovi similmente trenta canzoni francese di Janequin.* Venice: A. Gardane, 1541 (rev. edn in *Gardane 1543[23]*)
Gardane 1543[23]	*Quaranta madrigali di Ihan Gero insieme trenta canzoni francese di Clement Janequin di nuovo ristampati a tre voci.* Venice: A. Gardane, 1543 (rev. edn of *Gardane 1541[13]*)
Josquin 1550	*Trente sixiesme livre contenant xxx. chansons tres musicales, a quatre cinq & six parties . . . le tout de la composition de feu Josquin des Prez. . . .* Paris: P. Attaingnant, 14 March 1549 (= 1550 n.s.)
Kriesstein 1540[7]	*Selectissimae necnon familiarissimae cantiones . . . .* Augsburg: M. Kriesstein, 1540
Le Roy & Ballard 1553[22]	*Tiers livre de chansons, composées a trois parties . . . .* Paris: A. Le Roy & R. Ballard, 3 June 1553
Le Roy & Ballard 1578[14]	*Premier livre de chansons a trois parties composé par plusieurs autheurs . . . .* Paris: A. Le Roy & R. Ballard, 1578
Le Roy & Ballard 1578[15]	*Second livre de chansons a trois parties composé par plusieurs autheurs . . . .* Paris: A. Le Roy & R. Ballard, 1578
Moderne 1539[19]	*Le Parangon des chansons. Quart livre contenant XXXII chansons a deux et a troys parties . . . .* Lyons: J. Moderne, 1539
Mouton 1555	*Ioannis Mouton Sameracensis musici praestantissimi selecti aliquot moduli, & in 4, 5, 6, & 8 vocum harmoniam distincti. Liber primus.* Paris: A. Le Roy & R. Ballard, 1555
Petreius 1541[2]	*Trium vocum cantiones centum à praestantissimis diversarum nationum ac linguarum musicis compositae. Tomi primi.* Nuremberg: J. Petreius, 1541
Petrucci 1501	*Harmonice musices Odhecaton A.* Venice: O. Petrucci, 15 May 1501
Petrucci 1502[2]	*Canti B. numero cinquanta.* Venice: O. Petrucci, 5 February 1501 (= 1502 n.s.)

Petrucci 1519[1]

Motetti de la corona libro secondo. Venice: O. Petrucci, 17 June 1519

Rhau 1542[8]

Tricinia . . . . Wittenberg: G. Rhau, 1542

Scotto 1535[8]

Il primo libro de le canzoni franzese, nuovamente stampate. Et per Andrea Antigo intagliate, et con diligentia corrette. Venice: O. Scotto, 1535 (tenor partbook missing)

Scotto [1535][9]

Del secondo libro della canzoni franzese . . . . Venice: O. Scotto, n.d. (tenor partbook missing)

2. Inventory

No.	Incipit	No. of voices	Foliation[a] Original	Modern	Composer	Concordances/Remarks	Scribe
1	Souvent je m'esbatz et mon cueur est marry (tenor and bassus only)	3	[0ᵛ]–(1ʳ)	[0ᵛ]–(1ʳ)	—	*London 5242*, fols. 17ᵛ–18ʳ *Antico 1520⁶*, fols. 5ᵛ–6ʳ	Main
2	Hélas, j'en suis marry	3	(1ᵛ)–2ʳ	(1ᵛ)–(2ʳ)	[A. de Fevin]	*Cambridge 1760*, fols. 51ᵛ–52ʳ (An. de Fevin) *London 5242*, fols. 24ᵛ–26ʳ *Uppsala 76a*, fols. 47ᵛ–48ʳ *Gardane 1541¹³*, p. 49 (Janequin; rev. edn *Gardane 1543²³*) *Petreius 1541²*, no. 86 (Janequin)	Main
3	Chescun mauldit ses jaleux	3	2ᵛ–4ʳ	(2ᵛ)–4ʳ	[A. de Févin]	*Cambridge 1760*, fols. 53ᵛ–55ʳ (Anth. de Fevin) *Uppsala 76a*, fols. 74ᵛ–76ʳ *Antico 1520⁶*, fols. 19ᵛ–21ᵛ	Main
4	Je m'en allé voir m'amye ung soir	3	4ᵛ–5ʳ	4ᵛ–5ʳ	—	—	Main
5	Pleust a la vierge Marie	3	5ᵛ–6ʳ	5ᵛ–6ʳ	—	—	Main
6	Je le levray puis qu'il m'y bat	3	6ᵛ–7ʳ	6ᵛ–7ʳ	[A. de Févin]	*Cambridge 1760*, fols. 52ᵛ–53ʳ (Anth. de fevin) *London 5242*, fols. 5–7ʳ (Anth. de fevin) *Uppsala 76a*, fols. 43ᵛ–44ʳ (A. de Fevin)	Main

2. Inventory – *continued*

No.	Incipit	No. of voices	Foliation[a] Original	Foliation[a] Modern	Composer	Concordances/Remarks	Scribe
7	On a mal dit de mon amy	3	7^v–8^r	7^r–8^r	[A. de Févin]	*Cambridge 1760*, fols. 47^v–48^r (Anth. de fevin) *London 5242*, fols. 41^v–43^r *London 35087*, fols. 93^v–94^r *Munich 1516*, no. 139 *St Gall 463*, no. 43 *Ulm 237*, fols. 23^v–24^r *Uppsala 76a*, fols. 76^v–77^r (A. de Fevin) *Antico 1520^c*, fols. 16^v–17^r *Attaingnant 1529^c*, fol. 12^v *Le Roy & Ballard 1578^{85}*, fol. 11^v (Fevin)	Main
8	Orsus, orsus, vous dormez trop (*Le chant de l'alouette*)	3	8^v–10^r	8^v–10^r	[C. Janequin]	*Barcelona 454*, fols. 155^v–157^r *Copenhagen 1848*, pp. 439–40 *St Gall 463*, no. 36	Main
9	Mais que ce fust le plaisir d'elle	3	10^v–11^r	10^v–11^r	[J. Mouton]	*Antico 1520^c*, fols. 22^r–23^r *London 5242*, fols. 41^v–45^r *Uppsala 76a*, fols. 31^v–32^r (Jo. Moston)	Main
10	Monseigneur le grant maistre	3	11^v–12^r	11^v–12^r	—	*Antico 1520^c*, fol. 19^v *Attaingnant 1529^c*, fol. 10^r	Main
11	Qui vous vouldroit entretenir	3	12^v–13^r	12^v–13^r	—	—	Main

No.	Incipit	No. of voices	Foliation[a] Original	Modern	Composer	Concordances/Remarks	Scribe
12	Vive le noble roy de France	3	13v–14r	13v–14r	[L. Compère]	*Segovia*, fol. 180r (Loysette Compere) *Uppsala 76a*, fols. 48v–49r	Northern 2
13	Adyeu soullas, tout playsir et liesse	3	14v–15r	14v–15r	[A. de Févin]	*Cambridge 1760*, fols. 63v–64r (Anth. de fevin) *London 5242*, fols. 20v–21r *London 35087*, fols. 53v–54r *Uppsala 76a*, fols. 35v–36r (A. de Fevin)	Northern 2
14	D'amour je suis desheritée	3	15v–16r	15v–16r	—	*Copenhagen 1848*, p. 156 *Uppsala 76a*, fols. 44v–45r *Attaingnant 1529a*, fol. 2v	Northern 2
15	Questo mostrarsi lieta	3	16v–17r	16v–17r	♭♮ iolla	*Florence 2440*, pp. 32–3 (F. Aiolles)	Layolle
16	Donne, per electione	4	17v–18r	17v–18r	Baccio Fiorentino	*Florence 230*, fols. 133v–134r *Florence 337*, fol. 53v	Baccio
17	Amy, soufré que je vous aime	3	18v–19r	18v–(19r)	Do Izagha	*London 31922*, fol. 90r *Attaingnant 1529a*, fol. 6v *Berg & Neuber [1560]*[1], no. 41 *Le Roy & Ballard 1553*[22], fols. 21v–22r (Moulu; Le Hurteur in table) *Le Roy & Ballard 1578*[14], fol. 18v (Moulu; Claudin in table)	Izagha

2. Inventory – continued

No.	Incipit	No. of voices	Foliation[a] Original	Modern	Composer	Concordances/Remarks	Scribe
18	[J'ay mis mon cueur en ung lieu seulement]	3	19v–20r	(19v)–20r	—	Rhau 1542⁸, no. 80 / Si placet settings a 4: / A. Basel F. IX. 59–62, no. 25 / Munich 1516, no. 16 / B. Regensburg 940/941, no. 105 / C. Ulm 236, no. 53 / —	Izagha
19	[Ces facheux sotz qui mesdisent d'aymer]	3	20v–21r	20v–21r	—	Copenhagen 1848, pp. 178, 419 / Attaingnant 1529⁴, fol. 5r / Berg & Neuber [1560]¹, no. 43 / Rhau 1542⁸, no. 82 / Si placet settings a 4: / A. Basel F. IX. 59–62, no. 33 / B. Cambrai 125–8, fol. 139r / Munich 1516, nos. 19, 35 / C. Regensburg 940/941, no. 103 / D. Basel F. X.17–20, no. 88 (altus lacking)	Izagha
20	[musical notation]	3 of 4	21v–(22r)	21v–22r	—	An incomplete attempt at copying no. 22	Izagha
'Informal' entries		—	(22v–23r)	22v–23r	—	—	Scribbler

2. Inventory – *continued*

No.	Incipit	No. of voices	Foliation[a] Original	Foliation[a] Modern	Composer	Concordances/Remarks	Scribe
21	[N'] a tu point veu la viscontine	4	(23v)–24r	23v–24r	[J. Richafort?]	*The Hague 74/h/7*, fols. 21r–22r; *Paris 4599*, fols. 2v–3r (Richafort)	Northern 2
22	[music incipit]	4	24v–(26r)	24v–26r	—	The complete, corrected version of the piece attempted in no. 20	Izagha
	'Informal' entries	—	(26v–27v)	26v–27v	—	—	Scribbler
	Missing	—	[28v–31v]	—	—	—	—
	'Informal' entries	—	(32v–33v)	28v–29r	—	—	Scribbler
23	Et mirelaridaine Regnauldin	3	(33v)–34r	29v–30r	—	—	Main
24	Triste et pensif suis sans mot dire (superius only)	3	34v	30v	—	*Paris 1597*, fols. 76v–77r	Main
	Missing	—	[35r–36v]	—	—	—	—
25	Sourdez regretz, avironnez mon cueur (tenor and bassus only)	3	37r	31r	[L. Compère]	*Brussels 228*, fols. 54r–55r; *Brussels iv 90/Tournai 94*, fols. 7–8r; *Florence 2439*, fols. 51v–52r (Compere); *London 35087*, fols. 71v–73r (Compere)	Main? Main
26	Venez regretz, venez, il est en heure	3	37v–38r	31v–32r	[L. Compère]	*Bologna Q 17*, fols. 31v–32r (Loyset Compere); *Brussels 11239*, fols. 4v–6r (Compere)	Main

2. Inventory – *continued*

No.	Incipit	No. of voices	Foliation[a] Original	Modern	Composer	Concordances/Remarks	Scribe
						Brussels IV 90/Tournai 94, fols. 5v–7r	
						Copenhagen 1848, pp. 124–5	
						St Gall 462, pp. 86–7	
						Zwickau 78,3, no. 16	
						Petrucci 1501, fols. 58v–59r (Compere)	
27	Allés regretz, vuidez de ma plaisance	3	38v–39r	32v–33r	[Hayne van Ghizeghem]	*Bologna Q 17*, fols. 30v–31r (Hayne)	Main
						Brussels 11239, fols. 2–4r	
						Brussels IV 90/Tournai 94, fols. 1v–2v	
						Copenhagen 1848, p. 414	
						Florence 27, fols. 97v–98r (Hayne)	
						Florence 107bis, fols. 43v–44r	
						Florence 178, fols. 42v–43r	
						Florence 229, fols. 242v–243r	
						Florence 2356, fols. 97v–98r	
						Florence 2794, fols. 58v–59r (Heyne)	
						London 20.A.XVI, fols. 20v–21r	
						London 31922, fols. 5v–6r	
						Paris 1597, fols. 11v–12r	
						Paris 2245, fols. 17v–18r (Hayne)	

2. Inventory – *continued*

No.	Incipit	No. of voices	Foliation[a] Original	Modern	Composer	Concordances/Remarks	Scribe
						Rome 2856, fols. 96ᵛ–98ʳ (Haine)	
						Segovia, fol. 163ᵛ (Scoen Heyne)	
						Turin I.27, fol. 12ᵛ	
						Uppsala 76a, fol. 1ʳ	
						Vatican C.G. XIII.27, fols. 20ᵛ–21ʳ (Hayne)	
						Verona 757, fols. 28ᵛ–29ʳ	
						Washington–Laborde, fols. 140ᵛ–142ʳ	
						Zwickau, 78,3, no. 11	
						Egenolff [c.1535]¹⁴, III, no. 26	
						Formschneider 1538⁹, no. 7	
						Petrucci 1501, fols. 62ᵛ–63ʳ (Hayne)	
28	Va t'en regretz, celluy qui me convoye	3	39ᵛ–40ʳ	33ᵛ–34ʳ	[L. Compère]	Brussels 228, fols. 53ᵛ–54ʳ	Main
						Brussels 11239, fols. 6ᵛ–7ʳ (Compere)	
						Brussels IV 90/Tournai 94, fols. 4ᵛ–5ʳ	
						Copenhagen 1848, pp. 104–5	
						Florence 107bis, fols. 46ᵛ–47ʳ	
						Paris 1596, fols. 2ᵛ–3ʳ	
						Paris 1597, fols. 13ᵛ–14ʳ	
						Paris 2245, fols. 9ᵛ–10ʳ (Compere)	

2. Inventory – *continued*

No.	Incipit	No. of voices	Foliation[a] Original	Modern	Composer	Concordances/Remarks	Scribe
29	Les grans regretz qui sans cesser je porte	3	40ᵛ–41ʳ	34ᵛ–35ʳ	[Hayne van Ghizeghem]	*Bologna Q 17*, fols. 36–37ʳ (Hayne) *Brussels 11239*, fols. 7ᵛ–8ʳ (Agricola) *Brussels IV 90/Tournai 94*, fol. 4ʳ (incomplete) *Copenhagen 1848*, p. 95 *Florence 107bis*, fols. 44ᵛ–45ʳ *Paris 1597*, fols. 12ᵛ–13ʳ *Paris 2245*, fols. 19ᵛ–20ʳ (Hayne) *Washington–Laborde*, fols. 143ᵛ–145ᵛ (Hayne) *Petrucci 1501*, fols. 77ᵛ–78ʳ	Main
30	Laudate Dominum, omnes gentes	4	41ᵛ–42ʳ	35ᵛ–36ʳ	♭ᴵᴵ iolla	—	Layolle
	'Informal' entries		42ᵛ	36ᵛ	—	—	Scribbler
	Missing		[43ʳ–44ᵛ]	—	—	—	—
	'Informal' entries		(45ʳ–46ᵛ)	37ᵛ–38ᵛ	—	—	Scribbler
	Missing		[47ʳ–61ᵛ]	—	—	—	—
	'Informal' entries		(62ᵛ–63ʳ)	39ᵛ–40ʳ	—	—	Scribbler
31	Rejuissés vous borgeses, belles filles de Lion	4	(63ᵛ)–65ʳ	40ᵛ–42ʳ	Jo. mouton	*Cambrai 125–8*, fol. 126ᵛ *Uppsala 76b*, fols. 134ᵛ–135ʳ	Layolle (music) Northern 2 (incipit and attribution)

2. Inventory – continued

No.	Incipit	No. of voices	Foliation[a] Original	Modern	Composer	Concordances/Remarks	Scribe
32	L'aultre jour parmy ces champs	4	65v–66r	42v–43r	—	—	Main
33	Consumo la mia vita	3	66v	43v	[J. Prioris]	*Cambridge 1760*, fol. 86v (*a 4*; Prioris); *London 35087*, fols. 27v–28r (*a 3*); *Paris 1597*, fol. 78r (*a 3*); *St Gall 462*, fol. 48r (*a 3*); *St Gall 463*, no. 170 (*a 4*); *Washington–Laborde*, fols. 136v–137r (*a 4*)	Northern 2
	'Informal' entries	—	67r	44r	—	—	Scribbler
34	Fortune la diverse m'est bien assaillir	4	67v–68r	44v–(45r)	—	—	Main
35	Si j'ayme mon amy trop plus que mon mary	4	68v–70r	(45v)–47r	—	—	Main
36	[La jeusne dame va au molin]	4	70v–71r	47v–48r	—	—	Main
37	Chantons dançons ceste saison nouvelle	4	71v–72r	48v–49r	—	—	Main
38	En attendant la bergerotte	4	72v–73r	49v–50r	—	—	Main
39	Noz bergers et noz bergeres	4	73v–74r	50v–51r	[T. Janequin?]	*Copenhagen 1848*, pp. 419–20 (Tomas Janequin; bassus missing); *Munich 1503a*, no. 6; *Scotto 1535b*, no. 9	Main

103

2. Inventory – *continued*

No.	Incipit	No. of voices	Foliation[a] Original	Modern	Composer	Concordances/Remarks	Scribe
40	Sire Dondieu, tant y sont aisés noz bergeres	4	74ᵛ–75ʳ	51ᵛ–52ʳ	—	*Cambrai 125-8*, fol. 138ᵛ	Main
41	L'aultre jour fu chenilée si doulcement	4	75ᵛ–76ʳ	52ᵛ–53ʳ	—	—	Main
42	La guille des luron lureau, triboulle marteau	4	76ᵛ–77ʳ	53ᵛ–54ʳ	—	*Paris 1597*, fols. 65ᵛ–66ʳ	Main
43	Trut trut trut, avant, il fault boire	4	77ᵛ–78ʳ	54ᵛ–55ʳ	—	—	Main
44	N'emez jamais une villaine	4	78ᵛ–79ʳ	55ᵛ–56ʳ	[A. de Févin]	*Cambridge 1760*, fols. 81ᵛ–83ʳ (A. de fevin) *Uppsala 76b*, fols. 133ᵛ–134ʳ	Main
45	M'y levay par ung matin	4	79ᵛ–80ʳ	56ᵛ–57ʳ	[J. de] La Fage	—	Main
46	Hélas, hélas madame, tant my donnez de peyne	4	80ᵛ–81ʳ	57ᵛ–58ʳ	[P. Moulu]	*Attaingnant [c. 1528]9*, fol. 7ʳ	Main
47	I . . . I . . .	2 of ?	81ᵛ–82ʳ	58ᵛ–59ʳ	—	Two voices of what would appear to have been a multi-voice composition. The piece was meant to be continued on the following folio but was not.	Main
48	Palle palle (altus and bassus of second half missing)	4	82ᵛ–83ʳ	59ᵛ–60ᵛ	Yzac	*Cortona 95-6/Paris 1817*, no. 40 *Florence 107bis*, fol. 43ʳ	Layolle

2. Inventory – *continued*

No.	Incipit	No. of voices	Foliation[a] Original	Modern	Composer	Concordances/Remarks	Scribe
		—	[84ʳ–84ᵛ]	—		*London 3051/Washington M6*, fols. 81ᵛ–84ʳ *Vatican C.G. XIII.27*, fols. 0ᵛ–2ʳ (H. Isach) In the *New Grove Dictionary* article on Isaac, Martin Staehelin cites another concordance for this work, in: Kraków, Klasztor OO. Dominikanów ['Capellae Leonis pape']. I have not seen this source, and I wish to thank Ms Johanna Pfund of the University of Illinois for calling my attention to the concordance.	Layolle
49	Missing [Plus nulz regretz] (altus and bassus only)	4	(85ʳ)	(61ʳ)	[Josquin]	*Augsburg 142a*, fols. 38ᵛ–40ʳ *Basel F. X. 1–4*, no. 113 (Josquin) *Brussels 228*, fols. 27ᵛ–28ʳ (Josquin des Pres)	Layolle

105

2. Inventory – *continued*

No.	Incipit	No. of voices	Original	Modern	Composer	Concordances/Remarks	Scribe
						Brussels IV 90/Tournai 94, fols. 17ʳ–18ᵛ	
						Florence 2442, no. 2 (Josquin des pres)	
						Florence 164–7, no. 67	
						London 41–4, fols. 3ᵛ–4ʳ	
						Munich 1508, no. 65	
						Munich 1516, no. 107	
						Regensburg 3/I, no. 135 (Josquin)	
						Regensburg 120, pp. 300–3 (Josquin)	
						Uppsala 76b, fols. 136ᵛ–137ʳ	
						Uppsala 76c, fols. 117ᵛ–118ʳ	
						Vatican 11953, fol. 4 (Josquin)	
						Vienna 18810, fols. 8ᵛ–9ᵛ (Josquin de. pres)	
						Egenolff [c. 1535]¹⁴, I, no. 3	
						Josquin 1550, fol. 16ʳ (Josquin)	
						Kriesstein 1540ᵉ, no. 53 (Josquin)	
50	[Sancta trinitas unus Deus]	4	(85ᵛ)–87ʳ	(61ᵛ)–63ʳ	[A. de Févin]	This composition was disseminated widely, both in the version *a 4* by Févin	Layolle

106

2. Inventory – *continued*

No.	Incipit	No. of voices	Foliation[a] Original	Foliation[a] Modern	Composer	Concordances/Remarks	Scribe
						and in the setting *a 6* by Nicolas Craen, which adds two voices to Févin's polyphony. For concordances, see: E. Lowinsky, 'A Music Book for Anne Boleyn', *Florilegium historiale: Essays Presented to Wallace K. Ferguson*, ed. J. G. Rowe and W. H. Stockdale (Toronto, 1971), p. 217. G. K. Diehl, 'The Partbooks of a Renaissance Merchant' (Ph.D. diss., University of Pennsylvania, 1974), pp. 627–9.	
51	Ave sanctissima Maria, mater Dei, regina caeli (altus and bassus of second half missing)	4	87^v–(88^v)	63^r–64^v	[J. Mouton]	*Attaingnant 1534*³, fol. 13^r (Jo. Mouton) *Mouton 1555*, fols. 2^r–4^r (Mouton; an 18th-century score of this edition survives in *London 5043*)	Last
	Missing	—	[89^r–?]	—	—	—	Last?

[a] Square brackets denote missing folios; parentheses, folio numbers missing from the manuscript.

107

STANLEY BOORMAN

SOME NON-CONFLICTING ATTRIBUTIONS, AND SOME NEWLY ANONYMOUS COMPOSITIONS, FROM THE EARLY SIXTEENTH CENTURY*

A surprisingly large number of early madrigals carry conflicting attributions in the printed sources of the 1530s and early 1540s. For example, twenty-four of the ninety-five settings listed in Hans Musch's recent book on Festa appear in various sources under at least two composers' names;[1] among other pieces in the same position are some ascribed to Arcadelt or Verdelot – or at least appearing in volumes dedicated to those composers and carrying no other names at the head of the page.

In a number of cases, these conflicting 'attributions' cause little concern for the present-day scholar. The presence of a madrigal in the early editions of Arcadelt's first book, published without ascriptions,[2] does not mean that the printers believed it to have been by

* I wish to express my gratitude to the Harvard University Center for Italian Renaissance Studies for awarding me a fellowship during the year 1983–4, and to the Director and Staff at Villa I Tatti for facilitating my research and making my stay so congenial.

[1] H. Musch, *Costanzo Festa als Madrigalkomponist*, Sammlung musikwissenschaftlicher Abhandlungen 61 (Baden-Baden, 1977), pp. 157–69. Additional pieces and some new concordances are cited in I. Fenlon and J. Haar, 'Fonti e cronologia dei madrigali di Costanzo Festa', *Rivista Italiana di Musicologia*, 13 (1978), on pp. 231–42.

[2] For a study of this volume and its multitudinous editions, see T. W. Bridges, 'The Publishing of Arcadelt's First Book of Madrigals' (Ph.D. dissertation, Harvard University, 1982). A modern transcription, with comments on the earlier editions, appears in *Jacobi Arcadelt opera omnia*, ed. A. Seay, Corpus Mensurabilis Musicae 31/ii (n.p., 1970). This edition will be cited hereinafter as *Arcadelt*.

For many of the printed volumes mentioned or discussed in this paper, the references and descriptions in RISM (K. Schlager, ed., *Einzeldrücke vor 1800*, Répertoire International des Sources Musicales A/i, Kassel, 1971–81 [designated by letter and number]; F. Lesure, ed., *Recueils imprimés, XVIe–XVIIe siècles*, ibid. B/iv/1, Munich and Duisburg, 1960 [designated by date with superscript number]) or the New Vogel (F. Lesure and C. Sartori, eds., *Bibliografia della musica italiana vocale profane pubblicata dal 1500 al 1700*, Pomezia, 1977; rev. edn of E. Vogel, *Bibliothek der gedruckten weltlichen Vocalmusik Italiens, aus den Jahren*

Arcadelt, as is made clear by the consistency of an attribution to, say, Corteccia, once names became normal. The situation is a little more complex with Verdelot's early books, during the period when Scotto was printing and publishing material from wood-blocks cut by Andrea Antico,[3] and was apparently following rather different principles for supplying composers' names.

It is the purpose of this paper to show that a number of these 'conflicting' attributions are really irrelevant, that one of the names involved is, in each case, the product of one of a limited range of printing-house procedures or errors, traceable through bibliographical analysis. Some of these variant attributions have not been seriously accepted by any modern scholar: however, the process of demonstration in those cases will also throw light on others that are more in need of resolution.

I

During the 1530s and the very early 1540s the processes of Italian music printing underwent changes far more drastic than those involved merely in the introduction of single-impression music type. No doubt this innovation was in some measure responsible for other changes; but they involve, as a whole, the conversion of music printing from a craft (which it clearly had been for both Petrucci and Antico) into a business, streamlined, relatively efficient and (eventually) systematic in its procedures.

One of the places where this is most immediately apparent is in the layout on the page, including the methods for handling head-lines, composer ascriptions and so on. The transition is quite marked, as

---

1500 bis 1700, Berlin, 1892) are not satisfactory or sufficient to enable the reader to distinguish editions or single copies. Therefore, at the first reference of substance to a new volume, I give below a transcription of the title-page, together with such notes as are necessary to supplement these reference works. In my transcriptions and notes, which are not intended to be comprehensive, the word 'flower' refers to a printer's flower, which need not represent a flower as such; the collation, when given, arranges the partbooks in the standard order of Cantus, Tenor, Altus, Bassus, Quintus, etc. Thereafter the volume is cited by its reference siglum in RISM (whenever possible) in order to save excessive duplication of bibliographical detail.

References to composers' names appearing in the early editions are here given in italics if they are direct quotations of the original form. In such cases, a final point may well appear (if part of the original), and this should not be confused with the end of a sentence in the present text.

[3] These are discussed by C. W. Chapman in her doctoral dissertation, 'Andrea Antico' (Harvard University, 1964).

can be seen from a comparison of any early Scotto edition (from the mid 1530s) with almost any madrigal volume from the presses of Gardane or Scotto of the later 1540s. The most obvious change is in layout, in the placing of the start of each piece. The various Scotto editions from Antico's blocks always start a new piece at the beginning of a new line,[4] although this could be any line on the page, including the last. Thus the twenty-one pieces in the Bassus part of the first surviving (and probably actually the first) edition of Verdelot's first book of five-voice madrigals[5] start variously on any of the five staves which occupy each page: only four madrigals actually open a page, while six begin on the last stave. By contrast, Gardane's edition,[6] which appeared in 1541, has already gone a long way towards arranging the pieces in a manner to which we are more

4   This is something that is not always found once single-impression type takes over from blocks. With wood-blocks, there was a strong incentive for starting new pieces at the beginnings of new lines, for this gave the printer the flexibility to alter the order of items in subsequent editions, in exactly the manner permitted by blocks prepared for a volume of drawings or of maps. There is no reason to suppose that the Antico–Scotto partnership did not anticipate the possibility of later editions: the history of earlier music printers – Petrucci, Antico himself, or the Dorico brothers – suggests that this was seen as a normal practice, while some of the first Scotto editions were themselves taken from Antico blocks previously printed by other men.

5   RISM V1223; New Vogel 2887. Both suggest the date *ca*[1535].
      The Altus and Bassus partbooks survive, labelled
          Madrigali a cinque Libro primo. / A [B].
      Oblong quarto-in-eights: EF[8]; GH[8].
          The *Tavola*, on the first verso, is in one column, in order of the compositions in the book, and is of the same setting of type for both parts. This setting was probably used for all four parts, for it lists the nineteenth piece as *Deh non gionger tormenti*; these words are the second phrase of the madrigal *Purtroppo donn'in van'*, and the first words sung by the Cantus, Altus and Quintus parts. This piece is misnumbered *20* in the Bassus, fol. H6r; *Altro non e'l mio amor*, the twelfth piece, is misnumbered *11* in the Altus.
          The copies consulted for this study were, Altus: Paris, Bibliothèque Nationale, Rés. Vmd. 30; Bassus: Bologna, Civico Museo Bibliografico Musicale, R140(2); both complete.
          For the actual date of this volume see below, note 62. *Pace* the New Vogel, these partbooks contain sixteen folios (i.e. thirty-two pages) each, as probably did the other partbooks; the last folio of the Bassus is completely blank.

6   RISM 1541[17]; New Vogel 2885.
          [flower] CANTVS [flower] / LE DOTTE, ET ECCELLENTE COMPOSITIONI DE I MA=/drigali di VERDELOT, A cinque Voci, & da diversi perfettissimi Musici fat=/te. Novamente ristampate, & con ogni diligentia corrette. / M.D. [Gardane's mark] xxxxi. / Excudebat Venetiis, apud Antonium Gardane.
      The title-page also carries the signature line:
          Primi, Verdelot a cinque. A
      The other voice parts carry the same title-page (with changed part-name) and signature line (with changed letter).
      Oblong quarto, 48 pages per part: A–F[4]; G–M[4]; N–S[4]; T–Z,AA[4]; BB–GG[4].
      The copy consulted is at Washington, D.C., Library of Congress. The Cantus partbook at Paris, Bibliothèque Nationale, Rés. 1169 is of the same press-run.

accustomed from later in the century. Of the forty-three pieces, the Bassus starts all but six at the top of the page. The sequence of pieces is almost certainly partly conditioned by the arrangement of the Cantus partbook, for here only three pieces start anywhere other than at the beginning of the page, while rather more have to do so in both the Tenor and Altus books.[7] It so happens that, in this volume, there is no opening carrying three pieces. Thus there is no reason to doubt that (other things being equal) the ascription at the head of the verso refers to the first composition on the opening, and that on the recto to the second.

However, in many volumes, both Gardane and Scotto contrived to fit three pieces onto an opening. The decision to do this seems again most often to have been made with the Cantus book in mind, for the spacing is often more tidy here than in the other partbooks. Occasionally, for example, the second or third piece will have to open in the middle of a stave for the Altus or Bassus part. This is normally not a problem for the reader, in so far as he can easily see the ornate blocks used for the initial letters. In one or two cases, however, the music is so cramped that even these are done away with, for only a type capital can be fitted into the available space.[8]

This point is worth mentioning, for it also affects the manner in which composers' names became attached to compositions. The common practice (when there were only two pieces on an opening) was for the composer's name, when present at all, to appear in the head-line to the page, set in type with the running head (comprising the part-name for that book) and with a numeral representing page or folio number or number of the composition in the volume. This name would then refer to the work which appeared below it, even if that piece did not start until the second or third stave on the page. Although this is what we as modern readers might expect, it has to be confirmed by comparing those partbooks where pieces start well down a page with the other books where the same pieces start at the beginning of the first stave.

---

[7]   This is one volume where the pieces do not always open at the start of a line: the need to fit Barre's *Come potro fidarmi* and Baldassare d'Imola's *Non vi gloriate* onto a single opening, as well as that of squeezing Verdelot's *Donne se fiera stella* after Barre's *I sospiri amorosi*, led to the start of each second piece appearing part-way along a line in one or two of the partbooks.

[8]   Examples would include fol. Y3r (p. 45) of the Altus of RISM 1541[18], or K1v (p. 26) of the Tenor of 1541[11].

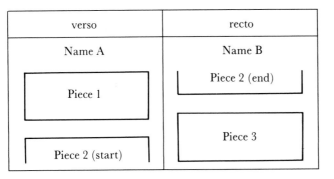

Figure 1

The implications of this for an opening with three compositions are clear (see Figure 1): name *A* was meant to refer to the first piece on the opening, and name *B* to the third. (This is apparently the normal situation, although I shall mention some exceptions below.) In theory (and, as will be shown, sometimes in practice) neither of these ascriptions need refer to the second piece on the opening: the printer's view of the composer of this piece has to be determined as much by bibliographical as by any other method. There are often two or three such situations in madrigal volumes of the early 1540s.

Printers were not unaware of the situation, with its potential for confusion, and they did sometimes supply an additional composer's name, immediately above the second piece. In many cases, however, they could not easily do this, for the text at the end of the previous piece occupied the relevant space in the forme; in other cases, they seem not to have bothered. On these occasions, the name of the composer of the second piece cannot necessarily be assumed to have been either *A* or *B*. We need to examine the manner in which the typesetter behaved throughout the volume, and also to determine the place of the volume in what appears to have been a gradual change in printer's habits.

RISM 1541[18], a collected edition of Verdelot's first two books,[9]

<hr />

9   RISM 1541[18] = V1229; New Vogel 2872.
    [flower] CANTVS [flower] / DI VERDELOT TVTTI LI MADRIGALI DEL PRIMO ET SE=/condo Libro, a Quatro Voci: Novamente ristampati, & da molti errori emen=/dati. Con la gionta de i Madrigali del medesmo Autore. / AGGIONTOVI ANCHORA ALTRI MADRIGALI / novamente Composti da Messer Adriano, & da Altri Eccellentissimi Musici. / M D [Gardane's mark] xxxxi / Excudebat Venetiis, apud Antonium Gardane.
    The lower voices have the same title (with the part-name changed) and with the addition of a signature line:

provides examples of all the points made above. On the opening K4ᵛ–L1ʳ of the Tenor book (the relevant pages are numbered 16–17 in all books), there are three pieces: *Lasso che se creduto havesse*, *Vostre dolce parole* and *Con lagrim'et sospir*.[10] The composer's name at the head of both pages is *Verdelot*, which, as I have said (and as other evidence in this volume confirms), means only that the first and third of these pieces were thought to have been by that composer. If only the Tenor book had survived, there might be some reason for believing Verdelot to be the composer of the second piece also. However, in all three other parts, the name *Iachet* has been fitted carefully above the opening stave of this second composition, low on the verso of the opening. The ascription is missing from the Tenor only because the previous piece has text (as well as music) that runs to the end of the last line, and therefore leaves no room for a composer's name. This pattern suggests that Gardane recognised the normal situation to be as I have described, with the name at the head of the following recto belonging to the work beginning on the page, and not to the second of the three madrigals.

In the same book, the Tenor also behaves differently on pp. 6–7 (fols. I3ᵛ–4ʳ). The three pieces involved are *Ogn'hor per voi sospiro*, *Non vi fidat'o simplicett'amanti* and *Quanto lagrime lasso*. Cantus, Altus and Bassus all carry the composer's names *Verdelot*, on the verso, and *Iachet Berchem*, on the recto. The Tenor alone moves the name of Berchem down, to the space above the start of the third piece. This confirms that, for the other three voices, the ascription on the recto applies to the piece that begins on that page, and not to the one that hangs over from the previous verso, even though that is what actually appears on the first stave.

Verdelot primi, & secundi. [with the appropriate signature letter]
Oblong quarto, 64 pages per volume: A–H⁴; I–Q⁴; R–Z,AA⁴; BB–II⁴.
The copy consulted is at Vienna, Österreichische Nationalbibliothek, SA.77.D.53.
    Typically, the composer listings in the entry in New Vogel are far from consistent. Of the pieces which straddle an opening, and which have no ascription of their own, *Non vi fidat'o simplicett'amanti* (pp. 6–7) is assigned to the composer on the verso (almost certainly incorrectly, as I am about to argue), while *Io son tal volta* (pp. 50–1) is left anonymous. *Igno soave* lies across two pages that both carry the name of Verdelot, and should perhaps be assigned to him in any account of this edition, while *Vostre dolce parole* (pp. 16–17) has the name *Iachet* fitted above its first stave in three of the four partbooks.

10 These three have survived elsewhere, without conflicting attributions, as the work of Verdelot, Jachet and Verdelot, respectively. The present discussion does not throw any doubt on this pattern, but is offered solely to draw attention to the procedure adopted by the printer.

In neither of these cases is there any problem in deciding on the intended ascription; both have at least one partbook making clear where the composer's name belongs, and, in both cases, this accords with the general pattern of ascriptions for the piece.[11]

RISM 1541[11] is the second edition of Arcadelt's third book of four-voice madrigals[12] and contains a large number of such problems of

---

[11] It has to be admitted that there is no firm bibliographical evidence here for the authorship of the second piece on pp. 6–7. My contention, supported by the concordance pattern and by other evidence (to be advanced), is that a piece in this position is normally, by this time, to be assigned to the composer named at the head of the verso, although by no means consistently following that pattern. Indeed, such a view raises questions about the opinion which Gardane held of the authorship of *Io son tal volta* (G1ᵛ–2ʳ): however, as I shall show, this kind of ambiguous situation is just that which led to changes of ascription as printer's habits became more settled and consistent. I shall return to this, and some other problems of ascription in the present edition, in connection with a different range of evidence.

[12] RISM 1541[11] = A1376; New Vogel 158.
    [flower] CANTVS [flower] / IL TERZO LIBRO DE I MADRIGALI NOVISSIMI / di archadelt a quattro voci insieme con alchuni di constantio festa & altri dieci bellissimi / a voci mudate novamente ristampati con nova gionta & nova corretione. / M.D. [Gardane's mark] L.XI. / Venetiis apud antonium gardane
    The other partbooks have the same title (with changed voice-name), plus a signature line:
    Terzo Libro d'archadelt. [plus signature letter]
    Oblong quarto, 48 pages per volume: A–F⁴; G–M⁴; N–S⁴; T–Z,+⁴.
    The copy consulted is at London, British Library, K.2.h.5. The second part of the date, L.XI., is changed in manuscript to XLI.
    Again, New Vogel is in error, or misleading, in its ascriptions for this volume: *E morta la speranza*, spread between pp. 12 and 13, is strictly anonymous – the caption *Archadelt.* heads p. 12, while *Con. festa.* appears on p. 13 (this might be another case for arguing that the piece starting at the foot of the verso was thought to be by the composer named at the head of that page, for this madrigal is ascribed to Arcadelt in 1539²³); *Se i sguardi di costei* is only attributed to *Con. festa* in the Cantus and Tenor books; *Lasso che pur hormai*, on pp. 26–7, is anonymous; *Madonna s'io credessi* (p. 29) is clearly attributed to *Archadelt.*; *Languir non mi fa amore* is only ascribed to *Corteccia.* in the lower three voices, while the Cantus reads *Archadelt.* (see below); and *S'altrui d'amor* is clearly ascribed to *Archadelt.* in all voices. (Some of these works will be discussed below. One must deplore the haphazard procedure adopted in New Vogel (for this and other volumes) whereby the name of the composer to whom the whole volume is dedicated is not repeated against individual madrigals: it does not allow the reader to distinguish between anonymous works and those that appear below the name of the composer given on the title-page, in this case, Arcadelt.)
    In stating that 1541[11] is the second edition of this title, I am making the following observations: (1) that RISM [c1556]²³, copy at Venice, Biblioteca Nazionale Marciana, Mus. 365–7 (Tenor, Altus and Bassus) is of the same edition as 1539²³ = A1374 (Tenor, Altus and Bassus of the copy at Munich, Bayerische Staatsbibliothek, 4⁰. Mus.pr. 95/2), as has been noted by other scholars (see *Arcadelt*, IV, p. ix, or New Vogel, no. 156), and that this is probably the first edition; (2) that the Cantus of the copy at Munich represents part of the same edition, although cited separately in New Vogel as no. 157; (3) that the remaining editions are as cited in RISM: 1541[11] = A1376; 1543²⁰ = A1377; 1556²² = A1378.
    The bibliographical evidence for asserting that the Cantus book at Munich is part of the same edition as the other partbooks is far from clear. The most difficult problem is a direct result of the Cantus carrying a dedication, on fol. A1ᵛ: although the music follows the same sequence as that found in the other partbooks, it cannot be arranged in the same manner, for it starts on a recto, rather than on a verso. Where the Cantus places three pieces on an

ascription: there are eleven pieces which carry, or appear to carry, a different composer's name in other sources, plus one more where the evidence of ascription is not as strong as we might like. So muddled

opening, it cannot reflect exactly the layout of the other three parts, for there these pieces would occupy a recto followed by its own verso, and would involve a page-turn in the middle of the second madrigal. The solution adopted was to use the same openings for three pieces, which results in these being different works: the following extract from a table of contents will make this clear, indicating the folio and (in roman numerals) the stave on which the pieces start in each book:

Piece	Cantus	Tenor	Altus	Bassus
24 *Liet'e seren'in vista*	D1ᵛ,i	d1ʳ,i	DD1ʳ,i	dd1ʳ,i
25 *Se la durezz' in voi fosse*	D1ᵛ,v	d1ᵛ,i	DD1ᵛ,i	dd1ᵛ,i
26 *Se tutto'l bel in questa sol*	D2ʳ,iii	d1ᵛ,iv	DD1ᵛ,v	dd1ᵛ,v
27 *Deh quanto fu pietoso*	D2ᵛ,i	d2ʳ,iii	DD2ʳ,iii	dd2ʳ,iii
28 *Madonna al volto mio pallido*	D3ʳ,i	d2ᵛ,i	DD2ᵛ,i	dd2ᵛ,i

This situation is most unusual, and would argue, at first sight, for the Cantus being part of a separate edition, potentially earlier than the others, despite the comment on the title-page that the pieces are 'corretti'. Perhaps supporting such a conclusion could be the different wordings found on the title-pages:
RISM 1539²³ = A1374; New Vogel 156–7.
    [Cantus:] IL TERZO LIBRO DE I MADRIGALI / NOVISSIMI DI ARCHADELTH A QVATTRO VOCI, / Insieme con alchuni di Constantio Festa, & altri dieci bellissimi a Voci mudate. / Novamente con ogni diligentia Stampati, & corretti. / [flower] / LIBRO TERZO [Scotto's mark] A QVATTRO VOCI. / VENETIIS / APVD HIERONYMVM SCOTVM. / [short rule] / 1539.
The other voices read:
    DEL TERTIO LIBRO DE I MADRIGALI / DI ARCHADELT, ET DI ALTRI ECCELLENTISSIMI / Authori. Con la gionta de alcuni Madrigali a Voci mutate bellissimi / A QVATTRO VOCI. / T / LIBRO TERTIO
or, for the Altus and Bassus:
    DEL TERZO LIBRO [. . .] A [B] / LIBRO TERZO
The presence of these differing title-pages is not a very strong argument for their belonging to different editions, for a number of volumes printed by the Scottos at this period carry different title-pages for the lower voices.
    However, there are three other features, each of which specifically leads me to believe that all four parts are probably of the same edition. One is the apparently random use of the word *Tertio* as opposed to *Terzo*, and that of *Arcadelth* as opposed to *Archadelt*, in the signature line for each gathering. *Tertio* is used only rarely, on fols. a1ʳ and 1ʳ and 2ʳ on gatherings b and c, as well as in the title of the Tenor book: *Terzo* appears everywhere else. *Arcadelth* is found more frequently: B1ʳ of the Cantus; b1ʳ, c2ʳ, d1ʳ, d2ʳ, e1ʳ, e2ʳ, f1ʳ and f2ʳ of the Tenor; throughout the Altus; and on ff1ʳ of the Bassus book. (Note that the Venice copy has the same pattern as that found in the Munich books.)
    Second is the state of the initial letters used in these partbooks. Those in the first three gatherings of the Tenor are marginally better than elsewhere. On the other hand, those in the Cantus are neither better nor worse overall than in the other books, tending merely to conform with the worst existing state elsewhere.
    The sum of these two pieces of evidence argues that the first three gatherings of the Tenor were the first to be prepared and printed. The rest of the Tenor then made one complete process, with the Altus and the Bassus: the Cantus was either part of the same process, or followed it immediately, without the intervention of any other printing.
    But the decisive factor is that of the *TAVOLA*, appearing at the end of each book: this shows quite clearly that all four copies were printed from the same setting of type, and that the Cantus was printed last. There are idiosyncratic spacings and alignments repeated

are some of the situations between this and the first and third editions of the book, and so interesting is the pattern that they suggest, that it is my suspicion that this was the point at which Gardane decided to sort out how to label compositions: certainly he found many difficult situations in working from the first, Scotto edition. Certainly, too, later volumes are much more systematic – even though they sometimes preserve wrong decisions, reached by working from the erroneous assumption that the earlier books were also systematic.[13]

I propose to leave aside three madrigals in this volume for which the first three editions all agree in their ascriptions (even within the constraints outlined above) against the new composer's name in RISM 1556[22], the fourth edition.[14] These are *Bramo morir*,[15] *Madonna al volto mio* and *Qual paura ho*, all of which are securely ascribed to Arcadelt in the earlier editions, and equally clearly to Festa in the fourth. All are accepted by Musch as being the work of Arcadelt,[16]

from book to book, as well as one or two places that have taken ink in identical manner. Apart from the normal and inevitable changes demonstrating that the Cantus was last in the sequence, there is a further detail: the tavola has, in addition to the normal two columns of contents, two additional columns flanking them, which contain the words *A voce pari.*, when needed. In the Cantus alone, the left column has slipped down half a line.

The apparent conclusion has to be that the Cantus was printed alone, and immediately after the other books, before the type for the tavola was dispersed. The probable reason for this is to be found in the presence of the dedicatory letter printed on fol. A1ᵛ. This letter, though signed *Geronimo Scotto*, draws attention to the desire of his brother, Ottaviano Scotto, to compliment the dedicatee, the Rev. Mons. Girolamo Verallo, then Papal Legate in Venice. Verallo was translated to the See of Bertinoro in February of 1539/40, which is sufficient to confirm that the date of 1539 on the title-page of the Cantus book is a genuine one, not falsified to conform with the other books. Gerolamo Scotto took over the printing shop from Ottaviano during 1539, and it is quite plausible that this dedication, with the consequent rearrangement of the Cantus book, represents one of his first publications as an independent printer.

[13] For this reason, I should expect 1541[18] to have been prepared for the press rather later in the year than was the present volume. The arrangement of the composers' names is more in line with later practice, although not completely straightforward. However, it is worth bearing in mind Mary Lewis's remarks about the extent to which Gardane seems to have worked on several volumes simultaneously: see her 'Antonio Gardane and his Publications of Sacred Music, 1538–1555' (Ph.D. dissertation, Brandeis University, 1979), pp. 139–58.

[14] This edition is not discussed in the present study. To demonstrate that the conventions outlined here continued in use for another fifteen years would require a considerable extension to this paper, an extension of no great relevance and, further, one which I am not yet in a position to offer.

[15] Despite the suggestion, in *Arcadelt*, IV, p. xii, this is not strictly anonymous in 1543[20], for the same name, *Archadelt*, is found at the head of both relevant pages, xx and xxi. By 1543, Gardane was regularly implying that the composer of the piece straddling the opening was the name he printed at the head of the verso, unless otherwise indicated.

[16] Musch, *Costanzo Festa*, pp. 158–67, and Fenlon and Haar, 'Fonti', pp. 237–8, both list the works, while Seay's edition of Arcadelt prints all three. It may be that all should be

and do not fit into the type of evidence being discussed here. *Si lieto alcun giammai*, apparently a similar case, will be discussed below.

One of the most interesting cases in Arcadelt's third book is that of *E morta la speranza*. In the first edition, 1539[23], it is to be found on fol. B2[v] of the Cantus and B2[r] of the other partbooks. There can be no doubt here that Scotto wished to assign the madrigal to Arcadelt: not only do all the folios say so, but the ascription in the Cantus is of a different setting of type from that found in the other three books. In 1541[11] and 1543[20], the madrigal appears split across an opening, at the foot of a verso and the top of the following recto (see Figure 2): in 1556[22], it is unequivocally ascribed to Costanzo Festa.

The pattern by which ownership of this madrigal was transferred from Arcadelt to Festa would seem to be fairly clear.[17] From occupying a page to itself in the first edition, it is reduced to fitting below other convenient pieces. In the edition of 1541, it happens to lie beneath a work surviving uniquely there (and therefore to be presumed to be by Arcadelt), and above *Se mort'in me potesse*.[18] If Gardane here were consistently following the pattern that he is apparently in the process of establishing (by which all pieces that begin on a page are by the composer whose name heads that page), he would be suggesting that *E morta la speranza* was still thought to be by Arcadelt.

However, the third edition, while retaining the madrigal at the foot of a page, happens to place it beneath a work securely by Festa.[19] (The need to place three pieces on some openings was a function of trying to control the total number of pages so that it might be divisible by eight, and thus use only whole sheets of paper: this in turn ensured that any pieces that were short enough to fit into a

---

reconsidered, in the light of the types of evidence to be offered in section III of this paper, below.

[17] Lest it be thought that the ascription in 1539[23] could be a simple error (as is, for example, that to *Madonna s'io credessi*; cf. J. Haar and L. Bernstein, eds., *Ihan Gero: Il primo libro de' madrigali italiani et canzoni francese a due voci*, Masters and Monuments of the Renaissance 1 (New York, 1980)), it is worth remarking that the pieces ascribed to Festa are all to be found on fols. B3[v]–C3[r], eight pages which form a discrete unit (and which, incidentally, may suggest something about how the music for this volume was collected). It should be added that both Musch and Seay (in his edition of Arcadelt) treat the ascriptions as if they were handled inconsistently by Gardane, in each case thereby supplying reinforcement of the author's position.

[18] For this madrigal, see below.

[19] In the first edition, this madrigal, *Lasso che pur hormai*, falls comfortably within the group of works assigned to Festa, while in the second there are no bibliographical grounds for rejecting the printed ascription to the same composer.

1541[11]

B2ᵛ	B3ʳ
Archadelt. Benedetto sia'l di	Con. festa. E morta la speranza
E morta la speranza	Se mort'in me potesse

1543[20]

C1ᵛ	C2ʳ
Con. festa. So che nissun mi crede	Archadelt. E morta la speranza
E morta la speranza	Lasso che pur hormai

Figure 2

group of three would normally do so – and the nine such pieces in 1541[11] would provide only a limited range of options for the next edition, particularly since *Benedetto sia'l di*, the piece previously above *E morta la speranza*, was not retained to the third edition.) The result is that Gardane, when later preparing the fourth edition, assumed that the new systematic procedures were then in place, and that both the pieces on fol. C1ᵛ were by Festa: since the first of these was not included in the new edition, he would not have had its presence to remind him of the problem.

In this situation, then, my contention is that the change of ascription from Arcadelt to Festa is not the result of a conscious change in the printer's view of authorship; the change in ownership of *E morta la speranza* is simply an unforeseen result of a refinement of procedures in the printing shop. The new attribution to Festa is, at least bibliographically, of no value.

In the same book (1541[11]), there are only two other openings where this situation arises: one of these will be discussed below, and the other, involving pp. 20–1 (fols. C2ᵛ–3ʳ of the Cantus), concerns *Se i sguardi di costei*. The opening contains *Se la durezz' in voi fosse*, with *Archadelt.* on the head-line; *Deh quanto fu pietoso* (starting on the fifth stave of the verso), with an attribution to *Archadelt.* above its first line in all partbooks; and *Se i sguardi di costei*, ascribed to *Con. festa* immediately above its opening line (the third stave of the recto) in Cantus and Tenor, although anonymous in both Altus and Bassus. This last madrigal had been securely attributed to Festa in the edition of 1539[23], but it forms the last of a group of three on an opening in 1543[20], with head-lines on both pages giving the name Arcadelt. My belief is that the unexpected placing of the attribution in 1541[11] resulted in the typesetter of 1543 missing it completely – it appears in the space normally reserved for the text of the previous piece, while referring to a piece whose ascription would now normally be at the head of the page. He therefore saw the work as one within a volume of Arcadelt and without any other name attached to it.[20] As a result, he transferred the work to that composer. However, as I believe, it is actually by Festa, and the later ascription is a printing-house error, followed up in the edition of 1556[22].

The printer of 1541[11], or his typesetters, clearly attempted to clarify the ownership of individual pieces. The case discussed in the previous paragraph is one example, while another concerns *O felix color*. This starts on the third stave of p. 39 of the Cantus, and has the ascription to *Con. festa.* – confirmed by the first edition – placed above that stave. In this way, Gardane had in fact adopted the best possible way to display the authorship of each piece, with the ascription placed above its first notes. Unfortunately, this system was not always practicable, and his later system, while easier for the typesetter, did not necessarily follow up all the clues offered by this practice (especially if the earlier edition had long runs of text at the ends of pieces), and encouraged many slips. I believe that the process followed here in 1541[11] was an interim one, before the establishment of the later, more enduring one, first to be found in 1541[18].

Of the remaining cases of doubtful identity affected by this volume, 1541[11], all but one can be resolved using different classes of evidence, and will be discussed later in this paper.[21] The remaining dubious ascription can be clarified by means of the bibliographical analysis described here: it concerns *Se mort'in me potesse*, also found in

---

[20] The wording of this phrase is in accordance with a point which I shall be pursuing in section III of the present study, to the effect that apparent ascriptions are sometimes no more than the use of a name to act as a running head-line, that is, as an internal title.

[21] They are *Amor s'al primo sguardo* and *Si lieto alcun giammai*, both to be discussed in section II below, and *Divelt'el mio bel vivo*, *Languir non mi fa amore* and *Poi che'l fiero destin*, all of which will be covered in section III.

1539[23] and 1543[20]. Musch suggests[22] that the piece is either anonymous or ascribed to Arcadelt in 1541[11]. Figure 2 (above) shows that it is probably not anonymous, but assigned to Festa, as beginning on a folio headed *Con. festa*, even though not starting at the head of that folio. There is no reason to doubt the ascription here, or its confirmation in 1539[23]. The pattern followed by Gardane confirms that there is in fact no conflicting attribution for this work.

The same can be said for *Apri'l mio dolce carcer*, found in the first two editions of Arcadelt's fourth book of madrigals (see Table 1).[23] In

[22]   Musch, *Costanzo Festa*, p. 166.
[23]   First edition: RISM 1539[24] = A1379; New Vogel 161.

   IL QVARTO LIBRO DI MADRIGALI D'ARCHADELT A / QVATRO VOCI COMPOSTI VLTIMAMENTE INSIEME CON / ALCVNI MADRIGALI DE ALTRI AVTORI NOVAMENTE CON / OGNI DILIGENTIA STAMPATI ET CORRETTI. / CANTVS [mark] CANTVS. / CON GRATIA ET PRIVILEGIO.

The other voices carry the same title, with the part-name changed. The word *Tenor* is misspelled TENNR to the right of the mark.

All parts carry a colophon on the last verso:

   IN VENETIA NELLA STAMPA D'ANTONIO GARDANE / Nellanno del Signore M.D. XXXIX. Nel mese di Setembre. / [mark] / CON GRATIA ET PRIVILEGIO.

Oblong quarto, 40 pages per part: A–E⁴; F–K⁴; L–P⁴; Q–V⁴.
Copy consulted: Munich, Bayerische Staatsbibliothek, 4⁰. Mus.pr. 95/3.

Second edition: RISM 1541[12] = A1380; New Vogel 162.

   [flower] CANTVS [flower] / IL QVARTO LIBRO DI MADRIGALI D'ARCHA=/delt, a Qvattro Voci, Composti vltimamente insieme con alcvni Madrigali d'altri aut=/tori, Novamente con ogni diligentia ristampati, & corretti. / M. D. [Gardane's mark] XXXXI. / NON SINE PRIVILEGIO. / Excudebat Venetiis, apud Antonium Gardane.

The lower voices have the same title, with the change of the part-name and the addition of a signature line:

   Quarto libro d'Archadelt. [plus signature letter]

Oblong quarto, 40 pages per part: A–E⁴; F–K⁴; L–P⁴; Q–V⁴.
Copy consulted: London, British Library, K.2.h.6.

Third edition: RISM 1545[18] = A1381; New Vogel 163.

   [flower] ARCHADELT [flower] / QVARTO LIBRO / DI MADRIGALI A QVATRO VOCI D'ARCHADELT / Insieme alcuni di altri autori novamente ristampato et corretto / A QVATRO [Gardane's mark] VOCI / Venetijs Apud Antonium Gardane / [rule] / M. D. XXXXV. / CANTVS

The lower voices have the same title, with changed part-name.
Oblong quarto, 32 pages per part: A–D⁴; E–H⁴; I–M⁴; N–Q⁴. Paginated in roman numerals from the second recto, I–XXIX, [XXX].
Copy consulted: Bologna, Civico Museo Bibliografico Musicale, R 58.

New Vogel again makes a number of errors in ascriptions for these three editions: *Dal bel suave ragio* is not ascribed to Layolle in the first edition – the word *Archadelt.* appears at the head of the relevant page (see below); *Col pensier mai* is anonymous in the first edition, as (strictly) is *S'era forsi ripreso*, for the latter appears at the foot of a page headed with Arcadelt's name; *Pace non trovo* is only ascribed to *Yvo* in the second edition; finally, New Vogel fails to point out that eight pieces (nos. 10, 14, 18, 23, 24, 26, 27 and 29) are anonymous in the third edition.

Table 1

RISM	Pages (folios)[a]	Verso (ascriptions and pieces)	Recto (ascriptions and pieces)
1539²⁴	iv–v (A2ᵛ–3ʳ)	Archadelt. Si grand'e la pieta Apri'l mio dolce carcer →	Archadelt. Dal bel suave ragio
	vi–vii (A3ᵛ–4ʳ)	Archadelt. Petrus organista. (in margin) Madonna per oltraggi Calde lacrime mie sospir →	[anonymous] Col pensier mai non maculai
1541¹²	21 (3ʳ)		Archadelt Madonna per oltraggi
	30–1 (D3ᵛ–4ʳ)	Archadelt Si grand'e la pieta Apri'l mio dolce carcer →	Layole Dal bel soave ragio
	35 (E2ʳ)		Archadelt Col pensier mai non maculai
	37 (E3ʳ)		Petrus organista. Calde lagrime mie sospir
1545¹⁸	i (A2ʳ)		Archadelt Si grand'e la pieta
	xxvii (D3ʳ)		[anonymous] Col pensier mai non maculai

[a] In this and subsequent tables, the folio numbers refer to the Cantus book.

122

both editions, it occupies a position straddling an opening, from the foot of a verso to the top of the recto following, and is accompanied by the same two other pieces. In 1539[24], both pages (numbered iv–v) have the heading *Archadelt.*: in 1541[12], while the verso (p. 30) is headed *Archadelt*, the following recto reads *Layole.*. The implications of this for the third madrigal on the opening, *Dal bel soave ragio*, will be discussed below; however, there seems no reason to doubt that *Apri'l mio dolce carcer*, starting low on each verso, was assigned in Gardane's plan to Arcadelt. In support of this is the manner in which Gardane handles the appearance of *Calde lagrime mie sospir*, by Petrus organista, on fol. vi of the first edition, where it starts beneath a work by Arcadelt. In so far as the new piece is not by the composer named at the head of the page, Gardane prints the new name in the left margin, against the start of the madrigal. (In the second edition, this work has a page to itself.)

On the same opening, *Col pensier mai non maculai* is affected by this approach. Since there is no ascription at the head of p. vii, the madrigal must be deemed anonymous in the first edition. The evidence of house practice also argues that the absence of a name above the same piece in the third edition is deliberate,[24] while I shall be arguing below that the treatment of the caption *Archadelt* in the running head-line of 1541[12] is no real argument in favour of authorship. My conclusion is that Gardane did not believe this piece to be

---

[24]   There are two elements to this argument. First is the evidence that two typesetters were involved in setting the head-lines, and probably all the text. One man set the outer forme of the first gathering of each book (A, E, I and N), and the other did the inner. If we call these men X and Y, then X set 1r, 2v, 3r and 4v, while Y was responsible for 1v, 2r, 3v and 4r. The second gathering (B, F, K and O) has all the captions re-set: X worked on the inner forme and Y on the outer. In the third gathering (C, G, L and P), as many captions as possible were retained: it appears that Y set both formes. The fourth gathering (D, etc.) has new captions: it is likely that Y set both formes again, although only two pieces have composers' names attached to them. Neither of these can have been retained from the previous gatherings. *Col pensier*, on D3r, in particular, does not retain the head-line *Archadelt*, found on C3r.

   Since there are no ascriptions on the outer forme of the last gathering (1r, 2v, 3r and 4v of D, H, M and Q – 4v contains the *TAVOLA Delli Madrigali*), one could suggest that all were omitted in error. However, the typesetter had another element to consider: five of the pieces in this gathering also have in the head-line the phrase *A voce Pari*. These five include two where the phrase does follow an ascription to *Archadelt*, and three (1r, 1v and 4r) where the work is anonymous. In these three cases, the phrase is placed in exactly the space that would otherwise have been occupied by a composer's name. It seems likely, therefore, that the typesetter did not simply forget to insert an ascription, but rather had to determine whether an ascription, or the new phrase, or both, were needed for each page in this gathering. As a result, it would seem that the omissions of composers' names were deliberate.

by Arcadelt, but did not know of any other name to put to it: it should stand as an anonymous work.

One other example may be taken from RISM 1545[19], a Verdelot anthology.[25] *Madonna io sol vorrei* is placed, as the second of three pieces, across pp. v–vi (fols. A3^v–4^r in the Cantus). Fol. A3^v is headed *Verdelot.*, and A4^r reads *Const. Festa*: the lower voices have the

---

[25] RISM 1545[19] = V1231; New Vogel 2874.

The first folio of the Cantus part is missing in the only surviving copy. The lower voices have identical titles, with the exception of the part-name:

TENOR / VERDELOT TVTTI LI MADRIGALI DEL PRIMO / ET SECONDO LIBRO A QVATRO VOCI NVOVAMENTE RI=/STAMPATI, ET CON DILIGENTIA CORRETTI. / A QVATRO VOCI / VENETIIS M. D. XLV.

Oblong quarto, 40 pages per part: A–F⁴; G–M⁴; N–S⁴; T–Z,+⁴.

Copy consulted: Florence, Biblioteca Nazionale Centrale, Mus.ant. 129: lacks fol. A1.

Mary Lewis discusses this and a number of other unsigned printed volumes of the period ('Antonio Gardane', pp. 314–29). She shows clearly that the typographical material for this volume was that normally used by Scotto, and assigns the book to him as publisher. However, the different treatment of certain details leads me to think that the book was edited (and possibly even set) by someone other than Scotto's normal house-men. Bridges, 'Publishing', pp. 119–29, reaches a similar conclusion, though for different reasons.

It may be significant that two of Lewis's 'Group 2' (to which the present volume belongs) are probably among those volumes that, as Richard Agee has recently shown, were supported by privileges issued in Venice – see his 'The Venetian Privilege and Music-Printing in the Sixteenth Century', *Early Music History*, 3 (1983), pp. 1–42: on pp. [29–30] are references to privileges issued to Rore for motets (22 November 1544, and therefore plausibly to be sought in the publications of 1545) and to Cambio for madrigals of Petrarch (2 June 1545). Others of these unsigned volumes, those by Festa, by Vicentino and of *Madrigali de diversi autori* (RISM 1547[13]) claim the existence of privilege. It is notable that, in the same period, Gardane received a privilege for the works of Jacques da Ponte, while in September 1544 Scotto gained a privilege for several different volumes. None of these has survived among the unsigned volumes that Lewis discusses: but they do indicate that both Gardane and Scotto were able and willing to apply for privileges on their own behalf during this period. It is not an unreasonable assumption that neither was involved in the petitions for privileges for the unsigned volumes.

However, both Rore and Cambio are among the musicians referred to by Andrea Calmo at just this period (1547) as being among the leaders of the period, alongside Arcadelt, Verdelot and Willaert. (The relevant extract from the later, 1580, edition of Calmo's letters is quoted and translated in Bridges, 'Publishing', pp. 57–8.) While neither Verdelot nor Arcadelt is known to have been in Venice at the time, all five composers are represented among the unsigned volumes discussed by Lewis, including Verdelot with the volume which stimulated this digression. It seems likely that a number of the unsigned volumes were published, or at least covered by privilege, by the composers concerned (as is suggested by the evidence of the privileges to Cambio and Rore), and merely printed by Scotto. This would certainly help to explain why no printer's name appears on the volumes, even after Scotto began inserting the salamander device on the title-pages. It would also raise interesting speculation as to where Verdelot was living during the 1530s and 1540s. If he was in Venice, this would to some extent help to remove the peculiar situation of a large number of volumes of music being published in Venice during the 1530s as the work of a non-resident. There is no parallel case during the period, if Arcadelt was resident, for he was not represented until the end of the decade (by which time the situation was changing rapidly): Festa had very few volumes to show, and, further, himself took out a privilege in 1538, as Agee shows (in 'Privilege', p. [29]). See Appendix, below.

same ascriptions, apparently re-set for the Tenor and Bassus. This madrigal survives in several other Verdelot anthologies, with the constant attribution to that composer. By the time of 1545, it had clearly been accepted as being by him. It would seem that the anonymous editor of 1545[19] also intended that ascription to be understood, rather than any possible suggestion that the work was by Festa. (The apparent reference to de Silva in the earliest editions will be discussed below, in section III).

The assumption in each of these cases has been that the composition beginning low on the verso, but ending on the recto, was thought of, by the Gardane of late 1541 and after (as well as by some other printers), as belonging to the composer cited on the verso. The evidence for this has been drawn not from the concordance pattern *per se*, but rather from the manner in which the printer himself interpreted the pattern when he came to prepare a later edition. For earlier volumes the procedure was clearly more fluid, and the transition from this to the more systematic has provided some of my evidence.

In the case of the Scottos working before 1541, the evidence is much less easy to interpret, because the family adopted different procedures for most of their editions from the 1530s. The following discussion of the situation in Scotto's 1540 edition of the combined contents of Verdelot's first two books,[26] while involving the same kinds of evidence, can therefore not produce the clear-cut pattern of

---

[26]   RISM 1540[20] = V1228; New Vogel 2871.
    [flower] DI VERDELOTTO [flower] / TVTTI LI MADRIGALI DEL PRIMO, ET SECONDO / Libro a Qvatro Voci. Con la Gionta de i Madrigali del medesmo / Auttore, non piu stampati. / AGGIONTOVI ANCHORA ALTRI MADRIGALI / novamente Composti da Messer ADRIANO, & de altri Eccellentissimi / Musici, Come appare ne la sequente Tavola. / [flower] / [device] / Apud Hieronymum Scotum. / [rule] / 1540.
    The lower voices have a different title, with the relevant part-name:
    MADRIGALI DEL PRIMO, ET SECONDO LIBRO / di Verdelotto a Quatro Voci. Con la Gionta del medesmo Auttore, & de / altri Eccellentissimi Musici, novamente Stampati. / [flower] / TENOR
    Oblong quarto, 60 pages per part: A–G⁴H²; a–g⁴h²; AA–GG⁴HH²; aa–gg⁴hh². Paginated from the second recto, I–LVIII.
    Copy consulted: Wolfenbüttel, Herzog August Bibliothek, 2.13.14–2.13.17. Musica.
    New Vogel does not correctly reflect the fact that eleven of the pieces lying across an opening are not specifically attributed, while the others are. Further, it suggests that the second setting of *Con lachrim'et sospir* (pp. XLIV–XLV, fols. F3ᵛ–4ʳ of each book) is by Verdelot: the names that appear at the heads of the relevant pages are *ARCHADELT* and *IACHET*, respectively. Finally, *Amor quanto piu lieto* (p. XLIII) is clearly ascribed to *VERDELOT* in all books. Both these pieces are discussed below.

typographical connections that makes the earlier argument so satisfying. In the eight gatherings of each partbook, there are eleven situations where an opening carries three madrigals. Eight of these are of no interest in the present connection, in so far as, in each, both pages carry the name *Verdelot*, and the three pieces involved are consistently attributed to him elsewhere. The other three cases can be tabulated as in Table 2.

Io son tal volta carries careful and deliberate ascriptions to Festa in all three of Scotto's early editions of Verdelot's second book.[27] When Gardane reprinted these volumes, in 1541[18] and 1544[18], he assigned the work to Willaert. He seems to have assumed that a piece occupying the position of this madrigal, even in an edition by Scotto, would be the work of the composer cited on the verso, in this case, Willaert; the evidence of Scotto's earlier editions suggests that he, on the other hand, thought it to be by the name cited on the recto following, that is, Festa. Scotto seems to have felt the same about *Madonna 'l bel desire*, which is specifically attributed to *Adrian* in the three earlier editions. I believe that, in both cases, the evidence offered here as to a bibliographical (or procedural) reason for the change of attribution argues strongly that there is support only for the earlier ascriptions, and that the later one has to be rejected.

(It might be thought that, if this were true, there should be some doubts as to whether the ascriptions on the rectos refer to two pieces (to the one across the opening as well as to that starting on the recto), or whether the second of these should not more properly be regarded as anonymous. However, the pattern seems to suggest that Scotto tried to arrange that the ascription could apply to both composers: the attribution of *Grat'e benigna donna* to Willaert and that of *D'amore le generose* to Festa are both securely supported by other sources. Further, that of *Vostre dolce parole* to *Iachet* is confirmed in Scotto's own earlier 1534[16].)

If this pattern holds, then questions need to be asked about the authorship of *Con lachrim'e sospir*. It would seem probable, working from the pattern proposed above, that Scotto believed this madrigal to be by *Iachet*. The fact that the work is assigned to Arcadelt in its only other source, Gardane's 1541[18], is of no value, for I have shown in more than one instance (including that of *Io son tal volta*) that

---

[27] Citations appear below, at note 45. For later sources, see the list in Musch, *Costanzo Festa*, p. 161, as supplemented by Fenlon and Haar, 'Fonti', p. 232.

Table 2

Pages (folios)	Verso (ascriptions and pieces)		Recto (ascriptions and pieces)	
32–3 (E1ᵛ–2ʳ)	VERDELOT	Lasso che se creduto Madonna'l bel desire →	ADRIAN Vuillaert.	Grat'e benigna donna
36–7 (E3ᵛ–4ʳ)	ADRIAN Vuillaert.	Signora dolce, io te Io son tal volta →	CON. FESTA.	D'amore le generose
44–5 (F3ᵛ–4ʳ)	ARCHADELT	Ardea tutt'a voi Con lachrim'e sospir →	IACHET	Vostre dolce parole

127

Gardane, when he tried to make things more systematic, took such a piece as belonging to the composer cited on the verso; that is probably what happened here, which would serve to render his attribution derivative – although in an eccentric sense. It does seem clear, therefore, that the bibliographical case for Jachet as the author of this madrigal is actually stronger than that for Arcadelt.

II

The rapid streamlining of the processes of music printing during the early 1540s had other effects, one of which directly concerns the head-lines and signature lines, and therefore the ascriptions. It had been the practice of many printers to preserve as much as possible of this material from one sheet to the next, retaining it in a skeleton forme, rather than redistributing the type and then setting it up again for the next sheet. However, this did not mean that the same head-lines could appear in the same setting of type on every sheet, still less on each side of every sheet, for a printer normally used more than one forme for each book in progress. Two were regarded as a minimum – one for each side of the sheet of paper – and many books show evidence of having been prepared with three or four such formes. This would allow the typesetter to start preparing one sheet while a previous one was still going through the press.[28] The material retained in the skeleton forme regularly comprised a running head (to which page or folio numbers were added), a signature line (to which the gathering letter could be added), and necessarily some of the furniture – the uninked pieces of wood which kept the text and staves in place.[29] This material can provide evidence of the order of printing: since more than one skeleton forme was normally in use, and since the elements of each were liable to shift slightly or to deteriorate during use (apart from usually being set in slightly different relative alignments), they can sometimes also help to reveal a break in the sequence of work, or the presence of a cancel leaf. For

[28] For a discussion of this in the output of a major early Italian printer, see my 'Upon the Use of Running Titles in the Aldus House of 1518', *The Library*, 5th ser., 27 (1972), pp. 126–31. I use the same evidence to help in the analysis of Petrucci's printing methods, in the forthcoming paper, 'A Case of Half-sheet Imposition in the Early Sixteenth Century'.

[29] Lewis, 'Antonio Gardane', pp. 117–18, has suggested that Gardane may have employed distinctively shaped formes in order to keep the staves in the same relationships from page to page. Some such system would have been essential for Petrucci and other multiple-impression printers.

the present discussion, the most useful element of the skeleton forme is the head-line, containing the name of the composer.

Most musical volumes, particularly anthologies, leave little scope for retaining a head-line, even though the signature line may stay the same. Scotto's early volumes occasionally use a consistent running head: *Verdelot* on every page of 1537[9], and also on all the versos but one of 1533[2]. In such cases, the presence of the caption at the head of any page is, of course, not an assertion that the pieces there belonged to that named composer – any more than the absence of any such captions in the first editions of Arcadelt's first book implies that all the pieces there are anonymous, or by Arcadelt.[30] However, the presence of some such patterns can yield bibliographical information, throwing light on the value (or otherwise) of the names that are printed, or of the blank space.

An innocuous example occurs in the book of Veggio madrigals printed in 1540 by Scotto.[31] Here, the formal pattern of the running head-lines was clearly systematised in the mind of the typesetter. The relevant part-name (*CANTVS*, etc.) appears on all rectos containing music. The composer's name (*CLAVDIVS Veggius.*) is to be found on all versos, except as mentioned below; in addition, it was to be set on the first recto of each gathering – where it would catch the binder's eye after he had folded the sheet, and confirm his choice. The book contains six madrigals by Arcadelt (according to the dedication, 'donated' by Scotto), on fols. C1^v, C2^r, D1^r, D1^v, D2^r and D2^v of each partbook. Each of these pages carries the word *ARCH-ADELT* in the running head, instead of Veggio's name, but, in the case of the three rectos, in addition to the part-name. In this volume the printer, faced with so simple a programme, was already keeping

---

[30] For more discussion of the implications of this procedure, see section III of the present paper, below.

[31] RISM 1540[19] = V1087; New Vogel 2844.

> [flower] MADRIGALI [flower] / A QVATTRO VOCI / Di Messer CLAVDIO Veggio, con la Gionta di sei altri di Arcadelth della / misura a breve. Nuovamente con ogni diligentia stampati. / [device] / VENETIIS / Apud Hieronymum Scotum. / [rule] / 1540.

The lower voices have a different title-page:

> MADRIGALI DI MESSER CLAVDIO / Veggio, a Quattro Voci. Nuovamente Stampati. / [flower] / TENOR / [etc.]

Oblong quarto, 40 pages per part: A–E⁴; a–e⁴; AA–EE⁴; aa–ee⁴. Paginated from the second recto, I–XXXVIII.

Copy consulted: Vienna, Österreichische Nationalbibliothek, SA.77.D.55.

J. Haar, 'The *Nota Nere* Madrigal', *Journal of the American Musicological Society*, 18 (1965), pp. 22–41, points out (on p. 25) that this is the first printed volume to refer to the new style.

as much material as possible in the head-line from one forme to the next: comparison of the same folio in different partbooks, or in consecutive gatherings of the same book, will rapidly confirm this. A natural, normal product of such a procedure is that the head-line would not always be checked for its accuracy: after all, the typesetter knew that it was normally retained, intact, from one gathering to the next. In this particular volume, there are two minor, though instructive anomalies. In gathering BB of the Altus, the formes were used in a different position from that found elsewhere: the forme that normally supplied the first recto of each gathering was here inverted. Therefore, the additional reference to the composer's name (which should have appeared on BB1^r) is found on BB3^r. The other head-lines in this forme confirm the nature of this slip as being purely procedural. In addition, the first recto of E in all partbooks lacks the additional reference to Veggio. Here, the probable explanation is rather different, for the typesetter had already had to take Veggio's name out of the skeleton forme for D1^r, when he inserted instead the name of Arcadelt. Apparently, when removing this latter name, ready for gathering E, he forgot to reinstate that of Veggio.

Clearly, there is no problem here over the ascription of the madrigal concerned, *Io son donna disposto di morire*. But, equally clearly, in books where the possibility of retaining a composer's name as part of the head-line exists, there also exists the possibility of making such an error where it becomes significant, omitting the name of a completely different composer, or alternatively forgetting to remove a now incorrect name. The obvious place to look for such possibilities is in those volumes largely devoted to the works of one composer – Arcadelt, Festa, Verdelot – rather than in a volume of *Madrigali diversi*, where the typesetter would expect to have to change the name in the head-line for each new page, and would therefore be less likely to forget about it.

Mary Lewis has drawn attention to a practice in Gardane's shop that, in fact, makes such errors even more likely: she has given the name of 'vertical setting' to a procedure whereby the second gathering, for instance, of every partbook was set in sequence, before work began on any of the third gatherings.[32] Clearly, this became a

---

[32] Lewis, 'Antonio Gardane', pp. 123–5. The evidence of the treatment of the head-lines in Veggio's book, which I have just outlined, argues that Scotto was following the same procedure.

convenient procedure only after printers had begun to lay out all partbooks consistently, with the same pieces lying on the same folios in each: equally clearly, once that had happened, part of every running head-line, the composer's name, could be retained from one partbook to the next, for four sheets with four-voice madrigals, for five with five-part music, etc. (It should also be no surprise that, under such a pattern of work, the part-name appears less frequently on the inner pages of a sheet, and more frequently only on the first recto: this reduces even further the number of elements needing to be changed when moving from one voice to another.) As a result, the habit of automatically checking the composer's name at the head of each page must have slipped from memory even more often, and the prospect of finding erroneous names, held over from the last part-book of one gathering to the first of the next, increases correspondingly.

Some excellent examples of this type of evidence occur in RISM 1541[16], another Verdelot anthology.[33] A setting of *Deh perche non e in voi, tante pietade* appears on p. 22 of each book. In the Cantus book only (fol. C3[v]), it is ascribed to *Archadelt*, while in the other five books the madrigal is anonymous.[34] The immediate assumption that the entry in the Cantus might be an error, then corrected in the lower voices, is confirmed by a simple analytical observation: the type appearing on C3[v] of the Cantus is identical, both in exact alignment and in the condition of the letter *l*, with that found on the correspond-

---

33   RISM 1541[16]; New Vogel 2890.
      VERDELOT / LA PIV DIVINA, ET PIV BELLA MVSICA, CHE SE / vdisse
      giamai delli presenti Madrigali, a Sei voci. Composti per lo Eccellentissi=/mi
      VERDELOT. Et altri Musici, non piu Stampati, & con / ogni diligentia corretti.
      Novamente posti in luce. / CANTVS / CON GRATIA ET PRIVILEGIO. / M.D.XLI. /
      VENETIIS APVD ANTONIVM GARDANE.
      The lower voices have different titles, with the appropriate part-name:
      TENOR / VERDELOT / M. D. [Gardane's mark] XXXXI. / Venetijs Apud Antonium
      Gardane. [plus signature line:] Madrigali primi, di Verdelot, a Sei [followed by the
      signature letter]
      Oblong quarto, 32 pages per part: A–D⁴; E–H⁴; I–M⁴; N–Q⁴; R–V⁴; X–Z,+⁴. Paginated
      from the first recto, [1], 2–31, [32] in all books.
      Copies consulted: Vienna, Österreichische Nationalbibliothek, SA.77.D.52; London,
      British Library, K.11.e.2(4) – Bassus only.
      Once again, there are serious problems with the list of ascriptions offered by the New
      Vogel: *Ultimi mei sospiri* is ascribed to Verdelot, as is *Ardenti miei sospiri*, while *In me cresce
      l'ardore* is anonymous. Four other pieces have ascriptions only in some of the partbooks,
      remaining anonymous in the others: all are discussed here.
34   On the strength of this ascription, the work is edited in *Arcadelt*, VII, no. 27. The folios in the
      other partbooks of this edition correspond: G3[v], L3[v], P3[v], T3[v] and Z3[v].

ing page of the previous gathering, p. 14 (fol. B3ᵛ of the Cantus, and corresponding folios in the other books). The error, then, was not even an active one on the part of the typesetter, that of deliberately inserting a composer's name – an act that would necessarily compel our attention. Rather, it was the passive error of leaving the name in place for one partbook too many.[35] The piece should not be regarded as by Arcadelt, but as anonymous, pending the discovery of further, independent sources.

There are three other pieces in this volume for which some of the partbooks lack an ascription, and which therefore might at first sight seem to fall into the same situation: for two of these, the presence of a name in some books has to be seen as an intentional entry on the part of the typesetter. *Cosi estrema de doglia* is ascribed to *Const. festa.* in all except the Tenor book, where there is no name.[36] This name does not appear anywhere else in the volume, so it can hardly have been retained in error. *Chi bussa*, fitted onto the lower staves of the last folio of music, has the name *Verdolot* [*sic*] above the stave on which it opens, only in the Cantus, Quintus and Sextus books. It is just possible to argue that the same ascription is lacking in the other three books only because of the presence of text from the end of the previous piece.[37] There is no reason to doubt the stated authorship of either piece.

More difficult is the case of *Madonna i prieghi mei*, on fol. A3ᵛ, ascribed to *Maistre Ihan*, only in the Cantus and Bassus books.[38] This madrigal has a heading which seems to me to be identical with that used for *Ditimi o diva mia* (the second setting, on p. 29, fol. 3ʳ of the last

[35] This must serve to underscore the extent to which we should adapt our view of 'errors', 'variants' and 'changes' in the surviving copies of early printed music – a view which is at present far from that of the contemporary purchaser of the volumes. For a printer to re-set a whole leaf or sheet, the errors had to be gross. For him to recall or correct pages that had slipped past him was virtually unknown. While Petrucci and other printers would regularly correct copies remaining unsold in their shop, supposing the errors to be serious musical ones, they felt almost no compulsion to correct non-musical mistakes. These were simply not deemed to be important enough, as is witnessed by the present erroneous ascription, which was merely 'corrected' for those partbooks which had not as yet gone through the press.

[36] Detailed analysis leads me to believe that the Tenor book was set first for the last gathering, which contains this madrigal: for earlier gatherings, the Cantus was certainly set first, perhaps followed by the Bassus.

[37] Despite the assertion of A.-M. Bragard, *Étude bio-bibliographique sur Philippe Verdelot, musicien français de la Renaissance*, Mémoires de la Classe des Beaux-Arts de l'Académie Royale de Belgique, 11 (1964), p. 58, this work is not to be found in later editions of Verdelot's six-voice madrigals. It is discussed and edited in D. Harrán, 'Chi bussa? or the Case of the Anti-madrigal', *Journal of the American Musicological Society*, 21 (1968), pp. 85–93.

[38] To be found on p. 6 – that is, fol. 3ᵛ of the first gathering – of each partbook.

gathering). If that were true, it would require that the first gathering of all the partbooks should have been set after the rest of the book (a by no means unknown occurrence, although without any evident reason in the present case), and also that the caption should have been moved from a recto to a verso (p. 6) – a most unreasonable assumption.

Instead, I think that one has to suggest that the attribution to *Maistre Ihan* on p. 6 was newly set, and that the pattern of preparing the head-line for this page was influenced by what the typesetter had just finished on p. 5. Here, Berchem's *Madonna se volete* begins at the top corner of the page only in the Cantus and Bassus books, and on the third stave in all others. In the Cantus and Bassus, therefore, the ascription to *Iachet Berchem* appears in its customary place in the head-line to the page. In the other four books, it is fitted above the opening of the piece, in the space that would otherwise have contained the last words of the text of the previous madrigal. It seems at least possible that the typesetter (or his editor) merely left the head-line blank on p. 6 because, in the same partbooks, it was also blank on p. 5. If this is so, and I admit it to be rather far-fetched, the omission of the composer's name in these four partbooks was not the result of second thoughts on Gardane's part, and the ascription to Maistre Jhan can be assumed to have been acceptable to him.[39]

Maistre Jhan fares poorly in this volume: there are two settings of

[39] This assumes that each gathering was set entirely through in consecutive order. One of the merits of the procedure proposed by Lewis is that the typesetter could not merely set the same gathering for each partbook before proceeding to the next, but he could also do the same for smaller units, certainly separate formes, and even possibly individual pieces. This last would in practice seem to have been unlikely, for, in the instance of the present volume, the music would have had to have been set for nearly six whole gatherings (one for each voice-part) before any one forme would have been completed and ready to go to press – to be precise, for thirty-seven pages of standing type. It is more likely that the procedure involved setting 'vertically' the individual pieces that made up one forme for each sheet. Then nineteen pages would have been set by the time the first forme was ready for the press. While this may seem still to make great demands on the amount of type, the number of sorts in the case, it must be remembered that one more page set would release another forme for the press, as that for the second partbook was finished, and another page would release the third, by which time the first would be returning from the press, and the type could be redistributed. Since fifteen pages of standing type would be required even under straightforward setting procedures (when each gathering was set straight through in order), this alternative arrangement does seem to have been feasible: indeed, it has the great advantage that each sheet would have time to dry from the first impression before the forme for the other side was printed, considerably greater time than that allowed by normal linear setting. However, this alternative method of vertical setting does weaken my argument for the attribution of Maistre Jhan's *Madonna i prieghi mei*, unless I assume that the lapse lies with the house editor or a shop supervisor, rather than with the actual typesetter.

Ditimi o diva mia ascribed to him (pp. 23 and 29), of which the second is retained for the second edition[40] and there attributed to Verdelot (piece 23). There is no chance that the presence of the name *Verdelot* in the second edition can be a simple technical slip: it cannot have been retained from elsewhere, and so must have been a deliberate act on the part of the typesetter. However, the second attribution to *Maistre Ihan* in the first edition (on p. 29) could have been, and probably was, retained from the first (on p. 23). It seems plausible to suggest that the typesetter, seeing the same words for an incipit, assumed (without thought) that he was dealing with a work by Maistre Jhan, for he would not have had the first setting before him – the type would have been dispersed, leaving only the running head. My belief, therefore, is that the two settings of *Ditimi o diva mia* in 1541[16] are by different composers, the first by Maistre Jhan, and the second by Verdelot, as attested in the second edition.

There are also a couple of examples of the same technique, or lapse in technique, in RISM 1543[20] (the third edition of Arcadelt's third book).[41] *Amor s'al primo sguardo* is here attributed to *Archadelt.* on p. xvii (fols. C1ʳ, H1ʳ, N1ʳ and S1ʳ). But the heading which gives the composer's name had been retained from p. viiii (B1ʳ in the Cantus), where it was used for all the partbooks, and was to be used further on p. xxv (fol. D1ʳ of the Cantus), where it appears above *Qual paura ho*. In the other editions of this volume, *Amor s'al primo sguardo* is unequivocally ascribed to Festa.[42] In exactly the same manner, the heading on p. xviii (fol. C1ᵛ) of the third edition, an ascription to

---

40   RISM 1546¹⁹; New Vogel 2891.

> VERDELOT A SEI / MADRIGALI DI VERDELOT ET / DE ALTRI AVTORI A SEI VOCI / novamente con alcuni madrigali novi ristampati & corretto / A SEI [Gardane's mark] VOCI / In Venetia Apresso di / Antonio Gardane. / [rule] / M. D. XXXXVI. / CANTVS

The other partbooks have the same title, with changed part-name.

This volume has the same collation as that of the first edition (see note 33, above). Not paginated; the pieces are numbered, I–XXIX.

Copy consulted: Munich, Bayerische Staatsbibliothek.

41   RISM 1543²⁰ = A1377; New Vogel 159.

> [flower] CANTVS [flower] / IL TERZO LIBRO D'I MADRIGALI D'ARCHADELT / A QVATRO VOCI INSIEME ALCUNI DI CONST. FESTA / & altri dieci a voci mudate novamente ristampato & corretto. / A QVATRO [Gardane's mark] VOCI / Venetijs Apud Antonium Gardane. / [rule] / M. D. XXXXIII.

The lower voices carry the same title, with changed part-name.

Oblong quarto, 40 pages per part: A–E⁴; F–K⁴; L–P⁴; Q–V⁴. Paginated from the first recto, [1], II–XXXIX, [40], in each partbook.

Copy consulted: Glasgow, Euing Music Library, lacking the last folio of the Bassus.

42   These editions, 1539²³ and 1541¹¹, are detailed in note 12, above.

Con. Festa., is retained for p. XXVI (D1ᵛ), where it changes the authorship of Arcadelt's *Si lieto alcun giamai*. In this case, it is little wonder that the next edition, 1556²², should retain Festa as the composer, for it displays a propensity for converting works to his property. However, the bibliographical evidence of the third edition shows that the changes of composer given there are not conscious decisions on the part of the printer, but merely technical slips. Both works should be regarded as belonging to their earlier authors – *Amor s'al primo sguardo* as the work of Festa, and *Si lieto alcun giamai* of Arcadelt.

Other cases can be found where an ascription is preserved from one folio to another, in all or some partbooks. Among them would be:

(1) the suggestion in the Bassus book of 1542¹⁶, *Madrigali de diversi autori libro primo*, that Alfonso de la Viola's *Ai pie d'un chiaro fonte* was by *Arnoldo*. This clearly erroneous ascription appears on fol. T4ᵛ as a relic from its correct use on T3ᵛ, which occupies a similar position in the arrangement of the inner forme for this sheet.⁴³

(2) the ascription to *Verdelot* of Festa's *D'amore le generose*, in the Verdelot anthology, 1541¹⁸, preserved in the Altus book.⁴⁴ This use, on fol. AA2ʳ, appears to be adapted from the same title employed on Z2ʳ and AA1ʳ. By contrast, the name of *Const. Festa.* is carefully applied to this work, not only in the other partbooks, but also in the Scotto edition 1540²⁰, in later anthologies, and in Ottaviano Scotto's earlier editions (1534, 1536 and 1537) of Verdelot's second book.⁴⁵

⁴³ This recurrence of identical captions on both formes of a single sheet tends to argue, as I discuss elsewhere in this paper, that some volumes were set more slowly, using only one or two formes for the work. This may be yet another reflection of Gardane's apparent habit of working on more than one title at a time.

⁴⁴ For this volume, see note 9, above. The Scotto edition, RISM 1540²⁰, is described in note 26.

⁴⁵ RISM 1534¹⁶ = V1220; New Vogel 2868.
The Bassus survives as
   Del Libro Secondo / B
with the colophon:
   Finisce il Secundo Libro de Madrigali di Verdelot, Nuovamente / Stampati, Et per Andrea Anticho intagliati, 7 con / summa diligentia corretti. / [Scotto's mark] / Venetijs Apud Octauianum Scotum / [rule] / M. D. XXXIII.
Oblong octavo, 32 pages: G–H⁸. Pieces numbered, 1–25. Tavola set in two columns, not headed. All but three composer ascriptions are set vertically in the left margin.
Copy consulted: Paris, Bibliothèque Nationale, Rés. Vmf. 40(2).

RISM 1536⁷ = V1221; New Vogel 2869.
   Il secondo Libro de Madrigali di Verdelot / insieme con alcuni altri bellissimi Madrigali di Adriano, 7 di / Constantino Festa, Nuouamente stampati, 7 con / summa diligentia corretti. / M. D. [large:]s XXXVI. / Con Gratia, 7 Privilegio.

(3) the misascription of two pieces in the Cantus book of 1540[18], repeated exactly in 1541[17], both editions of Verdelot's five-voice madrigals.[46] In the earlier, Scotto, edition, Verdelot's *Quand'havran fin* is ascribed to *Archadelt* on fol. C1[v], while Arcadelt's *Se'l foco in cui sempr'ardo* is given to *Verdelot* on C2[r]. The clear implication is that these two head-lines, which lie close to each other in the forme, were exchanged in error, and were then corrected for the remaining voices. In the later edition, the two pieces appear on pp. 24 (fol. C4[v]) and 20 (C2[v]) respectively: the repetition here of the error found in 1540[18] is almost enough to determine that the later edition was copied directly from the earlier.

(4) the faulty ascription, on fol. cc3[r] of the Bassus of 1539[23], of

The lower voices have variants of a different title:
¶Del Libro Secondo di Verdelotto / T
Del Libro Secondo di Verdelot. / A
¶Del Libro Secondo di Verdelot. / B
On fol. H7[v]:
[Scotto's mark] / [short rule] / ¶Venetijs Apud Octauianum Scotum.
Oblong octavo, 32 pages per part: A–B[8]; C–D[8]; E–F[8]; G–H[8]. Pieces numbered, 1–25.
Tavola in two columns, headed. Running head: part-name. Ascriptions at the head of the page in some instances.
Copy consulted: Bologna, Civico Museo Bibliografico Musicale, u 309.

RISM 1537[10] = V1222: New Vogel 1870.
Il secondo Libro de Madrigali di Verdelotto / insieme con alcuni altri bellissimi Madrigali di Adriano, 7 di / Constantio Festa: Nuouamente stampati, 7 con / somma diligentia corretti. / m d [large:]s xxxvii. / Con Gratia, 7 Privilegio.
The lower voices have a consistent title, with relevant part-letter:
¶Del Libro Secondo de Madrigali di Verdelotto. / [large:]T
On fol. H7[v]:
[Scotto's mark] / [short rule] / Venetijs Apud Octauianum Scotum.
Oblong octavo, 32 pages per part: A–B[8]; C–D[8]; E–F[8]; G–H[8]. Pieces numbered, 1–25.
Tavola in one column, headed and with ascriptions. Running head-line: part-name, extended on the first recto of gatherings B, D, F and H.
Copies consulted: Munich, Bayerische Staatsbibliothek, 8⁰. Mus.pr. 40/2, lacks the last folio of the Bassus; Paris, Bibliothèque Nationale, Rés. Vmd. 23 (an Altus book); Bologna, Civico Museo Bibliografico Musicale, r 140/1 (a Bassus).

46   RISM 1540[18]; New Vogel 2884.
LE DOTTE ET ECCELLENTE COMPOSITIONI / DE I MADRIGALI A CINQVE VOCI DA DI/versi perfettissimi Musici fatte. Nouamente raccolte, / & con ogni diligentia Stampate. / AVTORI. / Di Adriano Vuillaert. & di / Leonardo Barri suo discipulo. / Di Verdelotto. / Di Constantio Festa. / Di Archadelt. / Di Corteggia. / Di Iachet Berchem. / De Ivo, & di Nolet, / Apud Hieronymum Scotum. / [rule] / 1540.
The lower voices have a consistent different title, with the appropriate part-names:
MADRIGALI A CINQVE VOCE DA PIV / Eccellentissimi Musici fatti. Nouamente raccolti, & / con somma diligentia corretti. / TENOR
Oblong quarto, 44 pages per part: A–E[4]F[2]; a–e[4]f[2]; Aa–Ee[4]Ff[2]; aa–ee[4]ff[2]; AA–EE[4]FF[2].
Paginated from the second recto, i–xlii.
Copy consulted: Munich, Bayerische Staatsbibliothek, 4⁰. Mus.pr. 52(7); Wolfenbüttel, Herzog August Bibliothek, 2.11.1–2.11.5 Musica.
For RISM 1541[17], see note 12, above.

Festa's *Divelt'e'l mio bel vivo* to *Archadelt*. This is probably retained from fol. bb3ʳ and the corresponding pages in the other voice parts, although the evidence is rather indistinct.[47]

(5) the ascription to Arcadelt, in all books of 1541[12], of Verdelot's *Io son tal volta* (not to be confused with the Festa setting, discussed above). The ascription, *Archadelt.* (with the final point) on p. 19 of all partbooks, has been retained from p. 11, that is, from B2ʳ to C2ʳ of the Cantus (and corresponding folios in the other books). The piece is correctly ascribed to Verdelot in other editions.

III

It might seem that my procedure in the first and second sections of this paper has been to demonstrate that the earlier of two surviving ascriptions to a madrigal should be the preferred one. That is, of course, by no means always the case; but it is in the nature of the evidence I have been offering that it should suggest that some subsequent changes in ascription were the result, not of conscious thought, but of unconscious error or of technical change. If this has been adequately demonstrated, it has been capable of showing no more than that the later ascription has no evidence in its favour. It may be, in a few of these cases, that the later change was in fact deliberate; but one has no way of discovering such a possibility from the surviving evidence. All that can be shown is that it is more likely that the change was not deliberate.

On the other hand, there are several cases where no bibliographical or technical reason can be adduced for an erroneous change in ownership. In such cases, one has initially to admit that the two ascriptions remain in conflict, and look elsewhere for reasonable evidence: to the style of the music, to the relations between composer and publisher, to the known biographies of both, even to the concordance pattern. Occasionally, though rarely, there is bibliographical evidence suggesting that the later ascription is in fact the correct one. I propose in the paragraphs that follow to give a few examples of such instances.

I have already discussed one or two cases in Arcadelt's fourth book of madrigals, but I wish to turn to the volumes again, for the

---

[47] For this volume, see note 12, above.

three editions[48] do not show the same basic approach to the provision of names at the heads of pages. In the first two, Gardane clearly wished to have a name at the head of every page: therefore, the word *Archadelt.* acted as a general running title and was retained on pages where no other entry could be made. Thus, in 1539[24], the setting of type for the head-line which appears on p. v (fol. A3^r) is to be found also on pp. XIII (B3^r) and XXI (C3^r), in each case with the corresponding folios in the other partbooks). This pattern can also be seen elsewhere in the volume. A few folios, A3^r, A4^r, E4^r and their corresponding pages in the other books (i.e. those numbered v, VII and XXXIX), carry the word *Residuum.* in the head-line. Other composers are only named at the heads of five pages (VIII, IX, XX, XXIII and XXXVII). In addition, no name at all is found on p. XXXVIII, for the start of the last piece of all, *Pace non trovo* (assigned to Yvo in the second edition).[49] This falls on the last opening of music in both editions, and it is plausible to assume (in the absence of any other evidence) that the name was merely forgotten in the first edition.

There are very few substantive changes made to the ascriptions for the second edition. As I have shown above, some apparent changes are the result either of trying to adapt practice when fitting three pieces to an opening, or of failing to change an obsolete ascription in the head-line: both are direct products of the printer's attempts at becoming more systematic. *Io son tal volta*, for example, is ascribed to Arcadelt only because the running head-line was not removed from the forme and changed: the same appears to be true of that composer's name as found above *Col pensier mai non maculai.*

This is hardly surprising: of thirty-eight captions, only seven are not to Arcadelt – only two of the first twenty-nine. One of these is the name *Layole.* on p. 31 (fol. D4^r of the Cantus). Well down on the page is the opening of *Dal bel soave ragio*, ascribed to Layolle in Moderne's editions of *Le parangon des chansons. Second livre . . .* (1538[16] and 1540[15]). Gardane's acceptance of Layolle as the composer in his edition of 1541 is but one more piece of evidence regarding his knowledge of Moderne's editions. However, the use of *Archadelt.* as a caption in the first edition (1539[24]) cannot be taken to imply that the printer originally thought the piece to be by that composer: it is probably no

---

[48] RISM 1539[24], 1541[12] and 1545[18], described in note 23, above.
[49] On this work, see J. Haar, '*Pace non trovo*: a Study in Literary and Musical Parody', *Musica Disciplina*, 19 (1965), pp. 95–149, especially pp. 110–19.

more than a statement that he knew of no other name to put above the work, but that it was in an edition with Arcadelt's name on the title-page.

Indeed, in such cases throughout the first two editions, it seems that the name *Archadelt* functioned only as a standard running headline, identifying the volume rather than the composer of any specific piece. If another composer's name was known to the printer, it could be used: otherwise, when nothing was known (or when Arcadelt was certainly known to be the composer) the running head could be left in place, and the word *Archadelt* would appear. In other words, this title was not intended as a statement of authorship so much as an identification of the volume. (The similar cases in early volumes devoted to Verdelot will be discussed below.)

By contrast, the third edition (1545[18]) follows an entirely different approach. This is highlighted by two features: one is the number of pieces without ascription – four that had appeared below the name of Arcadelt in the earlier editions, plus one, *Col pensier*, that had started well down a page, and another three not found in the first two editions. The second feature is an additional element in the headlines, the phrase *A voce Pari*, accorded to nine madrigals. Where there is no ascription, for three of these works, this phrase occupies exactly the space reserved for the composer's name. This, by itself, is sufficient to support an assertion that these three pieces were not left anonymous by error – for the typesetter did have to give attention to the space in the head-line into which a name would have been fitted.[50] Therefore, the editor seems to have added to his responsibilities the additional decision of whether to leave a piece anonymous: in so doing, he had ceased to see the head-line merely as a running title. This is a most important change, for it gives a new range of significance to any composer's name appearing there.

Despite these points, there are, of course, occasions when the composer's name could legitimately be retained from one gathering to the next, and for some of these the same setting of type was retained in use. Those on pp. 9, 12 and 13 (fols. B2^r, B3^v and B4^r of the Cantus) are retained throughout all four partbooks and then re-used on pp. 17, 20 and 21 (C2^r, C3^v and C4^r), again for all four parts.

Such evidence might seem to weaken my case for precision on

---

[50] This point was used, above, in determining the printer's view of the authorship of *Col pensier mai non maculai*.

Gardane's part, but for the fact that he did not follow up several other opportunities to retain captions. It is further negated by two other occurrences: one is the reappearance of the name *Verdelot* against *Io son tal volta*, and the other is the use, for the first time, of an ascription to *Leonardus Barre.*, against *Tengan dunque ver me*. Neither of these names appears elsewhere in the volume: both have to have been deliberately inserted.

A few other compositions in this book need consideration at the present stage. Almost all appear in earlier editions ascribed to Arcadelt, and all, I believe, suffer from the use of that composer's name as a running head in the make-up of those editions (see Table 3). Seay accepts these works as being by Arcadelt, specifically so in the case of *Io son tal volta*, while according a 'probably' to *Tengan dunque ver me*.[51] I suspect that none of them is in fact by Arcadelt. In the case of *Tengan dunque ver me*, I have already hinted that the evidence is fairly strong against the ascription to Arcadelt. It is, in addition, likely that Barre was little known in Venice in 1539, so that Gardane could plausibly not have discovered his authorship until some years later. *Io son tal volta* has already been discussed. (The retention of Arcadelt's name from one forme to another in the second edition, affecting this piece, and discussed above at the end of the second section of the present study, is only a particular instance of the general case being stated here.) For similar reasons, I believe that the appearance of Arcadelt's name above the other five works carries much less weight than does its deliberate omission in the third edition: its use is no more than an admission on Gardane's part that he knew of no other composer to whom to give these pieces.

I fully recognise that a name in the hand is worth more than two – or none – in the murky undergrowth of bibliographical analysis. However, these names, and others, are hardly in the hand: they have to be taken as examples of decoys, names supplied to attract, if not other names (i.e. composers), then at least purchasers. They are statements that Gardane had no other name to offer. This may seem an unduly pessimistic position to adopt. On the other hand, to view these works as anonymous should allow us to examine more pre-

---

[51] *Arcadelt*, v, pp. xiii–xx. D. Hersh, 'Verdelot and the Early Madrigal' (Ph.D. dissertation, University of California at Berkeley, 1963), p. 289, suggests that *Io nol disse giamai* was composed by Verdelot. Bridges, 'Publishing', pp. 27–8, uses the fact that *Tronchi la parca* sets a poem of Lorenzo Strozzi to reinforce a suggested link between Arcadelt and the Strozzi family.

Table 3

Madrigal	1539[24]		1541[12]		1545[18]	
	Page (folio)	Ascription	Page (folio)	Ascription	Page (folio)	Ascription
Col pensier	VII (A4ʳ)	[anonymous]	35 (E2ʳ)	Archadelt	XXVII (D3ʳ)	[anonymous]
Dolcemente s'adira	XXIIII (C4ᵛ)	Archadelt.	16 (B4ᵛ)	Archadelt	XVIII (C2ᵛ)	[anonymous]
Donna s'ogni beltade	XXXXIII (E1ᵛ)	Archadelt.	27 (D2ʳ)	Archadelt	XXIIII (D1ᵛ)	[anonymous]
Io nol disse giamai	XXI (C3ʳ)	Archadelt.	18 (C1ᵛ)	Archadelt.	XIII (B4ʳ)	[anonymous]
Io son tal volta	XXIIII (C4ʳ)	Verdelot.	19 (C2ʳ)	Archadelt.	XV (C1ʳ)	Verdelot
Tengan dunque	XIII (B3ʳ)	Archadelt.	6 (A3ᵛ)	Archadelt	VIII (B1ᵛ)	Leonardus Barre.
Tronchi la parca	XXXIII (E1ʳ)	Archadelt.	23 (C4ʳ)	Archadelt	XXIII (D1ʳ)	[anonymous]

141

cisely the style, not only of these specific pieces, but also of those that are securely attributable to Arcadelt.

For the same reasons, I believe that *Amor quanto piu lieto* was thought to be by Verdelot, rather than by Arcadelt. It is, to be sure, assigned to Arcadelt in the crucial third edition, 1545[18], on p. IX (fol. B2[r]): but this can be seen as an extension of the same attribution found in the first two editions (1539[24], p. XIII; 1541[12], p. 4). By contrast, the attributions to Verdelot are not found in those volumes where Scotto is using his name as a running head; rather, they are in 1540[20], as well as in the two earlier editions of *Libro primo de la serena*.[52] These two editions, where composer's names appear only in the *TABVLA*, are not identical in contents or in bibliographical detail. It is apparent that the ascriptions of the second edition are taken from those of the first. However, the statement of Verdelot's authorship found in 1540[20] is independent of both, and there seem to be no bibliographical grounds for rejecting it.

There is a similar range of cases in Arcadelt's third book,[53] where it is again evident that the first edition, 1539[23], used the word *ARCHADELT* as a running title. This may also be true of the second edition, 1541[11]: by the time of the third, 1543[20], however, Gardane had settled his procedure. A number of pieces gain new ascriptions in the progress through these editions. Some of these have already been discussed,[54] but two others remain:

---

[52]   RISM 1530[2].
   Of this edition, only the Altus partbook survives, with (as title):
      A
   Oblong quarto, 36 pages: J–L⁴M⁶. Presumably the Cantus and Tenor books also had four gatherings each.
   Copy consulted: Seville, Biblioteca Colombina, 12–1–31(6) (Altus only).
      Chapman, 'Andrea Antico', no. 64, identifies this with a book cited in Colon's catalogue as printed in Rome in 1530. S. Cusick, 'Valerio Dorico, Music Printer in Sixteenth-century Rome' (Ph.D. dissertation, University of North Carolina, 1975), pp. 61 and 81, believes that the volume was printed by Pasoti and Dorico, and suggests there and in subsequent correspondence with the present writer that there was some connection with the Colonna family. See also K. Jeppesen, 'Die neuentdeckten Bücher der Lauden des Ottaviano dei Petrucci und andere musikalische Seltenheiten der Biblioteca Colombina zu Sevilla', *Zeitschrift für Musikwissenschaft*, 12 (1929–30), pp. 73–89.

[53]   For these editions, see above, note 12.

[54]   Despite Seay's assertion, in *Arcadelt*, IV, pp. xii–xiii, that these pieces are anonymous in 1543[20], both can be assigned to composers. The pieces are *Bramo morir* and *È morta la speranza*, and have been discussed above, in section I.
      I am not entirely satisfied that Gardane intended to regard the composer's name, *Archadelt*, as a free running-title in the second edition. As I am about to show, it was certainly retained from gathering to gathering, but this, of course, is not the same thing. However, the question does not affect the present issue.

Poi che'l fiero destin is ascribed to Arcadelt in the first edition (p. xxxix), but to *Iachet Berchem.* in the second and third (pp. 44 and xxxii, respectively): *Languir non mi fa amore,* also ascribed to Arcadelt in the first edition (p. xxxxi), is given to *Corteccia.* in the third (p. xxxiiii). In the second it carries the name *Archadelt.* in the Cantus but *Corteccia.* in all three other voices (p. 38). There is no other use of either name, Corteccia or Berchem, in the second or third edition, so that they cannot appear as the result of a lapse on the part of the typesetter, but have to reflect a conscious action. This cannot be said for the retention of the name Arcadelt in the first edition, or in the Cantus of the second (where its appearance on fol. E3^v (p. 38) is a relic from that on D3^v and corresponding places in the other partbooks). I am satisfied that neither of these madrigals was ever thought of, by the printer, as having been composed by Arcadelt.

Arcadelt's second book of madrigals does not present such problems. There are no ascriptions or running head-lines in the first two editions, and the ascriptions to other composers in the later editions are consistent. This may not mean that all the other works there are in fact by Arcadelt: but, if Gardane did not know of any other name to assign to them, he also left us with no bibliographical evidence to suggest any.

IV

The same pattern of using a composer's name as running head-line is found occasionally in the early editions of Verdelot. The first book of four-voice madrigals uses the rubric *Verdelot.*, or the part-name, or both.[55] However, the first book *à 5* has no composers' names, either in the head-line or in the tavola.[56] The second four-voice book is more interesting:[57] the first edition, 1534[16], has the composers' names in the left margin of the page, next to the start of the piece and set vertically (in an old-fashioned style that was soon abandoned by Scotto). The three exceptions are for pieces which open at the head of the page. In the third edition, 1537[10], the attributions have been transferred to the tavola, and the music pages carry only a part-name in the head-line. The second edition, 1536[7], is more complex in its treatment of the names, which are still on the music pages. Only

---

[55] For details of this title, see below, notes 60 and 61.
[56] See above, note 5.   [57] Details are above, note 45.

ten of the twenty-five pieces have names in all four partbooks: the Cantus has only fourteen composers' names, all but one at the head of the page, and the remaining one above the first stave of the piece. At the other extreme, the Altus labels twenty-three and the Bassus nineteen of the pieces, and the great majority of their composers' names are in the left margin. The evidence suggests that the typesetting was shared between two craftsmen, with a major point of division coming half-way through the Tenor book – although I do not believe that this represents any hiatus in the preparation of the edition. It does, however, help to explain two anomalies in the ascriptions preserved in this edition, both the result of this lack of a systematic approach:

On fol. D2^v (in the Tenor book) of 1536[7], the head-line *Adrian* appears above the second page of Verdelot's *Ne per gratia giamai*. There is no reason to believe that Scotto thought this work (much less a part of it) was by Willaert: the word *Adrian* was left in place from fol. C2^v, while Verdelot's name is entered at the start of the piece, on D2^r.

At the head of B5^r (Cantus) of the same edition, there is the caption *Andreas de Sylva*. Parts of two madrigals lie on this page: *Qual maraviglia o donna*, which had begun on the fifth stave of B4^v and is there ascribed to *Verdelot* (as it is in the tavola of 1537[10]); and *D'amore le generose*, starting on the fourth stave, and ascribed to Festa (as it is almost everywhere else).[58] There is therefore no apparent reason for any reference to de Silva.

It is clear that a typesetter would not actively insert a new name, going through the process of selecting the type sorts and fitting them into the forme, without some reason. On the other hand, as I have shown, he might very easily leave one in place, if it were already in the forme and his attention were not specifically drawn to it. This suggests that one should look for the chance that this erroneous caption had been left over from an earlier forme, in use at the printing house immediately before gathering B of this edition was set up in type. Of course, gathering B is not the first in the book – but there is no reference to de Silva in the first gathering, A, of the Cantus, or indeed anywhere else in this title.

However, gathering A does have a different anomaly in the

---

[58] The single surviving partbook that names Verdelot as the composer has been discussed above, in section II.

running titles, and one that helps to explain the appearance of de Silva's name. All the partbooks carry the part-name at the head of the page. The first gathering of the Cantus has the word *Altus* appearing on the majority of pages of the outer forme. This argues for that forme, at least, having been used immediately before as part of an Altus book. While it is just possible that this could have been an Altus gathering of the present title, the type sorts suggest that to be unlikely. Coupled with the erroneous head-line in gathering B, the evidence suggests rather that Scotto was using at least four skeleton formes at this stage of his career, and that both errors are relics of the use of these two formes at the end of a previously printed volume.[59]

On the basis of this evidence alone, I began searching other editions of 1535 or 1536 for an attribution to Andreas de Silva, at the top of a page, on the correct page in the forme, and at the end of a volume, whence it could have passed to the present book. There is, in fact, no such case. But there is an important related instance: the first book of Verdelot's four-voice madrigals.[60] In the surviving Bassus of

[59] The incorrect use of the word *Altus* is on fols. A2ᵛ, A3ʳ, A6ᵛ, A7ʳ and A8ᵛ. Of the other pages on this forme, the word is replaced on A4ᵛ and A5ʳ by the word *Cantus*, and of course would not have been allowed to remain on A1ʳ, the title-page. The presence of this error, in gathering A of a book, suggests that this forme had been used for part of an Altus book of some previous publication. The additional presence of another error, the retention of the name of de Silva, in a different forme, suggests that both formes came from another volume, and that they represent only part of the total number of formes (probably four) currently in use by the printer – so that some formes might appear first in this volume in a correct state.

The argument that the reappearance of the word *Altus* might be from the Altus book of the present title is a weak one, for the following reason: it is probable that at least the inner forme used for gathering A (the first of the Cantus) would be preserved as far as possible, for the first gatherings of the other partbooks, for it contained the *Tavola*. Indeed, the tavola shows the same type and the same setting in all four partbooks, confirming that it was indeed retained for all. However, the setting of the word *Altus* in gathering A does not correspond to those in the Altus partbook. Further, the retention of the same formes throughout the first gathering of each partbook implies that not all four (or more, if the printer used more) would be needed for the first gathering: this helps to explain why the reference to de Silva need not have appeared until the second gathering of the Cantus, presumably being set up while the first gathering was going through the press.

As a result, the most simple explanation is that the forme preserving a different setting of the word *Altus*, together with another forme containing a reference to an irrelevant composer, represent elements of two gatherings at the end of work on some previous title, printed immediately before the present one.

[60] RISM 1533² = V1218; New Vogel 2866.

The surviving Bassus is headed with a capital *B* and has a colophon:

Finiscono li Madrigali de Verdelot. Stampati novamente / in Vinegia per Zovan Antonio 7 i Fratelli da Sa/bio: Ad instantia de li Scotti: 7 per An/drea Anticho da Montona inta/gliati: 7 con somma dili/gentia corretti. / Con Gratia 7 Privilegio. / [Scotto's mark] / M. D. XXXIII.

Oblong octavo, 32 pages, signed G–H⁸. Pieces numbered, 1–28. The tavola is in two

the first edition, 1533[2], a very careful ascription to *Andreas de Silva* is accorded the madrigal *Madonna io sol vorrei*, entered above the fourth stave on fol. H4[v], with the piece continuing to H5[r]. From the evidence of the edition of 1537[9], the Cantus partbook would start this piece at the head of B5[r], and so would probably present the ascription as part of the head-line. I felt justified, as a result, in postulating an edition of the first book of Verdelot's four-voice madrigals that would be dated in late 1535 or early 1536, printed immediately before the second edition of the second book. The edition would probably have the name *Andreas de Sylva* at the top of B5[r], and perhaps of the other partbooks: this name would then have been left in place, along with the *Altus* headings and the correct running head of *Verdelot*, when work began on 1536[7].

This analysis was completed, and the new/lost edition was postulated, while I was beginning to study all the surviving copies of the Antico–Scotto publications of the 1530s. Among them is a single partbook belonging, indubitably, to my conjectured edition. This is, unfortunately, not a Cantus, but a Bassus book, and is to be found in the Biblioteca Nazionale in Florence (Mus.ant. 229).[61] My attention

columns with no head-line. A running head-line gives the part-name on the recto and the composer's name on the verso. There are errors on G3[r] and H7[r–v].
Copy consulted: Paris, Bibliothèque Nationale, Rés. Vmf. 40(1).

RISM 1537[9] = V1219; New Vogel 2867.
    Il primo libro de Madrigali di Verdelotto. / Novamente stampato, 7 con somma dili-/gentia corretto. / M D [large:]s xxxvii. / Con Gratia, 7 Privilegio.
The lower voices are differently titled, with their corresponding part-names:
    ꝗDel primo Libro de Madrigali di Verdelotto. / [large:]T
The last recto of the Bassus has a colophon:
    [mark of Scotto] / Venetijs Apud Octauianum Scotum. [with, in the only surviving copy, the manuscript addition of a date:] M D xxxvii
Oblong octavo, 32 pages per book: A–B[8]; C–D[8]; E–F[8]; G–H[8]. Pieces numbered, 1–28. *Tavola* in one column, and headed. Running head-line on all pages, of the part-name at the outer edge and the composer's name, centred: an extended form is used on the first recto of gatherings B, D, F and H.
Copies consulted: Paris, Bibliothèque Nationale, Rés. Vmd. 22 (Altus); London, British Library, к.8.b.11 (Altus); Oxford, Bodleian Library, Harding (vii) (imperfect Cantus); Bologna, Civico Museo Bibliografico Musicale, u 308.
    The table of contents offered by New Vogel for this edition seems to have been printed in error, for it bears no resemblance to the copies that I have seen.
[61] [1536]. Cited in RISM at 1537[9] = V1219, and in New Vogel at 2867.
The Bassus partbook is entitled:
    Del primo Libro de Madrigali di Verdelotto. / [large:]B
Oblong octavo, 32 pages: G–H[8]. Pieces numbered, 1–28. Tavola in two columns, no head-line. Running head-line on all folios from G2[r], as in the edition 1537[9].
Copy at Florence, Biblioteca Nazionale Centrale, Mus.ant. 229. Bassus only, misbound, and lacking H8.

was first drawn to it because neither the title-page nor the tavola corresponds with those of either 1533[2] or 1537[9]. On inspection, it is clear that all the pages have been re-set, and that the music blocks show a level of damage lying between that of these two other editions; further, the font of the text type employed here was adopted by Scotto only after the first edition. Detailed analysis of the states of individual sorts and capitals reveals that this volume has to be dated either at the end of 1535 or early in the following year.[62] (If I incline to early 1536, it is only because the second edition of the second volume carries that date.) It is probable that a Cantus book, should it ever surface, would have de Silva's name on fol. B5[r].

All three editions set out to use the name of *Verdelot* as a running title, with the part-name. In the first edition, there are some minor anomalies, while the second and third both carry the two elements at the top of each page of music. However, both the first and the second edition take care to enter the name of de Silva at the start of *Madonna io sol vorrei*. While the second edition is clearly derivative of the first, there seems to have been no reason in the mind of Antico or Scotto

---

[62] Unfortunately, the surviving Bassus book lacks the last folio, which would (if the normal procedure of Scotto and Antico was followed here) have carried at least Scotto's mark, and probably a colophon line, giving the date of printing. However, a few details of the analysis should suffice to demonstrate the dating of this volume – independently of its proposed close connection with 1536[7].

The state of the music blocks is already showing deterioration, though by no means as badly as in the 'second' (now known to be the third) edition of 1537[9]. An excellent example is at the end of the last stave in the book, on fol. H7[v]. But other obvious cases can be found on G2[v], G6[r], H1[r] or H4[v], to mention only one page in each forme of the book.

Several of the initial letters, showing progressive deterioration from 1533 to 1538, can be used to date this edition. Some are particularly vulnerable – and particularly valuable for analysis: the *J* that appears here on fol. G4[v] can be clearly seen to be in a worse condition than that displayed in 1534[16], 1535[8] or 1535[9], and in much the same state as that found in 1536[7]; the *M* on fol. G3[r] is also worse than in 1534[16] or 1535[8], though it is close to the example on H3[v] of 1535[8]; the *G* on H1[v] is again worse than in 1534[16], but it is marginally better than in 1536[7] and markedly better than in RISM V1224 (also dated 1536), while unfortunately not appearing in the other 1535 editions; of the different forms of the letter *L*, that found on H6[r] is very similar in state to its appearance in 1536[7], while that on H6[v] corresponds in condition to its state in V1223 (the first volume of Verdelot's madrigals *à5*); the letter *N* in the new edition is in fact a new letter, which is next to be found only in 1536[7] and later, while the *V* on H1[r] is in a state close to that of 1534[16] and 1535[8], markedly better than in 1536[7] and the succeeding V1224.

The sequence of printing that emerges from this is clear, and incidentally provides an admirable confirmation of the RISM date of [1535] for V1223: in 1535, RISM 1535[8] precedes 1535[9] and V1223, all to be followed by the new edition; then 1536[7] precedes V1224, and 1537[10] probably precedes 1537[9] and 1537[11]. It is therefore likely that the newly recovered edition of the first book of Verdelot madrigals should be dated [1536], pending the discovery of more parts, or of a Bassus part carrying a colophon.

for changing this name: my suspicion is that whichever of the two was responsible thought that the work was indeed by de Silva.

The minor anomalies of the first edition, 1533^2, seem, without the benefit of more than one surviving partbook, to be no more than inconsistencies. The intention seems to have been to put the part-name, *Bassus*, on the rectos, and the caption Verdelot on the versos. However, the part-name appears only on the first four rectos of each gathering (excluding the title-page, and including an *Altus* on G3^r). Almost all other pages with music carry the composer's name as running head: the exception is the appearance of the name *Maistre Ian* on H7^{r-v}, above *Lasso che mal accorto*. It is virtually impossible to suggest that this entry arose as did the reference to de Silva in 1534[16]. Apart from the position of this ascription, well into the volume, there is no other plausible title from which such a head-line could have been retained. The only two candidates, books with any reference to Maistre Jhan, are the *Libro primo de la Serena* (1530^2) and Verdelot's third book. Apart from the probability that the Antico–Scotto partnership had not been active before the surviving 1533^2, the first of these remote possibilities was put out by a different publisher (Dorico), while the second would presuppose three earlier lost editions, one of each of Verdelot's three books, simply so that one of the third book might have been lost.

It is much simpler, and much more plausible, to suggest that the typesetter of 1533^2 intended this ascription. Then it becomes comprehensible that the easy (or careless) retention of a running title in the second edition would lead to the suppression of any reference to Maistre Jhan in that (and therefore the third) edition.

I therefore believe not only that *Madonna io sol vorrei* is by Andrea de Silva, but also that *Lasso che mal accorto* was thought to be by Maistre Jhan. Certainly, the retention of the one ascription has to be seen as important, while the loss of the other is easier to explain than is its first appearance. (It is perhaps also significant that none of the other works in this volume have conflicting attributions elsewhere. While this does not confirm that they are all by Verdelot, it may help to reinforce the evidence that these two are not his work.) There is, in any case, no valid reason why de Silva should not have written a few madrigals, either for Rome (where he certainly would have come into contact with Verdelot's music) or perhaps as a result of his contact with the Duke of Mantua in 1522.[63] It is, after all, tempting to see some significance in the presence of only two extraneous works in a volume devoted to Verdelot, works possibly with connections to Mantua or Ferrara.

V

There are, of course, many muddled attributions which cannot be resolved by the methods developed here, either because the techniques are inapplicable or because, even though they may seem at first sight to be fruitful, they yield evidence which does not fully resolve the problem. Examples of the latter situation can be found in 1542[17], the first edition of Gardane's anthology, *Il primo libro di madrigali de diversi . . . a misura di breve*.[64]

A little can be inferred about how this volume was prepared, and that little does throw some light (though scarcely enough) on the question of the attributions in both this and subsequent editions. In gathering B of the Cantus, the second of the volume, five ascriptions are lacking – all present in the lower voices. Three of those missing are in the outer forme – on fols. 1[r] (*Archadelt.* in the other partbooks), 2[v] (*Ferabosco.*) and 4[v] (*N. Vbert.*); the remaining page in this forme, 3[r], has an ascription to *Yvo* which lacks the otherwise ubiquitous final point, and which (I suspect) may have been added at the last moment. Logically, this forme would only be finished and then prepared for the press after the inner forme (for this volume was probably set up consecutively, page by page), and it is perhaps

---

[63] See A. Bertolotti, *Musici alla corte dei Gonzaga in Mantova...* (Milan, [1890], reprinted Geneva, 1978), p. 34.

[64] RISM 1542[17].
[flower] D. AVTORI [flower] / IL PRIMO LIBRO D'I MADRIGALI DE DIVERSI ECCELLENTISSIMI AVTORI A MISVRA DI BREVE / NOVAMENTE CON GRANDE ARTIFFICIO / COMPOSTI ET CON OGNI DILIGENTIA / STAMPATI ET POSTI IN LVCE. / QVATVOR [Gardane's mark] VOCVM. / CON GRATIA ET PRIVILEGIO. / Venetijs Apud Antonium Gardane. / [rule] / M. D. XXXXII.
The lower voices have a different title, each with its relevant part-name:
TENOR / QVATVOR [Gardane's mark] VOCVM. / CON GRATIA ET PRIVILEGIO. / Venetijs Apud Antonium Gardane. / [rule] / M. D. XXXXII. [with the addition of a signature line:] Madrigali primi de diuersi autori a 4 [plus signature letter] Oblong quarto, 40 pages per part: A–E[4]; F–K[4]; L–P[4]; Q–V[4]. Paginated in roman numerals from the first recto of each voice-part: [i–ii], iii–xxxix, [xl].
Copy consulted: Verona, Società Accademia Filarmonica, Busta 208; gathering R is misbound.

significant that the two missing head-line names in the inner forme are for the last two pages – 3ᵛ and 4ʳ, both *N. Vbert.* in the other parts. These names were added to the formes before the lower voices were printed, and it is apparent that the caption *N. Vbert.* found on the equivalent of B4ᵛ (p. xvi in all parts) uses the same setting of type to be found on the equivalent page in the inner forme (B3ᵛ, p. xiv).

This suggests several interlocking elements of procedure in the printing shop. One, implied by the pattern of omissions in the Cantus alone, is that the typesetter was using a version of 'vertical setting', working through the whole gathering in the Cantus, then through the corresponding gatherings in the lower voices, before going on to the next Cantus gathering. Secondly, he was probably working with only one skeleton forme. (This is supported by the evidence of skeleton formes being retained for all voices, as demonstrated by the retention of the names in the running head-lines, as well as by the manner in which one setting of a composer's name can appear on both sides of one sheet of paper.) Thirdly, it would appear that the work was not progressing very fast. If the typesetter did have access to only one skeleton forme, there would be occasions when either he or the press-man was out of work, one waiting for the other.[65]

The significance of this for the present context is that we can possibly trace occasions when a head-line was left unchanged from one forme to the next,[66] especially since the evidence of gathering B points towards a certain carelessness on the part of the typesetter. There are few occurrences which could be plausible – after all, an anthology such as this will not often produce works by the same composer in the same position in different formes, even when allowing for the careless retention of a composer's name, itself less likely in such a volume. However, all these possible cases do produce situations in which the madrigal later through the press has an ascription which Gardane rejected in subsequent editions – itself a

---

[65] Gardane's shop certainly had more skeleton formes available, and, in any case, would not have wanted to have a press frequently standing idle. It may be that each typesetter could be working with fewer formes than normal whenever the shop was printing more than one title concurrently.

[66] The sequence of transfer from one forme to another would be as follows: inner forme of gathering A (2ʳ, 1ᵛ, 4ʳ, 3ᵛ) to the corresponding outer forme (1ʳ, 2ᵛ, 3ʳ, 4ᵛ), and thence to the inner forme of gathering B; as a result, improbable-looking sequences can occur, such as B4ʳ to B3ʳ, or B1ʳ to C2ʳ.

suggestive factor. Table 4 shows these cases, where an ascription seems to have been retained from one forme to another.

Two of these are immediate candidates for correction: the erroneous retention (as I propose) of *N. Vbert.* from p. xiiii to p. xvi produces an ascription for *S'io credessi* which is corrected in all Gardane's next three editions to *Anselmo de Reulx*: the apparent error of leaving *Per Dio tu sei cortese* anonymous is also corrected in these later editions. For one work here, there is no further information, for it does not reappear elsewhere. For the remaining three, the situation is slightly more complicated, since the change in ownership does not occur until the third edition, 1546[15]. However, the probability seems strong that these, too, belong to the composer cited in the later editions, and were misattributed in the second merely because Gardane did not spot an error in the first.

If the evidence has perhaps solved two problems and made claim to solving three more, it can do no more than suggest solutions for others in the same book. It is tempting to claim, on the basis of the above analysis, that ascriptions in the third (1546[15]) and subsequent Gardane editions are to be preferred to those in the first two. Some support for this could be derived from the Scotto editions: the first, 1547[13], is without printer's name[67] and follows Gardane's first two editions for nearly all its ascriptions. However, later Scotto editions, from 1550[15], gradually accept more of the new attributions to be found in Gardane's 1546[15], suggesting that these were winning a general acceptance.

But I believe this to be one area where the bibliographical evidence cannot be of any assistance, especially in such cases as *Con lei fuss'io*: the ascriptions to Corteccia in 1542[17] and to Arcadelt in 1543[17] are both beyond question on purely bibliographical grounds; that to Arcadelt in Scotto's 1547[13] is derivative; but Gardane's 1546[15] and later editions propose the name of *Jaques de Ponte*, equally clearly a deliberate choice on the part of the typesetter. The argument that the more obscure the name, the more likely the correctness of the attribution may well be valid here: but it is not one that will find support from an analysis of printing procedure.

Nor is it possible to determine, on these grounds, the probable author of *Per alti monti*, ascribed in 1540[20] (Scotto) to *Con. Festa.*, and

[67] Lewis, 'Antonio Gardane', pp. 317–26, and Bernstein, 'Burning Salamander', p. 500.

Table 4

Page (folio)[a]	Contents	Ascription on both folios	Page (folio)	Contents	Ascription of second piece in later editions[b]
[II] (A1v)	[Dedication]	[anonymous]	IIII (A2v)	Per inhospiti boschi	2: [anonymous] 3, 5: Festa
XIIII (B3v)	Ben che la donna mia	N Vbert. (T, A, B)	XVI (B4v)	S'io credessi	2, 3, 5: Anselmo de Reulx
XIII (B3r)	Deh dolce pastorella	Yvo	XXIII (C4r)	Troppo scorsa madonna	2: Yvo 3, 5: Berchem
XVII (C1v)	Tant'e l'ardor	N. Vbert.	XX (C2v)	Cesarea gentil	[not present in 2, 3, 5]
XVII (C1r)	Se la presenta vostra	[anonymous]	XXVII (D2r)	Per Dio tu se cortese	2, 3, 5: Naich
XXXI (D4r)	Perche la vita e breve	Corteccia.	XXIX (D3r)	Non ved'hoggi'l mio sole	2: Corteccia 3, 5: Pietro Brachario

[a] The folio numbers refer to the Cantus books and can be extended to the other parts.
[b] The later editions are: 2: 1543[17]; 3: 1546[15]; 5: 1548[6], all printed by Gardane. (The fourth edition, 1547[13], is one of the unsigned volumes, printed by Scotto.)

in 1541[18] and subsequent Gardane editions to *Verdelot*. The piece also appears, as one of two anonyma, in 1534[16], 1536[7] and 1537[10], the three early Scotto editions of Verdelot's second book. There is no evidence in any of this as to who was the correct composer. In both 1540[20] and 1541[18], the ascriptions could possibly have been kept over from previous gatherings, although the evidence is not conclusive: for both, the evidence that I have presented earlier has almost no relevance. There is a slight suggestion that the two anonymous pieces in 1534[16] were not truly anonymous in Scotto's eyes: they appear on fol. G3ʳ (*Con soave parlar*) and G3ᵛ (*Per alti monti*). These would correspond to fols. G1ʳ (title-page) and G1ᵛ (tavola) in the immediately preceding formes – neither of which would have carried a head-line. It is possible, therefore, that the absence of an ascription for these two pieces was merely an oversight. But we cannot know which name would have been inserted for either of the two madrigals concerned; nor can we read anything further into the juxtaposition of the two pieces, even though *Con soave parlar* is elsewhere regularly ascribed to Verdelot.[68]

It will immediately be noted that there has been no discussion of the style of any of the pieces mentioned. That has been an inevitable, if unwelcome, constraint on the present paper. There is no doubt that some of the points made here would have been more easily acceptable if stylistic arguments had been summoned in their support. On the other hand, such evidence could as easily be misleading. For example, the madrigal *Ditimi o diva mia* that I believe to be by Maistre Jhan is a remarkably inept piece of work, going far beyond the bounds that we would normally accept for music that is 'stiff, almost awkward':[69] so much so, that I had hoped to be able to demonstrate that it had to be, not the work of Maistre Jhan at all, but rather consigned to the limbo of anonyma. There are similar problems among the pieces regularly ascribed to Arcadelt. For this reason, as for one other (to be mentioned), it has seemed preferable to restrict this essay to a study of the evidence presented by the sources.

[68] The evidence that might seem to be offered by the Florentine manuscript, Florence, Biblioteca Nazionale Centrale, Magl. xix 122–5, is of little value if, indeed, the source is largely derived from printed editions.

[69] G. Nugent and J. Haar, 'Maistre Jhan', *The New Grove Dictionary of Music and Musicians*, ed. S. Sadie, 20 vols. (London, 1980), xi, p. 541.

What these sources tell us, after bibliographical analysis, is who the printer thought was the composer of a particular piece. For this reason, the existence of conflicting attributions – even if one is merely the significant absence of any attribution – is of more use than a regular series of ascriptions to the same composer. Such variant attributions can be studied from the point of view of the provenance of the volumes concerned, giving weight to the different sources, in much the manner that stemmatics can be applied to the readings. But they have to be studied as bibliographical objects, as well.

In fact, in these books a statement of anonymity is often at least as deliberate an act as is the attribution to Verdelot or Arcadelt.[70] The printer is potentially saying that he knows the madrigal was not written by Verdelot – or by the name that appears elsewhere as a running title. By contrast, the preservation of that name in a head-line is likely to be, in the volumes principally discussed here, no more than a statement of ignorance on the part of the printer: 'The pieces in this book (or on this page) are associated with the name of Verdelot; some I know are by Festa, and I say so; some I know are not by Verdelot, and I can give no name to them at all; some I know are by him; for the rest, I know nothing. But I have to provide a running title, so I retain the name found on the title-page, Verdelot.' By implication, indeed demonstrably (as a result of my analysis), the name of Arcadelt or of Verdelot can therefore be found over a number of pieces for which the printer had no strong feelings as to authorship. It is only when volumes contain anonymous pieces that we can believe that the typesetter was being instructed *when* to use the name that appears on the title-page, and when to omit it. Without such evidence of care, we have to question every work in the earliest volumes of Arcadelt and Verdelot not attributed to anyone else.

Further, many of these pieces survive with the same name in every printed edition, some of which can be shown to have been copied from others. As a result, the presence of the same name, even in later, more carefully controlled editions, is still only evidence against any other name, evidence that the printer and typesetter knew of no reason for change. Therefore, a piece ascribed to Arcadelt in every

---

[70] An exception would be RISM [c1530]¹, the *Libro primo de la fortuna*, where we cannot tell whether the attributions stop mid-way down the tavola because the printer left his anonyma to the end, or because he lost interest.

edition of one of his madrigal volumes is less necessarily his than a piece ascribed to Festa in the same books is Festa's.

This may not be a major problem in the case of Arcadelt. Firstly, he may have been living in Venice during the period of the early editions of his madrigals, even though he was in Rome before the later ones.[71] Secondly, he does not appear in printed editions until the end of the decade, as a representative of the new generation, and when the evidence suggests that printers were spreading their nets more widely. However, it must be disturbing that madrigals printed in the first editions of all four books are later transferred to other composers; and one has to wonder how many of the others (especially among those deleted from later editions) have remained with Arcadelt's name to the present day solely because Gardane had no other information. The problem is even more extreme in the case of Verdelot, who is not known to have been in Venice, and perhaps was no longer alive, when the first Scotto editions appeared, but whose anthologies were reprinted for well over ten years. With the very limited pattern of manuscript transmission and circulation (and the absence of attributions in some of the more important manuscripts), the best authority for ascribing a work to Verdelot in any edition of the 1540s was likely to have been an earlier edition.

Here we have the second reason why it is unsafe to use the style of any piece discussed above as part of the evidence for authorship. Colin Slim can write:[72] 'The style of the madrigals [of Verdelot] varies from chordal, mostly syllabic settings for four voices to highly imitative ones; most of them, however, lie between the two extremes.' Despite the perceptive assessments of style by Slim and other writers (such as Haar), it is still difficult to characterise the personal style, particularly of those composers who have left a smaller corpus, or to pinpoint the stylistic features that distinguish a single work. For this reason it has seemed dangerous to attempt to analyse any one work, and thereby eliminate any one composer,

---

[71] Bridges, 'Publishing', p. 43, adduces some evidence for suggesting that Arcadelt may have been in Rome in 1538. Certainly, he argues well that Arcadelt was probably not still in Florence.

[72] H. C. Slim, 'Verdelot, Philippe', *The New Grove Dictionary*, xix, p. 633. See also J. Haar, writing of Verdelot's influence on the development of the madrigal, and of the two extremes of style that had existed: 'he may be thought to have followed, and occasionally combined, both trends'. This appears in his 'The Early Madrigal: a Re-Appraisal of its Sources and its Character', *Music in Medieval and Early Modern Europe: Patronage, Sources and Texts*, ed. I. Fenlon (Cambridge, 1981), p. 78, fn.

when our perception of that composer's style is built up from pieces that may not be his, even allowing for the local knowledge of the printer.

I recognise that a similar position exists for almost all early music: we have to rely on what the scribe or printer thought, and we rarely have any other evidence – from theorists or from correspondence, for example. In this situation, we must necessarily take the copyist at his word, weigh it (if we can), and then decide – act upon it. My contention is that, once printing techniques for music became more systematic, negligence and the need for a consistent layout sometimes played as great a part as did conscious thought and action in producing the printed attribution. In such situations, many ascriptions lose their force.

By contrast, the majority of cases I have discussed here gain in strength, simply because they show evidence of this negligence or of a desire for consistency. In these cases, we can take a step beyond a pessimistic, passive acceptance of. rather weak bibliographical evidence for authorship, a step towards a surer awareness of those occasions when, as we can demonstrate, the printer, at least, believed in the name he was putting at the head of music.

New York University

APPENDIX

This appendix lists those cases, discussed in the preceding article, where the bibliographical evidence points strongly away from one ascription, and therefore towards another. (For comments on the extent to which this can confirm one ascription, see the article.) Only those sources relevant to the present argument are cited.

Madrigal	Rejected ascription	Preferable ascription
Ai pie d'un chiaro fonte	Arnoldo: 1542[16] (B)	Alfonso de la Viola: 1542[16]
Amor quanto piu lieto	Arcadelt: 1539[24], 1541[12], 1545[18]	Verdelot: 1530[2], 1534[15], 1540[20]
Amor s'al primo sguardo	Arcadelt: 1543[20]	C. Festa: 1539[23], 1541[11]
Apri'l mio dolce carcer	Layolle: 1541[12]	Arcadelt: 1539[24], 1541[12]
Chi bussa?	[anonymous]: 1541[16] (T, A, B)	Verdelot: 1541[16] (C, 5, 6)
Col pensier mai non maculai	Arcadelt: 1541[12]	[anonymous]: 1539[24], 1545[18]
Con lachrim'e sospir	Arcadelt: 1541[18]	Jachet: 1540[20]
Cosi estrema di doglia	[anonymous]: 1541[16] (T)	Verdelot: 1533[2], 1536[8], 1537[9]
		C. Festa: 1541[16]
Dal bel suave ragio	Arcadelt: 1539[24]	Layolle: 1538[16], 1540[15], 1541[12]

156

Non-conflicting attributions and newly anonymous compositions

D'amore le generose	A. de Silva: 1536[7] (T) Verdelot: 1541[18] (A)	C. Festa: 1534[16], 1536[7], 1537[10], 1540[20], 1541[18]
Deh perche non e in voi	Arcadelt: 1541[16] (C)	[anonymous]: 1541[16]
Ditimi o diva mia	Maistre Jhan: 1541[16]	Verdelot: 1546[19]
Divelt'e'l mio bel vivo	Arcadelt: 1539[23] (B)	C. Festa: 1539[23]
Dolcemente s'adira	Arcadelt: 1539[24], 1541[12]	[anonymous]: 1545[18]
Donna s'ogni beltade	Arcadelt: 1539[24], 1541[12]	[anonymous]: 1545[18]
E morta la speranza	C. Festa: 1543[20], 1556[22]	Arcadelt: 1539[23], 1541[11]
Io nol disse giamai	Arcadelt: 1539[24], 1541[12]	[anonymous]: 1545[18]
Io son tal volta	Willaert: 1541[18]	C. Festa: 1534[16], 1536[7], 1537[10], 1540[20]
Io son tal volta	Arcadelt: 1541[12] Willaert: 1545[18] (T)	Verdelot: 1539[24], 1545[18]
Languir non mi fa amore	Arcadelt: 1539[23], 1541[11] (C)	Corteccia: 1541[11], 1543[20]
Lasso che mal accorto	Verdelot: [1536], 1537[9]	Maistre Jhan: 1533[2]
Madonna i prieghi mei	[anonymous]: 1541[16] (A, T, 5, 6)	Maistre Jhan: 1541[16] (C, B)
Madonna io sol vorrei	C. Festa: 1545[19] Verdelot: 1537[9], 1545[19]	de Silva: 1533[2], [1536]
Madonna'l bel desire	Verdelot: 1540[20]	Willaert: 1534[16], 1536[7], 1537[10], 1540[20]
Ne pergratia giammai	Willaert: 1536[7] (T)	Verdelot: 1534[16], 1536[7], 1537[10]
Non ved'oggi'l mio sole	Corteccia: 1542[17], 1543[17]	Brachario: 1546[15], 1548[6]
Pace non trovo	[anonymous]: 1539[24]	Yvo: 1541[12]
Per dio tu se cortese	[anonymous]: 1542[17]	Naich: 1543[17], 1546[15], 1548[6]
Per inhospiti boschi	[anonymous]: 1542[17], 1543[17]	C. Festa: 1546[15], 1548[6]
Poi che'l fiero destin	Arcadelt: 1539[23]	Berchem: 1541[11], 1543[20]
Qual maraviglia o donna	de Silva: 1536[7] (C)	Verdelot: 1534[16], 1536[7], 1537[10]
Quand'havran fin	Arcadelt: 1540[18] (C), 1541[17] (C)	Verdelot: 1540[18], 1541[17]
Se i sguardi di costei	Arcadelt: 1543[20]	C. Festa: 1539[23], 1541[11]
Se'l foco in cui sempr'ardo	Verdelot: 1540[18] (C), 1541[17] (C)	Arcadelt: 1540[18], 1541[17]
Se mort'in me potesse	Arcadelt: 1541[11]	C. Festa: 1539[23], 1541[11]
Si lieto alcun giammai	C. Festa: 1543[20]	Arcadelt: 1539[23], 1541[11]
S'io credessi	Naich: 1542[17] (T, A, B)	de Reulx: 1543[17], 1546[15], 1548[6]
Tengan dunque ver me	Arcadelt: 1539[24], 1541[12]	Barre: 1545[18]
Tronchi la parca	Arcadelt: 1539[24], 1541[12]	[anonymous]: 1545[18]
Troppo scorsa madonna	Yvo: 1542[17], 1543[17]	Berchem: 1546[15], 1548[6]

Addendum to note 25: J. Bernstein, 'The Burning Salamander: Assigning a Printer to some Sixteenth-century Music Prints', *Notes*, 42 (1985–6), pp. 483–501 (which appeared after this paper was completed), clarifies many points regarding these volumes. She leaves open the question why the interconnected group of printers and patrons should wish (most unusually among partnerships) to leave the volumes unassigned, as also any reason why these particular books should be involved. My discussion needs to be read in conjunction with her analysis, and with further detailed study of editorial practice.

JAMES W. McKINNON

ON THE QUESTION OF PSALMODY IN
THE ANCIENT SYNAGOGUE

Music historians are virtually unanimous in attributing the source of
early Christian psalmody to the synagogue. In this they follow the
vast majority of liturgical scholars, Protestant and Catholic alike.
There is, after all, considerable plausibility to the view: nascent
Christianity was a Jewish sect and its first liturgical gatherings
shared with the synagogue its most revolutionary characteristic – the
coming together of co-religionists in a meeting room rather than the
witnessing of sacrifice in a temple court. Moreover, the liturgical
practices of these gatherings resembled those of the synagogue; in
particular the so-called 'liturgy of the Word' that preceded the
Eucharist appears to have been modelled after the scripture-centred
order of synagogue worship. And when one observes that the
principal vehicle of early Christian chant was the Old Testament
Book of Psalms it seems a natural assumption that the singing of
those psalms was a practice borrowed from the synagogue. The
present author shared this assumption until coming to question it
when pursuing a related topic.[1] The study that follows is a fulfilment
of the intention stated then to explore the subject more thoroughly.[2]
In doing so it is necessary to begin with a general examination of

[1] J. McKinnon, 'The Exclusion of Musical Instruments from the Ancient Synagogue',
   Proceedings of the Royal Musical Association, 106 (1979–80), pp. 84–5.
[2] *Ibid.*, n. 43. The article in progress mentioned there, 'The Myth of Psalmody in Early
   Synagogue and Church' was presented as a paper in December 1980 at Duke University;
   the present article is a revision of the portion of that paper dealing with the synagogue. In
   the meantime John A. Smith, who was present at the Royal Musical Association meeting
   where the paper on the exclusion of musical instruments was read, decided to pursue the
   subject of synagogue psalmody on his own and published his findings in an article, 'The
   Ancient Synagogue, the Early Church and Singing', *Music and Letters*, 65 (1984), pp. 1–16.
   I agree with virtually all Mr Smith's conclusions and shall try to avoid duplication here of
   his argument.

Jewish liturgy in the time of Jesus, both the liturgy of the Temple and that of the synagogue.

The second Temple of Jerusalem was founded on the site of Solomon's original Temple by those Jews who returned from the Babylonian exile in 539 B.C. It was at first a comparatively modest structure, but with renovations climaxing in Herod's vast rebuilding begun in 20 B.C. it became one of the foremost shrines of the ancient world. As such it attracted the attention of numerous chroniclers, both Jewish and gentile, so that we are well informed about it during the period before its destruction by the Romans in A.D. 70.[3] By far the most important of these sources is the Talmud, that massive collection of rabbinic commentary which had its first redaction in the Mishnah of about A.D. 200. There are literally hundreds of relevant passages scattered throughout the sixty-three tractates of the Mishnah, but two tractates in particular give us a remarkably detailed knowledge of both the Temple itself and its public worship. These are the tractate Middot, literally 'measurements', which describes the Temple with its precise dimensions and the tractate Tamid, literally 'perfect' or 'perpetual', which goes step by step through its daily sacrificial services. The information in each tractate is thought to derive from eye-witness accounts.[4]

The Temple was situated on the Temple Mount, a massive colonnaded platform of masonry about a quarter of a mile square, the outlines of which exist still today along with sections of its great lower walls. Such a vast concourse was needed to accommodate the throngs that visited Jerusalem, particularly for the three week-long pilgrimage festivals of Passover, Weeks and Tabernacles. The immediate Temple area was an architecturally elaborate enclosure of about 75 by 175 metres. It was made up of two courts, a square-shaped one to the east, the outer court or Court of the Women, and a larger rectangular one to the west, the inner court referred to in Hebrew as simply 'the court' (ʿazara). They were separated by the splendid Nicanor Gate, which was approached from the outer court

---

[3] For a summary of ancient references to Herod's Temple, see S. Safrai, 'The Temple and the Divine Service', *The World History of the Jewish People*, III, *The Herodian Period* (New Brunswick, N.J., 1975), pp. 282–4.

[4] *Ibid.*, p. 282. But see also J. Neusner, 'Dating Mishnah-Tractates: The Case of Tamid', *Method and Meaning in Ancient Judaism*, III, ed. J. Neusner, Brown Judaic Studies 16 (Chico, Ca., 1981), pp. 103–16.

by fifteen semi-circular steps. To one entering the inner court by this route the altar was to the left (i.e. to the south), and the Temple in the most proper sense, a lofty free-standing building housing the Sanctuary and Holy of Holies, was directly ahead taking up much of the western portion of the court.

The participants in the Temple liturgy were representatives from twenty-four regions of Israel who twice yearly served for a week in the Temple. They were made up of three classes: priests, Levites and Israelites. The priests performed the majority of the sacred rites, while the Levites served as musicians, and the Israelites, that is the lay citizens, witnessed the sacrifice in their role as representatives of those who had contributed the gifts. *Ma'amadot*, literally 'divisions', is the term applied to the twenty-four representative groups.[5] During their stay in the Temple they were supervised by a resident staff. There was the High Priest, of course, and a sort of executive officer, the *segan*, who deputised for him during the daily services, and several lesser officers with authority in specific areas: among these were one who was 'over the cymbals' and another 'over the singing'.[6]

On every day of the year the perpetual (*tamid*) sacrifice was celebrated. This took the form of a solemn morning service and an essentially similar one in the afternoon. Between the two, various offerings were brought in by the people, while on Sabbaths, festivals and days of the new moon there were additional (*mussaf*) public sacrifices. It is the daily sacrificial liturgy that is described in the tractate Tamid.[7] Preparation for it began early in the morning when

---

5 On the *Ma'amadot*, see especially M. Ta'anit 4, 2–3. (Thus the standard method of citing passages from the Mishnah indicating in this case Mishnah, tractate Ta'anit, chapter 4, paragraphs 2 and 3.) There is a convenient edition of the Mishnah with Hebrew and English translation in adjoining columns: *Mishnajoth*, ed. P. Blackman, 6 vols. (3rd edn, Gateshead, 1973). The Hebrew Mishnah, redacted in about A.D. 200, was followed by two extended Aramaic commentaries, one compiled in Palestine and one in Babylonia, each referred to as *Gemara*. The Mishnah together with Palestinian *Gemara*, redacted in the fourth century, is called the Jerusalem Talmud, and the Mishnah with Babylonian *Gemara*, redacted in the fifth century, is called the Babylonian Talmud. The more often cited Babylonian Talmud exists in an English translation published in London by the Soncino Press from 1936 to 1960. All translations in the present article will be taken from this work unless otherwise indicated. There is no complete translation of Jerusalem Talmud, but a monumental edition of both Talmuds with translation and commentary has been undertaken by A. Ehrman, ed., *Babylonian and Jerusalem Talmud* (Jerusalem and New York, 1965–).

6 The Temple offices and the individuals who held them in the last years of the Temple are given in M. Shekalim 5.

7 The description of the daily service given here is selective, emphasising those elements of relevance to the subject at hand. It follows the Mishnah Tamid and will give citations for

the priests were summoned from the various chambers and gates of the Temple where they slept or stood guard. They made ready the altar fire and drew lots for the more privileged functions of the service such as the slaughter of the lambs, one each for the morning and afternoon sacrifices. The service proper began when the 'eastern sky was alight as far as Hebron'. The priests blew three blasts on their silver trumpets,[8] the great gate of the sanctuary was opened, the lamb was slaughtered and its limbs made ready for the sacrifice. At this point the participants retired for prayer to the Chamber of Hewn Stone, a building along the south wall of the inner court where the Sanhedrin convened. They recited three items: (1) the Ten Commandments; (2) the Shema, 'Hear, O Israel'; and (3) a number of benedictions which constituted the nucleus of what would become the eighteen benedictions of the Tefillah, literally 'prayer'.[9] The latter two, the Shema and Tefillah, eventually came to constitute the core of all synagogue liturgies, and indeed many scholars have tended to view the interlude just described as a synagogue service within the Temple service and similarly to speak of a synagogue building within the Temple precincts.

The service continued as two priests chosen by lot went to the Sanctuary for the solemn incense offering before the Holy of Holies. As they moved across the court towards the Sanctuary an officer threw down a large rake, the *magrefah*, with a legendary great clatter.[10] This was the signal for the participants to prepare for the final acts of the service, and accordingly the Levite musicians assembled on the *duchan*, a platform adjoining the people's portion of the inner court towards the east. While the incense was being offered the people both within and without the Temple court prayed.[11] After performing the offering the chosen priests withdrew from the Sanc-

---

individual events only if derived from other tractates. Of the many secondary works consulted the most helpful was that of S. Safrai cited above.

8 M. Sukkah 5, 5.

9 Tefillah will be the term used in this study; synonyms used with comparable frequency are *'Amidah*, literally 'standing', the traditional posture for the prayer, and *Shemoneh 'Esreh*, literally 'eighteen'. The modern syngaogue follows Babylonian usage with its nineteen benedictions.

10 There is a musical curiosity involved here: the *magrefah* came eventually to be confused with a monstrous pipe organ and was considered to be such by musicologists as late as A. Z. Idelsohn, *Jewish Music in its Historical Development* (New York, 1929), p. 14. The confusion was finally unravelled by J. Yasser, 'The Magrepha of the Herodian Temple: a Five-Fold Hypothesis', *Journal of the American Musicological Society*, 13 (1960), pp. 24–42.

11 Luke 1: 10.

tuary and together with the other priests blessed the people from the Sanctuary steps. The limbs of the lamb were then carried up the altar ramp and cast upon the fire. Two priests gave three blasts on their trumpets, the *segan* waved a cloth, the Temple officer who was 'over the cymbals' clashed them together, and as the libation of wine was poured on to the fire the Levites sang a psalm accompanied by the string instruments *nevel* and *kinnor*. The morning service – and the afternoon service as well – ended with the conclusion of the psalm.

There are a number of observations about the daily Temple psalmody that cast some light on the question of synagogue psalmody. Temple psalmody in the last century of its existence was a highly formalised liturgical action. There was one proper psalm appointed for each of the seven days of the week.[12] It was performed by a minimum of twelve Levite musicians.[13] Most significant was its placement: it came at the climax of the service as an accompaniment to the act of sacrifice. Its manner of performance seems peculiarly adapted to this function. The psalm was divided into a number of sections, and between the singing of each the priests sounded their trumpets and the people fell prostrate. The essential relationship between Temple psalmody and the act of sacrifice is further indicated by legislation which permitted the playing of instruments in the Temple on the Sabbath precisely because the instrumentally accompanied psalmody was performed as part of the sacrifice.[14] This intimate connection between sacrifice and music, particularly instrumental music, comes as no surprise to the observer of other religious rites of the ancient Mediterranean region. Animal sacrifice seems actually to have required musical accompaniment, a circumstance suggesting some deep religious or magical link between the two. Explanations as to what this might have been are not particularly convincing, but the phenomenon itself should be borne in mind throughout the course of this study.[15]

---

[12] They are given in M. Tamid 7, 4 (actually a *baraita* – an item from the mishnaic period but not included in the Mishnah – appended to Tamid): Sunday, Ps. 24; Monday, Ps. 48; Tuesday, Ps. 82; Wednesday, Ps. 94; Thursday, Ps. 81; Friday, Ps. 93; Sabbath, Ps. 92. See also Rosh ha-Shanah 30b–31a (thus the standard manner of reference to a passage from the *Gemara* of the Babylonian Talmud; 30b–31a indicates folios of the standard Venetian edition of 1548).

[13] M. ʿArakin 2, 3–6.

[14] M. Sukkah 5, 1; Sukkah 50b–51a. On the question of a Sabbath prohibition of instruments, see McKinnon, 'Exclusion', p. 82.

[15] The credit for making the phenomenon known goes to J. Quasten, *Musik und Gesang in den*

There is one other psalmodic practice of the Temple of Jerusalem sufficiently relevant to require mention; it is associated not with the daily sacrifice but with important festivals. This is the singing of the Hallel, a group of psalms – 113 to 118 – characterised by an Alleluia refrain. The Hallel was sung in the Temple on about eighteen days of the year: the eve of Passover, possibly the first day of Weeks, the eight days of Tabernacles and probably the eight days of Hanukkah.[16] The sources present the clearest picture of its use at Passover. Here it was sung during the slaughter of the people's personal sacrifices in the afternoon. The Levites sang it as often as was necessary to cover the sacrificial activity although the third singing of it was never known to have been completed.[17] On this occasion, and on others when the Hallel was sung, the aulos-like *halil* was added to the Temple instrumentarium.[18]

In A.D. 70 the Roman legionaries under Titus razed the Temple after a cruel siege that brought to a climax five years of fierce revolt. It was a catastrophic event for Israel because the Temple had stood at the centre of her political and religious life. George Foot Moore, however, expressed a somewhat contrasting view when he wrote in his classic study of ancient Judaism: 'The cessation of the sacrificial cultus, which in any other religion would have been in a short while the end of it, was in Judaism not even a serious crisis, so completely had the worship of the synagogue come to satisfy its religious needs.'[19] It is difficult to reconcile this position with R. Eleazar's anguished cry that with the destruction of the Temple 'an iron wall intervened between Israel and its Father in Heaven';[20] difficult to reconcile it with Israel's desperate attempt to restore the Temple in the Bar Kokhba rebellion of A.D. 132–5; and in fact difficult to reconcile it with what follows in this study. It is true that Judaism eventually adjusted very well to the destruction of the Temple, but it

Kulten der heidnischen Antike und christlichen Frühzeit, Liturgiewissenchaftliche Quellen und Forschungen 25 (Münster, Westphalia, 1930), pp. 36–44. Although his explanation of the phenomenon as apotropaic magic is widely accepted, the present author finds it unsatisfactory; see 'The Church Fathers and Musical Instruments' (Ph.D. dissertation, Columbia University, 1965), pp. 11–17.

16 There are minor discrepancies among the numerous talmudic references; here 'Arakin 10a especially is followed.
17 M. Pesahim 5, 7.
18 M. 'Arakin 2, 3; 'Arakin 10a.
19 *Judaism in the First Centuries of the Christian Era*, 3 vols. (Cambridge, Mass., 1927–30), II, p. 13. See also H. Rowley, *Worship in Ancient Israel* (London, 1967), p. 241.
20 Berakhot 33b.

is a large assumption indeed that the adjustment took place before the destruction.

Precise as are the sources for the Temple liturgy at the time of Jesus, just so elusive are they for the liturgy of the contemporary synagogue. One best approaches the subject by consideration of a similarly elusive topic, the question of synagogue origins. The conventional wisdom has it that the synagogue was founded during the Babylonian captivity of the sixth century B.C.: the exiled Jews, deprived of their national shrine, are thought to have devised synagogue meetings as a substitute for Temple worship. It is a plausible and attractive view, even if unbuttressed by positive evidence, and it enjoys near unanimous support in both popular writings and, until recently, scholarly writings as well. In the past two decades support has gathered for a dissenting position that places the origins of the synagogue considerably later. The most compelling argument for it is the complete failure of exilic and post-exilic sources to mention the synagogue. The New Testament, however, presents it as a thriving institution, and hence the task of the scholar to provide a convincing hypothesis to account for its origin some time in the centuries immediately preceding the Christian era. Solomon Zeitlin,[21] for long a solitary voice in maintaining the late origin of the synagogue, associated it with the institution of the *Ma'amadot* mentioned above, the sending of representatives from the twenty-four districts of Israel to participate in Temple services. Those remaining behind gathered in the local meeting places to read the passages of the Pentateuch which treat of Temple sacrifice; they did so on the Sabbath and also on the market days, Monday and Thursday, when the people from the countryside were gathered in the towns.[22] Two points are essential to Zeitlin's view. One is that these meeting places were secular in origin and maintained their secular character for centuries, a fact supported by the Hebrew term for synagogue, *beth ha-knesset*, 'house of assembly'. (*Synagogē*, in turn, is the Greek translation of *beth ha-knesset*, meaning literally 'a coming together'.) The second point is the involvement of the Pharisees. They fostered the synagogue as a means of educating

21 'The Origin of the Synagogue', *Proceedings of the American Academy for Jewish Research*, 2 (1930–1), pp. 69–81.
22 See especially M. Ta'anit 4, 2–3.

the people in the Law, both the written Law of the Pentateuch and the oral Law of its interpretation – this, in opposition to the Sadducees who controlled the Temple and maintained the primacy of the written Law, free of interpretation.

Ellis Rivkin,[23] Zeitlin's student, considerably refined Zeitlin's position. He laid particular stress upon the *Wisdom of Ben Sira*, probably written shortly before the Maccabean revolt of 167. *Ben Sira* is rich in its description of contemporary Jewish institutions such as the Temple and the scribes, but fails to mention either the synagogue or the Pharisees. Rivkin speculates, then, that both came into existence during the religious revolution accompanying the Maccabean revolt. The Temple and its cult became no less important to the religious life of Israel, but they served broader needs like the maintenance of a national religious identity and the fertility of the land. The new religious consciousness, embodied in the Pharisaic movement, was concerned just as much with the salvation of the individual soul and this was to be achieved by adherence to the Law, which was to be read and interpreted in meeting places throughout the country. Thus the existing meeting places, which came to be known as synagogues, were given new focus and definition by regular assemblies to learn and ponder Israel's venerable Law.

This dissenting view of synagogue origins, whether or not it has penetrated the popular consciousness, has made its mark upon historians of the synagogue.[24] It must be kept in mind during what follows because of its implications for the conventional notion of synagogue liturgy at the time of Jesus.

According to the conventional view the synagogue liturgy was a revolutionary one which abandoned the typical animal sacrifice of antiquity in favour of a simple coming together (*synagogē*) to partici-

---

[23] 'Ben Sira and the Nonexistence of the Synagogue: a Study in Historical Method', *In Time of Harvest: Essays in Honor of Abba Hillel Silver*, ed. D. Silver (New York and London, 1963), pp. 320–54. Rivkin, moreover, is convincing in arguing that the Jewish *proseuchē* (prayer-site), referred to in a frequently mentioned third-century B.C. Egyptian inscription, was not a synagogue but a dedicatory shrine. He acknowledges his debt to Zeitlin in 'Solomon Zeitlin's Contribution to the Historiography of the Inter-testamental Period', *Judaism*, 14 (1965), pp. 354–67.

[24] See J. Gutmann, 'The Origin of the Synagogue: the Current State of Research', *The Synagogue: Studies in Origins, Archaeology and Architecture*, ed. J. Gutmann (New York, 1975), pp. 72–6; and 'Synagogue Origins: Theories and Facts', *Ancient Synagogues: the State of Research*, ed. J. Gutmann (Chico, Ca., 1981), pp. 1–6.

pate in a service consisting in four activities: the reading of Scripture, discourse upon it, prayer and psalmody.[25] There is much that is valid and indeed profoundly important about this generalisation. What could be more significant for the subsequent religious history of Europe and the Middle East than a religious institution which substituted a group of canonical writings and the practice of statutory congregational prayer for the universal ancient custom of bloody sacrifice? Yet there are serious problems with the precise shape the generalisation takes. There are problems of chronology with certain of the four elements when considered individually, and there are problems with the way that the four relate to each other. It is necessary that each in turn be examined with a view to the question of their existence at the time of Jesus or, to define the period more properly, during the formative years of Christianity from the death of Jesus to the fall of Jerusalem in A.D. 70.[26]

There can be no questioning that the first two of these elements, the reading of Scripture and discourse upon it, were important activities in the synagogue at this time. The New Testament provides vivid testimony to this. There is the famous passage in the Gospel of Luke (4: 14–30) where Jesus returns to Nazareth and goes to the synagogue 'as his custom was on the Sabbath'. He stood up to read and was given the Book of Isaiah; after reading he returned the scroll to the attendant, sat down, and began to speak on the passage that he had read. Very similar is the description in the Acts of the Apostles (13: 14–43) of participation by Paul and his companions in Sabbath synagogue activities at Antioch in Pisidia. They sat through readings from 'the Law and the prophets', after which Paul stood up and preached in answer to the invitation of the synagogue rulers, 'Brethren, if you have any word of exhortation for the people, say it.' Philo of Alexandria, writing somewhat earlier in the century, describes Essenes gathering on the Sabbath: 'and on it they abstain from all other work and proceed to sacred spots which they call synagogues'; they sit attentively while 'one takes the books and reads aloud and another of especial proficiency comes forward and expounds what is not understood'.[27]

[25] References to the relevant secondary literature appear below.
[26] On the significance of the date for Christianity, see S. Brandon, *The Fall of Jerusalem and the Christian Church* (2nd edn, London, 1975).
[27] *Quod omnis probus liber sit* 81–2; see also Philo, *Hypothetica* 7, 12–13, and Josephus, *Contra Apionem* 2, 175.

The most important synagogue reading was of course from the Torah, that is, the Law, the first five books of the Bible. The Mishnah gives explicit instructions for the reading of the Torah,[28] including proper readings for the three great pilgrimage festivals, minor festivals, fast days, days of the new moon and the four Sabbaths preceding the month of Nisan. For ordinary Sabbath morning meetings there were no proper readings and the Torah was read according to the 'regular order'.[29] The same term is applied to the lesser weekly meetings of Sabbath afternoon, and the market days of Monday and Thursday, although here the qualification is added that 'it is not taken into account', suggesting that these readings are repeated on Sabbath morning.[30] This 'regular order' is commonly construed as the Triennial Cycle, a strictly regulated series of readings which completes the Torah in precisely three years. The question of the Triennial Cycle has a direct bearing on the issue of psalmody and will be taken up again below.

The Torah readings were divided among several readers ranging from three at the Sabbath afternoon service to seven on Sabbath morning. Any male member of the congregation was permitted to read although precedence was given first to a priest and secondly to a Levite if any were present. The reading was in Hebrew from the Torah scroll, and it was followed immediately by an extempore translation into the Aramaic vernacular by some competent member of the congregation. The readings from the prophets, the second canonical group of biblical works which included in addition to the prophets as such early historical works like the Books of Joshua and Judges, were called *haftarot*. They were less carefully regulated than the Torah readings. Indeed, it should be emphasised that many of the details given here from the Mishnah must surely reflect practices developed after the destruction of the Temple; one imagines considerably less regularised customs before that time.

The Mishnah makes no attempt to regulate synagogue discourse as it does scripture reading, and therefore we have less precise knowledge of its early history. It is sufficient for present purposes to observe from the passages quoted above that it was a typical if not obligatory practice and that the speaker's starting point – wherever his didactic or hortatory penchant might lead – was biblical read-

---

[28] M. Megillah 3, 4–6; 4, 2–6.   [29] *Liksidran; ibid.*, 3, 4.   [30] *Ibid.*, 3, 6.

ing.[31] And one should not hesitate to make the broader observation that such discourse – in a word, the sermon – is an important innovation of the synagogue that is continued in the early Christian homily.

With the third element, prayer, we come to an area where the conventional view can be called into question. Prayer in this context means something both less and more than the word normally connotes. It means less in the sense that it refers only to the two basic formulations of the Shema and Tefillah, mentioned above in connection with the Temple liturgy. The Shema, actually, is not prayer in the strict Jewish sense, but more a confession of faith. It is a series of three brief passages from the Pentateuch, beginning with Deuteronomy 6: 4: 'Hear [*shema*ʿ], O Israel, the Lord our God, the Lord is One, and thou shalt love the Lord thy God with all thy heart...'. The Tefillah, prayer in the strictest sense, is a series of benedictions, eventually eighteen in number, although probably less in the time of Jesus. A benediction (*berakhah*) is the nuclear Jewish unit of prayer. It opens with a doxological section beginning 'Blessed art thou, O Lord', hence its name. It continues with other material, frequently petitionary, and in its fullest form closes with additional doxological material. In addition to the eighteen benedictions of the Tefillah, the pious Jew recites numerous others in the course of the day such as those before and after meals.

The term 'prayer' as used here exceeds its normal connotation in that it implies the existence of a regulated worship service. If prayer in the restricted sense of Shema and Tefillah is recited at regular times and in prescribed order by a congregation, it amounts, then, to more than two prayer formulae – it constitutes a liturgy. This is certainly the way it is construed in the conventional view.[32] According to it the synagogue at the time of Jesus was the site of daily prayer services consisting essentially of the Shema and Tefillah. Before the final benediction of the Tefillah the priestly blessing was given in imitation of the priestly blessing of the Temple liturgy. On market days and Sabbaths the service was expanded to include a 'liturgy of

---

[31] The classic work on synagogue homiletics is L. Zunz, *Die gottesdienstlichen Vorträge der Juden* (Frankfurt am Main, 1892). For a more recent attempt to describe the character of early synagogue sermons, see I. Bettan, *Studies in Jewish Preaching* (Cincinnati, 1939), pp. 3–48.

[32] A good example is P. Billerbeck, 'Ein Synagogengottesdienst in Jesu Tagen', *Zeitschrift für neutestamentliche Wissenschaft*, 55 (1964), pp. 143–61. He does not, however, mention psalmody; for several advocates of the conventional view who do, see below.

the Word': a Torah pericope was read according to the schedule of the Triennial Cycle, preceded and followed by special benedictions; an *haftarah* selection was read; and a homily followed. The precise time at which psalms were sung is not clear, but one must assume they were somehow included. There was, of course, no prayer book yet in existence,[33] but the service followed well-ordered conventions; it had been developing, after all, since the time of the Babylonian exile, or at least from the time that Ezra instituted the public reading and exposition of the Torah.[34]

Against the conventional view it is possible to take the extreme opposite position that the synagogue remained exclusively a secular institution until after the destruction of the Temple, and that while regular reading and discussion of the Torah took place there, it was not a place for prayer. Among that group of revisionist scholars who argue the late establishment of the synagogue and its secular origins, Zeitlin and Rivkin would not go quite so far in postponing its religious development, but Sidney Hoenig would.[35]

The positions of these authorities aside, there is a *prima facie* case for the extreme negative position. Consider first the New Testament evidence. The synagogue appears there as the proper venue for judicial and penal activities but not for prayer. Jesus warns his disciples that 'they will deliver you up to councils, and flog you in their synagogues' (Matthew 10: 17), and Paul recalls his pre-conversion activities: 'Lord, they themselves know that in every synagogue I imprisoned and beat those who believed in thee' (Acts 22: 19).[36] As for prayer, Jesus gives this advice: 'when you pray, you must not be like the hypocrites; for they love to stand and pray in the synagogues and at street corners, that they may be seen by men . . . But when you pray, go into your room and shut the door' (Matthew 6: 5–6). This passage is typically cited as evidence for the conventional view, but surely it speaks to the contrary. Individuals are told to avoid places like street corners and synagogues for their prayer and to pray at

---

[33] Not until Amran Gaon's, in the ninth century.

[34] Nehemiah 8: 1–8; see W. Oesterle, *A History of Israel* (London, 1934), II, p. 138.

[35] Zeitlin mentions prayer, if only in passing, 'The Origin of the Synagogue', p. 76; as does Rivkin, *A Hidden Revolution* (Nashville, 1978), p. 250; while Hoenig appears to exclude it, 'The Supposititious Temple-Synagogue', *Jewish Quarterly Review* [hereafter *JQR*], 54 (1963), p. 130, n. 71. For more on Hoenig's related views see 'Historical Inquiries: I. Heber Ir II. City-Square', *JQR*, 48 (1957), pp. 123–39.

[36] See also Luke 12: 11; Acts 9: 1–2 and 12: 11.

home instead. The implication is that a synagogue is a public place like a street corner, not a proper place for prayer.

Another passage occasionally cited in favour of the conventional view[37] is that in Acts 16: 12–13, where Paul and his companions visit a *proseuchē* (place of prayer) in Philippi of Macedonia: 'and on the Sabbath we went outside the gate to the riverside, where we supposed there was a place of prayer; and we sat down and spoke to women who had come together'. The argument is that a synagogue is described here as a 'place of prayer', but surely the context in which the term is used is incompatible with the ancient synagogue. It would be different if the passage spoke of Paul's group as remaining in the town where they knew the place of prayer to be and where, after listening to the readings, they engaged the men of the congregation in a discussion of their meaning.

There are many other references to synagogues in the New Testament. The typical gospel reference has Jesus visiting a syna-gogue, generally on the Sabbath, to teach and occasionally to heal: 'Now he was teaching in one of the synagogues on the Sabbath. And there was a woman who had a spirit of infirmity for eighteen years...' (Luke 13: 10).[38] In the Acts of the Apostles Paul visits synagogues to argue the case for Jesus with the Jews, while he uses other forums to speak to the gentiles. In Athens, for example, 'he argued in the synagogue with the Jews and the devout persons, and in the market place every day with those who chanced to be there' (Acts 17: 17).[39] But never does the New Testament speak of anyone praying in the synagogue. On the other hand, one does so in the Temple. We read of Peter and John 'going up to the Temple at the hour of prayer, the ninth hour' (Acts 3: 1), and of Paul who recalls the time shortly after his conversion, 'when I had returned to Jerusalem and was praying in the Temple' (Acts 22: 17).[40] Several other occasions and venues for prayer are mentioned: the followers of Jesus prayed together in the upper room at Jerusalem (Acts 1: 14);[41] Cornelius prayed frequently in his home (Acts 10: 2, 30); Judaeo-Christians prayed at the Jerusalem home of Mary, the mother of

[37] Even by J. Smith, 'The Ancient Synagogue, the Early Church and Singing', p. 4. I differ from Smith only in that I believe he accepts too easily the common assumptions about prayer in the synagogue of the period.
[38] See also Matthew 4: 23; Mark 1: 21, 6: 2; and Luke 4: 14, 6: 6.
[39] See also Acts 9: 20, 13: 5, 14: 1, 17: 1–3, 17: 10–11, 18: 4, 18: 19, 18: 16 and 19: 8.
[40] See also Acts 2: 46.   [41] See also Acts 4: 31.

Mark (Acts 12: 12); Paul prayed with the elders of the church of Ephesus (Acts 20: 36); and he and his companions prayed on the beach at Tyre before embarking (Acts 21: 5). There is no lack of references to prayer in the New Testament, only to prayer in the synagogue.

The overall impression conveyed by the New Testament is that the synagogue was the place of public assembly in each town and village. What we would call secular legal proceedings took place there, and in keeping with the character of Jewish society at the time, the Torah, at once divine and earthly law, along with the prophets, was read at regular Sabbath meetings. Afterwards various individuals might speak on matters related to the readings. It is entirely possible – as will be suggested below – that the synagogue was to a limited extent also a place of prayer, but it is difficult to reconcile with the New Testament evidence the notion that a regular synagogue prayer service played a central role in Jewish religious life at this time.

The other contemporary evidence, that derived from the writings of Josephus and Philo of Alexandria, fails to counter the impression given by the New Testament. The passages cited above emphasise the institution of the Sabbath as a day of rest on which Jews gathered in the synagogue to hear and ponder the Torah. Again there is no mention of prayer. It is true that Philo uses the term *proseuchē* occasionally to refer to Jewish religious establishments. However, as Rivkin has pointed out, the Egyptian *proseuchai* were not synagogues but dedicatory shrines by which Jews demonstrated their loyalty to the divine emperors; they were, in Philo's own words, 'manifestly bases for their expression of piety toward the house of Augustus'.[42] It is true also that on another occasion Philo uses the term in reference to what are apparently Roman synagogues,[43] but it is easy to imagine an Alexandrian Jew using the term loosely in the same way that, say, the terms temple and synagogue are used to describe modern synagogues. In any case this isolated usage of the term is hardly sufficient grounds for reconstructing a synagogue prayer service.

It is to the rabbinic evidence that one must turn to reconstruct the ancient synagogue liturgy, but here one is faced with the fundamen-

---

[42] *In Flaccum* 49; Rivkin's discussion of the meaning of *proseuchē* appears as an appendix to 'Ben Sira and the Nonexistence of the Synagogue', pp. 150–4.
[43] *Legatio ad Gaium* 155–6; again I follow Rivkin's argument.

tal chronological problem that the earliest rabbinic document, the Mishnah, was not redacted until about A.D. 200, considerably later than the period in question. The central text is the Mishnah Megillah 4, 3:

It is not permitted 'to recite the *Shema*'', nor to step before the *Tebah*, nor to lift up the hands (for the priestly benediction), nor to read the Law, nor to read the concluding prophetical lesson, nor to make ceremonial halts on the return journey from a funeral, nor to recite the benediction over the mourners nor over the newly married, nor to use the name [of God] in the preface to the Grace after Meals when there are less than ten [men] present.[44]

There are two basic questions to be asked concerning the text: does it in fact describe a synagogue service, and if so, to what date does one assign the service? The first can be answered with a relatively uncomplicated yes. It is true that the passage does not describe the service explicitly, rather it gives a series of ritual acts – nine in number – that one may not perform publicly with less than the traditional *minyan* of ten adult males. Moreover, only the first five acts pertain to the synagogue service; the final four, beginning with the 'ceremonial halts on the return journey from a funeral' clearly do not.

On the other hand, the five initial items are not simply any five that one might associate with synagogue liturgy; they are five essential acts of the Sabbath service as we know them from later sources, given, moreover, in proper order, and hence a description of the service by implication. The second item requires a word of explanation: 'to step before the *Tebah*' (the Ark of the Torah scroll) is a common phrase in rabbinic literature indicating recitation of the Tefillah; it refers to a member of the congregation rising and standing before the Ark for the recitation.[45] Actually the phrase suggests a liturgical act, as does that for the fifth and final item, 'to read the concluding prophetical lesson', literally 'to conclude in a prophet' (*maphtirin benabi'*). Finally, the text immediately succeeding that quoted above confirms the impression by dwelling on the first five items to the exclusion of the others and by adding regulations that make little sense outside the context of a liturgical service: for

---

[44] Text, translation and critical commentary in J. Rabbinowitz, *Mishnah Megillah* (London, 1931), pp. 114–21.

[45] See Rabbinowitz, p. 117.

example, 'A minor may read the Law or may translate but he may not recite the *Shema*'nor step before the *Tebah* nor lift up his hands.'[46]

If this is the proto-description of a synagogue service, then, to what date does it apply? The Mishnah, of course, was redacted in about A.D. 200, but since it is a compilation and digest of orally transmitted material we can entertain the possibility of an earlier date. For present purposes the question is whether to opt for a date before the destruction of the Temple in A.D. 70 or not. The popular view, of course, sees everything contained in this description and much more – psalmody, needless to say – as being regular features of a synagogue service in the time of Jesus and much earlier. The radically negative view, on the other hand, absolutely excludes prayer from the pre-destruction synagogue. Are there not contemporary scholars offering a more carefully nuanced view of synagogue liturgical origins? Joseph Heinemann[47] and Jacob Petuchowski[48] come immediately to mind, but understandably they are not concerned primarily with Christian origins and hence do not treat the crucial date A.D. 70 as explicitly as one might wish. The historian of Western music, then, is left to his own devices in attempting at least a provisional answer to the question.

Surely all probability points to those elements cited in the Mishnah Megillah 4, 3 as coming together in a recognised liturgical order no earlier than the first decade after the destruction of the Temple. At that time a group of rabbis gathered around Johanan ben Zakkai at Jabneh with the aim of salvaging some political and religious order after the disastrous conclusion of the revolt.[49] Characteristic of Johanan's activity was the decision to proclaim the new moons and leap years, crucial calendric matters hitherto reserved to Temple authorities. He was deeply grieved at the Temple's fate and shared the universal Jewish hope that it be rebuilt, but he recognised the need to maintain Israel's religious life and hence set about adapting various Temple practices to synagogue usage. His was not the only position one might adopt in the circumstances. The more inflexible

---

[46] M. Megillah 4, 6; Rabbinowitz, p. 125.

[47] *Prayer in the Talmud*, Studia Judaica 9 (Berlin and New York, 1977).

[48] 'The Liturgy of the Synagogue: History, Structure and Contents', *Approaches to Ancient Judaism*, III, ed. W. Green, Brown Judaic Studies 27 (Chico, Ca., 1983), pp. 1–64.

[47] Berakhot 5a.

[48] Berakhot 4b.

[49] The best source for Johanan's activity is J. Neusner, *A Life of Yohanan ben Zakkai, Ca. i–80 C.E.* (Leiden, 1970).

Eliezer ben Hyrcanus 'could conceive of no piety outside of that focused upon the Temple' and continued to legislate as if it were still in existence.[50] Johanan's position would, of course, prevail in the end, but we do not know how thoroughly it was worked out at this early stage nor how widely accepted. It is conceivable that he might have ordered a daily synagogue service as a surrogate for the *tamid* sacrifice, but we have no evidence to that effect.

It might be somewhat more plausible that this took place in the time of his successor Rabban Gamaliel II, who assumed leadership at some time around A.D. 80. He was a figure who commanded wider respect than Johanan[51] and who consolidated the authority of the rabbinic council at Jabneh during his rule of several decades. He was, moreover, associated by tradition with the establishment of synagogue liturgy. The key passage in this respect reads: 'Our Rabbis taught: Simeon ha-Pakuli arranged the eighteen benedictions in order before Rabban Gamaliel in Jabneh.'[52] The significance of the passage can be exaggerated as an argument for both the late and the early development of synagogue liturgy. On the one hand, it does not suggest an original institution of the Tefillah but merely the final selection and ordering of its eighteen benedictions. On the other hand, it does not mention the synagogue and hence could refer to private recitation of the Tefillah as well as congregational. It represents, nevertheless, at least one more step in that process of extra-Temple liturgical legislation begun by Johanan ben Zakkai and is an indication that Gamaliel II figures in the process.[53]

Some might wish to postpone the ordering of the synagogue service to the period after the Bar Kokhba revolt (132–5) when the rabbinic council came to be held at Usha in Galilee. They might argue that the need was more clearly indicated then because there was considerably less hope than before of rebuilding the Temple in the immediate future and because the Romans no longer allowed

---

[50] On Eliezer ben Hyrcanus, see J. Neusner, *Eliezer ben Hyrcanus: The Tradition and the Man*, 2 vols. (Leiden, 1973). The issues discussed here have been summarised recently by Neusner in 'The Formation of Rabbinic Judaism: Methodological Issues and Substantive Theses', *Formative Judaism: Religious Historical and Literary Studies*, III, ed. J. Neusner, Brown Judaic Studies 46 (Chico, Ca., 1983), pp. 99–146. The quotation is from the latter work, p. 139.

[51] On opposition to Johanan, see Neusner, *Yohanan ben Zakkai*, pp. 215–18.

[52] Berakhot 28b and Megillah 17b.

[53] He had a hand in other liturgical developments, for example the ordering of the Passover seder; see M. Pesahim 10, 5.

Jews to visit the site of the Temple where they might offer private sacrifices.[54] One can only speculate, but one at least speculates on some grounds when considering these different post-destruction dates. The contrasting positions of Eliezer ben Hyrcanus and Johanan ben Zakkai demonstrate that the adaptation of Temple liturgy to the synagogue had become an issue after the destruction, whereas there exist no such indications from before the destruction.

Another central point to consider is that the Tefillah, the core of the synagogue service, was to be recited at the same times of the day and the week as the sacrificial rites had been performed in the Temple. Indeed, this recitation was to 'replace' the daily sacrifice.[55] With respect to the question of chronology the conception can be read in two ways: the Tefillah can be looked upon as a substitute for the Temple sacrifice after its cessation, or as a substitute during its existence for those who could not journey to Jerusalem. The latter has a degree of abstract plausibility, but certainly the former better suits the historical circumstances just alluded to – that we have evidence of a movement to create ritual substitutions for the Temple after its destruction but only surmise for anything of the sort before the destruction. It is true that the *Maʿamadot* fasted in the villages and recited portions of the Torah relating to the Temple sacrifice. In a sense this was a contemporaneous substitute for Temple sacrifice, but more properly viewed it was an extension of participation in the Temple cult, whereas the establishment of a synagogue liturgy while the Temple still stood would seem to have created a rival for it. Eleazar, the prominent mid-second-century rabbi who was quoted above to the effect that 'a wall of iron intervened' between Israel and God after the destruction of the Temple, lamented also that 'from the day on which the Temple was destroyed the gates of prayer have been closed'.[56] It is difficult to reconcile such an attitude with the existence of a synagogue liturgy which had long since been accepted as a substitute for the Temple sacrifice.

Perhaps the most telling argument comes from a fresh – indeed, naïve – reading of the tractate Berakhot, which is largely taken up with the subject of the Shema and Tefillah. The overwhelming impression gained from this exercise is that the obligation to recite them is more often spoken of as individual than corporate. This is

---

[54] See A. Guttmann, 'The End of the Jewish Sacrificial Cult', *Hebrew Union College Annual*, 38 (1967), pp. 137–48.   [55] Berakhot 26b.   [56] Berakhot 32b.

especially true of the Shema. The opening chapters of the Mishnah
Berakhot are devoted exclusively to the obligation to recite the
Shema every morning and evening with little if any suggestion that a
common recitation is involved, and even in the accompanying
Gemara private rather than common recitation continues as a rule to
be implied. For example, it is deemed appropriate to recite the
evening Shema after retiring: 'If one recites the *Shema*ʿ upon his bed,
the demons keep away from him.'[57] However, there is a danger that
one might fall asleep in such circumstances and, therefore, 'Rather
should a man, when returning home from the field in the evening, go
to the synagogue. If he is used to read the Bible, let him read the
Bible, and if he is used to repeat the Mishnah, let him repeat the
Mishnah, and then let him recite the *Shema*ʿ.'[58] But note in this
second passage that although he recites the Shema in the synagogue,
he appears to do so on his own, along with other pious acts of his
choice, not as part of a public service. Passages suggesting a
congregational recitation of the Shema, such as that from the
Mishnah Megillah quoted above, are the exception, not the rule.

The situation with respect to the Tefillah is roughly analogous, yet
quite different in degree. The Mishnah Berakhot, after dealing with
the Shema, devotes two entire chapters to the Tefillah. Much of this
seems to apply to an individual obligation as when it provides: 'If he
is riding on an ass he dismounts and prays.'[59] Similarly, in the
accompanying *Gemara* one reads: 'If a man erred and did not say the
evening Tefillah, he says it twice in the morning.'[60] But there are
many passages that reveal a congregational recitation: 'If a man had
already said the *Tefillah* and went into a synagogue and found the
congregation saying the *Tefillah* . . .'.[61] Indeed, there are a number of
extended passages that strongly suggest a congregational recitation
to be preferable: a brief extract, for example, reads: 'Whosoever has
a Synagogue in town and does not go there in order to pray, is called
an evil neighbour.'[62] Still there are rabbis, even if exceptional ones,
who refuse to pray in the synagogue: 'R. Ammi and R. Assi, though
they had thirteen Synagogues in Tiberias, prayed only between the
pillars where they used to study.'[63] Their reason for thus refusing

---

[57] Berakhot 5a. [58] Berakhot 4b. [59] M. Berakhot 4, 5.
[60] Berakhot 26a. [61] Berakhot 21a.
[62] Berakhot 8a; see also Berakhot 3a; Berakhot 6a, quoted below, and Berakhot 30b.
[63] Berakhot 8a.

was that since the destruction of the Temple Israel's sole possession was the Torah, which one studied more deeply not in the synagogue but 'between the pillars' of the house of study (*beth ha-midrash*).

Just as the synagogue came to be the preferred venue for recitation of the Tefillah, so too did it come to be looked upon as a sacred place where the Lord was present: 'How do you know that the Holy One, blessed be He, is to be found in the Synagogue? For it is said: *God standeth in the congregation of God.*'[64] Yet one is reminded of the synagogue's secular past when it remains necessary to remonstrate:

> Synagogues must not be treated disrespectfully. It is not right to eat or to drink in them, nor to dress up in them, nor to stroll about in them, nor to go into them in summer to escape the heat and in the rainy season to escape the rain, nor to deliver a private funeral address in them. But it is right to read [the Scriptures] in them and to repeat the Mishnah and to deliver public funeral addresses.[65]

There are two further points to consider before attempting to summarise the evidence on the question of synagogue prayer. The first concerns the supposed existence, alluded to above, of a synagogue within the Temple itself, and the second introduces the subject of archaeological evidence for the early synagogue. The existence of a synagogue within the Temple has traditionally been cited as an argument for the liturgical significance of the synagogue before the destruction. Recently, however, Zeitlin[66] followed by Hoenig[67] have quite thoroughly disposed of the notion. Their basic argument is simply that the sources like the Mishnah Middot which describe the various buildings and chambers of the Temple fail to mention it. Moreover, Torah readings, when required in the Temple as on the Day of Atonement, were conducted from a wooden dais erected in one or the other of its courts rather than in a building of any sort. And finally it is gratuitous to claim that the Temple prayer sequence held in the Chamber of Hewn Stone was in reality a synagogue service; the sources present it simply as part of the Temple service even if it did find place eventually in the synagogue.[68]

---

[64] (Ps. 82: 1), Berakhot 6a; the immediately preceding passage has a reference to song that will be discussed below.

[65] Megillah 28a–28b.

[66] 'There Was No Synagogue in the Temple', *JQR*, 53 (1962), pp. 168–9.

[67] 'The Supposititious Temple-Synagogue'.

[68] For the philological aspect of the argument, which is too complex for brief summary, see especially Hoenig, *op. cit.*, pp. 118–23.

The subject of synagogue archaeology pursues a similar historiography to that of the Temple synagogue. For some time the established view was that of an orderly evolution in the history of early synagogue architecture, reflecting the institution's liturgical functions. However, a more critical evaluation of the purported synagogue sites in recent years has seen a dramatic revision in thinking on the subject. In general, dating tends to be later, and the buildings in question are viewed as more heterogeneous in design.[69] In particular five first-century A.D. Palestinian buildings claimed to be synagogues and claimed to represent a homogeneous type have been shown – whether synagogues or not – to be widely divergent in size, shape and detail, thus rendering untenable the proposition that they reflect uniform first-century liturgical practices.[70]

The specific question under consideration here remains the date of the synagogue service described in the Mishnah Megillah, but an attempt to answer it best takes the form of a summary of the entire question of early synagogue liturgy. In the pre-rabbinic evidence, particularly that of the New Testament, the synagogue appears in precise conformity to its name as a local meeting place. It is the venue for judicial proceedings and also for an exercise unique to Jewish society – at once religious, educational and civic – the reading and explication of the Torah. Prayer is not mentioned in connection with it, while it is with home and Temple. The destruction of the Temple was the occasion for profound change in the ritual life of Israel. A conservative like Eliezer ben Hyrcanus resisted, but most saw the need for adaptation. The period of Gamaliel II's ascendancy at Jabneh towards the end of the first century would seem a likely time for the ordering of the synagogue service as given in the Mishnah Megillah, but even then the process seems not to have been complete. There is something isolated about the Mishnah Megillah passage; the other rabbinic evidence presents a much less orderly and stable picture. The overwhelming majority of references to the Shema as an individual obligation creates the suspicion that it was not a constant element of the synagogue service until post-mishnaic times.[71] The Tefillah appears as the congregational prayer *par*

---

[69]   See Gutmann, *Ancient Synagogues: The State of Research*, especially A. Seager, 'Ancient Synagogue Architecture: An Overview', pp. 39–47.

[70]   M. Chiat, 'First-Century Synagogue Architecture: Methodological Problems', *Ancient Synagogues*, pp. 49–60.

[71]   See Petuchowski, 'The Liturgy of the Synagogue', p. 20.

excellence and the congregation as the preferred medium for its recitation, but only in the *Gemara*, and even then there is some dissent. Similarly, the synagogue came to be looked upon as a sacred place, but strictures against disrespectful conduct there recall its secular past.

All in all one gains the impression that for some centuries after the destruction of the Temple the synagogue service was still in the process of achieving the stability and centrality generally attributed to it for the time of Jesus. This might seem to support the validity of the extreme negative position, but the very lack of fixity and homogeneity suggested by the sources should caution against it. Who is to say, for example, that there was not a sufficiently sacral aura surrounding the reading of the Torah to call for benedictions to precede and follow it? Or who is to say that pious fellowships did not gather periodically for recitation of the Tefillah at home or at some quiet moment reserved for them in the local synagogue? But in the final analysis the evidence appears not to support the existence of an established synagogue worship service that was available to be taken over *en bloc* in the early Christian liturgy.

There are at least three reasons for having lingered over the question of ancient synagogue prayer in a study concerned primarily with psalmody. For one, the existing secondary literature provides no focused discussion of the chronological factors that are relevant here. For another, there is the dialectical point that if statutory congregational prayer can be shown not to have been a standard practice of the synagogue in the time of Jesus, then *a fortiori* psalmody must have been similarly absent. But the third and most important reason is that an attempt to deal with the question of prayer – however provisional – provides the only proper context within which to consider the question of psalmody. It provides an overview of the early development of synagogue liturgy, an introduction to the relevant primary sources, and some acquaintance with the more important secondary sources. It does all this, moreover, within the context of synagogue liturgy itself, not from the viewpoint of Christian liturgical practice in search of Jewish precedents.

This last point reminds one of the modern historiography of the psalmody question. That psalmody flourished in the ancient synagogue is a notion created primarily by Christian liturgical and musical historians. Louis Duchesne described a synagogue service corresponding precisely to the contemporary consensus and concluded: 'These four elements – lection, chants, homilies and prayers – were adopted without hesitation by the Christian Churches.'[72] Shortly before, Peter Wagner had stated: 'At the religious exercises in which for a long period they joined with the Jews in the synagogues, the Christians without doubt joined in the psalmody which was customary and in use there.'[73] But it was probably that group of Anglican liturgical historians writing in the second quarter of the century – W. O. E. Oesterly,[74] Clifford Dugmore[75] and Dom Gregory Dix[76] – who did the most to popularise the view among English-speaking scholars. These ordinarily cautious scholars wrote with great sympathy for the ancient synagogue, and perhaps it was an excess of such sympathy that caused them to make assertions on the subject of psalmody without benefit of primary sources. Oesterly's blithe remark is typical: 'The liturgical use of psalms in the Jewish Church in pre-Christian times is too well known to need many words. The adoption of the Temple liturgy by the Synagogue took place while the Temple was still standing.'[77]

The authors of music history surveys have been virtually unanimous in subscribing to this view. They have expressed it with remarkable similarity, offering only minor variations on Duchesne's four elements.[78] Specialists in the area of Jewish music have maintained a similar position but expressed it with more individuality. Abraham Idelsohn stated rather guardedly that 'the intonations of the [Temple] Psalms' were 'most likely retained and transplanted into the Synagogue';[79] while Alfred Sendry asserted less cautiously: 'Psalm-singing, the tonal aspect of religious expression, was always considered an indispensable stimulant for adoration, and therefore it

---

[72] *Christian Worship: Its Origin and Evolution* (5th edn, London, 1919), p. 48. The first French edition appeared in 1903.
[73] *Introduction to the Gregorian Melodies* (trans. A. Orme and E. Wyatt, London, 1907), p. 7. The first German edition appeared in 1895.
[74] *The Jewish Background of the Christian Liturgy* (London, 1925), p. 75.
[75] *The Influence of the Synagogue upon the Divine Office* (London, 1944), pp. 8 and 80–1.
[76] *The Shape of the Liturgy* (2nd edn, London, 1945), p. 45; and more recently, *Jew and Greek* (London, 1953), pp. 92–3.
[77] *Op. cit.*, p. 75.
[78] These authors are too numerous to cite. The most recent is G. Cattin, *Music of the Middle Ages*, I (trans. S. Botterill, Cambridge, 1984), p. 5. For my own commitment to the view, see 'The Church Fathers and Musical Instruments', pp. 113–14.
[79] *Jewish Music in its Historical Development*, p. 19.

must have been introduced without much delay into Synagogue worship.'[80] Eric Werner went so far as to indicate the particular psalms that were sung at the various synagogue services throughout the course of the week and of the liturgical year.[81] All three involved the institution of the *Maʿamadot*; they assumed that the Levite members would bring the Temple psalm melodies back to the synagogues. Sendry took the most extreme position. He reversed the commonly understood role of the *Maʿamadot* by describing it not as a means of bringing the people to the Temple but as a device for propagating Temple liturgical practices, including psalmody, in the countryside.[82]

There is but one group of scholars that have failed to claim an important role for psalmody in the ancient synagogue: Jewish liturgical historians. They have little to say on the matter for the simple reason that the primary sources provide no occasion to discuss it.[83] This is the crux of the argument against psalmody in the ancient synagogue – the lack of documentary evidence. The argument for psalmody, conversely, is an assumption based on its supposed appropriateness: 'It would seem natural', writes Moore, 'that with other features of the temple worship the songs of the levites at the morning and evening sacrifices should be imitated in the synagogues.'[84] It was argued above that these 'other features of the temple worship' cannot be assumed to have been imitated in the synagogue before the destruction of the Temple. Sources such as the Mishnah Megillah indicate that items like the Shema, Tefillah and priestly blessing were eventually imitated, but at no time do they suggest this for 'the songs of the levites at the morning and evening sacrifices'. As one ponders the abundant evidence – whether from before or after the destruction – relevant to reading, discourse and prayer in the daily and weekly synagogue service, the silence on psalmody appears increasingly significant. It is a silence of some 500

[80] *Music in Ancient Israel*, p. 180.
[81] *The Sacred Bridge* (New York, 1959), pp. 7–10, 144–5.
[82] *Op. cit.*, pp. 184–7.
[83] The standard history of Jewish liturgy is I. Elbogen, *Der jüdische Gottesdienst in seiner geschichtlichen Entwicklung* (3rd edn, Frankfurt am Main, 1931); see his brief remarks on pp. 249 and 252. Heinemann, *Prayer in the Talmud*, does not mention psalmody, while Petuchowski, 'The Liturgy of the Synagogue', p. 25, simply mentions the 'Verses of Song' as one among several practices not yet established in the talmudic period. The one scholar who deals with the issue at length, L. Rabinowitz, 'The Psalms in Jewish Liturgy', *Historia Judaica*, 6 (1944), pp. 109–22, takes a strongly negative position.
[84] *Judaism in the First Centuries of the Christian Era*, I, p. 296.

years extending from the New Testament period to the final redaction of the Talmud. Surely if it had been customary to recite the daily Temple psalm in the synagogue, this vast literature would have made some reference to the practice.

Such reference does finally appear in the eighth-century tractate Sopherim,[85] which includes the seven daily psalms in the synagogue service, citing the incipit of each. Interestingly enough the innovation of reciting them is not attributed to some authority but to the people. More significantly for present purposes, it is found necessary even at this late date to contrive some justification for their use in the absence of sacrifice. This, in contrast to the easy assumption that such a transfer of psalmody from Temple to synagogue was something that one could take for granted even before the destruction. These psalms, incidentally, are still recited today towards the close of the synagogue service, where the proper psalm for the day is introduced by the rubric: 'This is the first [second, etc.] day of the week, on which the Levites in the Temple used to say.'[86]

Sopherim mentions a second daily usage of psalms in the synagogue, one that might pre-date the seven Temple psalms.[87] These are the six psalms, 145–50, which today form the nucleus of the 'Verses of Song', a kind of prelude to the service proper.[88] There are two reasons suggesting a somewhat earlier date for them: (1) unlike its treatment of the Temple psalms, Sopherim seems to take them for granted, offering no justification for their introduction, and (2) they appear to have been mentioned once in the Talmud, albeit as a private rather than congregational practice.[89] If this passage does in fact refer to them, the circumstance of private recitation suggests that our hypothetically earlier date for their synagogue usage would still be a matter of some centuries after the destruction of the Temple.

Up to this point daily, as opposed to festive, psalmody has been stressed. This is entirely proper in the present context where the

---

[85] Sopherim 18, 1. What follows here on Sopherim owes much to the discussion of Rabinowitz, 'The Psalms in Jewish Liturgy'. Sopherim is available in English translation as part of a supplement to the Soncino translation of the Babylonian Talmud.

[86] J. Hertz, *The Authorized Daily Prayer Book* (revised edn, New York, 1948), p. 218.

[87] Sopherim 17, 11.

[88] Hertz, *op. cit.*, 84–96.

[89] Elbogen, *Der jüdische Gottesdienst*, p. 82, determined that a phrase in Shabbath 118b refers to these six psalms, but L. Hoffman casts serious doubt on the identification: *The Canonization of the Synagogue Service* (Notre Dame, Ind., and London, 1979), pp. 127–8.

question at issue is the supposed adoption of an elemental synagogue service by the primitive church. Nevertheless, the employment of psalmody on special occasions would not seem entirely without significance, and something of the sort appears to have taken place in the form of the Hallel, Psalms 113–18, mentioned above in connection with the Temple. There are some forty references to the Hallel in the Mishnah and the Babylonian Talmud.[90] Of these roughly a quarter refer to its performance in the Temple,[91] and another quarter to its recitation at the Passover seder.[92] Of the rest, several do not give a clear indication of the circumstances in which it was said,[93] while a few seem to speak of private recitation.[94] There are, however, a number which clearly point to public recitation, presumably in the synagogue; of these the passages from the *Gemara* of Rosh ha-Shanah and Sotah are the most revealing.

We read in Rosh ha-Shanah: 'In the recital of the Torah [in synagogue] one may read and another translate; what is not allowed is that one should read and two translate.... In the recital of *Hallel* and *Megillah* even ten may read.'[95] Interesting about this passage, in addition to the fundamental point of the Hallel's usage in the synagogue, is the circumstance that it is treated less as a discrete musical item than as a scripture reading like the reading of the Torah and the Megillah (the Book of Esther).

The passage from Sotah is an inquiry into the manner in which the canticle of Moses (Exodus 15) might have been performed. Rabbi Akiba likens it to the manner of an adult's reading of the Hallel, while another rabbi likens it to a minor's reading.[96] The difference is that when an adult reads, the congregation responds with only the refrain Alleluia; whereas when a minor reads, it is thought necessary to repeat each verse. These are two recognisable modes of responsorial psalmody, a circumstance of considerable significance for both Jewish and Christian music history, but at the same time the passage

---

[90] That is, those sufficiently developed to appear in the indexes of the Soncino translation.
[91] Especially: M. Pesahim 5, 7; M. Taʿanit 4, 4–5; M. Sukkah 4, 1 and 8; Sukkah 37b; 42b; 54b.
[92] Especially: Berakhot 9a; M. Pesahim 9, 3; 10, 6–7; Pesahim 85b–86a; 115b; 117a.
[93] For example, ʿArakin 10a–10b and Taʿanit 28b.
[94] For example, a reference to David's supposed recitation, Megillah 21b, and another on the question of kneeling during the recitation, Berakhot 34b.
[95] Rosh ha-Shanah 27a; see also 34b and M. Rosh ha-Shanah 4, 7.
[96] Sotah 30b. I. Slotki discusses this and related passages at length: 'Antiphony in Ancient Hebrew Poetry', *JQR*, 26 (1936), pp. 199–219.

confirms the impression of the passage from Rosh ha-Shanah that the performance of the Hallel at this time was more in the nature of scripture reading than elaborately melodious psalmody. It is some undefined adult or minor from the congregation who reads the Hallel, not a skilled officiant. Yet this point of psalmody as reading should be considered positively rather than negatively in the context of early synagogue and church relationships. One is reminded of St Augustine's description of the Athanasian style of psalmody – 'more like speaking [*pronuncianti*] than singing [*canenti*]'[97] – and indeed students of early Christian chant are increasingly of the opinion that until the later fourth century psalms figured in the Christian liturgy as readings rather than set musical pieces.[98]

But the central point here is the appearance of psalms – whatever their mode of performance – in the ancient synagogue, and the earliest such appearance seems to be that of the Hallel. Perhaps this is due in part to the heterogeneity of its usage. It is true that it was performed during the sacrifice on special occasions such as the people's offering on the Passover and the additional sacrifices on the eight days of Tabernacles, yet it was also performed at home during the Passover seder. Thus, lacking the rigid association with sacrifice of the seven daily psalms, there might not have been so strong an inhibition to its adaptation for use in the synagogue. As for the date of that adaptation, one of the sources cited above is from the Mishnah, again suggesting that it was relatively early. Nevertheless, to place it before the destruction requires making the sort of assumptions objected to throughout this study.

It should be noted further – and here it is necessary to digress – that there are no signs of the Hallel's adaptation to the liturgy of the early church except for the significant exception of the Hallel sung at the Passover seder. It is significant because it is a matter of neither Temple nor synagogue liturgy but rather a ceremonial meal. The gospels of Matthew and Mark end their descriptions of the Last Supper with the identical sentence: 'And when they had sung a hymn, they went out to the Mount of Olives' (Matthew 26: 30; Mark 14: 26). If the Last Supper took place on the first night of Passover as

97 *Confessions*, x, 33, 50.
98 See especially P. Jeffery, 'The Introduction of Psalmody into the Roman Mass by Pope Celestine I (422–32)', *Archiv für Liturgiewissenschaft*, 26 (1984), p. 159. It is the central point of my paper, 'The Fourth Century Origin of the Gradual'; see *Abstracts of Papers Read at the First Joint Meeting of the American Musicological Society ...* (Vancouver, 1985), pp. 27–8.

the synoptic gospels indicate, then it was a Passover seder, and in all probability the hymn sung by Jesus and the Apostles was the Hallel.[99] Some centuries later there is a suggestion, however slight, that the practice might have been retained. The *Apostolic Tradition*, which describes the Roman liturgy of the third century, refers to the singing of psalms with Alleluia refrain at the *agape*.[100] The *agape*, 'love feast', is in direct line of descent from the Last Supper; it was a ceremonial meal that continued to be celebrated in Christian communities after the Eucharist had been separated from it and placed in the early morning. As for the psalms with Alleluia refrain, while there are many others in the Psalter besides Psalms 113–18, this is the most prominent such grouping. But Hallel or not, it is still a matter of psalmody in these passages, and thus there exists a verified link between Jewish and Christian practice in psalmody at ceremonial meals.[101] To complete the digression, one recalls the frequently cited singing of the Jewish Therapeutai, described by Philo of Alexandria.[102] They were quasi-monastic communities of Egyptian men and women, reminiscent of the Palestinian Essenes, who came together at the Feast of Weeks to participate in a sober religious banquet in which psalmody figured prominently. The practices described are so similar to those of subsequent Christianity that Eusebius of Caesarea claimed – falsely, of course – that Philo was really talking about early Christians.[103] Only somewhat less obviously false is the modern claim that Philo was describing psalmody in the Egyptian synagogue.[104] A monastic assembly for a festive meal can scarcely be identified with a synagogue meeting of lay congregants. To make such claims, moreover, diverts attention from the positive significance of the passage: psalmody at Jewish meals is significant for the question of Jewish and Christian musical links because the Christian evidence of the first three centuries shows

---

99 The Gospel of John, which suggests to some that the Last Supper took place on the previous day, gives pause. Still there are liturgical historians who view the matter with certainty: for example, J. Jungmann, *The Early Liturgy* (trans. F. Brunner, Notre Dame, Ind., 1959), p. 12.

100 *La tradition apostolique de Saint-Hippolyte*, ed. B. Botte (Münster, Westphalia, 1963), p. 6.

101 An important point for which one is indebted to Smith, *op. cit.*, p. 16.

102 *De vita contemplativa*, 64–90.

103 *Ecclesiastical History*, II, 17, 22. Compare the Philo passage with Tertullian, *Apologeticum*, 39, 16–18.

104 M. Hengel, 'Proseuche und Synagoge', *Tradition und Glaube: Das frühe Christentum in seiner Umwelt: Festgabe für Karl Kuhn zum 65. Geburtstag*, ed. G. Jeremias and others (Göttingen, 1971), p. 163.

common meals to be the principal venue of Christian psalmody.[105]

To return to the question of synagogue psalmody, it is a generally negative picture that the sources present. The proper psalm for each day of the week seems not to have been adopted until many centuries after the destruction of the Temple and the 'Verses of Song' only somewhat earlier, while the festive reading of the Hallel was considerably earlier but still shortly postdating the destruction in all probability. Yet it runs contrary to the nature of the evidence to deal in absolutes, and there are a number of talmudic passages that suggest a somewhat less bleak picture. We read, for example, that 'R. Shefatiah further said in the name of R. Johanan: If one reads the Scripture without a melody or repeats the Mishnah without a tune, of him the Scripture says, *Wherefore I gave them also statutes that were not good.*'[106] Whatever the date of this passage it suggests that scripture reading – and certainly the recitation of the Hallel – was not always as totally unmusical as modern reading but might have amounted to a sort of cantillation. Even more significant perhaps is the passage cited above where Abba Benjamin says: 'A man's prayer is heard [by God] only in the Synagogue. For it is said: *To hearken unto song and to the prayer* [Ps. 82: 1]. The prayer is to be recited where there is song.'[107] Again, an ideal reader is described by R. Judah as: 'One having a large family . . . whose youth was unblemished, who is meek and is acceptable to the people; who is skilled in chanting, who has a pleasant voice, and possesses a thorough knowledge of the Torah, the Prophets and the Hagiographa, of the Midrash, *Halachoth* and *Aggadoth* and of all the Benedictions.'[108] These references are all relatively late and they may have more to do with cantillation in general – of Scripture, benedictions, etc. – than with psalmody in particular, but they serve to counter any suggestion that the synagogue was an absolutely unmusical institution during the years after the destruction of the Temple when its liturgy was beginning to take shape. The argument here is only against the opposite extreme notion of a regularised synagogue psalmody existing in the time of Jesus.

Before attempting a summary of that argument there remains a final point to consider: the notion of a three-year cycle of synagogue

---

[105] In addition to the passages cited above from Tertullian and the *Apostolic Tradition*, see Clement of Alexandria, *Paedagogus* 2, 4 and Cyprian, *Ad Donatum*, 16.
[106] Megillah 32a.   [107] Berakhot 6a.   [108] Taʿanit 16a.

psalmody, a corollary to the Triennial Torah Cycle mentioned above. It has been invoked as an argument for early synagogue psalmody most recently by Eric Werner.[109] The theory of the Triennial Torah Cycle was introduced by Adolph Büchler[110] towards the end of the nineteenth century and developed later by Jacob Mann.[111] According to it the five books of the Torah were read consecutively at morning Sabbath services lacking proper readings. The cycle assigned specific sections of Scripture to each Sabbath and was completed in precisely three years. Corollary to the theory is the idea that the prophetic *haftarot* were similarly assigned to a precise three-year schedule. Here, however, there was not a consecutive reading, but readings were selected to correspond in theme to the seasons and the Torah readings. Psalmody enters in by way of a further corollary: the 150 psalms were to be read consecutively, one on each of the Sabbaths of the Triennial Cycle.[112] According to the theory, not only does the number 150 correspond neatly with the three years of the cycle, but the Hebrew division of the Psalter into five books corresponds with the five books of the Torah. The theory is developed by a complex web of subject-matter relationships among the three classes of readings and among early medieval commentaries, homilies and poetic cycles, which were composed, supposedly, with the Triennial Cycle in mind.

The psalter cycle corollary has a number of serious flaws. Some of the thematic correspondences with Torah or prophetic readings are apt enough, but their significance is rendered dubious by the circumstance that the arithmetic of the theory allows a flexible synchronisation of the Psalter with the Torah cycle. One psalm can be matched with as many as four readings, thus giving the scholar a

---

[109]   *The Sacred Bridge*, ii (New York, 1984), pp. 73, 97–100.

[110]   'The Reading of the Law and Prophets in a Triennial Cycle', *JQR*, 5 (1893), pp. 420–68; 'Reading of the Prophets in a Triennial Cycle', *JQR*, 6 (1894), pp. 1–73. Both articles are reprinted in J. Petuchowski, *Contributions to the Scientific Study of Jewish Liturgy* (New York, 1970), pp. 181–229; 230–302.

[111]   *The Bible as Read and Preached in the Old Synagogue*, 2 vols. (Cincinnati, 1940–55; vol. ii completed by I. Stone).

[112]   The principal advocates of the theory are: E. King, 'The Influence of the Triennial Cycle upon the Psalter', *The Journal of Theological Studies*, 5 (1904), pp. 203–13; N. Snaith, 'The Triennial Cycle and the Psalter', *Zeitschrift für die alttestamentliche Wissenschaft*, 51 (1933), pp. 302–7; L. Rabinowitz, 'Does Midrash Tillim Reflect the Triennial Cycle of Psalms', *JQR*, 26 (1936), pp. 349–68. The inclusion of this last scholar is surprising in view of his later opposition to the idea of psalmody in the early synagogue; see 'The Psalms in Jewish Liturgy', cited above.

suspicious advantage in his search for correspondences. A more obvious flaw lies in the alleged correspondence between the five divisions of the Psalter and the five books of the Torah. While there is a rough proportion between the length of Genesis and Exodus and the first two divisions of the Psalter, the remaining quantities are so divergent as to force one scholar to rearrange the latter three divisions of the Psalter.[113] A similarly extreme instance of sacrificing evidence to theory comes from a Christian exponent of the triennial psalter cycle, who notes that the talmudic evidence stands against synagogue psalmody and resolves the contradiction by claiming that rabbinic authorities did away with psalmody in about A.D. 100 because the Christians had adopted it.[114]

One suspects the psalter corollary at the outset as the creature of internal evidence; it is advocated not on the grounds of any documentary evidence but because of its seeming appropriateness. Doubt grows as internal inconsistencies mount, but ultimately it must be rejected for a still more compelling reason – it collapses along with the original theory of the Torah cycle on which it is based. Heinemann,[115] followed by Ben Zion Wacholder,[116] have demonstrated that the notion of any uniform cycle of Torah readings in the earliest centuries is contradicted by the talmudic evidence. To take a single example, a passage from the Mishnah Megillah prescribes a minimum number of verses to be read each Sabbath but leaves the maximum open.[117] This means, of course, that different synagogues would read from different places in the Torah each Sabbath. The most that can be said for the Triennial Cycle is that later evidence suggests it took about three and a half years to complete the reading of the Torah in Palestine as opposed to just one in Babylonia, and even then the three-and-a-half-year reading seems not to have been simultaneously observed from place to place until the sixth century at the earliest. As for the earlier period, Heinemann appears not to have stated the case too strongly when he says that the hypothesis of

[113] Rabinowitz, 'Does Midrash Tillim Reflect the Triennial Cycle', p. 358.

[114] A. Arens, *Die Psalmen in Gottesdienst des Alten Bundes*, Trierer Theologische Studien 11 (Trier, 1961), p. 202.

[115] 'The Triennial Lectionary Cycle', *The Journal of Jewish Studies*, 19 (1968), pp. 41–8.

[116] In the 'Prolegomenon' to the 2nd edn of Mann, *op. cit.*, I (New York, 1971).

[117] M. Megillah 4, 4. For another example, the passage from Mishnah Megillah (3, 4) quoted above, which counts only Sabbath morning readings in the cycle, is directly contradicted by other rabbinic evidence; see Heinemann, *op. cit.*, p. 45. For a summary of the issue, see Petuchowski, 'The Liturgy of the Synagogue', p. 29.

a three-year cycle of proper Sabbath readings 'belongs clearly to the realm of fiction'.[118]

To summarise, then, the evidence against psalmody in the synagogue at the time of Jesus appears overwhelming. This is not to assert categorically that psalms were never heard. The Book of Psalms was securely fixed in the Hebrew biblical canon, and it is conceivable that portions of it might have been read as scripture. It is true that it belonged to the third division of the Bible, the Hagiographa, and as such would appear to have been excluded from the prophetic readings, but one wonders if such distinctions were rigidly observed in the first century. If the present study teaches us one thing about the early synagogue, it is that we cannot think about it in terms of absolutes. Anything was liable to happen there, of either a secular or a religious nature, and who is to exclude the possibility of occasional psalm-singing? But what the evidence assembled here does refute is the conventional notion that psalmody was a discrete event in an established synagogue liturgical order before the destruction of the Temple. Daily synagogue psalmody as generally understood was not instituted until several centuries into the Christian era. This is a cautious enough finding and one that corresponds well with the recent work of Jewish liturgical historians. Where the present study departs from such caution is in its suggestion that there may not have existed a synagogue liturgical order of any sort before the destruction of the Temple. If it is correct in this respect, then it is correct *a fortiori* in regard to psalmody, but if not, the findings on psalmody can stand on their own.

If these findings are negative in the narrow sense, they must be considered positive in the broader perspective of synagogue and church relationships. It goes beyond what can be demonstrated here, but it seems fair to say that the same general fluidity we observe in ancient synagogue liturgy, and the same tendency for specific liturgical items to become established later than generally assumed, can be observed also in the primitive church. The earliest description of the pre-eucharistic 'liturgy of the Word' – that portion of the Christian liturgy thought to derive directly from the synagogue – appears in a mid-second-century document, Justin Martyr's first Apology.[119] Reading and discourse are present there and prayer also

---

[118] *Op. cit.*, p. 46.   [119] *Apology*, I, 67.

but, as Smith points out, the prayer comes at the opposite end of the service from where it appears in the synagogue.[120] Psalmody is absent altogether, and in fact we lack unequivocal evidence for it at this point in the liturgy until the last quarter of the fourth century.[121]

What Christian liturgy does derive from the synagogue is more important than a liturgical order. It inherits the synagogue's unique liturgical setting of a meeting house for religious associates as opposed to a temple square for the witnessing of sacrifice. And it owes to Judaism – not necessarily the synagogue – many specific items of comparable uniqueness and significance: a canon of sacred books, the practice of reading them and discussing them in public, the institution of congregational prayer and a matchless collection of 150 hymns. But church and synagogue have less in common than is frequently claimed with respect to the process by which these items came to be fixed in liturgical orders. Their liturgies incorporated specific practices such as psalmody – indeed, especially psalmody – in their own way and their own time.

State University of New York at Buffalo

---

[120] *Op. cit.*, p. 7.
[121] See Jeffery, 'The Introduction of Psalmody into the Roman Mass', and McKinnon, 'The Fourth Century Origin of the Gradual'.

EDWARD NOWACKI

TEXT DECLAMATION AS A DETERMINANT OF MELODIC FORM IN THE OLD ROMAN EIGHTH-MODE TRACTS*

This essay presents a close examination of the Gregorian eighth-mode tracts in Old Roman transmission.[1] Its main objective will be to show that the apparent diversity of the genre as a whole is due largely to conditioned variation, and that within subsets characterised by identical textual conditions, melodic shape is uniform, or thrifty, to a degree that is as remarkable as it is unexpected. Particular attention will be paid to the regular and, in some cases, predictable ways in which the accentuation, phrasing and syntax of the text determine melodic form. The essay will take up the subject of text expression in its classic formulation by Dominicus Johner[2] and show how he was prevented from arriving at a satisfactory result by the very terms in which he framed the question. Finally and incidentally, some comparative observations will be made about the

---

* This essay is presented to Michel Huglo on the occasion of his sixty-fifth birthday.

[1] Eighth-mode tracts are transmitted in four sources of the Old Roman manuscript tradition: Vatican City, Biblioteca Apostolica Vaticana, MSS Vat. lat. 5319, San Pietro F 22 and San Pietro F 11 (*De profundis* only), and Cologny bei Genf, Martin Bodmer Collection, MS 74 (*olim* Phillips 16069). They are catalogued and indexed to their respective folio numbers in P. F. Cutter, *Musical Sources of the Old-Roman Mass*, Musicological Studies and Documents 36 (Neuhausen-Stuttgart, 1979). The folio numbers for the examples in the Bodmer–Phillips manuscript, not given by Cutter, are listed here: *Qui regis israhel*, fol. 8ᵛ; *Qui seminant*, fol. 31ᵛ; *Desiderium*, fol. 32; *Beatus vir*, fol. 32ᵛ; *De profundis*, fol. 34; *Commovisti*, fol. 35ᵛ; *Iubilate deo*, fol. 36ᵛ; *Laudate dominum*, fol. 47ᵛ; *Ad te levavi*, fol. 52; *Qui confidunt*, fol. 57ᵛ; *Sepe expugnaverunt*, fol. 63ᵛ. Space limitations prevent me from illustrating all of the analytic observations made in the article. Readers are referred to the complete edition of the Old Roman gradual by B. Stäblein, *Die Gesänge des altrömischen Graduale Vat. lat. 5319*, Monumenta Monodica Medii Aevi 2 (Kassel, 1970). The musical examples in the article are my own transcriptions from Vat. lat. 5319.

[2] D. Johner, *Wort und Ton im Choral*, 2nd edn (Leipzig, 1953).

counterparts of the Old Roman tracts in Frankish transmission (i.e. Gregorian chant in the narrow sense) with a view to showing the aesthetic superiority of the Old Roman versions in certain respects.

In an analytic study of this kind, why should one choose the Old Roman tradition of Gregorian chant instead of the more familiar standard, or Frankish tradition? One answer to that question is simple: Gregorian chant in Old Roman transmission is intrinsically interesting and deserves no less attention than its much-studied Frankish counterpart. The wealth of scholarly articles devoted to Old Roman problems in the last four decades has been limited for the most part to comparative studies that attempt to define the relative positions of the two traditions in the history of Gregorian chant generally. Now that most of the historical arguments have been stated, the time has come to devote some attention to the Old Roman tradition as a cultural artefact in its own right, apart from its evidentiary value in support of this or that theory of origins.

Another reason lies in the value of the Old Roman manuscripts as witnesses to their tradition. The melodic forms transmitted in these manuscripts exhibit a certain casual indifference in the employment of decorative detail, yet are remarkably uniform in the way that their structural elements are adapted to the given texts. These qualities point to a vigorous tradition, where tolerance of variation in non-essential matters is consistent with confidence in the organising power of well-understood structural principles. Moreover, the Old Roman manuscripts are all Roman in origin and were copied, it would seem, under native auspices, probably by scribes who were themselves authorities on the current tradition. I do not have the confidence to make such strong claims about the Frankish manuscript tradition, and several published studies have urged caution in accepting Frankish manuscripts as witnesses to a pure tradition in spite of the avowed intention of Frankish liturgists to transmit the *cantus romanus* unchanged.[3]

---

[3] T. Klauser, 'Die liturgischen Austauschbeziehungen zwischen der römischen und der fränkisch-deutschen Kirche vom achten bis zum elften Jahrhundert', *Historisches Jahrbuch*, 53 (1933), pp. 169–89; reprinted in Klauser, *Gesammelte Arbeiten*, ed. E. Dassmann (Münster, Westphalia, 1974), pp. 139–54. H. Hucke, 'Die Einführung des gregorianischen Gesanges im Frankenreich', *Römische Quartalschrift für christliche Altertumskunde und Kirchengeschichte*, 49 (1954), pp. 172–85; *idem*, 'Gregorianischer Gesang in altrömischer und fränkischer Überlieferung', *Archiv für Musikwissenschaft*, 12 (1955), pp. 74–87. T. H. Connolly, 'Introits and Archetypes: Some Archaisms of the Old Roman Chant', *Journal of the American Musicological Society*, 25 (1972), pp. 157–74.

Similar objections might be raised against the witness value of the Old Roman manuscript tradition if one were seeking from it information about the seventh-century Gregorian prototype from which both it and its Frankish counterpart are descended. However, the demands that I place on the evidence are not nearly so strong as that. I require of it only that it bear witness to a living tradition of plainchant untouched by the potentially distorting effects of a foreign redaction. Since the Old Roman manuscript tradition appears to satisfy that relatively modest requirement, I find it an excellent source of data for an analytic study of plainchant.

I

Tracts consist of several psalm verses declaimed with a melodic pattern that is repeated for each verse. Although the Old Roman manuscripts transmit only eleven eighth-mode tracts in the native style,[4] these tracts comprise thirty-five psalm verses and therefore provide more material for comparison than may be apparent at first sight. The basic melodic pattern consists of four phrases with cadences on G, F, G and G, in that order. The medial cadence on the *subfinalis* creates a strong tonal contrast that effectively organises the four phrases into two larger units corresponding to the typical division of psalm verses into hemistichs. In the declamation of any given verse, this medial cadence ordinarily coincides with the break between the hemistichs, while the lower-ranking internal cadences are made to coincide with lesser internal divisions of the text. In this way the musical declamation reinforces the prosodic structure of the verse and helps to make manifest the meaning of the words by providing the main syntactical breaks with musical punctuation.

To simplify the discussion I shall label the four phrases V (for verse-initial), M (for medial), P (for post-medial) and K (for cadential). There are also tract-initial (I) phrases, which replace V in the first verse, and tract-final (F) phrases, which replace K in the last verse. A normal tract of three verses has the form:

I	M	P	K
V	M	P	K
V	M	P	F

---

4 The Old Roman tradition lacks versions in the native style of the four tracts for the Easter vigil: *Cantemus domino*, *Vinea facta est*, *Attende caelum* and *Sicut cervus*. The versions of these tracts given in the Old Roman manuscripts are Frankish (i.e. standard Gregorian).

In addition, there are three other phrases, R, K_1 and K_2, that are relatively infrequent. R occurs in various initial and internal positions, and K_1 and K_2 are alternatives to K. They are not variants of K; they simply occur in the same environment. The labelling is a shorthand intended to convey that elements with the same label are the same in an obvious way. Ordinarily the similarity of the particular versions bearing the same label can be verified at sight by consulting the tables. Phrases labelled I and V, however, present an exception: in their case the validity of the cover label is not so apparent and depends on arguments showing the variation to be conditioned in some way by the text. These arguments will make clear that phrases of types I and V exhibit only a little more real, or contrastive, variation than do phrases of the more obviously uniform types.

While some variants are contrastive and others non-contrastive, still others, which I call casual, must be denied any variant status at all. The grounds for this assertion are both intuitive and empirical. It would defy common sense in such a prolix melodic idiom to attribute variant character to such minimal alternations as those involving passing notes, auxiliary notes and note repetitions. Passing notes do not affect melodic goals, ambitus or contour; auxiliary notes have no effect on melodic goals and only the most superficial effect on ambitus and contour; note repetitions are a matter of articulation only and do not affect pitch structure at all. In this category I include also alternations involving the transposition of consecutive notes, and alternations involving the omission of certain structural notes (e.g. G) between the subsidiary notes (e.g. F and a) that they generate. In performance, the effect of such variation on the identity of the chant is negligible.

Empirical support for this view of casual variation comes from the distribution of casual variants in the Old Roman sources. Consider, for instance, the ascending figure in column h of Table 1. The observed alternation between the forms $F–a–c–b$ (rows III and V–XI) and $G–a–c–b$ (rows I and IV) in Vat. lat. 5319 appears to have no environmental motivation and raises the suspicion that it is casual, occurring randomly from performance to performance. This suspicion is borne out by the testimony of the other two sources. The Bodmer–Phillips manuscript gives the version $F–a–c–b$ instead of $G–a–c–b$ in rows I and IV, and San Pietro F 22 gives $F–G–a–c–b$, a

Table 1 *Phrase F (tract-final)*

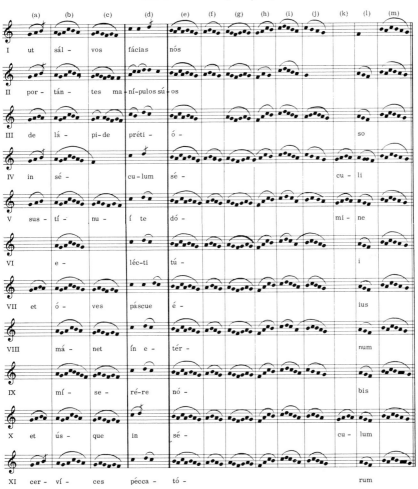

version combining both alternatives, in row VIII and *G–a–b–c–b*, a realisation entirely in conjunct motion, in row X. Even the version in row II, *F–a–G* (*F–a* in San Pietro F22), is another form of gapped ascent spanning the interval from *F* to the *c* in the following segment. The line passes through *a* first and then *G* in a temporary reversal of the usual ascending order, and fails to reach *c* before the end of the segment as the other versions do. However, since the omitted *c* is nothing more than the anticipation of a melodic goal reached in the following segment, alternation in its employment has no more claim to variant status than other more obvious casual variants.

One last argument for the non-variant status of casual variants is, again, an intuitive one. Consider how difficult it is to detect alternations between such variants by ear without the help of a visual guide. Clearly, they make a much bigger impression on the eye than on the ear, and their ubiquitousness in Old Roman transmission suggests that the test for correctness in that tradition was not visual, but auricular. Even in the copying of the Old Roman manuscripts, where, I believe, written exemplars were employed, the copyists evidently consulted them only as *aide-mémoire*, referring to them for text underlay and phrase structure, but then turning away and writing down whole phrases in the form already assimilated from years of exposure to the tradition. In order to discuss the Old Roman eighth-mode tracts in a way that is true to their nature, it will be necessary to adopt the same attitude towards them that their performers and copyists had, and to consider casual variants captured in a written medium as non-variants in terms of the oral medium in which they freely occurred.

Take once again the example of Table 1 and consider the melodic segments in vertical alignment. (The segmentation, while loosely following the original notation, has no other purpose than to facilitate visual comparison and should not be taken as a statement about the melodies' constituent structure.) The basic identity of the segments may be verified with a glance down each column. In column m, for example, the only variation is in the note repetition on the penultimate pitch, *a*, in rows IX and XI (undoubtedly a notational difference only). In column j all the segments except the one in row II, which appears to be a real variant, consist of an ascent to *c* from the *a* at the end of the preceding segment and a descent to *G*. The only difference consists in whether the initial ascent to *c* is by leap or employs a passing *b*. The descending figure in column i is likewise limited to gapped and conjunct versions in which a passing *b* is the optional pitch. The figure in column h has already been discussed. The passage spanning columns e, f and g exhibits no variation at all, except that the internal segment in column f, being redundant, is omitted in one case. Column d contains various forms of embellished pitch repetition on c. In column c, aside from some non-contrastive pitch repetitions, the only variant is in row IV, where a single F stands in place of the more usual embellished descent to F. Although the verification of these details may be tedious, it is important that readers have confidence in the graphic presentation as an index of basic similarity. Segments that do not seem to belong in their column will be commented on in due course.

Phrase F. Now consider the melodic structure of phrase F (Table 1) and its relationship to text declamation. The melodic pattern declaims the words in such a way that the final accent normally coincides with the long melisma extending from column e through to column j. This is true even in the relatively infrequent case occurring in row I, where the accent is on the ultima. The weak final syllable, when there is one, falls in column l, while the figure $G–a–b–a$ in column k is reserved for the extra weak syllable that occurs when the final accent is on the antepenult. The table reveals at a glance the consistency of these mappings. The syllable placement in row II, which represents the only departure from the norm, may be an error. The fact that all three surviving sources transmit it suggests that they may depend, at least for text underlay, on a written tradition. The three manuscripts also give the phrase in row II abnormal melodic forms, reacting in all probability to the anomalous absence of a weak final syllable near the end of the phrase. Those versions, in other words, are not instances of contrastive variation, but conditioned responses to a change in the textual environment.

As in the preceding example, the peculiar reading in row I, column l, is a response to a change in the normal textual conditions: the absence of a weak final syllable. In this case, however, the syllable in column e (*nos*) is corrrectly placed. There are no additional weak syllables for the melodic material in columns k and l because the phrase ends on an accented ultima (*ut sálvos fácias nós*).[5] We must

---

[5] The rules of accentuation in standard Gregorian psalmody, as described in the *Antiphonale monasticum* (Tournai, 1934), p. 1225, treat stressed final monosyllables as unaccented:

Aliter diceres: monosyllabica vox in ultimo loco posita semper accentu privatur. Unde cum haec spondeum sequitur, ambo simul efficere putantur dactylum: v.g. *Fáctus sum = Dóminus*; cum autem dactylum sequitur, ambo simul efficere censentur dispondeum: v.g. *génuí te = Déus méus*.

The Old Roman example is consistent rather with the practice of Dominican psalmody, as

assume, therefore, that the example is regular, though only one instance of its type survives, and that similar melodic solutions would be produced whenever similar textual conditions prevailed.

The section of the phrase projected on columns a to d is the most variable part of the pattern. This is typical of all phrases of the eighth-mode tracts, where endings are uniform and textual differences are accommodated with flexible adaptation procedures at the beginning of the phrase. Even here, though, the variation is only an index of the variety of textual environments and not a sign of any tendency to create unmotivated melodic diversity. The melodic figures in columns b and d are associated with stressed syllables when the number of syllables permits such a distribution.[6] In rows IV and X it does not, and that accounts for the weak syllables in column d. The figures in columns a and c always declaim weak syllables and are omitted when the number of syllables does not suffice to require their use.

Phrase K. (See Table 2.) The section of the melodic pattern projected on columns a, b and c is anacrustic and is employed as needed. This is followed by a segment of plain or embellished recitation on *c* in column d. The anacrusis and recitation are arranged in such a way that the final accent comes out on the melisma beginning in column e. Observe that the final accent is on the ultima in row 2. The scribes of the Old Roman manuscripts consistently treat trisyllabic Hebrew words, such as *manasse*, *beniamin*, *cherubim* and *israhel*, in this way.[7] The normal place for the ultima, which is ordinarily weak, is on the final six-note figure in

set forth in the *Processionarium iuxta ritum S. Ordinis Praedicatorum* (Rome, 1949), which claims to transmit thirteenth-century usage. For a full discussion of this entire matter, see M. Y. Chen, 'Toward a Grammar of Singing: Tune–Text Association in Gregorian Chant', *Music Perception*, 1 (1983), pp. 84–122.

[6] Primary and secondary stress have been determined by the trisyllable rule: all polysyllables are proparoxytone if the penult is light or weak; otherwise they are paroxytone. In longer words, secondary stress is placed on all even-numbered syllables preceding the primary stress (Chen, 'Toward a Grammar of Singing', p. 89). Atonic polysyllables (prepositions, particles and true copulative conjunctions), exemplifying Chen's Rule 4 (*ibid.*, p. 93), are declaimed as if they bore normal stress. The same rule specifies that monosyllables are declaimed as stressed or unstressed according to phrasal patterns. An example of the former is *nos* in line I; an example of the latter is *te* in line V.

[7] Again, the Old Roman practice is consistent with thirteenth-century Dominican usage as transmitted in the modern liturgical books of the Dominican rite, rather than with the modern Gregorian practice described in the *Antiphonale monasticum*, p. 1225. See Chen, 'Toward a Grammar of Singing', p. 108.

Text declamation as a determinant of melodic form

Table 2 *Phrase K (verse-final)*

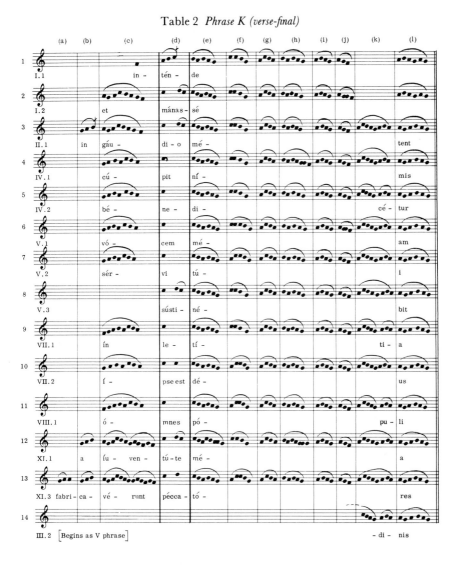

column l, and the preceding figure in column k is subdivided (see rows 5, 9 and 11) when an extra weak syllable occurs between the final accented syllable and the ultima. In this respect the version in row 5 is clearly in error, an error preserved in all three sources, since it misreads *benedicétur* as proparoxytone. The version in row 1 does not observe the normal accent placement, but is prevented from doing so by an insufficient number of syllables.

The melisma projected in columns e to j exhibits no variants except casual ones of very low status. The leap from *G* to *c* across the boundary of columns e and f alternates between direct and partly filled-in versions employing *a* as an incomplete passing note. The remaining casual variants are routine and in any case infrequent. The uniformity of this melisma, like its counterpart in phrase F, is remarkable. In rows 1 and 2, the absence of the figure in column k and the reversal of the normal figure in column l (*a–b–a–G–a–G* instead of *a–G–a–b–a–G*) are conditioned variants coincident with the lack of a weak final syllable at the end of the phrase. Within their sub-category as defined by the textual environment, they are uniform.

Phrase P. (See Table 3.) Observe first of all the uniformity of the short flourish on the final syllable (column h). The first twenty-four examples are invariant. The version in row 25, which substantially weakens the cadential effect of the figure normally occurring in that position, may be conditioned by a reluctance to make a caesura between *quis* and *sustinebit*, reflecting the strong syntactical link between predicate and pronominal subject. The version in row 26 is a special case. Although it begins as a P phrase, it cannot end as one, because it falls at the end of a verse. The brevity of the text *quia mota est* must have presented the cantor with a problem. He cannot be faulted for beginning the passage as a P phrase, since the medial cadence that precedes it has a tendency to stimulate P phrases that is practically never suppressed; M and P phrases go together as antecedent–consequent pairs. Still, he must have seen the end coming much too fast. He deals with the situation by carefully avoiding the characteristic melisma that marks the end of P phrases and employing instead a unique melisma specially formed so as better to resemble the endings of phrases that normally occur in verse-final positions: the twice-sung figure descending to *E* a third below the final is particularly suggestive of a similar repeated figure in the verse-final phrase K_1.[8]

---

[8] The agreement of the three sources in the transmission of this unique melisma adds further weight to the speculation that the copyists had a written tradition to which they could refer in non-standard cases. For examples of phrase K_1, to which the passage in question is

Table 3 *Phrase P (post-medial)*

Apart from these exceptions, treatment of the final accent is regular. When it falls on the penult, it is declaimed by the figure in

compared, see the Stäblein edition, p. 236 on the words *mittentes semina sua*, p. 237 on *dominorum suorum*, p. 238 on *domine sue* and p. 240 on *in hierusalem*.

Table 3 *continued*

column g beginning on the pitch *c*. Accented antepenults are accommodated by repeating the *c* (column f). The only departure from this norm is in row 2, where the anomaly of an accented ultima (*beniamín*) makes the familiar solutions for treatment of the accent inapplicable.

Moving now to the middle section of the phrase, observe that the employment of the melodic segment spanning columns b to e depends on the number of syllables. When there are too few of them, parts of that segment may be omitted. Note in row 3 that the graph itself can create certain specious problems. The ascending figure *a–c–b* that spans the interval from *F* at the beginning of the phrase to the stressed *c* near the end of the phrase belongs equally in column e and in column b; having to make a decision between these two projections when the figure occurs only once is an artificial by-product of the graphing technique.

The section of the melody projected in column d consists of various flexible recitation forms on *G*, on *c*, and in the *G–b* trichord that are characteristic in general of the Old Roman melodic idiom. They are employed as needed according to the number of syllables. The segment in column c exhibits only casual variants. There has been an attempt to employ the figure in column b to declaim an accented syllable when the number of syllables permits such a distribution. The segment in column a consists of the pitch *F* articulated as often as necessary to declaim the anacrusis of the phrase.

Phrase M. (See Table 4.) The most vivid punctuation in the verse is the medial cadence on *F* at the end of phrase M. The cadence functions as a point of reference, helping listeners and performers to orient themselves as they make their way through the circuitous melody. Having such an important structural and practical function, it is rarely omitted, and the frequency of its employment has resulted in a particular version of it becoming habitual. As Table 4 shows, the final approach to the cadence, comprising all the notes in column h and the last eight notes in column g, is utterly uniform in all twenty-seven examples. Having stereotyped solutions at orientation points must have been extremely useful to singers, since they could employ them without thinking and thus achieve effortless

Table 4 *Phrase M (medial)*

206

Table 4 *continued*

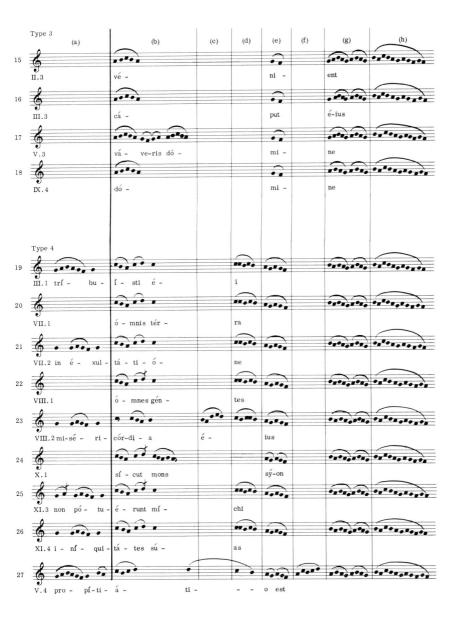

fluency while saving their concentration for parts of the verse that required more particular attention.

In spite of the uniformity of the final melisma, a cursory examination of the beginning and middle sections may give the impression that M phrases are subject to a rather liberal amount of variation. A closer look, however, reveals that the variation can be reduced to differences occurring between four sub-categories. Within the sub-categories variation is actually quite minimal. To the extent that the sub-categories can be distinguished on the basis of textual and contextual determinants, the melodic differences between them may be considered an index of those variables rather than manifestations of purely melodic contrast. It is important, therefore, to determine whether, and to what extent, the four observed varieties are independently distinguished by those other variables.

Phrase length is the chief distinguishing criterion; phrases of types 2 and 4 (the reference is to the four sub-heads into which Table 4 is divided) have more syllables on average than those of types 1 and 3, and the melodic differences between them are in part a conditioned response to that feature. Observe in particular that the phrase types with longer texts employ a distinct segment of recitation (column b), while the phrase types with shorter texts, having no need for it, lack a distinct recitation segment. Besides their brevity, the shorter phrase types are distinguished also by the manner of their articulation; they declaim psalm verses in which the first hemistich does not admit an internal caesura. Whereas phrases of types 2 and 4 occur with hemistichs consisting of two distinct grammatical or prosodic units:

Ita oculi nostri / ad dominum deum nostrum
Desiderium anime eius / tribuisti ei

phrases of types 1 and 3 are employed in the declamation of hemistichs which, for reasons of syntax or sheer brevity, are only weakly, or not at all, divisible into distinct phrases:

Excita potentiam tuam
Sana contritiones eius

M phrases are adapted to these shorter, more continuous texts by emerging somewhere in the middle of the phrase with little or no phrase articulation separating them from the I or V melody with which the phrases begin.

Although approximately equal in length, types 1 and 3 are distinguished from each other by their phrase environment. Type 1 phrases follow initial phrases of several types, but type 3 phrases invariably follow initial (V) phrases of type 3. In fact, the phrase sequence V (type 3) – M (type 3) is really one indivisible unit. Its division into two labelled constituents is merely a quantitative way of stating that it comprises both initial and medial phrase functions along with the salient features of each. There is no distinct phrase boundary; one observes simply that the melody, having begun as a V phrase, has assumed by the last or penultimate syllable the characteristic form of the medial punctuation melisma (i.e. the part common to all medial cadences projected in columns g and h).

I am unable to discover any textual or contextual conditions that may have motivated the melodic differences between types 2 and 4; they appear to exhibit genuine melodic contrast. Nevertheless, the tendency towards variety is constrained by a parallel tendency to limit variety within single tracts, as the clustered distribution of the two types shows (see Table 5; roman numerals denote tract numbers,[9] arabic numerals, verses).

Summing up, we can observe that symmetrical psalm verses comprising two balanced hemistichs, each divisible into two phrases, will tend to employ in the second phrase position an M phrase of type 2 or 4, and will be influenced in the selection by the type of M phrase employed elsewhere in the same tract. Psalm verses whose articulation is in three parts with the main caesura after the first part will usually avoid a melodic articulation before the caesura by employing an M phrase of type 1 or 3. The selection of types 1 and 3 is not random but is environmentally conditioned by the type of the V phrase that begins the verse.

As mentioned earlier, once allowances are made for conditioned variants that divide the examples into four sub-categories, it is fair to observe that M phrases are remarkably uniform. This can be verified by consulting Table 4. Observe, for example, the consistent treatment of word stress in phrases of types 1 and 4 (column b) and of type 2 (column c). In these three sub-categories the part of the final melisma that is invariant is actually much greater than the minimum common to the whole class, comprising the melodic

---

[9] The tracts discussed in this essay are numbered I to XI; the complete list is given below at the beginning of part II.

Table 5

Type 2	Type 4
I.2	III.1
IV.1	VII.1
IV.2	VII.2
IV.3	VIII.1
IX.4	VIII.2
X.1	X.1
X.2	XI.3
X.2	XI.4

segments in columns d, e, g and h. One could say, in fact, that this string forms the normal medial punctuation melisma and that the version in phrases of type 3 is abbreviated.

I have discovered no environmental motivation for the figure in column f; alternation in its use appears to be genuinely contrastive. Another variant unconditioned by the textual environment occurs in column c, mostly in phrases of type 2, where a prefix to the final melisma ascending eloquently to high *e* appears to compensate for the plain, psalmodic style of recitation in the first part of the phrase. In phrases of type 4 the anacrusis and recitation are already somewhat elaborate and therefore do not need that additional embellishment; nevertheless, one performance, the one in row 23, employs it anyway, thereby bringing about a kind of internal harmony with the preceding V phrase, which includes that same figure as an extraordinary constituent of its melodic make-up (see Table 6, row 9). Though not conditioned by the text, these variants may be conditioned by their melodic environment in complex and mutually complementary ways whose investigation goes beyond the scope of this article. Whatever the case may be, these examples of variation are isolated and do nothing to contradict the overwhelming impression of uniformity given by M phrases, an impression deriving from invariance within textually defined sub-categories that are every bit as uniform as phrases of types P, K and F.

I and V phrases. Phrases in tract-initial (I) and verse-initial (V) positions are presented in Tables 6 and 7. V phrases have been divided into three types and are relatively uniform within each type; note in particular the consistency of treatment of the principal word stresses. Types 1 and 3 have no discrete final boundary. Being

Table 6 *Phrase V (verse-initial)*

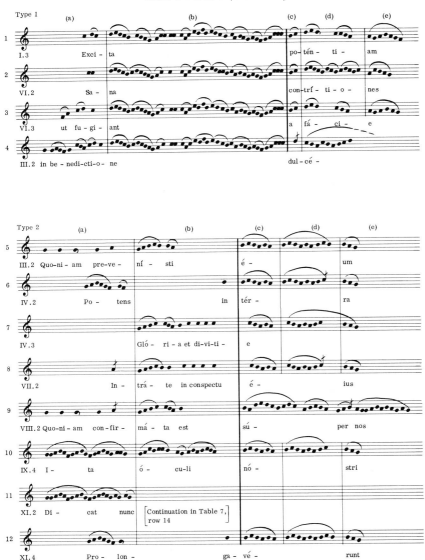

adapted to texts in which the first hemistich has no internal caesura, these versions of the V phrase flow into the following phrase, usually an M, with only a slight articulation or none at all.

Type 1 and type 3 phrases declaim texts of the same length; accordingly, the reason for the contrast between them must be

Table 6 *continued*

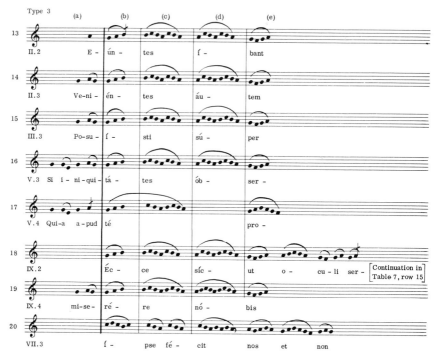

Table 7 *Phrase I (tract-initial)*

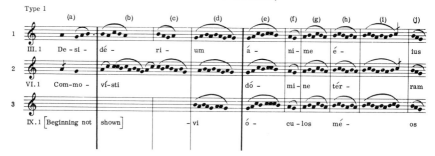

Table 7 *continued*

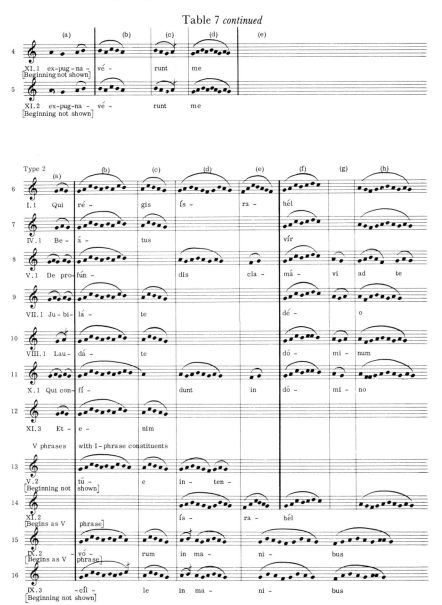

sought elsewhere than in the number of syllables. Texts of type 3 are narrative and, for the most part, in the indicative mood. (The example in row 19 is an exception.) Type 1, on the other hand, conspicuously displays texts in the imperative mood. Even the subjunctive in the purpose clause in row 3, *fugiant*, has the force of a volitive because of its dependence on the imperative *sana* in the main clause:

> Sana contritiones eius, quia mota est;
> Ut fugiant a facie arcus, ut liberentur electi tui.

In all probability, the extraordinary internal melisma in type 1 was motivated by the need for rhetorical emphasis on these words in the form of entreaty, whereas the more normal solution, when the text is merely narrative, is to employ the relatively less melismatic version of type 3. This is not a case of word-painting in the usual sense; the melisma in type 1 does not represent the semantic content of the words. The meanings of *excita* (arouse), *sana* (heal) and *fugiant* (escape) could hardly be more different. It is rather the case that the florid–non-florid alternation in the melody is coincident with the volitive–narrative alternation in the text. The music, in other words, mirrors not the direct referents of the words, but formal relations between the words. To the extent that such formal relations are a necessary condition for the communication of meaning, the music may be said to express the meaning of the words by mapping its formal relations congruently onto theirs. Moreover, these mappings are empirically verifiable in a way that can never be claimed by those who profess to find in plainchant instances of word-painting in the more familiar sense.[10]

V phrases of type 2 declaim texts from verses in which the first hemistich is relatively long and can be subdivided into two parts. The boundary between the parts is marked with a distinctive punctuation melisma that is basically uniform in pitch structure and syllable distribution (see Table 6, type 2, columns c, d and e). This melisma is the same one employed in I phrases of type 1 (Table 7, type 1, columns h, i and j), revealing the basic functional identity of the I and V phrase types. The melisma, like the ones punctuating the ends of F, K, P and M phrases, functions as a position marker, being associated in this case with the first of the four major cadence points in the verse. All V phrases have it, provided they have a cadence at all; in I phrases it alternates with a second punctuation melisma in a way that is coincident with phrase length. I phrases of type 2 are

---

[10] E.g. Johner, *Wort und Ton im Choral*, pp. 435–6. See also P. Ferretti, *Estetica gregoriana* (1934; repr. New York, 1977), p. 104.

shorter on average than those of type 1, and their different punctuation melismas are a consistent index of that textual contrast. It is to be emphasised that all five types of initial phrase are independently characterised by textual and contextual factors, and that the pattern of variation in five sub-categories cannot be accepted as evidence of variety or novelty sought for its own sake. Within the sub-types, where environmental conditions are roughly constant, the opportunity for novelty is rarely seized.

This is not to say that compositional novelty is shunned entirely. V phrases and especially I phrases exhibit more unconditioned variation than phrases of any other type. The initial phrase of tract II, *Qui seminant in lacrimis* (not shown), is unique, and the initial phrase of tract VI, *Commovisti*, contains a unique internal detail (Table 7, columns b and c). Tracts IX, *Ad te levavi*, and XI, *Sepe expugnaverunt me*, employ a distinctive prefix that occupies the extraordinary range of a fifth below the final, before regaining the normal starting position on *G* and proceeding to follow the more typical melodic outlines of the I phrase type.[11] *Sepe expugnaverunt me*, moreover, exhibits the unusual procedure of repeating this prefix, associated with the tract-initial position, at the beginning of an internal verse. The explanation in this case is clear. The internal verse repeats the text *Sepe expugnaverunt me* with which the tract begins; anything but an exact melodic repetition would obscure the syntactic and prosodic parallelism of the words:

Sepe expugnaverunt me a iuventute mea, dicat nunc israhel;
Sepe expugnaverunt me, etenim non potuerunt michi.

Wherever they occur, the instances of this special figure are virtually invariant, illustrating that even departures from the norm merge and form other norms within their own sub-group.

In the foregoing discussion, a distinction has been made between contrastive and non-contrastive variation. In order for variants to contrast with one another, they must alternate in the same environment. Variants that never occur in the same environment, whose

---

[11] The examples may be found in the Stäblein edition, pp. 236–40. The passage in question, treated here as a constituent of a larger I phrase, is identical with the motif that elsewhere forms the core of the phrase labelled R. Although contextual differences may justify the inconsistency of labelling, a more thorough study of the phrase, and of the composition of I phrases generally, may yet yield a more elegant, less *ad hoc* solution to this analytical problem. However, since the passage occurs only five times in the whole corpus of eighth-mode tracts, the resolution of its status will have no great effect on the general outcome.

distribution coincides exactly with that of the textual conditions, cannot be considered as melodically distinctive; they reflect only the different ways in which the same underlying melody is processed by the declamation rules so as to produce a good delivery of the text. Even when not realised, they must be regarded as latent in the basic melodic forms, as merely waiting, in a manner of speaking, for the right textual conditions to activate them.[12]

The first impression given by the Old Roman eighth-mode tracts is one of profuse variation. Even after generous allowances are made for casual variation, the impression remains of a tradition prodigal and undisciplined in its employment of melodic detail. Only after a persistent search for textual determinants do we discover the intricate patterns of coincidence that account for all but a small fraction of the observed variation. Most of the variation taken at its face value as evidence of the tracts' lack of thrift must be thrown out on the grounds that the variants are not true alternatives: they cannot be substituted for one another in the same environment. Only in the few remaining cases can we say that the variation is truly distinctive and therefore evidence of a purely melodic impulse to enrich the scope of the repertory. On balance, the Old Roman eighth-mode tracts reflect little esteem for the values of novelty and creative originality. On the contrary, they exhibit as high a level of discipline and thrift as one may find in any plainchant tradition.

II

One of the purposes of the foregoing discussion has been to establish the validity of the various phrase units as legitimate analytic categories. Within the terms of their definitions, which include the various automatic ways in which they adjust to textual conditions, they are fundamentally uniform. This uniformity within classes

[12] The notion of contrastive variation presented here is related in important ways to the linguistic concept of the phoneme. For a useful general introduction to this subject, see V. Fromkin and R. Rodman, *An Introduction to Language*, 2nd edn (New York, 1978), pp. 101–137.

More specific parallels to the phenomenon of contrast in plainchant may be found discussed in A. B. Lord's work on the oral epic, in which supposed departures from the expected prosody and vocabulary are shown to coincide with subtle disturbances in the poetic environment. Lord observed that singers, once they had solved a particular problem in verse-making, generally did not seek additional ways of expressing the same essential idea, so long as the poetic environment did not motivate them to do so. See *The Singer of Tales* (Cambridge, Mass., 1960), pp. 50–3.

makes distinctions between classes especially sharp, permitting contrast and ruling out the possibility of mistaken identity. Now it is possible to use these categories, indexed to simple cover symbols (M, P, K etc.), as a means of analysing the large-scale phrase structure of whole tracts without getting bogged down in small-scale differences that are irrelevant to phrase identity. The analyses, presented below, are mapped onto the texts in such a way as to show how the musical phrase structure responds to, and makes manifest, the phrase structure of the words.

I.   [$^\mathbf{I}$Qui regis israhel]   I   K
        [$^\mathbf{K}$intende]
    [$^\mathbf{P}$Qui deducis velud ovem ioseph]   P   M   P   K
       [$^\mathbf{M}$qui sedes super cherubim]
       [$^\mathbf{P}$appare coram effrem beniamin]
       [$^\mathbf{K}$et manasse]
    [$^\mathbf{V}$Excita potentiam tuam$^\mathbf{M}$]   V – M   P   F
       [$^\mathbf{P}$et veni] [$^\mathbf{F}$ut salvos facias nos]

II.   [$^\mathbf{I}$Qui seminant in lacrimis]   I   K
       [$^\mathbf{K}$in gaudio metent]
    [$^\mathbf{V}$Euntes ibant] [$^\mathbf{R}$et flebant]   V   R K_1
       [$^{\mathbf{K}1}$mittentes semina sua]
    [$^\mathbf{V}$Venientes autem venient$^\mathbf{M}$] [$^\mathbf{P}$in   V – M   P   F
       exultatione]
    [$^\mathbf{F}$portantes manipulos suos]

III.   [$^\mathbf{I}$Desiderium anime eius] [$^\mathbf{M}$tribuisti ei]   I   M   P K_2
       [$^\mathbf{P}$et voluntate labiorum eius]
       [$^{\mathbf{K}2}$non fraudasti eum]
    [$^\mathbf{V}$Quoniam prevenisti eum]   V   V – K
       [$^\mathbf{V}$in benedictione dulcedinis$^\mathbf{K}$]
    [$^\mathbf{V}$Posuisti super caput eius$^\mathbf{M}$]   V – M   P   F
       [$^\mathbf{P}$coronam] [$^\mathbf{F}$de lapide pretioso]

IV.   [$^\mathbf{I}$Beatus vir] [$^\mathbf{M}$qui timet dominum]   I   M   P   K
       [$^\mathbf{P}$in mandatis eius] [$^\mathbf{K}$cupit nimis]
    [$^\mathbf{V}$Potens in terra] [$^\mathbf{M}$erit semen eius]   V   M   P   K
       [$^\mathbf{P}$generatio rectorum]
         [$^\mathbf{K}$benedicetur]
    [$^\mathbf{V}$Gloria et divitie] [$^\mathbf{M}$in domo eius]   V   M   P   F
       [$^\mathbf{P}$et iustitia eius manet] [$^\mathbf{F}$in seculum
       seculi]

v.   [$^\mathbf{I}$De profundis clamavi ad te domine$^\mathbf{M}$]   I – M   P   K
      [$^\mathbf{P}$domine exaudi] [$^\mathbf{K}$vocem meam]
    [$^\mathbf{V}$Fiant aures tue intendentes$^\mathbf{M}$]   V – M   P   K
      [$^\mathbf{P}$in oratione] [$^\mathbf{K}$servi tui]
    [$^\mathbf{V}$Si iniquitates observaveris domine$^\mathbf{M}$]   V – M   P   K
      [$^\mathbf{P}$domine quis] [$^\mathbf{K}$sustinebit]
    [$^\mathbf{V}$Quia apud te propitiatio est$^\mathbf{M}$]   V – M   P   F
      [$^\mathbf{P}$et propter legem tuam] [$^\mathbf{F}$sustinui
      te domine]

vi.   [$^\mathbf{I}$Commovisti domine terram]   I   K$_2$
      [$^\mathbf{K2}$et conturbasti eam]
    [$^\mathbf{V}$Sana contritiones eius$^\mathbf{M}$]   V – M   P – K
      [$^\mathbf{P}$quia mota est$^\mathbf{K}$]
    [$^\mathbf{V}$Ut fugiant a facie arcus$^\mathbf{M}$]   V – M   P   F
      [$^\mathbf{P}$ut liberentur] [$^\mathbf{F}$electi tui]

vii.   [$^\mathbf{I}$Iubilate deo] [$^\mathbf{M}$omnis terra]   I   M   P   K
      [$^\mathbf{P}$servite domino] [$^\mathbf{K}$in letitia]
    [$^\mathbf{V}$Intrate in conspectu eius] [$^\mathbf{M}$in   V   M   P   K
      exultatione]
      [$^\mathbf{P}$scitote quod dominus] [$^\mathbf{K}$ipse est
      deus]
    [$^\mathbf{V}$Ipse fecit nos et non ipsi nos$^\mathbf{M}$]   V – M   P   F
      [$^\mathbf{P}$nos autem populus eius] [$^\mathbf{F}$et oves
      pascue eius]

viii.   [$^\mathbf{I}$Laudate dominum] [$^\mathbf{M}$omnes gentes]   I   M   P   K
      [$^\mathbf{P}$et collaudate eum] [$^\mathbf{K}$omnes populi]
    [$^\mathbf{V}$Quoniam confirmata est super nos]   V   M   P   F
      [$^\mathbf{M}$misericordia eius]
      [$^\mathbf{P}$et veritas domini] [$^\mathbf{F}$manet in
      eternum]

ix.   [$^\mathbf{I}$Ad te levavi oculus meos]   I   K$_2$
      [$^\mathbf{K2}$qui abitas in celo]
    [$^\mathbf{V}$Ecce sicut oculi servorum in manibus]   V   K$_1$
      [$^\mathbf{K1}$dominorum suorum]
    [$^\mathbf{V}$Et sicut oculi ancille in manibus]   V   K$_1$
      [$^\mathbf{K1}$domine sue]
    [$^\mathbf{V}$Ita oculi nostri] [$^\mathbf{M}$ad dominum deum   V   M   P   V – M   F
      nostrum]
      [$^\mathbf{P}$donec misereatur nobis]
      [$^\mathbf{V}$miserere nobis domine$^\mathbf{M}$]
       [$^\mathbf{F}$miserere nobis]

x.   [^{I}Qui confidunt in domino] [^{M}sicut   I   M   R – M   P   K$_1$
       mons syon]
     [^{R}non commovebitur in eternum^{M}]
     [^{P}qui abitat] [^{K1} in hierusalem]
     [^{K2} Montes] [^{M}in circuitu eius]   K$_2$ M   P   M   P   F
     [^{P}et dominus] [^{M}in circuitu populi
       sui]
     [^{P}ex hoc nunc] [^{F}et usque in seculum]

xi.   [^{I}Sepe expugnaverunt me] [^{K} a   I   K
       iuventute mea]
     [^{V}Dicat nunc israhel]   V   I   K$_1$
       [^{I}Sepe expugnaverunt me] [^{K1} a
         iuventute mea]
     [^{I}Etenim] [^{M}non potuerunt michi]   I   M   P   K
       [^{P}Supra dorsum meum]
       [^{K}fabricaverunt peccatores]
     [^{V}Prolongaverunt] [^{M}iniquitates suas]   V   M   P   F
       [^{P}dominus iustus concidet] [^{F}cervices
       peccatorum]

Tracts IV, V, VI, VII and VIII are basically regular and require no comment. The remaining six tracts all exhibit irregularities of phrase structure that could easily lead casual observers to conclude that they are unsystematic. In almost every case, however, it will be seen that the irregularities of musical phrasing correspond directly to irregularities of prosody or syntax that rule out declamation according to the standard four-phrase melodic pattern and demand special treatment.

I. *Qui regis israhel* (Ps. 79): The most peculiar aspect of the reading that the Old Roman tract imposes on these psalm lines is the full stop after *intende*. A more natural reading would place a caesura after *intende* and save the full stop for *ioseph*. Such a reading would produce more balanced prosody and would observe the procedure, typical of the psalms, of placing in the second hemistich (*qui deducis . . . ioseph*) a paraphrase of the first (*Qui regis israhel*). Be that as it may, the reading imposed by the Old Roman tract is not arbitrary or meaningless. The first two verses of this tract contain three noun clauses governed by the vocative case and two verb phrases in the imperative mood in the following order:

[N]   [V]   [N]   [N]   [V]

219

(The second verb phrase, *appare coram effrem beniamin et manasse*, is taken to include its prepositional modifier.) The reading imposed by the melody emphasises the implicit parallelism in the passage by arranging the two imperative verb phrases at the ends of their respective verses, thus giving them identical positions in the prosodic structure and enabling them to be declaimed with the same melodic inflection. This arrangement produces a first verse that is too short to be declaimed with the normal four-phrase melodic pattern. For that reason, a shorter version of the pattern is substituted in which only the first and fourth components (I and K) are used.

I can find no intrinsic explanation for the employment of a P phrase at the beginning of the second verse. It may be a vestige of an older performance in which the preceding segment, *Qui regis israhel intende*, was declaimed as a half-verse ending with a medial cadence. That such performances actually occurred is shown by the version in Frankish transmission, which declaims the passage in exactly that way.[13] The Frankish version, however, is evidently garbled. Instead of continuing after the medial cadence on *intende* with the music expected for normal second hemistichs ending on a full stop, it declaims the words *velut ovem Joseph* with another medial cadence, thus failing to define the passage ending on *Joseph* as a discrete verse, even though the following text, *Qui sedes super cherubim*, declaimed as a V phrase, is clearly a new verse beginning. Confusion continues in the second verse, where a full stop, clearly marked by the Frankish version of the K phrase, is placed in mid-sentence after *Ephraim*, obliging the singer to declaim the remaining text in that phrase as a discrete verse, employing another V phrase on *Benjamin* and another K phrase on *Manasse*.

Although the Old Roman version is not nearly so irregular as the Frankish, both versions show signs of confusion in the performances that preceded them in transmission, caused perhaps by the ambiguous phrase structure of the words. In Frankish transmission, however, a particularly bad performance was not recognised as such and became the basis for the officially sanctioned version, frozen in musical notation for all time. On the Old Roman side, despite an unsteady transmission evident in the traces of an earlier form that interpreted the present second verse as the second hemistich of verse

---

[13]   *Liber usualis* (Tournai, 1953), p. 351.

1, the version that was eventually written down has managed to make sense of the text by declaiming it in a reasonable way. The Old Roman tradition, because it was a living tradition, was self-correcting. Bad performances undoubtedly occurred, but single performances, whether bad or good, rarely had the opportunity to initiate a new stemma. The continuation of the tradition depended on knowledge of structure which the carriers of the tradition inferred from many examples of the given type. In such a tradition single bad performances would have the tendency to be dismissed as anomalous.

II. *Qui seminant* (Ps. 125): The initial verse is too short to be subdivided into four parts; it is declaimed with the first and last segments of the four-phrase pattern, employing the same solution already observed in the first verse of *Qui regis israhel*. Combining this verse with the following one to make a single larger verse is out of the question, because the next phrase, *Euntes ibant...*, introduces the first half of a parallel construction, of which the complementary half, *Venientes autem venient...*, occurs at the beginning of the third verse. Declaiming the *Euntes* phrase as the second hemistich of the first verse and the *Venientes* phrase as the first hemistich of the following verse would have obscured the parallel structure obviously intended by the psalmist.

The parallelism also explains why *Euntes* and *Venientes* are both declaimed with V phrases of type 3. A more balanced phrasing of the third verse:

> [Venientes autem venient] [in exultatione]
> [portantes] [manipulos suos]

would have required a V phrase of type 2 (i.e. the type used to declaim long initial phrases that are separated from the following M phrase with a clear caesura). Such a V phrase would have spoiled the parallelism with the preceding verse. By choosing the parallel V phrase of type 3, the cantor obligates himself to run it into the following M phrase without an intervening cadence. This, in turn, requires that he declaim the verse in three phrases: [V M] [P] [F], placing the medial cadence before the natural midpoint of the verse, and combining *portantes manipulos suos* into one long phrase at the end. In this way the prosodic balance of the verse has been compromised for the sake of emphasis on the *Euntes–Venientes* parallelism, which, after all, is one of the excerpt's most salient features.

The second verse employs an R phrase in its interior instead of the usual M and P phrases.[14] The choice of this phrase, with its characteristic descent to low *C*, to declaim the word *flebant* (they wept) exemplifies text expression in the special sense discussed above in the section on I and V phrases. The word *flebant* has a certain meta-linguistic quality, describing something actually done by the voice. It does not require a stretch of the imagination to suppose that singers, when they came upon such words, might choose to act out their meaning in some stylised way. No one would claim, of course, that the melodic setting of *flebant* bears any resemblance to the sound of weeping. The special setting of this word, spanning the rarely occurring fifth below the final, merely sets it apart, putting it, as it were, in quotation marks. To the extent that this is a case of text expression at all, it is text expression of a structural kind. The contrast in the music between ordinary and special melodic ranges is mapped congruently onto the textual contrast between ordinary words and words used meta-linguistically to refer to actual vocal sounds.

III. *Desiderium* (Ps. 20): The Old Roman version of this tract reflects a decision to declaim the segments beginning *Quoniam* and *Posuisti* as separate verses, even though the form and content of the poetry strongly favour their interpretation as paired hemistichs of a single verse. Perhaps singers did not favour the long phrases that a simple division of the excerpt into four parts would have created. Having made that decision, however, the singer confronts the fact that there is too little text to accommodate a subdivision into twice four parts, which the interpretation of the two main constituents as separate verses would normally entail. The peculiar melodic structure reflects the singer's predicament. It is perhaps a sign of indecision as to whether the segment *Quoniam ... dulcedinis* is really a discrete verse that it has an extended beginning employing two versions of the V phrase consecutively, and then closes in haste by simply adopting the last thirteen notes of the normal full stop (K).

---

[14] The example may be found in the Stäblein edition, p. 236; see also p. 240 on the words *non commovebitur*. For further discussion of the R phrase, see n. 11.

IX. *Ad te levavi* (Ps. 122): The declamation of lines 2 and 3 as discrete verses, in spite of their brevity, and the melodic identity of the last two-thirds of each verse, employing a special form of the closing phrase (K_1 instead of K), give special emphasis to the formal repetition embodied in the two *sicut* clauses. The simpler form:

[**V**Ecce sicut oculi servorum] [**M**in manibus dominorum suorum]
[**P**Et sicut oculi ancille] [**K**in manibus domine sue]

would have obscured the formal repetition and would also have implied stronger closure at the end of the second clause than at the end of the first. This effect is clearly undesirable, since it would have misrepresented the equal dependence of the two *sicut* clauses on the following *ita* clause that complements them. The unusual melodic phrasing of the long final verse of this tract reflects the division of the text into twice three phrases, too few to be organised into two ordinary four-phrase verses, but too many to be declaimed as an ordinary single verse.

X. *Qui confidunt* (Ps. 124): The peculiarities in the order and distribution of melodic constituents in verse 1 of this tract may not be novelties at all, but simply the most natural response to the poetic environment. The text consists of two noun clauses acting as subjects of their respective sentences: *Qui confidunt in domino* and *qui abitat in hierusalem*, and two predicates: *sicut mons syon* (the verb *to be* understood) and *non commovebitur in eternum*, arranged in chiastic order (subject–predicate–predicate–subject). The music responds to the chiasmus by placing medial cadences at the ends of the two internal constituents, balanced on both sides of a central R phrase. Although the musical chiasmus cannot be complete, reflecting a given of the system that requires I and K phrases respectively at the beginnings and ends of verses, a vivid chiastic pattern spanning the entire verse does obtain between the main cadence notes (*G* on *domino*, *F* on *syon*, *F* on *eternum* and *G* on *hierusalem*).

The second verse likewise exhibits the repetition of an M phrase after an intervening middle constituent. In this case, the text expresses a proportional relationship in which the elements compared (*Montes* with *dominus* and *eius* with *populi sui*) are placed in the same position in the prosodic structure. The music reinforces the proportional relationship by declaiming the two predicates with identical melodies (both are M phrases of type 2). Ordinarily this would not be possible, because the second predicate would have to end with a full stop (K or F); here, however, the tag phrase *ex hoc nunc et usque in seculum* permits the final cadence to be postponed, making room for the repetition of M where it can reinforce the syntactical parallelism.

XI. *Sepe expugnaverunt* (Ps. 128): The most immediately evident pecularity of this tract is the declamation of the two phrases containing the words *a iuventute mea* as K phrases despite the poetic structure, which places them at the ends of half-lines followed in each case by a complementary hemistich. Accepting that as a given, however, the declamation of *Dicat nunc israhel* and *Etenim* as initial phrases is obligatory; the conclusion of the preceding phrases with full stops leaves no other alternative. If the singer then insists on emphasising the repetition of the opening words *Sepe expugnaverunt me* by singing them to the same music with which they were declaimed in the first verse – or, perhaps, if he simply follows the path of least resistance – the result will be the employment of two initial phrases in a row, a procedure that is relatively rare, but certainly not outside the bounds of normal practice in so far as we can infer it from the surviving examples. Frankish sources transmit a different solution to the problem. There the phrase *Dicat nunc Israel* is declaimed as a normal first hemistich, employing I and M, and concluding with a medial cadence. This obliges the following *saepe expugnaverunt me* to be recited as a post-medial (P) phrase, thereby vitiating the rhetorical effect of the textual repetition. Indeed, the Roman cantor on whose performance the Old Roman version is based may have seen the textual repetition coming and deliberately avoided the medial phrase that would normally occur before it just so that he could avoid the post-medial phrase on the critical words and declaim them instead with a repetition of the opening music (I).

Old Roman and Frankish sources both transmit the same reading of the last two verses, which incorrectly groups *Etenim non potuerunt michi* (for truly they were powerless against me) with *Supra dorsum meum fabricaverunt peccatores*, the beginning of an entirely new sentence. It is easy to imagine better readings of these lines and of the whole tract for that matter, and our ability to do so, based on knowledge abstracted from the other examples, was undoubtedly matched by the ability of the best Roman singers to produce such readings in performance. In criticising the particular version that is transmitted in writing, we must be careful to remember that it is only one example of what the tradition was capable of producing. In a living tradition, where examples are the result of the application of rules rather than repetitions by rote of fixed exemplars, especially in the performances of the best singers, the forms that any given chant may assume are limited only by the formal constraints that all the examples in its mode and genre jointly embody. To the extent that we are able to learn those constraints, we are in a better position to appreciate the repertory's true scope and to put mediocre and bad examples transmitted in writing in the proper perspective.

III

In his monograph *Wort und Ton im Choral,* Dominicus Johner set himself to the task of showing that Gregorian chant, like all great vocal music, is expressive of its texts. At the outset one is struck by Johner's candour in observing that two-thirds of Gregorian chants are incapable of expressing their texts in any of the expected ways. The overpowering rigour of their formal constraints, which he characterised as a *Wille zur Form,* was an obstacle, in his view, to the kind of melodic freedom that he regarded as necessary for true text expression; accordingly, the tendency of chants to be expressive of their texts, their *Wille zum Ausdruck,* could be realised only to the extent that the *Wille zur Form* was suppressed.[15] It followed from this view that chant types with the strongest formal constraints, tracts being the foremost example, were the least likely to conform to the demands of text expression.[16]

There is considerable irony in Johner's determination to conceive of expressiveness and formal rigour as mutually exclusive principles, since it caused him to rule out the most pertinent category of evidence and to exclude from consideration the very genres of plainchant that offered his investigation, at least presumptively, the greatest hope of success. Lacking our structuralist perspective, he took no notice of the indispensable role of structure in the expression of meaning. Just as it is the formal properties of sentences that enable

[15]   Johner, *Wort und Ton im Choral,* pp. 429–32.
[16]   *Ibid.,* p. 213.

225

words to form meaningful utterances, so it is precisely the most routine formal properties of plainchant that give it the capacity to project the poetic and syntactic structures of its texts in a way that makes them plain to the understanding and vivid to the imagination.

It is unfair to chide Johner for failing to achieve more than he did. The assumptions shared by all chant scholars of his day effectively limited the study of text expression to the search for those rare and debatable instances where the melody might be regarded as forming an analogue to the semantic reference of the words. Johner rationalised the meagreness of his findings with the observation that Gregorian chant is sacred music and that the decorum of the liturgy required it to employ only the most subtle forms of text expression. In a sense he was right. The means of expression in plainchant are so unspectacular as to be commonplace. In directing us to look for those means in the most ordinary material, the words of Adalbert Stifter cited by Johner as a reminder of plainchant's expressive restraint assume for us a renewed validity: 'The sublime does not present itself with fanfare.'[17]

Brandeis University

---

[17] 'Das Erhabene posaunt sich nicht aus'. *Ibid.*, p. 430.

JO-ANN REIF

MUSIC AND GRAMMAR: IMITATION AND ANALOGY IN MORALES AND THE SPANISH HUMANISTS

The relationship of mass composition to the study of rhetoric has occupied many writers interested in perceiving the two as analogous in organisation, vocabulary and persuasive goals. Grammar belonged to the choirboy's education but, more importantly, the method of grammar permeated the general teaching method for other subjects as well. Material, such as questions or disputations, was organised into the similar and the dissimilar, so that working from a model and transfer by analogy were the principal means of making connections between statements and ideas. This essay is concerned with the opportunities available in sixteenth-century Spain for the study of grammar and music and how these possibilities affected the leading Spanish composer of the time, Cristóbal de Morales. In this discussion, Juan Bermudo's treatise *Declaración de instrumentos*[1] is important. Not only does it name leading humanists and composers, and present its theoretical remarks in the language of rhetoric; Morales, who had been in close contact with Bermudo at the Marchena estate of the Duke of Arcos, recommended the treatise. Thus Bermudo, a young Minorite monk, reveals a good deal about Morales by both direct quotation and analogy, and in effect provides a more rounded intellectual impression of the composer, who otherwise expressed himself only in his musical works and their dedications. It can be deduced from musical quotations that Morales is Bermudo's model composer, and by analogy that Morales, versed in rhetoric and imitation, understood the application of these rules in musical composition. In his thorough

[1] J. Bermudo, *Declaración de instrumentos* (Osuna, 1555); facs. ed. M. S. Kastner, Documenta Musicologica, series I/11 (Basle, 1957).

appraisal of musical tradition, theory and practice, Bermudo assumes the function of a critic in the modern sense.

Morales was born in Seville which, by the sixteenth century, was very cosmopolitan. The Casa de Contratación, the only custom-house for treasure from the New World, was founded there in 1503, but Seville had always been a city of traders, rich merchants and aristocratic families who owned fleets of trading ships. This native population was increased after 1503 by an influx from other parts of Europe (Genoese, Germans, Flemings and Portuguese), while Spaniards from other parts of the peninsula also moved to Seville. By 1553, fifty years after the founding of the Casa de Contratación, and the accepted year of Morales' death, the population of Seville had doubled.[2] This increased population intensified the already hetero-geneous character of the city's inhabitants which included *Moriscos* (Moslems living under Christian rule) and *conversos* (Jews nominally converted to Christianity). The *conversos*, who counted among their number some of the members of the richest merchants and nobility, made frequent alliances with important families to underwrite ventures to the New World. In intellectual circles, they made up a good proportion of the clergy and frequently had the best university educations, often in legal studies. In contrast to these groups, Seville had its share of drifters, beggars and landless peasants who had come to seek a living in the city, an aspect of life most memorably portrayed in Mateo Alemán's picaresque novel, *Guzmán de Alfarache*.[3]

Educational opportunities in Seville at the beginning of the sixteenth century existed in monasteries and convents, and within the next two decades new schools were founded. For advanced studies one went to Salamanca or to Italy. In the early years of the sixteenth century, a charter was drawn up for a *colegio* and university in Seville at the instigation of the archdeacon Rodrigo Fernández de Santaella, but he died in 1509, his project uncompleted. He had

---

[2]   R. Pike, *Aristocrats and Traders: Sevillian Society in the Sixteenth Century* (Ithaca, N.Y., 1972), pp. 6–7.

[3]   The picaresque novel had its genesis in the conditions of the poor in many Spanish cities of the period. The two non-censored (i.e. printable) examples are *Lazarillo de Tormes*, set in Salamanca, and *Guzmán de Alfarache*, written by the Sevillian Mateo Alemán. In these novels the central character, who is also the narrator, is born in extreme poverty, usually illegitimate, and lives by instinct and his wits, surviving encounters with swindling masters and criminals in the most sordid conditions, particularly hunger.

studied at the Spanish school in Bologna and had brought Italian ideas about education back to Seville. The university project was finally realised by the cathedral chapter, which acted to admit the first students in 1518.[4] Other schools in Seville included the Colegio Mayor de Santo Tomás Aquino, founded in 1516. Run by the Dominicans, it was meant for members of their order, although non-ecclesiastics were admitted to study Latin and scholastic philo-sophy. A little later the Jesuits founded a school, the Colegio de San Hermenegildo, where studies of a more humanist orientation were offered.[5] In addition, the thirty-eight religious houses in and around Seville offered some kind of instruction. The Hieronymite and Minorite houses, outside the city, appear to have been centres of learning for the unlikely reason that they were suspected of Protes-tant (i.e. reformist) leanings. (The Hieronymite movement, which pressed for reforms and more critical readings of the texts of St Paul and St Augustine, was active in Spain; it is interesting to note that there was a strong covert Protestant community in Seville.) At the cathedral school itself the choirboys lived in a large house of their own; they assisted at the daily cathedral services, and studied the subjects of the trivium – logic, grammar and rhetoric. They were also frequently engaged to sing and act in entertainments at the houses of noble and rich families, such as the wedding of Charles V and Isabella of Portugal on 10 March 1526.[6]

Morales was a chorister at the cathedral from some time after 1503 until 1526, the time of his first appointment as *maestro de capilla*, and he refers to this good education in the dedication of his *Missarum liber primus* of 1544. Here he states that he devoted himself to the study of the liberal arts so that no one in his own discipline would question his proficiency in the other fields.[7] His remarks imply that his fellow musicians had certain expectations in education and that these must have included proficiency in the subjects of the trivium. The Latin of

---

[4] Pike, p. 56. Although a curriculum of the time could not be found during research for this paper, it may be assumed that the programme of study was similar to that of Alcalá de Henares, founded in 1508 with humanist aims.

[5] Pike, pp. 66–7.

[6] R. Stevenson, *Spanish Cathedral Music in the Golden Age* (Berkeley, 1961), pp. 8–9.

[7] 'Cuius si in maximis, praestantissimisque rebus haud quaquam cognita est industria, certe in his, que liberalium artium disciplinis continentur, cum meae me vitae ratio ab ineunte aetate intentum exercuisset, elaboravi sedulo, ut ne hoc meum studium ab his contemni possit, qui artem Musicam tractarent.' H. Anglès, ed., *Cristóbal de Morales: Opera omnia*, Monumentos de la Música Española 11 (Madrid and Barcelona, 1952), pp. 48–9.

Morales' dedication to the *Missarum liber primus* is a model of humanist style, while his use of Spanish, particularly in correspondence with Juan Bermudo, suggests a solid training in the use of language. During Morales' youth, Seville was probably the best place in Spain to study music; since the later fifteenth century it had ranked with Salamanca in importance for musical study. Two treatises and the first two printed Spanish music books appeared in Seville, in 1492 and 1494.[8] Several composers who had been active at the court of the Catholic Monarchs, Ferdinand and Isabella, also served in turn as *maestro de capilla* of Seville Cathedral.[9] It seems that the city was second only to the court as a musical centre. The *maestros* between 1503 and 1526, the most likely period of Morales' choir membership, were Francisco de la Torre, Alonso de Alva, Juan de Valera, Fernando de Solís, Pedro de Escobar and Pedro Fernández de Castilleja, and it was Castilleja who was still *maestro de capilla* in 1545, when Morales returned to Spain from Rome. All of these composers, with the exception of de Solís, are represented in the *Cancionero musical de Palacio*. But of all the composers born in Seville, Francisco de Peñalosa is the best-documented and also the most prolific. He had connections at the court of the monarchs and, although not a *maestro de capilla*, served at Seville Cathedral; he also sang in the papal choir from 1517 until 1521, the year of Leo x's death. In 1516, the cathedral chapter required that Peñalosa return directly to participate in cathedral administration. Peñalosa's first duty was to report on the teaching of Latin to the choirboys. Secondly, he was to draw up a curriculum for ex-choirboys, who were educated at the expense of the cathedral. Both of these requests by the chapter show their concern for the quality of education at the cathedral. The second, more interesting project suggests that the school had ambitious educational aims and perhaps offered more

---

[8] R. Stevenson, 'Morales, Cristóbal de', *The New Grove Dictionary of Music and Musicians*, ed. S. Sadie, 20 vols. (London, 1980), xii, p. 553.

[9] Ferdinand and Isabella held court in various places, although Toledo was their principal seat. Isabella reigned over Castille-León from 1474; Ferdinand, over Aragon from 1479. His holdings included the Kingdom of the Two Sicilies and, later in his reign, most of Navarre. Isabella died in 1504, Ferdinand in 1516. Their issue became the first ruler to inherit a unified Spain. Unfortunately, this was Juana 'la Loca' who was married to Felipe 'el Hermoso' of Austria, the son of Maximilian of Austria; the son of Felipe and Juana was Charles i of Spain and v of the Holy Roman Empire. Felipe el Hermoso died in 1506, and Ferdinand was called back as regent. He reigned as Ferdinand v. The 'Catholic' in the title 'Reyes Católicos' referred to the universality and oneness of the monarchy.

subjects than other choir schools. Peñalosa must have been considered an authority by the chapter as he was in touch with at least one Italian humanist, Lucio Marineo (who taught at Salamanca), and commanded good Latin. He evidently sympathised with humanist ideas and probably implemented them in his curriculum. Peñalosa's works show that his musical interests were wide. In his *Missa Ave Maria peregrina* the Agnus Dei combines the plainsong 'Salve regina' with the tenor, in retrograde, of Hayne van Ghizeghem's *De tous biens plaine*. That Peñalosa's *Sancta Mater istud agas* has been attributed to Josquin is evidence of his skilful polyphonic style, probably the most competent of any Spanish composer before Morales.[10] Peñalosa returned to Seville Cathedral for a last sojourn in March 1525, when he presented papal bulls ordering that he be made treasurer of the cathedral. He stayed until his death in 1528.

Although it is not known with whom Morales studied (the notices for him in the capitular acts are few), Peñalosa and Escobar are the most likely candidates. That Morales did not have a specific teacher or may have had only an adviser would fit with the concept of *imitatio*. Working from a musical model does not necessarily mean that the author of the model must be present, and most humanists' models were drawn from the remote past. When first-rate models are available, a guide through the material is a priority, and in Peñalosa and Escobar, the cathedral services and the school, Morales had the necessary models and guides.

In addition to religious institutions, a certain amount of private patronage existed in Seville. The most prominent member of the nobility was the Duke of Medina Sidonia, owner of extensive lands and a fleet of trading vessels to the New World, and an income estimated at 55,000 ducats in the early years of the reign of Charles v.[11] The Duke of Medina Sidonia is of some importance here because in 1503 one of his household singers was a Cristóbal de Morales, who may well have been the composer's father.[12] The principal rival to Medina Sidonia was the house of Arcos, one of whose members, Don Luis Cristóbal Ponce de León, Duke of Arcos (1518–73), was a patron of Morales. The duke was a young man when Morales

---

[10] R. Stevenson, 'Peñalosa, Francisco de', *The New Grove Dictionary*, xiv, pp. 347–8.
[11] Pike, p. 27. The next income below the duke's was 40,000 ducats.
[12] Stevenson, *Spanish Cathedral Music*, p. 8.

entered his service in 1548, three years after returning from Rome. His annual income is documented for 1539 at 25,000 ducats, and he provided well for Morales and his household singers.[13] At his country palace at Marchena, thirty miles from Seville, Don Luis Cristóbal offered a pleasant environment to Morales, who had just left his post as *maestro de capilla* of Toledo Cathedral in strained circumstances. (It is also possible that the climate agreed with Morales, who is thought to have suffered from malaria.) Morales remained with the duke from 1548 until 1551. Interestingly, Don Luis Cristóbal also had a connection with Bermudo. In his earlier treatise of 1549, *El arte tripharia*, Bermudo mentions that Morales was *maestro de capilla* to his lord, the duke, and it is possible that both composer and theorist were employed by the duke at that time.

Far from being closed or cut off from Europe, as sixteenth-century Spain in general has often been portrayed, Seville was a lively and cosmopolitan city during Morales' lifetime. Trade and a mobile population gave it a character analogous to the Italian trading cities or the free cities of the north. The new educational institutions were receptive to ideas from Italy, and Morales' own education at the cathedral school followed a humanist emphasis on language, evident in his good Latin style. During the composer's youth a group of composers worked in Seville as well as Toledo and the other areas visited by the court of the Catholic Monarchs. Competitive patronage existed as well in the two ducal houses of Medina Sidonia and Arcos. Seville during the half-century of Morales' life was on a par with any model Renaissance city.

To this picture of the Seville of Morales' lifetime should be added the evidence of Bermudo's *Declaración de instrumentos*, a work known to Morales and one that addresses specific questions of musical composition and rhetoric. Morales is a primary figure in Bermudo's work. The dedication page bears his name as having examined and approved it, and at Marchena, on 20 October 1550, Morales wrote the commendatory letter which Bermudo placed before book 5, the last section of the treatise. The author makes reference to the composer at important points in his discussion, for appropriate use of modes and preparation of dissonance. He suggests that Morales' masses are good material for vihuela intabulations, and keyboard

---

[13]   L. M. Siculo, *De rebus Hispaniae memorabilis* (Alcalá de Henares, 1533), fol. 17ᵛ; quoted in Stevenson, *Spanish Cathedral Music*, nn. 61 and 174.

players are advised to start with the villancicos of Vasques and then proceed to the music of Willaert, Gombert, Figueroa and Morales. One of Bermudo's musical examples is from Morales' Requiem (the introit 'Votum in Hierusalem'), and he also selects Morales' hymn *Sacris solemniis* for its use of canon and quotes from the *Magnificat a sexti toni*. Bermudo's epithets for Morales range from 'Luz de España' to 'egregio musico' to 'excelente musico'. Morales is cited, together with Willaert and Gombert, in the third book (chapter 26) as having augmented the species of consonances as well as the genera of music. Later, in book 5, Bermudo writes: 'For composing polyphony I had as my master the works of Adriano, Cristóbal de Morales and Gombert. In Spain there are excellent musicians whose works you can imitate.'[14] Following this, Bermudo implies a parallel context by noting those who have improved the use of language, naming 'the most learned Antonio de Lebrixa [Nebrija], who improved the art of grammar; Ludovico Vives, the Latin language, chaste and natural; and the most expert and scholarly Erasmus, the manner of language'.[15]

Antonio de Nebrija, born in 1442 near Seville, published a Latin–Castillian dictionary of 30,000 words, the *Interpretatio dictionum ex sermone latino in hispaniensem* in 1492, and in the same year brought out the *Gramática sobre la lengua castellana*, the first grammar of its kind for a Romance language. Nebrija left Salamanca for the new University of Alcalá de Henares in 1513; since Bermudo studied at Alcalá, it may be assumed that he came into contact with Nebrija's works there. Luis Vives is considered the greatest of the Spanish humanists. Born in 1492 in Valencia, he lectured at Louvain and at Corpus Christi, Oxford, was tutor to both Catherine of Aragon and Princess Mary (later Queen), and corresponded with More and Erasmus. Vives' writing includes letters, commentaries, polemics and dialogues. In the *De disciplinis*, a treatise on education, Vives devotes two chapters of book 4 to rhetoric and imitation. A few citations from his outline of these procedures will clarify the intellectual context of rhetoric and imitation that Bermudo assumes in his treatise.

---

[14] 'Para componer canto de organo tuve yo por maestro las obras de Adriano, de Christoval de Morales, y de Gomberth. En España ay excelentes musicos, cuyas obras podeys immitar.' *Declaración*, bk 5, chap. 9, fol. cxxix^v.

[15] 'Quanto el doctissimo Antonio de Lebrixa augmento el arte de la grammatica, el latinissimo Ludovico Vives la lengua latina, casta y natural, el peritissimo y estudiosissimo Erasmo el modo de dezir...'; *ibid.*, 4.8, fol. lxvi^v.

Jo-Ann Reif

Vives introduces 'The Art of Good Speaking' with general remarks on the requirements of oratory:[16]

The word is the cause of the greatest good and evil. How important it is, then, to use decent language that is appropriate to the person, the subject, the time and the place so that nothing may escape which is bad, trivial or indecorous. And nothing other should be the orientation that we follow in this study than that which comes down to a sonorous gathering of words, combed, trimmed, and brilliant, grouped softly and sweetly, without expressing ourselves affectedly, ineptly or unsuitably, so that it may remain manifest that this art is the principal part of prudence ... The proposed end [of oration] is to teach, persuade and move.

Thus a serious moral basis is necessary to oratory in order to effect the instructive and mediating power of the word. An oration must be suited to both the speaker and the audience in order to persuade. This propriety is a sign of the speaker's prudence, discretion, and concern for both his subject and his listeners. Suitability also applies to the orator's capacity to please through choice of words, use of voice and gesture. Vives, as Bermudo does in relating these ideas to music, implies the double context of a moral–intellectual basis, and grace of execution.

Later in chapter 3 Vives offers a classroom scene as an example of the rhetorical process:[17]

Every week, the preceptor will make a critique of a declamation in the presence of the whole class; first, he will decide on the subject and then on the speaker, on what occasion and to whom he is directing himself; next, he will examine the words individually and as a whole, the phrases, the proofs, the order, the quality of each one of these elements in itself; next, the consistency that they keep with the subject and the suitability to time, place, audience and the orator.

Thus the method implied moves from the simple to the more complex, from single words to phrases. By now the student is fluent in rhetorical exercises, can cite passages on rhetoric in Quintilian, Cicero and Aristotle, and is ready to advance to the study of imitation. This is the subject of the following chapter, where Vives states that 'Imitation is nothing more than the accommodation of a thing to a proposed model.' Here the assumption is that the

---

[16] L. Riber, ed. and trans., *Luis Vives: Obras completas*, II (Madrid, 1948), p. 621 [my translation].

[17] *Ibid.*, p. 625.

proposed model will be the best possible, chosen by a student who has the expertise to recognise that quality. He will view the model with a critical awareness ('the imitator looks at the example ... with the most awakened attention') of the procedures followed in it: 'He does this in order to conclude satisfactorily, with analogous criterion and technique, the work that he himself has proposed.' At this advanced level, the student's method is analogy, matching technique and situation in order to shape his own material. In this way Vives constructs a philosophy of imitation. Following his own rules, he draws the most important qualities from classical, late Christian, medieval and contemporary authors, and provides them with a context in order to demonstrate a method of education and to make them relevant to the thought of his own time. His purposes are simultaneously pedagogical, moral, historical and political. The goal of Vives' system is persuasion, and the ideal, eloquence. Calling for virtuous eloquence among rulers, theologians and practitioners of law, Vives sees mediation in the issues of his time – free will, divine and temporal powers – through the efficacy of the word.

With this in mind it is instructive to return to Bermudo, whose methodology and goals are similar to those of Vives. In the *Declaración de instrumentos*, Bermudo cites the most important classical, Christian, medieval and contemporary writers on music. He introduces each chapter with a definition and proceeds to give his own elaboration or musical example. His method in itself resembles that of a grammar, with citations of a rule followed by instances of its use and practical examples. Like Vives, Bermudo is demonstrating an educational method for questions of music theory, playing keyboard instruments and the vihuela, and composing plainsong and polyphony. At the same time, he is relating these issues to the music of his own time by including his own organ pieces, referring to the music of Figueroa, Gombert and Morales, and by his own remarks on theory. Bermudo creates a context that is historical, theoretical, practical and critical. In this process grammar and rhetoric serve as a constant metaphor throughout the *Declaración*. Bermudo assumes that the reader understands this intellectual framework, and this allows him to make the analogy between language and music, so plain to him that his remarks often seem casual. For example, Bermudo remarks that an error in counterpoint is like an error in grammar; that is to say, to the language of counterpoint it *is* a grammatical error.[18] Similarly, singing without noticing B or B♭, or the deduction, is like making a syllogism out of figure and mode.[19] 'Contra rhetorica' is Bermudo's critical remark on anything against the sense of the composition.[20]

Within the five books of the *Declaración*, the subjects are treated in a graduated order, proceeding from introductory discussions to more involved theoretical elaborations and practical applications.[21] In book 1, chapter 4, Bermudo explains the necessity of modes by making an analogy with diction. As speaking is something *of* orators, diction is particularly suited to them; it is something that is particular to orators. In the same way, Bermudo reasons, mode is particular to music. He continues to say that even if one follows rules of consonance and proportions but errs in suiting the work to place, time or mode, the resulting work is not good or well done: 'Not only have we to do good things, but they are to be well done, with each thing put in its place and home. One has to look not only at the nouns but also at the adverbs.'[22] The idea of modal propriety appears again in chapter 7; here classical legends are cited to introduce the idea that mode must be related to the emotion, so that the music may act positively and appropriately on the listener. In book 2, the reader goes on to the rudiments of the modal system; in book 3, its application in plainchant; and in book 4, the theoretical possibilities and implications for polyphony of the system. In book 5, chapters 2–8, the student reads a history of how modes came to be; how their characteristics are tied to emotion; and the properties ascribed to them by Cicero. These sections are all meant to emphasise the importance of suitability in choice of mode in composition. It is only in chapter 6, by which time he is addressing the advanced student, that Bermudo allows the possibility of mixed modes. These may be admitted under two conditions: if the sense of a text changes, and in conformity with the rules of music and good rhetoric.[23] Bermudo,

---

18   *Declaración*, 5. 16, fol. cxxviii^v.
19   *Ibid.*, 1. 18, fol. xviii^r.
20   *Ibid.*, 5. 6, fol. cxxiii^r; 5. 7, fol. cxxiii^v; 5. 9, fol. cxxv^r.
21   For a comparison of the range of Bermudo's citations, discussions and examples with those of other European and Spanish theorists, see R. Stevenson, *Juan Bermudo* (The Hague, 1960).
22   'No tan solamente avemos de hazer buenas cosas: sino que han de ser bien hechas, poniendo cada cosa en su lugar y casa. No tan solamente se miran los nombres: mas tambien los adverbios.' *Declaración*, 1. 4, fol. iiii^r.
23   *Ibid.*, 5. 6, fol. cxxiii^r.

like Vives on the preparation of an oration, states in chapter 7, entitled 'Donde pueden los modos começar y clausular', that one should consider the beginning, middle and end of any composition in order to establish and carry out the mode correctly.[24]

Bermudo presents his most significant discussion of rhetoric in book 1, chapter 5.[25] Here he is differentiating between the *cantante* (popular or virtuoso singer), the *cantor* (serious or church singer) and the *musico* (musician) and, in effect, is evaluating these three types of musician. As a critical yardstick Bermudo uses the degree to which each understands music theory and, by extension, rhetoric. Speaking of the *cantante* he writes: 'Lightness of the fingers in players and facility in pronouncing points among singers proceed from use, not from art. The name *cantante* is suited to such and they remain well served [by it] because they have not advanced.'[26] The *cantante* does not advance because he lacks an understanding of theory. Significantly, the only word Bermudo takes from the rhetorical vocabulary in this extract is *pronunciar*, to pronounce. This has to do with the clear use of the voice and applies to singing as well as speaking, but pronunciation belongs to the performance of oratory, not to the intellectual exercise of rhetoric.

The *cantor* has two places within Bermudo's hierarchy. At a lower level, he must execute a work in accordance with what the *musico* has determined, because he himself does not know the causes or the theoretical basis of the work: 'Singers [may] know how to compose in all modes and show much beauty and ability in them, even by improvisation (which is to be admired), but they cannot tell us the causes.'[27] Bermudo goes on to clarify the better position for the *cantor*, indeed the best position within the hierarchy: 'Anyone who could compose polyphony and could tell the causes of all that was done may be called a singer *par excellence* for having proceeded in his

---

24 'Hablando estrechamente, clausula llamo a la que los griegos dizen perihodo, que es fin de sentencia. Ay otras, que en la musica pueden hazer clausulas, y son en medio de sentencia, la qual los griegos dizen collum, y los latinos membrum, o parte principal de la oracion: y los musicos llaman punto de mediacon.' Note his use of the word oration. *Ibid.*, 5. 7, fols. cxxiii–v.

25 'Que differencia ay entre cantante, cantor y musico', *ibid.*, 1. 5, fols. iiii^v–v^v.

26 'La ligereza de los dedos en los que tañen, y la facilidad de pronunciar los puntos en los que cantan: del uso y no del arte procede. A estos tales conviene el nombre de cantante, y quedan bien pagados: porque no passaron adelante.' *Ibid.*, 1. 5, fol. iiii^v.

27 'Los cantores saben componer todos los modos, y en ellos hazer grandes primores, y abilidades, y aun de improviso (lo que es de admiracion) ... pero no os diran la causa dello.' *Ibid.*

composition in the best manner of learning that there is ... Only the theoretician is called musician. As he has the science of music in his intellect, he attains this renown.'[28] Bermudo's distinction is essentially one of faculty. Only the theoretician is called simply a musician, whereas the singer may also be called a musician if he has theoretical understanding and uses it to enrich his execution of the musical work. Bermudo makes his distinction clearer through analogy with rhetoric: 'The difference that exists between the orator and the rhetorician is the same as that between the singer and musician. No one ought to be called an orator if he is not first a rhetorician. Similarly, no one merits the name of singer if he is not first a musician.'[29] Thus rhetoric and music both have the purpose of projecting a theoretical process into a practical result. Rhetorician and musician both have the ability to think in a compositional process, while the orator and singer translate this process into persuasion or performance. In this same discussion Bermudo uses the word *razon* (*ratio*), a word with specific scholastic meanings. It could be defined as the governing principle of a composition of any kind, or the principle that effects balance of parts. Bermudo uses the word in conjunction with *juzgar*, to judge. Reason is a condition necessary for judgement, which is a quality the rhetorician (i.e. musician) must possess. In effect, Bermudo is setting a standard of judgement, and in this way he functions as a critic, rhetoric having supplied him with a methodology, a vocabulary and a set of expectations.

The question 'How much did Morales know of rhetoric?' is answered by Morales himself in his recommendation of Bermudo's treatise, in effect a review of Bermudo's work.[30] Morales says that, given the merit and worth of the young friar, he set himself to examining the young man's work. As soon as he began, he understood from experience that it would be no labour to read 'such a fruitful work', but 'a great pleasure and joy for the mind and spirit'.

[28] 'Todo aquel que canto de organo compusiere, y diere las causas de todo lo que hizo: llamarse ha cantor por excelencia, por aver procedido en su composicion en el mejor modo de saber que ay.... Solo el theorico es dicho musico. Por tener la sciencia de la Musica en su entendimiento: alcança este renombre.' *Ibid.*

[29] 'La differencia que ay entre el orador y el rhetorico: essa mesma dezimos aver entre el cantor y el musico. Ninguno merece ser dicho orador, si primero no es rhetorico: assi ninguno merece el nombre de cantor, si primero no fuere musico.' *Ibid.*

[30] *El arte tripharia* (1549), which Morales must have seen at Marchena, was expanded into the *Declaración*.

The style of writing 'put will and soul to reading it with delight'. Morales next comments: 'The manner of proceeding I understood to be artificial, because it proceeds from the imperfect to the perfect, as is natural.'

This critical remark is made by opposing the artificial to the natural, which refers to the skilful inventiveness of the writer for copying the natural order of things in the steps of his treatise.[31] As Morales states: 'An art is so much the more perfect when it imitates and copies the natural.'[32] Morales finds this in Bermudo's treatise in the discussions of plainsong, mode, consonance and proportion, which he considers to be complete.

The last lines of Morales' review, which recognise the need for a sound theoretical text for what it can offer to the practical musician, make clear his understanding of Bermudo's aims:

Read this book advisedly and with care and you will find in it all that you can desire in composition. Theory set in practice, and practice run together with theory: until this time we have not seen such a thing in Spain. Now practical musicians can no longer say truthfully that theory is contrary to practice: how excellently, then, friar Juan Bermudo shows both sciences coming together in consonance and proportion.[33]

Theory set in practice is analogous to rhetoric voiced in oratory. Morales applauds Bermudo's musician who makes performance complete through theoretical understanding, and tacitly recognises here the qualities of artifice which he has already emphasised. The theoretical basis, the imitation, is the artifice that allows the natural (consonance, proportion) to be seen through its copy, the musical work. Artifice is the composer's handiwork. It aids the clear presentation of what is already there – the natural. Morales can speak of artifice and imitation together because both signify a means for bringing out the coherence of the musical composition. They also

---

[31] The artificial and the natural became the subject of discussion and element of style in the works of Cervantes, Lope and, ultimately, Góngora.

[32] 'Tanto es mas perfecto un arte: quanto imita y contrahaze a lo natural.' Letter by Morales, written in 1550, placed before book 5 of the *Declaración*, no folio number.

[33] 'Leed con aviso y cuydado este libro: y hallareys en el todo lo que en composicion podeys dessear. Theorica engastada en practica, y la practica corriesse junctamente con la theorica: hasta ahora en nuestra España no avemos visto. No pueden pues con verdad dezir los musicos practicos ser la theorica contraria a la practica: pues que tan excelentemente muestra fray Juan Bermudo ... venir ambas sciencias a consonancia y proporcion.' *Ibid*.

239

signify the system of reference in the composition, its suitability to occasions and patrons temporal or spiritual.

It is this kind of abstract understanding of imitation that best suits Morales' *Missarum liber secundus* of 1544. Morales himself prepared the volume for publication and dedicated it, perhaps in the expectation of a papal benefice, to Pope Paul III, a man noted for his learning.[34] To emphasise the range of his compositional abilities, Morales included masses composed according to different techniques. The way in which these are presented suggests that each technique is a sub-category or a genre in itself within the larger designation of mass composition. The index reads as follows:

Quatuor vocibus	Quinque vocibus
Tu es vas electionis	De beata Virgine
Benedicta es caelorum Regina	Quem dicunt homines
Ave Maria	Pro defunctis
Gaude, Barbara	
L'Homme armé	

Of these, two are tenor masses, three are paraphrase and three masses *ad imitationem*. Morales' total output of masses includes one canonic mass, one 'treble', three tenor, seven *ad imitationem* and nine paraphrase masses. Twelve of these are *a* 4, seven *a* 5 and two *a* 6. Six of his masses use secular tunes (three Spanish and two French – *L'homme armé* being used twice); his models are principally plainsong and motets (though not his own). Thus the masses of the *Liber secundus* include stylistic traits representative of his mass composition as a whole, while some make learned references both through their style and in their texts. The *Missa Tu es vas electionis*, for example, refers to Paul III through its choice of source material, being based on a versicle from a Hieronymite *Liber processionarius* published in Alcalá de Henares in 1526. The Hieronymite order was active only in Spain and Italy, had a house near Seville and attracted its members, even from other orders, through an active reformist life. The choice of Spanish material is unusual for Morales. The versicle is for 29 June, the Feast of Saints Peter and Paul, with a text deriving from the Acts of the Apostles 9 (also read on 25 January, the Conversion of St

[34] According to one biographer he had read Ptolemy's *De musica* in the original Greek. See R. Stevenson, 'Cristóbal de Morales', *Journal of the American Musicological Society*, 6 (1953), p. 22.

Paul).[35] 'Tu es vas electionis' was the phrase that Pope Paul III used as a motto for himself, and on the engraved title-page of the *Liber secundus* it is inscribed under the music that Morales is presenting to the pope. On an immediate level the material is perfectly appropriate to the pope since it refers to St Paul. But there is also a more involved meaning. The sense of the full Biblical text is that of mission to spread the name of Christ to all people, and since St Paul took on a special importance for reformers both inside and outside the Church, the sense of the text was an epitome of the issues of the day. Morales' choice of musical quotation, therefore, brought together the composer himself as a Spaniard, a Catholic reformist group (the Hieronymites), the memory of St Paul, and the present Paul, who would soon be convening the Council of Trent. In addition, the *Missa Tu es vas electionis* is one of two published masses by Morales that employs triple metre throughout (O). This was unusual for Morales and may be considered a learned usage that the pope would appreciate. The significance of the number 3 corresponds also to the ancient Paul, the times of Pope Paul, and his efforts towards the future that are implied in the choice of the versicle text. The *Missa Quem dicunt homines* is related to the textual references of the *Missa Tu es vas* in that it too pays homage to the papacy. Its main phrase 'Tu es Petrus', Christ's dictum of foundation of the Church, is a text that also appears in the liturgy for the Feast of Saints Peter and Paul. The *Missa L'homme armé* (*a* 4) is Morales' other published mass written in triple metre throughout. Also like the *Missa Tu es vas*, it is marked by an insistent repetition of the tune, as if the composer is leading his premise through the steps of the disputation. At the end of the *Missa L'homme armé* Morales achieves a kind of *peroratio*. The Agnus I is written in O mensuration but Agnus II, the last one, is notated in ₵. Both have three semibreves to a bar, but those in Agnus II are faster, thus emphasising the conclusion.

On the subject of mode, Morales was consistent in ending each principal movement of the mass on the same tone. For the initial or intermediate sections he regularly used tones related either plagally or authentically to those of the ending, and all but two masses in the *Liber secundus* follow such a scheme. His consistency conforms to the rhetorical practice of dividing the oration clearly into beginning,

---

[35] 'But the Lord said unto him, Go thy way: for he is a chosen vessel unto me, to bear my name before the Gentiles, and kings, and the children of Israel.'

middle and end, and such a clear arrangement also allows the composition to correspond to the appropriate mode. The *Missa L'homme armé* (*a* 4), for example, in the Phrygian mode, corresponds to the martial character assigned to Mode III by Ramos de Pareja. By contrast, the *Missa L'homme armé* in the *Liber primus*, which is dedicated to Cosimo de' Medici, is in Mode V, associated with good fortune. In the *Missa Benedicta es caelorum regina* Morales quotes from two models, both famous motets of the same name. His mass was generally thought to be based on Mouton, but the opening of the Benedictus is based on a quotation from Josquin's six-voice motet. Morales, by working with both motets, chose the requisite models for treating this antiphon while showing reverence to both composers and placing his work in their tradition. A kind of *peroratio* also occurs in this mass. In the last Agnus, Morales adds two voices to the existing four and sets off the borrowed material by the use of canon. The same procedure is followed in the second Marian mass *a* 4 of the collection, the *Missa Ave Maria*. His elaborate conclusion in both masses heightens the sense of devotion reserved for this celestial patron. In quoting Gregorian material Morales is frequently literal; his usual practice is to quote the plainsong but to invent a short motif around it as an accompanying phrase. In the *Missa Ave Maria*, for example, the figure ♩ ♪♪♩ ♩♩ ♪♪♪, invented by the composer, can be found throughout the voices while a canon proceeds in notes of greater value. Morales displays his canonic ingenuity to its fullest when it is linked to plainsong. The strictness of the techniques he employs and the ensuing brilliance in composition, embodying the exercise of *inventio*, demonstrate his imaginative capacity through artifice.

If we consider the *Missarum liber secundus* once more we see something rhetorical in its arrangement. The book opens with 'Tu es vas electionis', a good *exordium*, containing all the necessary themes, and paying proper reverence, even in apostrophe ('sancte Paule!'). For the *disputatio* we have a view of the Church and of the world at the time. The *Missa L'homme armé* suggests Charles V, the man with whom Paul many times attempted a reconciliation. We may also see in the figure of the Armed Man the Church Militant, the faithful on earth in the fight to reach Heaven. Sustaining us through our argument is the Virgin Mary, the ever present recourse for the militant and for the souls in torment. She is the 'caelorum regina' and as such brings Heaven into the scheme.[36] Barbara, a martyr, is herself an example of the Church Militant who joined the Church Triumphant. Thus we come round to the main theme of the Church on earth as an institution in the *Missa Quem dicunt homines*, the associations of titles culminating in their own *peroratio*. One last view is that of the dead, the *Missa pro defunctis*, which stands like the skull on the scholar's desk, a 'vanitas' or *memento mori*. The argument is fully concluded, in structure and significance. Morales has presented us with a cosmos, an ordering in the Greek sense, and in these works we see his world reflected.

Columbia University

---

[36] Bermudo expresses similar sentiments: 'The most powerful reason for learning to sing is that we may use music in the service of God to which the holy angels incite us who in the Church Triumphant praise God with song, and the saints of the Church Militant (in imitation of the heavenly that is our mother) ordain that there shall be song.' ('La potissima causa porque aviamos de saber cantar: es para emplear la musica en el servicio de Dios: a lo qual nos incitan los sanctos angeles, que en la iglesia triumphante alaban a Dios con canto, y los sanctos en la militante (a imitacion de la celestial que es nuestra madre) ordenaron que vuiesse canto.' *Declaración*, 1. 15, fol. xiii*v*.)

PETER WRIGHT

ON THE ORIGINS OF TRENT 87$_1$ AND 92$_2$*

In their pioneering study of the Trent codices, Adler and Koller divided the six manuscripts then known to them into two distinct and separate groups: a younger group, Tr88–91, which they believed to have been compiled 'in or for Trent' by the scribe Johannes Wiser; and an older group, Tr87 and Tr92, which they described less specifically as 'unquestionably north Italian' in origin.[1] Recent findings have tended to confirm Trent as the place of origin of the former group,[2] while at the same time indicating that the blanket description 'north Italian' can no longer suffice for the latter. This group comprises in effect three sources which once existed independently of each other: a principal source divided into two parts, Tr87$_1$ and Tr92$_2$, here referred to jointly as *TR*;[3] and two

* This is an expanded version of a paper read at the Eleventh Annual Conference on Medieval and Renaissance Music, held at Pembroke College, Oxford, in July 1983. I wish to record my particular gratitude to Sig. Danilo Curti and Don Ivo Leonardi, curator of the Archivio e Biblioteca Capitolare, Trent, for their generous and invaluable assistance. I wish also to thank the staffs of the Archivio di Stato, Trent, and the Tiroler Landesarchiv, Innsbruck, for their kind co-operation.

A key to the abbreviations used in this study may be found on pp. 264–5.

[1] G. Adler and O. Koller, eds., *Sechs Trienter Codices: Geistliche und weltliche Compositionen des XV. Jahrhunderts, Erste Auswahl*, Denkmäler der Tonkunst in Österreich, Jg VII, 14–15 (Vienna, 1900), pp. xiii–xxi. Tr93, which stands apart from Tr88–91 in the sense that Wiser's contribution to it is only an incidental one, was rediscovered some years later than Tr87–92 (see A. Carlini and others, *Dalla polifonia al classicismo: il Trentino nella musica* (Trent, 1981), pp. 28–9); its existence was first made known by R. von Ficker and A. Orel, eds., *Sechs Trienter Codices: Geistliche und weltliche Compositionen des XV. Jahrhunderts, Vierte Auswahl*, Denkmäler der Tonkunst in Österreich, Jg XXXI, 61 (Vienna, 1924), p. vi.

[2] See in particular G. Spilsted, 'Toward the Genesis of the Trent Codices: New Directions and New Findings', *Studies in Music*, 1 (1976), pp. 55–70; and G. Spilsted, 'The Paleography and Musical Repertory of Codex Tridentinus 93' (Ph.D. thesis, Harvard University, 1982).

[3] This is an unusually complex source which was compiled piecemeal over a period of about twenty years. The two parts, Tr87$_1$ and Tr92$_2$, are related by papers, scribes and repertory, and in several instances a layer is divided between them. It has therefore been

smaller sources, Tr87$_2$ and Tr92$_1$.[4] The few attempts that have been made to determine the individual provenances of these manuscripts rest more on informed hypothesis than hard fact,[5] with the result that their precise origin and the reason for their association with the later codices have remained as much of a puzzle as they were when the first six manuscripts were rediscovered just over a century ago. Now, with the help of new evidence, it is possible to clarify several important aspects of the origin of the main manuscript, *TR*, thereby explaining how it and its companion sources Tr87$_2$ and Tr92$_1$ reached Trent, and to show that some of the issues respectively concerning the older and younger groups can no longer be regarded as mutually exclusive.

Adler's and Koller's assessment of the younger group was based on two main factors: Wiser's documented connection with Trent; and the presence in the manuscripts of poems with local associations, two of them apparently addressed to Georg Hack who was bishop there from 1444 to 1465.[6] Their view was firmly rejected by the Austrian historian Richard Wolkan,[7] who, writing at the very time when the Austrian and Italian governments were engaged in the delicate process of negotiating the future of the codices, argued that Hack was too unpopular a figure to be the dedicatee of these poems, and that a musical backwater such as Trent would not have been conducive to the production of an anthology of this scope and character. According to Wolkan, the manuscripts were more likely

considered both appropriate and convenient to view the two parts as one source, although there is no evidence that they were ever bound together. For details of the make-up of *TR* see P. Wright, 'The Compilation of Trent 87$_1$ and 92$_2$', *Early Music History*, 2 (1982), pp. 237–71.

[4] On the former see R. White, 'The Battre Fascicle of the Trent Codex 87' (Ph.D. thesis, Indiana University, 1975); on the latter see T. Ward, 'The Structure of the Manuscript Trent 92-I', *Musica Disciplina*, 29 (1975), pp. 127–47.

[5] Ward, 'The Structure', pp. 144–7, suggests that Tr92$_1$ was probably copied in the Strasbourg–Basle region; and Wright, 'The Compilation', pp. 270–1, speculates that *TR* may also have originated in this area – a possibility which is somewhat diminished though not ruled out by the evidence presented here. White, 'The Battre Fascicle', pp. 5 and 18, proposes that Tr87$_2$ originated in the province of Namur, Belgium, on the basis of the fact that two of the texts set in the manuscript are related to this region.

[6] Adler and Koller, eds., *Sechs Trienter Codices*, pp. xvii–xviii. Translations of these poems are given in Spilsted, 'Toward the Genesis', pp. 64–5. For a useful account of the history of Trent at this time, and in particular of the often difficult relations between the Bishop of Trent and the Count of the Tirol, see J. Kögl, *La sovranità dei vescovi di Trento e di Bressanone* (Trent, 1964), pp. 151–78. A more general account is given in A. Zieger, *Storia della regione tridentina* (Trent, 1968), pp. 138–62.

[7] R. Wolkan, 'Die Heimat der Trienter Musikhandschriften', *Studien zur Musikwissenschaft*, 8 (1921), pp. 5–8.

to have been copied in Vienna, reaching Trent under the auspices of Hack's successor, the humanist and bibliophile Johannes Hinderbach. In response to these arguments, which were undocumented and politically motivated, the Trent musicologist Renato Lunelli put forward a case for Tridentine origin,[8] drawing attention to the important fact of Wiser's appointment as master and rector of the cathedral school during the very years when he would have been compiling much of his collection.[9] He also cited the names of a number of local musicians – and the activities of one man in particular – as evidence of a flourishing musical life in quattrocento Trent capable (he implied) of sustaining sophisticated polyphony. The two men's claims were, of course, exaggerated at times, and tinged with chauvinism; yet the issues they raised are critical ones. If recent thinking favours Trent rather than Vienna as the place where most of the repertory of Tr88–91 was copied, the more important questions of where this repertory came from, why and for whom it was written down, have still to be answered. But it is the unexpected relevance of some of the issues raised by Wolkan and Lunelli to the older group of manuscripts that is of more immediate concern.

The principal musician cited by Lunelli was a priest named Johannes Lupi,[10] known also by the German equivalent of his name, Wolf. Among documents relating to him is a lengthy will in which he bequeathed to various friends, colleagues and institutions a number of legacies, clothes, household items, books, musical instruments and sundry personal effects.[11] Its existence was first made generally known through a description and partial transcription published at the turn of the century by the then curator of the Archivio

---

[8] R. Lunelli, 'La patria dei codici musicali tridentini', *Note d'Archivio per la Storia Musicale*, 4 (1927), pp. 116–28. Lunelli first presented some of his arguments in a newspaper article, 'Intermezzo comico', *Il Nuovo Trentino* (Trent, 19 February 1921), pp. 33–4, in which he apparently took account of Wolkan's views, although it is doubtful whether the latter's article had yet been published.

[9] This institution was probably one of the cathedral schools of grammar and song which were widely established in northern Italy by the early part of the fifteenth century (see G. Cattin, 'Church Patronage of Music in Fifteenth-century Italy', in *Music in Medieval and Early Modern Europe: Patronage, Sources and Texts*, ed. I. Fenlon (Cambridge, 1981), pp. 23 and 29). In a document of 22 December 1460 (TAC, Instr. Cap. x, fol. 65^r), for example, Wiser is described as 'artium gramatice professor'.

[10] He is not to be confused with his sixteenth-century namesakes: see B. J. Blackburn, 'Johannes Lupi and Lupus Hellinck: a Double Portrait', *Musical Quarterly*, 59 (1973), pp. 547–83.

[11] TAC, Capsa dei Testamenti, unnumbered document. A complete transcription of the will is given in the Appendix on pp. 265 and 268–70.

Capitolare, Vigilio Zanolini, and it was probably from this rather than the original that Lunelli worked.[12] Whereas Zanolini's interest had been in the socio-historical value of the document, Lunelli's was confined to its musical contents, and it was one clause in particular which attracted his attention: a bequest of six books of figured song (*cantus figuratus*) to the parish church of Bolzano,[13] an important town in the German-speaking part of the Trent diocese. Since *cantus figuratus* was a term commonly applied to polyphony in the fifteenth century, it was natural for Lunelli to speculate on the possibility that this was a reference to the celebrated codices, and he even ventured to suggest that Lupi may have had a hand in their compilation.

His equation of the codices with the books in the will – a matter to be considered more fully later – has provoked further speculation; not surprisingly, however, his notion of Lupi as a participant scribe has never been pursued. Federhofer dismissed the idea,[14] and in so doing was, of course, correct to point to the lack of numerical correspondence (seven manuscripts, 'sex libri'); but his observation that Lupi's name does not appear in the codices, and his suggestion that an organist (such as Lupi is known to have been) would have had little interest in vocal polyphony, cannot be counted valid objections. It happens that Lunelli was nearer the truth than even he might seriously have imagined.

Zanolini described the will as a holograph, and all the evidence supports his judgement. The document was never witnessed or notarised, and is written on paper – a fact which is itself significant since all the other medieval wills in the Archivio Capitolare are on parchment. The author's statement that it is written in his own hand (Appendix, line 8) may be mere convention; but the informal layout of the document, its deletions and omissions, the poor quality of its Latin (full of errors of grammar and syntax), and the lack of a seal

---

[12] V. Zanolini, 'Spigolatura d'archivio', *Programma del Ginnasio Privato Pr[incipe] Vescovile di Trento per l'anno scolastico 1902–3* (Trent, 1903), pp. 40–3. Apparently the will went missing for a long time. It is not known when it disappeared, but quite possibly it was not available to Lunelli. Spilsted searched for it in vain ('The Paleography and Repertory', p. 183, n. 26), as did the present writer in 1980. It finally resurfaced *c.* 1982, having been incorrectly filed in a later part of the archive.

[13] See Appendix, lines 74–7. Cited in Lunelli, 'La patria', p. 122; and quoted in Zanolini, 'Spigolatura d'archivio', p. 42, n. 2, and Spilsted, 'The Paleography and Repertory', p. 184.

[14] H. Federhofer, 'Trienter Codices', *Die Musik in Geschichte und Gegenwart*, ed. F. Blume, 16 vols. (Kassel, 1949–79), xiii (1966), cols. 670–1.

(despite the author's reference to its presence (line 9)), make it amply clear that this was Lupi's own draft.

The chief interest of the will, however, lies not in its form or contents, but in its handwriting, which bears a strong resemblance to that of the main scribe of *TR*. Because of the wide degree of script variation throughout his work (which in *TR* often creates the impression that several hands are present rather than one), and because there are few opportunities for sustained comparison between the will and the musical manuscript, this resemblance may not be immediately obvious. But closer examination shows that most of the regular features of the hand, as well as a number of more idiosyncratic characteristics, remain constant from one source to the other. Figure 1 illustrates some of the individual letter-forms. The initials 'E' and 'T' are included merely for their similarity of design, whereas all the other examples – among which the majuscules 'A', 'F' and 'V' are arguably the most striking – have been chosen on grounds of identity or near-identity. The examples in the right-hand column are taken from four different layers of *TR*; but it is one layer in particular, a late one comprising Tr87, fols. 109–20 and 197–200, that most closely resembles the will (see Figures 2–3). From the thickness of the pen-strokes, the generally solid appearance of the hand, and the occasional use of looped ascenders (usually absent from earlier stages of the scribe's hand), it would appear that the scripts are roughly contemporary, although a few features – notably the small 'i' which sometimes looks more like an 'r' (for example, the first word of Figure 3, line 2) – suggest that the will represents a slightly more advanced stage of the hand.

The evidence of these examples should demonstrate, it is hoped unequivocally, that Johannes Lupi was the compiler and principal scribe of *TR*, and hence of *ZW* also;[15] and that it was he, therefore, who was responsible for subdividing *TR*, amalgamating its respective parts with Tr87₂ and Tr92₁, and appending to the volume which became Tr92 his own 'comprehensive' index of its contents.

Lupi's will is undated and contains no reference to specific events. Zanolini suggested that it must have been written some time between about 1450 and Lupi's death in 1467, but in fact it is possible to establish a much earlier *terminus ante quem*, on the basis of

---

[15]   The surviving fragments of this once large and formal choirbook are in the hand of the main *TR* scribe (see Wright, 'The Compilation' (n. 3), pp. 265–8).

Lupi's will

TR

recto,
line 3

Tr87, fol. 39ᵛ/1

recto,
line 1

Tr87, fol. 15ᵛ/6

verso,
line 34

Tr87, fol. 197ᵛ/2

250

Lupi's will		TR
verso, line 21		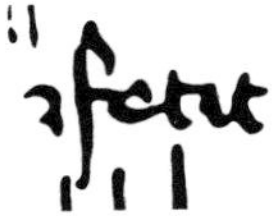 Tr87, fol. 46ᵛ/2
recto, line 20		 Tr92, fol. 165ᵛ/7
recto, line 28		 Tr87, fol. 197ᵛ/3
recto, line 46		 Tr87, fol. 111ʳ/6
recto, line 13		 Tr87, fol. 197ᵛ/3

Figure 1 Comparative samples of Johannes Lupi's hand (the examples in the right-hand column are slightly reduced)

251

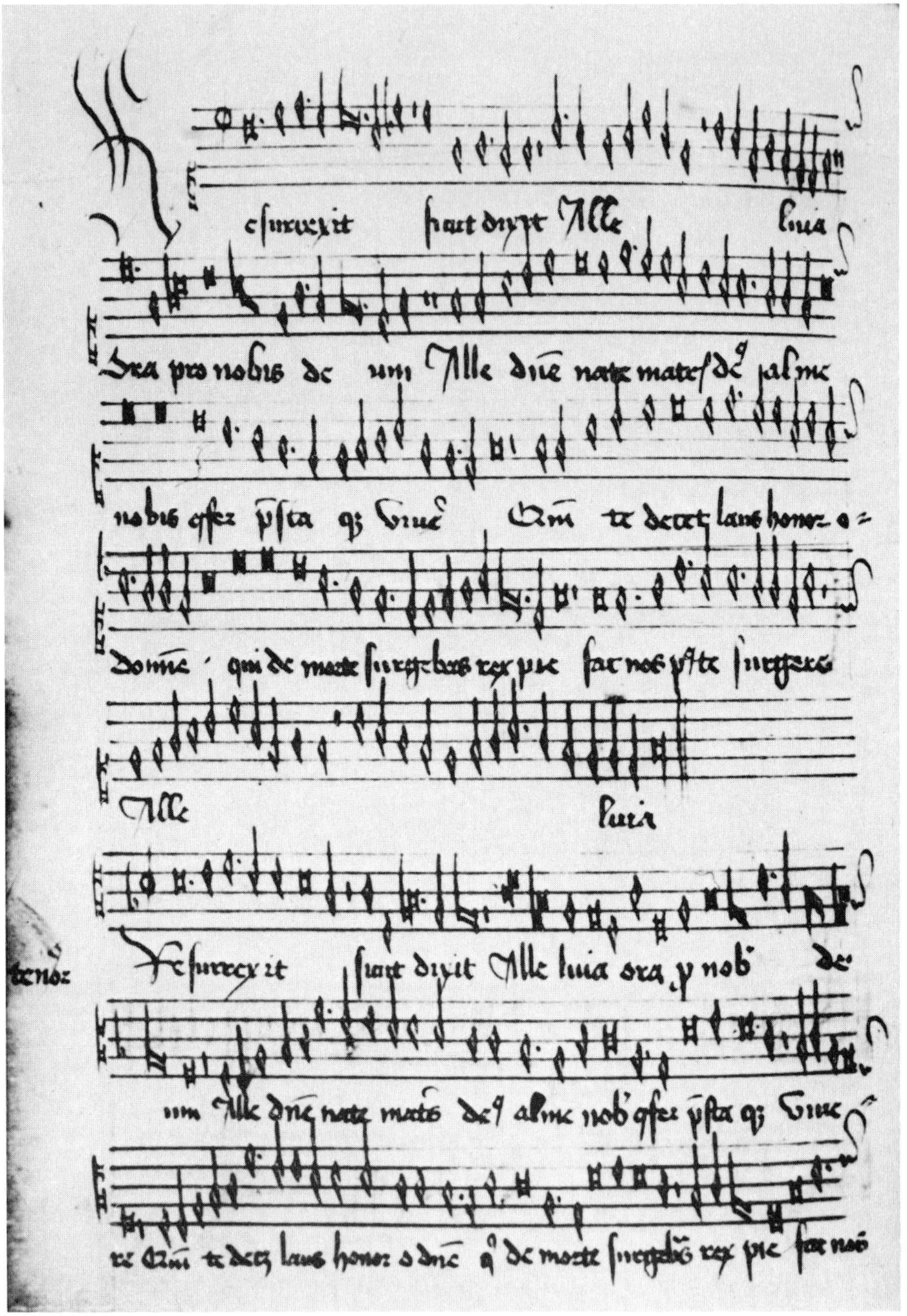

Figure 2 Tr87, fol. 197ᵛ (reduced)

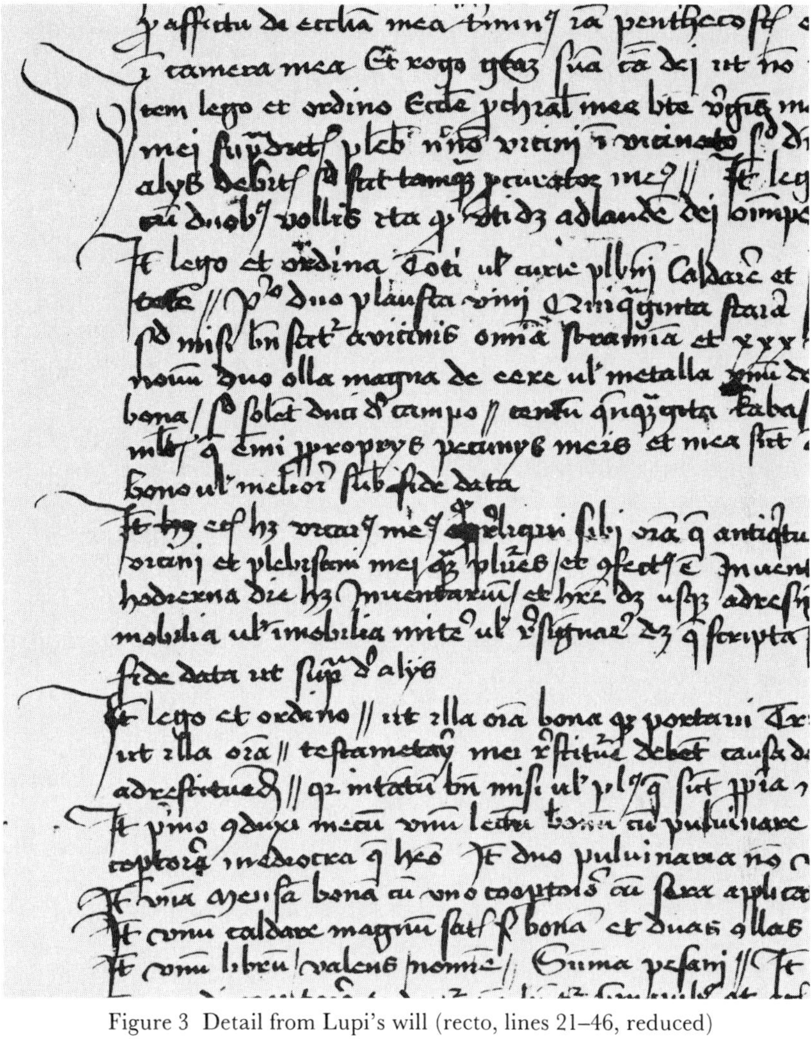

Figure 3 Detail from Lupi's will (recto, lines 21–46, reduced)

information concerning one of its beneficiaries: a certain Andrea Augenlicz, who was rector of the local parish of Livo in the Val de Solis.[16] He is known to have died some time between 22 April and 30 July 1455,[17] and it is therefore pertinent that his name and bequest

[16] He is thus described in the document recording Lupi's investiture at Caldaro (cf. n. 23), at which occasion he was present.

[17] He was still alive on 22 April (TAC, Instr. Cap. IX, fol. 275ʳ), but had died by 30 July (*ibid.*, fol. 284ʳ). In a document of 19 March (*ibid.*, fol. 271ʳ) he is described as 'Magister Andreas'. L. Santifaller, *Urkunden und Forschungen zur Geschichte des Trientner Domkapitels im*

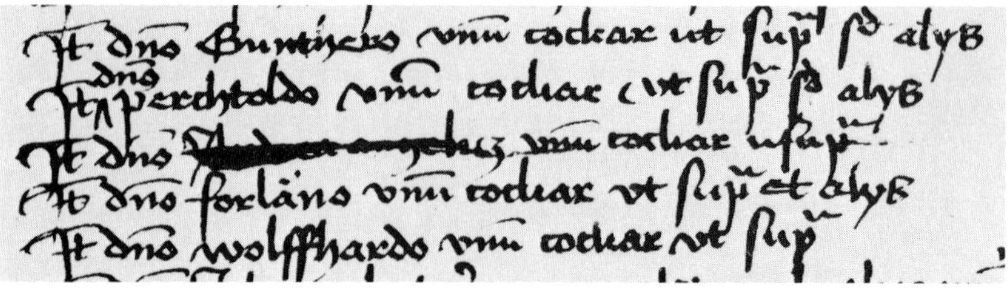

Figure 4 Detail from Lupi's will (verso, lines 40–4, reduced)

should have been deleted from the will (see Figure 4 and Appendix, lines 130–1). Unless news of his death was slow to reach Lupi, it would seem safe to assume that the document had been drawn up by 30 July. No comparable evidence has yet been found to support a *terminus post quem* later than 1447 (the year of Lupi's investiture as a parish priest), but this may in any case not matter greatly since there are good reasons – to be considered shortly – for believing that 1455 was itself the year in which he made his will.

His many possessions included only five non-musical books: a volume entitled *Summa Pesani* (Appendix, line 70), a *Flores Sanctorum* (lines 70–1) and three breviaries according to the uses of Salzburg, Passau and Rome. The proceeds of the first two breviaries were to be donated to the hospital at Bolzano and the poor priests of the town (lines 82–6), while the third was to be kept in the cathedral church at Trent for the benefit of those priests who were unable to purchase their own copies (lines 113–16). Judging by the small number of his books and his poor knowledge of Latin as evidenced in both *TR* and the will, Lupi was no bibliophile. Instead, he seems to have preferred to use his not inconsiderable personal resources for the purchase of musical instruments. To his church at Caldaro he left a positive organ with two bellows (lines 39–41); to various friends a portative organ, two clavichords, two lutes, a clavicembalo and a *schaffpret* (lines 116–22). Clearly this was a substantial collection for any individual to possess, and one which might be seen as presupposing considerable musical versatility. Rather than being incompatible with an interest in vocal polyphony, as Federhofer suggests, such implied instrumental skills would appear highly

Mittelalter, I: *Urkunden zur Geschichte des Trientner Domkapitels 1147–1500*, Veröffentlichungen des Instituts für Österreichische Geschichtsforschung 6 (Vienna, 1948), gives a short summary of the latest of these documents (p. 348, no. 477) as well as a number of others cited here.

appropriate for a man so obviously in touch with the mainstream musical developments of his day.

Lunelli included in his study a summary of Lupi's life based on just a handful of documents. Through a closer examination of these sources, and with the addition of a number of others, it is now possible to construct a somewhat fuller biography. The earliest known reference to Lupi is in the records of the University of Vienna, where he matriculated in the winter semester of 1428–9. He is described as a member of the Austrian nation, and is said to have come from Bolzano.[18] The date of his matriculation, and that of his death (1467), suggest that he must have been born in about 1410. On 27 May 1431 Duke Friedrich IV of Austria wrote to the then Bishop of Trent, Alexander Masowien, in order to present Johannes Lupi, a clerk of the Trent diocese, for the benefice of St Jacob, a chapel belonging to the parish church of Bolzano.[19] A few days later, on 4 June, the benefice was conferred upon him by Johannes Anhang, a member of the Trent chapter.[20] Thereafter Lupi's name is apparently absent from Tridentine documents until 1447,[21] the year

---

[18] 'Anno domini millesimo cccc°xxviii° in die beati Colomanni martiris electus fuit in rectorem alme universitatis studii Wiennensis Mag. Johannes de Pawmgarten, arcium et medicine professor. In cuius rectoria intitulati sunt infrascripti: Nacio Australium ... Johannes Lupi de Bolzano 4 gr.'. Quoted from L. Santifaller, ed., *Die Matrikel der Universität Wien*, I: *1377–1450*, Publikationen des Instituts für Österreichische Geschichts-forschung, ser. VI, 1/I (Graz and Cologne, 1956), p. 162, no. 4; also cited in L. Santifaller, 'Studenti della diocesi di Trento all'Università di Vienna nel medio evo', *Studi Trentini di Scienze Storiche*, 3 (1922), p. 166, no. 24. According to Santifaller (*Die Matrikel*, I, p. xxii), four groschen was the standard matriculation fee from the summer semester of 1414 to the winter semester of 1450. Since this fee varied according to social standing, it seems fair to assume that Lupi was not born into a high-ranking family. (I have not yet had the opportunity to check the graduation records of the university, hitherto unpublished for the period in question, for Lupi's name.)

[19] TASAPV, Sezione Latina, Capsa 46, N. 31: 'Salutem cum bonorum omni incremento, ad cappellam Sancti Jacobi ... nobis fidelem Johannem Wolff de Bolzano, clericum predicte vestre diocese'. Cited in Lunelli, 'La patria', p. 121, n. 1; and summarised in F. Schneller, 'Beiträge zur Geschichte des Bisthums Trient aus dem späteren Mittelalter', *Zeitschrift des Ferdinandeums für Tirol und Vorarlberg*, ser. III, 38 (1894) [part 1], p. 186, no. 64a.

[20] TASAPV, Sezione Latina, Capsa 46, N. 32 (there are two copies of this document): 'Johannes Anhang de Bopphingen, canonicus Tridentini ... discreto viro Johanni Lupi de Bolzano, Tridenti diocesi, salutem in Domino sempiternam, vacanda cappella Sancti Jacobi situata in cimiterio parochialis ecclesie Sancte Marie Virginis in Bolzano'. Cited in Lunelli, 'La patria', p. 121, n. 2; and summarised in Schneller, 'Beiträge zur Geschichte', p. 186, no. 64b.

[21] An incomplete and undated document records that Lupi was the representative of Andreas Prehenberger when the latter was elected to the Trent chapter (see TAC, Instr. Cap. IX, fol. 229^r; and Santifaller, *Urkunden und Forschungen*, p. 345, no. 465). According to [B. Bonelli], *Monumenta Ecclesiae Tridentinae* (Trent, 1765), p. 283, Prehenberger's election took place in 1446; if this is the case, it would imply that Lupi was then already present in Trent.

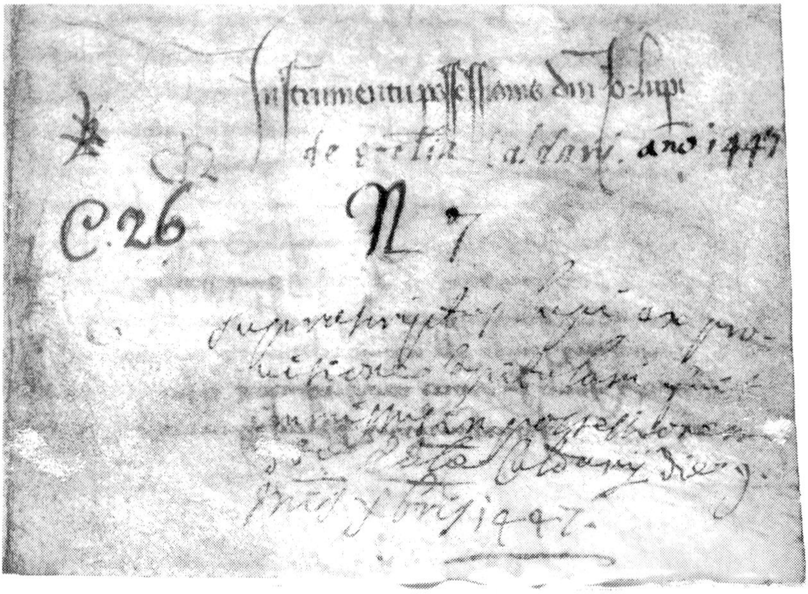

Peter Wright

Figure 5 Detail from TAC, Capsa 26, N. 7 (reduced)

in which he was installed as rector of Caldaro (near Bolzano), one of the principal parishes in the diocese.[22] The documents recording his formal nomination (6 December) and investiture (9 December) describe him as altarist of San Maxentia (the highest altar in the cathedral) and a chaplain of Sigmund, Duke of Austria.[23] Inscribed on the reverse side of the later document are the words 'instrumentu[m] possessionis dni Jo. Lupi' apparently in Lupi's own hand

[22] ,Lupi's appointment is cited in Lunelli, 'La patria', p. 121; in K. Atz and A. Schatz, *Der deutsche Antheil des Bisthums Trient*, 5 vols. (Bozen, 1902–10), ii (1904), pp. 78 and 96, as part of a detailed history of the parish; and in O. Stolz, *Die Ausbreitung des Deutschtums im Lichte der Urkunden*, 4 vols. (Munich and Berlin, 1927–34), ii (1928), pp. 79–80, who concludes that by the time of this appointment German was the language spoken in Caldaro.

[23] TAC, Capsa 26, N. 43–1, records Lupi's nomination; TAC, Capsa 26, N. 7, records his investiture. The second of these documents (part of which is transcribed, somewhat erratically, in Stolz, *Die Ausbreitung*, 2, p. 103) describes him as follows: 'Honorabilis vir dominus Johannes Lupi de Bolzano, Tridenti diocesi, cappellanus altaris Sancte Maxencie in ecclesia Sancti Vigilii Tridenti, necnon serenissimi principis domini domini Sigismundi ducis Austrie etc. cappellanus habens ac in suis tenens manibus quandam investitura per modum instrumenti sigillo'. Copies of these documents are found, together with German summaries of their contents, in ITL, Urkundenserie i, MS 4058, fols. 8ᵛ–11ʳ; they are also summarised in MS 5525, fols. 27ᵛ and 29ʳ. All of these documents are cited in Schneller, 'Beiträge zur Geschichte', pp. 237–8, nos. 261a–b.

(Figure 5), a neat book-hand which contrasts sharply with the rather quavery script of the will.

On 4 March 1452 the chapter granted Lupi an indefinite lease on a house in the centre of Trent.[24] He is described as [cathedral] organist, an appointment which is confirmed in at least two other documents.[25] His duties as organist may not have begun until 1452, though it is much more likely that they commenced with his investiture as altarist of San Maxentia, since it was customary for these two posts to be held by the same person.[26] The precise date of Lupi's investiture cannot be established, as the chapter acts for this period were never completed; what is certain is that he was already altarist when he took possession of Caldaro and that he continued to occupy this position for the rest of his life.

Several documents written in April and May 1467 testify to Lupi's recent death, which may be presumed to have occurred earlier the same year.[27] However, some confusion arises from the fact that on 26 February 1456 Duke Sigmund wrote to the Bishop of Trent (Georg Hack) in order to present a priest named Georg Marschalk for the benefice of St Jacob which had fallen vacant 'through the death of Johannes Lupi'.[28] This was a formal letter written on parchment. In a subsequent (undated) letter, this time a draft written on paper, Sigmund presented an alternative candidate, Dionysus Haidelberger, for the same benefice, but left the choice between him and

---

24 TAC, Instr. Cap. ix, fol. 19ʳ: 'Locatio perpetualis facta per dominos canonicos domino Johanni Volf de una domo'.
25 *Ibid.*, fol. 20ᵛ (4 March 1452) and fol. 32ᵛ (4 March 1453), each of which records his presence at a meeting of the chapter. On 7 May 1452 Lupi served as a witness at the reading of the will of Hertvicus of Passau (TAC, Capsa dei Testamenti, unnumbered document (formerly Capsa 50, N. 10); quoted in Santifaller, *Urkunden und Forschungen*, p. 347, no. 474), in which he is described simply as altarist of San Maxentia.
26 See Spilsted, 'The Paleography and Repertory', pp. 186–9. The three documents describing Lupi as organist are in a different hand from any of the other documents in which he is cited, and it may be that the scribe who wrote them chose to state what other scribes took for granted.
27 On 4 April Lupi's successor as altarist of San Maxentia was appointed (TAC, Instr. Cap. xi, fol. 107ʳ; Santifaller, *Urkunden und Forschungen*, p. 382, no. 516); on 15 April his successor at Caldaro was elected (TAC, Instr. Cap. xi, fol. 108ʳ, and Capsa 26, N. 43–2; a later copy is found in ITL, Urkundenserie i, MS 4058, fols. 11ʳ–12ʳ; see Santifaller, *Urkunden und Forschungen*, p. 383, no. 517); and Schneller, 'Beiträge zur Geschichte', p. 239, no. 266); and on 13 May the benefice of St Jacob was transferred (TASAPV, Sezione Latina, Capsa 46, N. 33; summarised in ITL, Liber Presentationum i (MS 3164), fol. 28ʳ; see Schneller, 'Beiträge zur Geschichte', pp. 189–90, no. 76).
28 ITL, Urkundenserie i, MS 5469; summarised in ITL, Liber Presentationum ii (MS 3165), fol. 4ʳ; see Schneller, 'Beiträge zur Geschichte', pp. 187–8, no. 69a.

Marschalk to the bishop.[29] These two documents must therefore have been based either on incorrect information or on an assumption of imminent death; and it is worth remarking that the earlier one lacks its validating seal. The many references to Lupi after 1456 confirm the erroneousness of these documents, and there is no evidence to support early transferral of the benefice. Furthermore, there can be no question that more than one man is involved here, since Lupi associates himself unambiguously in his will with the three ecclesiastical positions at Bolzano, Caldaro and Trent. Interestingly, it was only a few months earlier, on 9 September 1455, that he leased the entire parish of Caldaro for a period of five years.[30] The proximity of this event and the subsequent records of Lupi's alleged decease is striking, to say the least, and strengthens the possibility implied by Sigmund's letters that the former's health had recently suffered a severe decline. If indeed this is what happened, it is most likely to have occurred in the course of 1455, which would encourage the belief that it was during the first half of that year that Lupi felt impelled to take the precautionary measure of making his will.

The latter part of Lupi's life is reasonably well documented;[31] but until now there has been a lack of information for the period from 1432 to 1446, the very years of his known activity as a music scribe. Assuming that he was not a mature student when he entered the University of Vienna, his work as a copyist is likely to have begun in about 1430. Most of *TR* and *ZW* must have been copied *c.* 1433–45, although the similarity mentioned earlier between the script of the will and that of one of the last layers of *TR* (Figures 2–3) may indicate a slightly later date for the completion of Lupi's contribution to that manuscript. *TR* probably received its final form in or

[29] ITL, Urkundenserie I, MS 5466; summarised in ITL, Liber Presentationum II (MS 3165), fol. 4ʳ; see Schneller, 'Beiträge zur Geschichte', p. 187, no. 69b. Remarking on the inconsistency between the documents of 1456 and those of 1467, Schneller suggests (p. 189, n. 1) that the benefice may not really have been occupied at all during this period, but I have found no evidence to support this idea.

[30] TAC, Capsa 26, N. 23–1: 'dominus Johannes Lupi in Kaldario plebem eandem locavit honorabili viro domino Johanni Institoris ad annos quinque immediate sequentibus annum primum incipiendum circa festum Sancti Martini'.

[31] In addition to those sources already mentioned, he is cited – mainly in connection with the business of his parish – in the following documents: TAC, Instr. Cap. IX, fol. 285ᵛ (14 October 1455), fols. 290ᵛ–291ʳ (17 February 1456), fols. 315ᵛ–316ʳ (1 August 1457), fol. 342ʳ⁻ᵛ (19 October 1458); Instr. Cap. X, fol. 17ʳ (17 May 1459), fols. 19ᵛ–20ʳ (3 June 1459), fol. 157ᵛ (16 December 1462); Instr. Cap. XI, fol. 41ʳ⁻ᵛ (18 May 1464); and there are doubtless others. It is also known, from his will (Appendix, lines 103–11), that Lupi was a member of the fraternity of Corpus Christi.

near Trent, and some of its later additions may even have been copied there, yet there is no evidence that the manuscript is a local product.[32]

Where, then, was it copied? One obvious possibility is Bolzano, but although Lupi enjoyed a lifelong association with his native town, there are as yet no grounds for supposing that he was ever required to be there continuously: his benefice, for example, would almost certainly have been held 'in absentia'.[33] A more fruitful line of inquiry is suggested by his position as chaplain to Duke Sigmund, the only mentions of which occur in the documents relating to his investiture as rector of Caldaro. From the lack of any later reference to this position it might be inferred that 1447 (or 1446) marked the occasion of Lupi's arrival in Trent following a period of royal service. Sigmund had inherited the title of Duke of Austria on the death of his father, Friedrich IV, in 1439. Since he was then only thirteen, his powers were entrusted to his cousin and guardian, Friedrich (IV, King of Germany, from 1440; III, Holy Roman Emperor, from 1452), who in violation of an agreement with Sigmund's advisers took the boy with him to the Habsburg court at Graz/Wiener Neustadt, where he kept him in a state of semi-captivity until 1446.[34] Two documents from Friedrich's chancery provide evidence that by the end of 1440 Lupi was already in the service not of Sigmund, but of the king himself. The first, written in Wiener Neustadt on 23 November, is a recommendation for the collation of the parish of Tramin, a parish comparable in size and importance with Caldaro.[35] Lupi, who is described simply as a clerk of the diocese, presumably was

---

32 None of its papers appear to have been in regular use in Trent, there are no local texts, and no composers' names which suggest a local connection. (The only possible evidence of an association between the compiler and one of the composers is the ascription of the Sanctus on Tr92, fols. 210ᵛ–211ᵛ, to 'Magister Andreas' (cf. n. 17), the one continental composer in *TR* to be identified by Christian name alone.)

33 Apart from other considerations, Bolzano would not have been a particularly salubrious place in which to live or work after 1443, the year in which a fire destroyed a large part of the town. Details are given in B. Klammer, ed., *P. J. Ladurner's Chronik von Bozen, 1844* (Bozen, 1982), pp. 300–1.

34 I am grateful to Professor Reinhard Strohm for drawing my attention to this point. For details of Sigmund's wardship see J. Chmel, *Geschichte Kaiser Friedrichs IV. und seines Sohnes Maximilian I*, 2 vols. (Hamburg, 1840), I, pp. 414–42; and J. Ladurner, 'Über Herzog Sigmund's Vormundschaft 1439–1446', *Archiv für Geschichte Alterthumskunde Tirols*, 3 (1886), pp. 23–140.

35 VHHS, Reichsregistraturbuch O, fol. 30ʳ: 'Item primariae preces Johanni Lupi de Poczen, ad collacionem communitatis Traminii, clericus Tridentinenti diocesi'; a marginal note reads 'vacat, recepit alibi'. See J. Chmel, *Regesta chronologico-diplomatica Friderici IV. Romanorum Regis (Imperatoris III)* (Vienna, 1838), p. 18, no. 168.

unsuccessful as there is no record of an association with this parish.[36] The second document, dated 1440 and written in Wiener Neustadt probably in December, records Lupi's receipt from the king of a letter of service with [safe] conduct.[37] Unfortunately the nature of his employment is not specified, and it cannot be assumed that his duties were connected with music; yet so striking is the coincidence between his royal service and his known musical activities at this time that it is hard to resist the hypothesis that Lupi was employed as a copyist for the royal chapel (*ZW* in particular has the character of a commissioned manuscript). The fact that *AO*, a manuscript closely associated with this institution, appears to have been the direct source for a number of pieces in *TR*[38] strengthens this hypothesis; and it cannot be fortuitous that *AO* and *TR* are the two principal sources for the music of the most distinguished member of the chapel at this time, Johannes Brassart. Clearly, however, further investigation of the Viennese archival holdings is necessary if Lupi's activities during the 1430s and early 1440s are to receive proper clarification, and for the moment any connection between him and the royal chapel must remain purely conjectural.[39]

Returning to the question of the six books of *cantus figuratus* mentioned in the will, it becomes clear that to equate them with some combination of the seven volumes of polyphony that happen to survive at Trent, as Lunelli and others have attempted to do,[40] is misguided. Quite apart from the difficulty of reconciling the dates of the codices with the date of the will (Tr93 and Tr90 are the only

---

[36] For an account of the system whereby the King of Germany was entitled to request the transfer of benefices under his jurisdiction, see L. Santifaller, 'Die Preces primariae Maximilians I', *Festschrift zur Feier des zweihundertjährigen Bestandes des Haus-, Hof- und Staatsarchivs*, ed. L. Santifaller, Mitteilungen des Österreichischen Staatsarchivs 1, Ergänzungsband 2 (Vienna, 1949), pp. 578–9. In 1441 the king recommended Lupi to the Bishop of Bressanone: 'Item preces pro Johanne Lupi ad collacionem Episcopi Brixensi' (VHHS, Reichregistraturbuch O, fol. 34ᵛ); but once again it is probably fair to assume that his recommendation was unsuccessful.

[37] VHHS, Reichregistraturbuch O, fol. 30ʳ: 'Item familiaritatis pro Johanne Lupi de Boczano, clerico Tridentinenti diocesi, sub forma communi cum conductu'. See Chmel, *Regesta chronologico-diplomatica*, p. 20, no. 192.

[38] See P. Wright, 'The Aosta–Trent Relationship Reconsidered', paper given at a conference to commemorate the life and work of Laurence Feininger held at Trent in September 1985, and to be published in the conference proceedings.

[39] Federhofer, 'Trienter Codices' (n. 14), col. 668, speculates that Tr87 and Tr92 may contain the repertory of the chapel of Emperor Sigismund III.

[40] See S. Saunders, 'The Dating of the Trent Codices from their Watermarks, with a Study of the Local Liturgy of Trent in the Fifteenth Century' (Ph.D. thesis, University of London, 1984), pp. 148–9; and Spilsted, 'Toward the Genesis' (n. 2), p. 62.

members of the younger group which could have been complete by 1455), one would need to presuppose that the young Wiser passed on his collection to the ageing and probably ailing Lupi, merely for it to be bequeathed to the parish church of Bolzano. Such a hypothesis clearly is unsustainable. What does seem to be implied by Lupi's bequest is that the 'sex libri' were manuscripts which he had copied or collected himself, and that Tr87 and Tr92 were therefore among them. This, however, is not to deny an association between Lupi and Wiser; indeed, it would be surprising if two men employed by the chapter at the same time, each with a consuming passion for collecting polyphony, had not known each other. Proof that they were in fact well acquainted is furnished by the document recording Wiser's investiture on 3 June 1459 as chaplain of the altars of SS. Dorothea and Nicolaus, for in it Lupi is himself named as collator of the benefice – the person responsible for its conferment and subsequent protection and administration.[41] The personal nature of his task, entrusted to one who was not a member of the chapter, bears witness to a close friendship.

This document, first cited by Lunelli on account of its mention of Wiser's appointment at the cathedral school, has long been thought to contain the earliest reference to him. Since it describes him as a young priest from Munich, it has reasonably been assumed that Wiser had arrived in Trent only very recently. However, a previously overlooked document describing him simply as a musician in the city indicates that he was already present there four years earlier, but in a humbler capacity.[42] It seems unlikely therefore that

---

[41] TAC, Instr. Cap. x, fol. 19ᵛ: 'comisserunt predicto domino Johanni Lupi ut dictum dominum Johannem Wiser in tenuram et corporalem possessionem dictorum altarium, ut premissum est sic sibi colatorum inducat et ponat, et inductum et positum tueatur, et defendat ac faciat sibi de fructibus reditibus'. Earlier in this document, which is summarised in Santifaller, *Urkunden und Forschungen*, p. 363, no. 486, Wiser is referred to as 'honestus et discretus iuvenis dominus Johannes Wisser de Monaco, Frisingensis diocesis, magister et rector scolarum'.

[42] TAC, Instr. Cap. ix, fol. 284ʳ (30 July 1455): 'Johannes Wissar, suonatore scolaris in dicta civitate'. The word 'suonatore' (the scribe has lapsed into the vernacular at this point) might be interpreted more specifically to mean 'player' or 'organist'. It would appear significant that this early mention of Wiser (so far the only reference to his status as a musician) occurs in a document relating to his predecessor as master and rector of the cathedral school, Johannes Prenner, since this suggests that Wiser may already have been employed there, perhaps as his assistant. The proximity of this earliest reference to Wiser to the matriculation of 'Johannes Organista de Monaco' at the University of Vienna (2 November 1454; see L. Santifaller, ed., *Die Matrikel der Universität Wien*, ii: *1451–1518*, Publikationen des Instituts für Österreichische Geschichtsforschung, ser. vi, 1/ii (Graz and Cologne, 1959), vol. 1, p. 31, no. 47) marginally strengthens the attractive if slight

Wiser was in Trent much before July 1455. To assume that he was might be to stretch the medieval definition of 'iuvenis', while perhaps also implying exceptional longevity (he was still alive in 1497).[43]

By 1459 the two men evidently knew each other well. Had they been thus well acquainted by 1455, one would expect Wiser to have been a beneficiary of Lupi's will. The fact that he apparently is not[44] seems therefore to suggest that their association began in about 1455, soon after Wiser's arrival in Trent. Such a date would not only allow time for their relationship to mature to a point of mutual trust, but would also provide a plausible *terminus post quem* for Wiser's scribal work on the codices, the early part of which reveals a distinct lack of experience. From a study of the repertory shared by *TR* and the later codices (Tr93, Tr90 and Tr88) it appears that Wiser never drew directly on the surviving material copied by Lupi. Nevertheless, it is quite possible that Lupi acted as Wiser's mentor, his own work perhaps serving as a stimulus and source of inspiration for the younger man, and that there was even some form of collaboration between them.[45]

Whether or not Lupi's original bequest of the 'sex libri' was ever carried out must remain a matter for conjecture;[46] but the very fact that his will survives in autograph form suggests that it was never executed, and it would be surprising if at some point during the remaining twelve or so years of his life he had not made another. In

possibility raised by Spilsted ('The Paleography and Repertory', p. 174, n. 9) that they are one and the same person.

[43] TAC, Instr. Cap. xiii, fol. 135ᵛ (12 April 1497). Cited in G. Boni, 'Origini e memorie della chiesa plebana di Tione', *Studi Trentini di Scienze Storiche*, 19 (1938) [part 3], p. 253.

[44] Unless he is either 'Johannes amicus domini decani' (Appendix, line 128) or 'Johannes lector ewangelii' (lines 133–4).

[45] This might be adduced from the fact (hitherto unnoticed) that the scribe who copied Tr87, fols. 167ᵛ–174ʳ, also entered the Gloria on Tr88, fols. 384ᵛ–386ʳ, and the Sanctus setting on Tr89, fols. 57ᵛ–58ᵛ, and may have copied other works into the later manuscripts. Many features of this hand (for example, the hairline stroke of the 'e' or the internal '2'-shaped 'r') seem to indicate that it is not Wiser's (as suggested in M. Bent, 'Some Criteria for Establishing Relationships between Sources of Late-medieval Polyphony', in *Music in Medieval and Early Modern Europe: Patronage, Sources and Texts*, ed. I. Fenlon (Cambridge, 1981), p. 303, n. 11), but that of one of his assistants. Tr87, fols. 167ᵛ–174ʳ, form part of a late addition to *TR* which differs from the later codices both in its papers and in its layout of staves.

[46] There is, for example, no record of their presence among the liturgical books listed in the various fifteenth-century catalogues of the parish church of Bolzano: see H. Obermair, 'Die liturgischen Bücher der Pfarrkirche Bozen aus dem letzten Viertel des 15. Jahrhunderts', *Der Schlern*, 59 (1985), pp. 516–36. I am grateful to Herr Obermair for sending me a copy of his article and answering a number of points.

all probability Lupi decided that it would be safer or more appropriate to leave his music books to Wiser, who, it appears, subsequently bequeathed his entire collection to the recently founded chapter library. A catalogue entry shows that the codices formed part of the library in the early eighteenth century,[47] and there is little reason to doubt that they had remained there undisturbed since Wiser's death in about 1500. One non-musical book may also be identified as having belonged to Wiser: a volume of Cassiodorus's letters, whose note of ownership provides the only other known specimen of his handwriting (see Figure 6).[48]

It cannot be certainly established whether Tr87 and Tr92 were used as performing manuscripts. At times these sources seem by their very nature to preclude such a possibility, while for the most part they provide perfectly adequate performing copies, many of which incorporate changes apparently born of practical experience. Although no documentary evidence has so far emerged to support the idea that polyphony was performed in Trent in the early to mid-fifteenth century, *cantus figuratus* probably was taught at the cathedral school[49] and, more importantly, the anthologies compiled by Lupi and Wiser (both of whom were practising musicians) are unlikely to have been intended as mere repositories without practical value. *TR* may, as has already been suggested, have had a specific function in connection with the Habsburg court. But that is not to imply that by the time Lupi arrived in Trent in the mid-1440s his manuscripts had necessarily outlived their useful purpose. Much of the music contained in Tr87 and Tr92 would still have been in

---

[47] TAC, manuscript catalogue, 'Repertorium omnium documentorum, quae in Archivio Cattedralis Ecclesiae Tridentinae Divi Vigilii custodienda asservantur, ad Reverendissimi Capituli commodum, et Ecclesiae predictae incrementum opera, ac studio Francisci Feliciis Comitis de Albertis Canonici Tridentini, interiectis materiarum titulis anno Domini 1746 absolutum', fol. 108^v: 'Liber Musicus MS. = alii consimiles = B.L.'. (Cited in Carlini and others, *Dalla polifonia al classicismo* (n. 1), p. 16.) R. Bockholdt, 'Notizen zur Handschrift Trient "93" und zu Dufays frühen Messensätzen', *Acta Musicologica*, 33 (1961), p. 40, noted the presence on the spine of Tr93 of the letters 'BL' and an inscription 'Cod(?) Musicus MS Libr . . .'. Unfortunately all the original bindings of the Trent codices were discarded during the restoration of the manuscripts in the 1970s, but photographs of Tr87–92 taken before 1934 and now kept at the Museo Provinciale d'Arte confirm that the same eighteenth-century shelfmark was present on the spines of other volumes in the group.

[48] This note reads: 'Et postea emptus per Johannem Wiser, iuris utriusque doctorem, in die exaltationis sancte crucis, Anno Domini M°C°C°C°C°9°'. The book in which it is found (TBC, MS 151, 'Cassiodori liber Variarum') is cited in V. Casagrande, *Catalogo del Museo Diocesano di Trento* (Trent, 1908), p. 90, no. 470.

[49] See Cattin, 'Church Patronage' (n. 9), esp. p. 29.

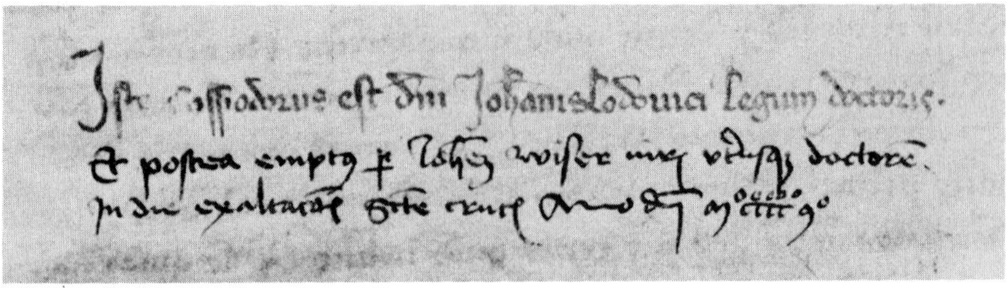

Peter Wright

Figure 6 Johannes Wiser's note of ownership of TBC, MS 151 (final page)

vogue, and as cathedral organist he would presumably have had the occasional opportunity to promote polyphonic performance. It is thus conceivable that the clearer and more reliable parts of these manuscripts continued to fulfil a practical need, and that they were perhaps even sung from by some of the ostensibly musical beneficiaries of Lupi's will.[50] Viewed in this light, Lunelli's admittedly ill-founded belief that there existed in quattrocento Trent the resources for realising complex polyphony seems distinctly more credible than it once appeared.

ABBREVIATIONS

AO	Aosta, Biblioteca del Seminario Maggiore, MS A¹D 19
Instr. Cap.	Instrumenta Capitularia
ITL	Innsbruck, Tiroler Landesarchiv
TAC	Trent, Archivio Capitolare
TASAPV	Trent, Archivio di Stato, Archivio del Principato Vescovile di Trento
TBC	Trent, Biblioteca Capitolare
Tr87–92	Trent, Museo Provinciale d'Arte, MSS 87–92 (now numbered 1374–9)
Tr87₁	Tr87, fols. 1–218
Tr87₂	Tr87, fols. 219–65
Tr92₁	Tr92, fols. 1–143
Tr92₂	Tr92, fols. 144–268
TR	Tr87₁ and Tr92₂
Tr93	Trent, Biblioteca Capitolare, MS 'BL'

---

[50] The rector of Tysens, recipient of a *schaffpret* and a portative organ (Appendix, lines 116–18); Johannes Freudental, recipient of a clavichord and lute (lines 118–20); Ambrosio [Slaspeck], recipient of a clavicembalo, clavichord and lute (lines 120–2); and the priest 'primo qui cantat' (lines 141–2). Also mentioned in the will are a *mansionarius* (lines 14 and 125) and a *succentor* (line 139); both of these offices often carried musical duties.

On the origins of Trent 87$_1$ and 92$_2$

University of Nottingham

APPENDIX[51]

Johannes Lupi's will (TAC, Capsa dei Testamenti, unnumbered document)

Testamentum Johannis lupi | plebano in Caldario et cetera | Ego Johannes lupi Plebanus in Caldario et Capellanus altaris sancte Maxencie in crippa ecclesie Cath(e)trali | Sancti Vigilii preciosi martiris Tridenti et cetera Recognosco et lego necnon ordino et hoc pro ultimo
5   testamento | meo // Si migrarem de hoc seculo avertat deus iam in via peregrinacacionis ut illa omnia infrascripta maniant semper | firma et rata sine dolo et fraude / usque qualitercumque revocarem illa in vita mea. et hoc libera et sana mente | propria manu mea hic conscripsi et hoc cum sigillo meo sigillavi et impressi ‖ **Item** pro omnibus constituo pro
10   testamentaribus meis primo Venerabilem necnon Egregium et cetera dominum Johannem Sulczpach | Decanum et Cancellarium gloriossissimi domini mei episcopi Tridenti Johannem ⌜de⌝ frewlental plebanum in fundo dominum | Johannem zeis plebanum in sancto petro dominum Leonhardum mensionarium ecclesie Tridentine et cetera Rogo causa
15   dei | supradictos testamentarios ut testamentum meum infrascriptum volunt distribuere assignare et dare pro salute | anime mee et eciam pro salute omnium fidelium defunctorum // ad loca infrascripta et hoc fideliter sicud volunt respondere deo ‖ **Item** primo lego et ordino fabrice

[51]   This is a transcription, not an edition. As many as possible of the original characteristics of the document (spelling, capitalisation, punctuation) have therefore been retained, in the hope that this will facilitate evaluation of Lupi's habits as a scribe. Abbreviations have been expanded and italicised. Occasionally a letter which is obviously missing has been supplied parenthetically. A vertical stroke indicates the end of a line, two vertical strokes the end of an item where the following item begins on the next line. (Oblique strokes represent original punctuation.) In addition the following symbols (borrowed from M. B. Parkes, *English Cursive Book Hands 1250–1500* (Oxford, 1969), p. xxviii) have been used: ⌜ ⌝ enclose words which have been inserted between lines or placed in the margin; [ ] enclose words or letters which have been deleted by the scribe by means of crossing out or erasure. I am grateful to Don Ivo Leonardi for allowing me to consult his unpublished transcription of the will, from which my own version differs in a number of respects; and to Dr Michael Jones and Professor Robin Storey of the University of Nottingham History Department for kindly checking my transcription and offering some useful suggestions.

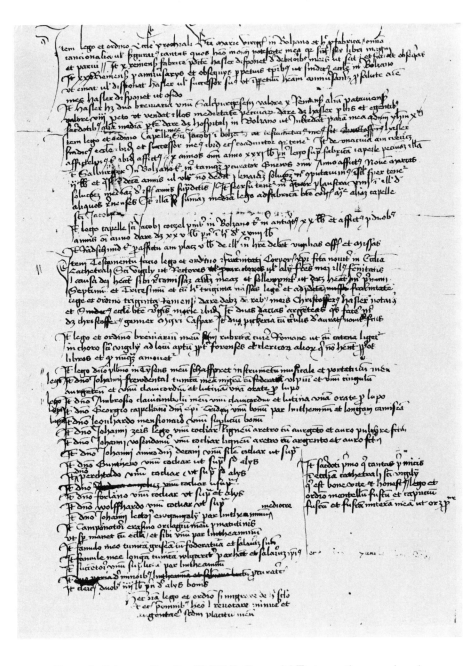

Figure 7a Johannes Lupi's will (TAC, Capsa dei Testamenti, unnumbered
document, reduced; original dimensions 400 × 290), mm recto

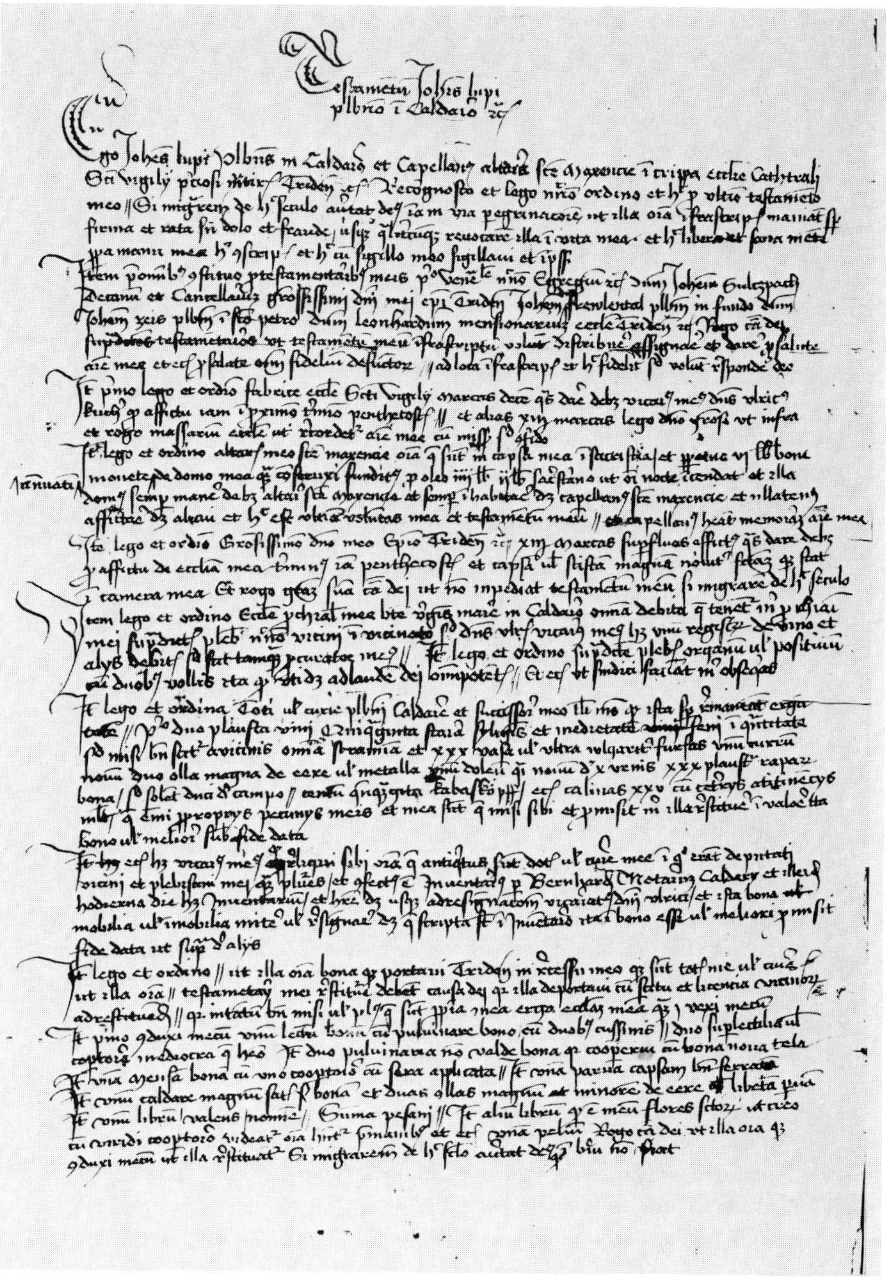

Figure 7b Johannes Lupi's will, verso

ecclesie Sancti Vigilii Marcas decem quas dare debet vicarius meus
20 dominus ulricus | kuchus pro affictu iam in proximo termino penthe-
costes // et alias xiij marcas lego domino glorioso ut infra | et rogo
massarium ecclesie ut recordetur anime mee cum missis sicud confido ||
Item lego et ordino altari meo sancte maxencie omnia que sunt in capsa
mea in sacristia / et perpetuo vj libras bone | monete ⌐annuatim⌐ de
25 domo mea quam construxi funditus pro oleo iiij libras ij libras
sacristano ut omni nocte incendat et illa | domus semper manere debet
altari sancte Maxencie et semper inhabitare debet capellanus sancte
maxencie et n(u)llatenus | affictare debet alicui et hoc est ultima
voluntas mea et testamentum meum // et capellanus habeat memoriam
30 anime mee || **Item** lego et ordino Gloriosissimo domino meo Episcopo
Tridentino et cetera xiij Marcas superfluas affictus quas dare debet | pro
affictu de ecclesia mea terminus iam penthecostes et capsam vel stistam
magnam noviter factam que stat | in camera mea Et rogo graciam suam
causa dei ut non inpediat testamentum meum si migrarem de hoc seculo
35 || **Item** lego et ordino Ecclesie parochiali mee beate virginis marie in
Caldario omnia debita que tenentur michi parochiani | mei supradicte
plebis necnon vicini in vicinato sicud dominus ulricus vicarius meus
habet unum registrum de vino et | aliis debitis secundum scit tamquam
procurator meus // **Item** lego et ordino supradicte plebi organum vel
40 positivum | cum duobus vollis ita quod uti debet ad laudem dei
omnipotentis // Et eciam ut sindici faciant michi obsequias || **Item** lego
et ordina Toti vel curie plebani Caldarie et successori meo tali modo
quod ista semper remaneant erga | totem // Primo duo plaust(r)a vini
Quinquaginta staria syliginis et medietatem [vini] feni in quantitate |
45 sicud misi bene scitur a vicinis omnia stramina et xxx vasa vel ultra
wlgariter furfas unum currum | novum duo olla magna de cere vel
metalla unum doleum quasi novum de x urnis xxx plaustra raparum |
bona / sicud solent duci de campo // centum quinquagi(n)ta kabasköpff
/ eciam calinas xxv cum ceteriis atitinenciis | multis que emmi pro
50 propriis pecuniis meis et mea sunt que misi sibi et promisit michi illa
restituere in valore ita | bono vel meliori sub fide data || **Item** (habet]
eciam habet vicarius meus quod reliqui sibi omnia que antiquitus sunt
dotis vel curie mee in qua erant deputati | vicini et plebisani mei quam
plures / et confectus est Inventarius per Bernhardum Notarium Caldarii
55 et ille idem | hodierna die habet Inventarium / et habere debet usque ad
resignacionem vicariatus domini ulrici / et ista bona [vel] | mobilia vel
immobilia mitere vel resignare debet que scripta sunt in Inventario ita in
bono esse vel meliori promisit | fide data ut supra de aliis || **Item** lego et
ordino // ut illa omnia bona que portavi Tridentum in recessu meo que
60 sunt tota me vel curie | ut illa omnia // testamentarii mei restituere

268

debent causa dei qui illa deportavi cum scitu et licencia vicinorum | ad
restituendum // qui intantum bene misi vel plus quam sunt propria mea
erga ecclesiam meam quam nihil(?) vexi mecum ‖ **Item** primo conduxi
mecum unum lectum bonum cum pulvinare bono / cum duobus cussinis

65 // duo superlectilia vel | copertoria mediocra que habeo **Item** duo
pulvinaria non valde bona qui cooperui cum bona nova tela ‖ **Item**
unam Mensam bonam cum uno coopertorio cum fera applicata // **Item**
unam parvam capsam bene ferratam ‖ **Item** unum caldare magnum
satis [s] bonam et duas ollas magnum et minorem de cere [et] libetam

70 parvam ‖ **Item** unum librum / valens / nomine // Summa pesani // **Item**
alium librum quod est meum flores sanctorum / ut cre(d)o | cum viridi
coopertorio videatur omnia habentur per manibus et eciam unam pelvim
Rogo causa dei ut illa omnia que | conduxi mecum ut illa restituantur Si
migrarem de hoc seculo avertat deus ⌐quod⌐ in brevi non fiat ‖ (VERSO)

75 **Item** lego et ordino Ecclesie parochiali Beate Marie Viriginis in
Bolzano et hoc pro fabrica // omnia | cancionalia vel figuratus cantus
quos habeo in omni potestate mea que sunt sex libri magni | et parvi //
Item x reinenses fabrice predicte hasler disponet de debitoribus meis ut
scit / et faciat obsequias | **Item** xxx Reinenses pro anniversariis et

80 obsequiis perpetuis temporibus ut sindicus ecclesie in Bolzano | ut emat
vel disponat hasler vel successor suus ut in perpetuum habeam anniver-
sarium pro salute anime | mee hasler disponet ut confido ‖ **Item** Hasler
habet duo breviaria unum Salczpurgensem valore x Reinenses alium
pataviensem | valore viij Peto ut vendat illos medietatem pecuniarum

85 dare debet hasler probis et egentibus | sacerdotibus aliam mediam
partem dare debet hospitali in Bolzano ut Intercedant pro anima mea
a(d) dominum jhesum Christum ‖ **Item** lego et ordino Capelle ⌐mee⌐
Sancti Jacobi in bolzano ut testamentarius meus sit Christofforus hasler
| sindicus ecclesie ibidem et successor meus ibidem eciam coadiuitor qui

90 tenetur **It(em)** de una curia am creücz | affictelinus tenetur ibidem
affictus [x]x annos omni anno xxxj libras pro(?) nobis(?) lego supra
fabricam capelle pecuniam illam ‖ **Item** Sal(z)burger In Bolzano
tenetur michi tamquam procurator Gnews omni Anno affictus Novem
Marcas | ij libras et quod si in decem annis v(e)l ultra non dedit

95 plenariam solucionem nec computavimus in simul semper tenetur | solu-
cionem mediarum de istis annis supradictis / **Item** seorsum tenetur
michi quatuor plaustra vini in illis de | aliquos reinenses **Item** illam [so]
summam mediam lego ad fabricam beate virginis Marie aliam capelle |
sancti Jacobi ‖ **Item** lego capelle sancti Jacobi coczel pintus in Bolzano

100 tenetur michi antiquitus xx libras et affictus pro duobus | annis omni anno
dare debet xxv libras pro(?) nobis(?) in hoc dixit xviiij libras ‖ **Item**
Radschmid tenetur pro affictu am placz v libras de illis michi habere
debent vigilias officia et Missas ‖ **Item** Testamentum facio lego et

ordino Fraternitati Corporis Christi facta noviter in Ecclesia |
105 Cathetrali Sancti Vigilii ut Rectores vel procuratores vel alii fratres mei
ill(i)us fraternitatis | nihil(?) causa dei habeant sibi recomissam animam
meam et sollempniter ut decet habeant michi primum | Sepetimum et
Tricesimum et cum hoc triginta missas legere et ad predictam [missam]
fraternitatem | lege et ordino triginta Reinenses dare debet de rebus
110 meis Christofferus hasler notarius | ut Si⌐ndi⌐cus ecclesie beate virginis
marie ibidem **Item** duas dacias argenteas quas facere michi | debet
christofferus genner Magistri Caspar **Item** duo pickeria cum circulis de
auratis noviter factis ‖ **Item** lego et ordino breviarium meum secundum
rubricam curie Romane ut cum catena ligetur | in choro sancti vigilii ad
115 locum aptum propter forenses et clericorum aliorum qui non habent
proprios | libros et quod nunquam amovetur ‖ **Item** lego domino plebano
in Tysens meum schaffpret instrumentum musicale et portativum
meum ‖ **Item** ⌐lego⌐ domino Johanni frewdental tunicam meam nigram
cum foderatum ulpium et unum cingulum | aurgenteum et unum
120 clavicordium et lutinam unam orate pro lupo ‖ **Item** ⌐lego⌐ domino
Ambrosio clavicimbolum meum unum clavicordium et lutinam unam
orate pro lupo ‖ **Item** ⌐lego⌐ domino Georgio cappellano domini
episcopi Tridenti unum bonum par lintheminum et longam camisiam ‖
Item ⌐lego⌐ domino leonhardo mensionario unum superlicium bonum ‖
125 **Item** domino Johanni zeis lego unum cocliar ligneum aretro cum
aurgento et auro pulchre factum ‖ **Item** domino Johanni vosendonum
unum cocliar ligneum aretro cum argento et auro factum ‖ **Item** domino
Johanni amico domini decani unum simile cocliar ut supra ‖ **Item**
domino Gunthero unum cocliar ut supra sicud aliis ‖ **Item** ⌐domino⌐
130 perchtoldo unum cocliar ut supra sicud aliis ‖ **Item** domino [Andrea
auge(n)licz unum cocliar u(t) supra] ‖ **Item** domino forläno unum
cocliar ut supra et aliis ‖ **Item** domino Wolffhardo unum cocliar ut
supra ‖ **Item** domino Johanni lectori ewgangelii par lintheaminum
⌐mediocre⌐ ‖ **Item** Campanatori erasmo orilagium meum pro
135 matutinis | ut semper mane(a)t cum ecllesia / et sibi unum par
lintheaminum ‖ **Item** famulo meo tunicam griseam cum foderatura et
salarium suum ‖ **Item** famule mee longam tunicam wlgariter parhant et
salarium ipsius et duas tunicas et unum lectum bonum sicut debet ‖ **Item**
succentori unum superlicium par lintheaminum ‖ **Item** domino paria de
140 minoribus [lintheamina et solummodo lectum] procuratorie ‖ **Item**
clericis duobus iiij libras pro(?) nobis(?) de aliis bonis ‖ ⌐**Item** sacerdoti
primo qui cantat primicis | in ecclesia cathetrali sancti vigilii | qui est
bone vite et honestus / lego et | ordino mantellum fustum et capucium |
fuscum et fuscam miteram meam ut oret pro me⌐ ‖ Hec omnia lego et
145 ordino si migrarem de hoc seculo | Et eciam pre omnibus habeo nihil(?)
revocare minuere et | aug(m)entare secundum placitum meum |

REVIEWS

IAN WOODFIELD, *The Early History of the Viol.* Cambridge, Cambridge University Press, 1984. xiii + 266 pp.

Writers have speculated about the early history of the viol for more than three centuries but until now have neither pinpointed its origins nor satisfactorily explained its rise to popularity as an ensemble and solo instrument. Ian Woodfield convincingly traces the beginnings of the viol to the late fifteenth century in the Spanish kingdom of Aragon by carefully examining a wealth of new archival and iconographical material and adding fresh interpretations of some familiar historical writings. He then charts the instrument's rise to prominence in the sixteenth century with its introduction into Italy, Germany, France, the Low Countries and England. He also brings a player's insight to a discussion of the music and technical matters of construction and playing technique.

In an entertaining and informative introduction, the author traces previous attempts to uncover the viol's obscure origins. Renaissance theorists such as Ganassi credited the viol with an ancestry reaching back to antiquity and the Greek and Roman civilisations, while twentieth-century organologists[1] have mistakenly speculated that it could be traced back to medieval times. Yet the viol's existence between the thirteenth and late fifteenth centuries has never been documented. One of the important contributions of Woodfield's study, therefore, is that it overturns the views advanced by Galpin, Bessaraboff and Hayes that a large twelfth-century bowed instrument with an hourglass shape and played downwards was a type of

---

[1] See, for example, F. W. Galpin, *Old English Instruments of Music* (London, 1910; fourth revised edition, 1965), pp. 64–5; N. Bessaraboff, *Ancient Musical Instruments* (Boston, 1941), p. 267; and G. R. Hayes, *Musical Instruments and their Music, 1500–1700*, 2 vols. (London, 1928 and 1930), II: *The Viols and Other Bowed Instruments*, p. 56.

early viol and related in some mysterious way to the Renaissance viol, despite the lengthy period which separated them. Thurston Dart proved to be closer to identifying the viol's true origin when he speculated that it grew up in Spain as a sort of bowed guitar, the result of 'cross-fertilisation between the 15th-century Spanish plucked instrument known as the *vihuela de mano* and the medieval fiddle'.[2] Woodfield's well-chosen plates, over a hundred in all, help to document the origin of the viol in Aragon and to trace its unbroken line of development beginning about 1480.

In the first part of the book, Woodfield addresses five main questions: the medieval instrumental traditions that contributed to the evolution of the viol, the precise origins of the instrument, the physical characteristics of the early viol and the emergence of the 'classic instrument', the music performed by the first viol players and the spread of the viol throughout Europe. The lack of conclusive results from previous historical research on the early viol can be attributed in part to the lack of any treatises or instruments surviving from the 'crucial period' of 1480 to 1520, when the instrument began to spread across Europe. Woodfield thus relies primarily on evidence from visual representations – paintings, miniatures and sculptures. Fortunately, there is a wealth of such iconographic evidence, extensive enough to allow one to observe trends in construction and the viol's physical characteristics and even some features related to its manner of playing. It also allows the author to identify representations that lie outside these norms and are therefore too artistically individual to be considered reliable as historical evidence. Woodfield adds some references to the instrument in archival documents and literary sources, but he correctly observes that many early names were generic (such as *vihuela*, *Geige* and *viola*) and therefore applied to several different instruments at the same time.

One of the distinctive features of the viol's playing technique is that the instrument is held downwards, supported on the knees or between the legs (*a gamba*), and bowed with the palm turned up (called 'underhand'). As bowed string instruments spread through Europe this technique and the *a braccio* method, with the instrument held against the arm or on the shoulder and bowed 'overhand' (palm down), were at first used on the same instrument but soon became

---

[2]   R. T. Dart, 'The Viols', in A. Baines, ed., *Musical Instruments through the Ages* (London, 1961), pp. 184–90; Woodfield, p. 3.

associated with different instruments and evolved separately. With the virtual dominance of the violin family by the mid-eighteenth century, the *a gamba* method gradually died out in Western countries, but even today it is still a common manner of playing many string instruments in North Africa, the Middle East, Central Asia and the Far East.

The earliest depiction of a bowed string instrument is found in a Mozarabic manuscript dating from *c.* 920–30 in the Biblioteca Nacional, Madrid. It shows four standing musicians playing 'large, bottle-shaped instruments which are held downwards and bowed with large, almost semi-circular bows' (p. 9). This *a gamba* position became associated by the twelfth century with waisted fiddles, and was a feature that led organologists to refer to them as 'medieval viols'. Woodfield examines the plentiful thirteenth-century depictions of similar instruments and is able to discover three main shapes; all three have a waisted and gently curved shape, without corners. He postulates from the smaller number of representations in the early fourteenth century that the instrument was already suffering decline and probably fell into disuse by the end of the century. The author also suggests that the occasional depictions of fiddles held *a gamba* in fourteenth- and fifteenth-century art prove upon closer examination to show the instrument being held downwards for tuning. Woodfield concludes that 'despite its undeniably viol-like appearance and playing techniques, the medieval viol was not the immediate ancestor of the renaissance instrument, which did not appear until the end of the 15th century' (p. 14).

The fifteenth century has long been a completely uncharted period in the history of bowed strings that were played *a gamba*. Thus Woodfield's chapter 2, 'The Moorish *rabāb* in Aragon', offers much new information and provides a link between the earliest depictions of bowed fiddles played *a gamba* and the spread of the viol during the sixteenth century, from which a continuous tradition is easier to trace. With the decline of the medieval fiddle, the *a gamba* posture was largely replaced with the *a braccio* playing position for most Western bowed instruments, but in southern Europe players of the Moorish *rabāb* introduced that instrument into certain areas of the Kingdom of Aragon, and it became 'a provincial tradition that proved an important factor in the eventual emergence of the renaissance viol' (p. 15). Early depictions of the instrument, such as a finely detailed angel found on a late fourteenth-century reliquary chest in Perpignan (pl. 4), show a *rabāb* being played in the usual downwards position. The instrument is long and thin with a straight-sided body, a curved lower end, reverse pegbox, two strings, and a distinct division between the two halves of the belly (the lower of parchment and the upper of wood), with ornamental roses on the upper portion. The growing popularity of a similar instrument, the rebec, in Western Europe slowly influenced the development of the Moroccan *rabāb* and altered some of its features, converting it by the 1470s and 1480s to an instrument with two to six strings and a completely wooden belly. Amplifying his discussion with some literary references and comments by the theorists Jerome of Moravia and Tinctoris, Woodfield illustrates the diversity of instruments as to size, stringing and type of bow, and he summarises significant trends in the relevant artistic depictions and even suggests how the instrument might have been tuned. Since Jerome attributed a range of a major ninth to the 'rubeba', it would have been possible for the two-string *rabāb* to have open strings a fifth apart (*c–g*), giving it a range of *c–d'*.

Plentiful iconographical evidence still offers little assistance in studying such specific technical matters as the manner of bowing or the instrument's function in ensembles, for artists' depictions of angel concerts cannot necessarily be taken as representative of actual practice. Woodfield occasionally relies too much upon evidence from the 'majority' of illustrations, a necessarily inaccurate representation of the total number that still survive and of the much greater number that once existed.[3] There is little evidence either to establish how the medieval *rabāb* functioned in its musical setting. Woodfield assumes that it served primarily as a drone instrument, and he draws support for this from references in sixteenth-century Spanish pastoral literature to the 'rabel' used by shepherds to accompany songs and from the remarkable similarity of this instrument to the modern Moroccan *rabāb*, an instrument still used for drone accompaniments. The author surmises that when the instrument came to be constructed entirely from wood, a development that can be documented with evidence from contemporary paintings, it may have been more suited to part-music. Outside Aragon the

[3]   These two points are also raised by Howard Mayer Brown in 'The Trecento Harp', *Studies in the Performance of Late Mediaeval Music*, ed. S. Boorman (Cambridge, 1983), p. 40.

instrument (known as the rebec) was played in the *a braccio* position and bowed overhand. Woodfield's conclusion thus finally sheds some light on a mysterious period in the viol's history: 'The Moorish musicians of the Kingdom of Aragon can thus claim the important distinction of having maintained in Europe the ancient, oriental method of string playing from which the viol was to copy its own playing techniques' (p. 37).

The other strong influence upon the early viol also came from Aragon, with the large, waisted plucked instrument of the mid-fifteenth century known as the *vihuela de mano*. Although Thurston Dart recognised the significant contribution of that instrument to the early viol, especially in details of construction and body shape, historians of the *vihuela* have devoted more attention to its sixteenth-century repertory and have ignored the preceding decades when it exerted a strong influence upon the viol. With plentiful iconographic support, Woodfield shows that the plucked *vihuela* was well established in the Kingdom of Aragon by the 1480s. Frequently included in scenes of angelic music-making, the instrument was generally shown with a reverse lute-like pegbox, a long thin neck, and waists with corners. The reverse pegbox (replacing the old circular pegbox) and the four-cornered, waisted shape were developments that originated before the middle of the fifteenth century and became typical features of its construction by the end of the century.

The next stage in the viol's development can be summarised as follows: 'In and around the city of Valencia two distinct offshoots of this instrument [the *vihuela de mano*] began to emerge: the bowed *vihuela de arco* or viol, structurally identical to its ancestor, but borrowing its playing techniques from local Moorish players of the *rabāb*; and the plucked *vihuela de mano* which reverted to the guitar shape and abandoned the use of corners' (pp. 44, 49). A brief transitional period in the 1480s and 1490s may have seen the early cornered *vihuelas* used for either bowing or plucking, but the playing technique soon became associated with a specific shape: the cornered shape was retained for the *a gamba* posture, while the gently curving, guitar-shaped waists were used for plucked instruments. One of these transitional instruments is shown on an Italian majolica plate (Figure 1), probably from the Duchy of Urbino in the mid-fifteenth century. In this accurately painted representation, Apollo is holding a six-string fretted *vihuela de mano* with a flat pegbox

Figure 1 Majolica plate depicting Apollo and Pan before the gods Timolus and
Midas, Italy, c. 1542; London, Wallace Collection, c 121

and four-cornered shape. Woodfield does not mention the plentiful
illustrations of *vihuelas* and early viols on majolica, but a study of
these representations would amplify his evidence for Moorish
influence upon the instrument's early development, for the highly
developed technique of majolica was also first brought across the
Mediterranean by Moorish craftsmen.

Having identified the antecedents of the viol in Valencia, Woodfield then traces the instrument's characteristic structure, playing
techniques and music, beginning with the earliest depictions of a
Valencian viol in a panel of a Madonna and Child with musicians in
San Felíu, near Játiva. From the large number of early depictions of

276

the instrument, a composite view of its shape, size and number of strings emerges. A tall, slender instrument with a long neck and thin ribs, the Valencian viol had a relatively small body and cornered shape. It had neither the raised fingerboard nor angled neck that the viol acquired later in the sixteenth century. Although it was shown with three to as many as six strings, five or six seem to have been the norm. Iconographic evidence even suggests the possibility that transverse barring was used under the flat belly of the instrument.

One of the critical points regarding the possible function of the instrument in musical ensembles is its bridge. On the basis of many early representations, a common method of string-fastening seems to have been that of the guitar and lute, in which the strings ran directly from the nut to a flat stringholder around which the strings were looped securely, without a bridge. Although modern builders may not have attempted to construct instruments of this type as yet, Woodfield's suggestion that the reader try the effect on a modern guitar is sure to cast doubt on his otherwise convincing iconographical evidence. It is hard to imagine that players, once equipped with a bow, would not immediately add a bridge as a necessity for producing sound. If indeed a flat bridge was occasionally added, as some of the iconographic evidence suggests, one wonders how instruments with five or six strings (the 'majority', according to Woodfield's survey of paintings) were used, if most of these strings had to be bowed together (p. 71). It is entirely possible, as some modern instrument makers have demonstrated, to construct two bridges for an instrument, one flat to allow the instrument to play drones, either with or without a melody on the top string, and another arched for single-line playing. The bridges can be easily exchanged by the player when re-tuning the instrument.

Having presented new evidence for the ancestor of the Italian Renaissance viol, Woodfield provides little encouragement for players who might want to experiment with such an instrument: 'The only way to bow such an instrument in practice is to play all the strings together which, to judge by experiments with a modern guitar, produces a soft, rather nebulous sound. The strings run so close to the belly that bowing the outer strings individually produces unsatisfactory results' (p. 78). One wonders why the instrument survived even twenty-five years if its characteristics made it so impractical. Without the evidence of surviving instruments, it is difficult to imagine how the Valencian viol might sound, but Woodfield is over-pessimistic about its potential. He concludes that 'the Valencian viol really was a most impractical instrument even for the relatively simple task of playing drones, and that its demise was fully deserved' (p. 78). Two decades ago viol players made the same observation about the postless Renaissance viol, but today many builders have convinced players of its mellow sound and excellent blend in sixteenth-century consort music. Perhaps the Valencian viol will eventually enjoy a similar revival of interest among enthusiasts.

Italy still claims a large share of the viol's early history, and this is reflected in Woodfield's study by the space devoted to it. Of nine chapters covering the dissemination of the viol, four deal with aspects of its Italian literature: the technique of playing, Italian tunings, and music for solo or consort. Solo playing is otherwise little in evidence, with the exception of the lyra viol repertory, which figures only at the end of the 'early' period in the final chapter on the viol in England. Even in the relatively well-charted history of the viol in England, Woodfield is able to adduce new evidence to show 'the fundamental importance of the choirboy viol players and their masters, both in the evolution of a repertory of music idiomatically conceived for viols and in the wide dissemination of the instrument' (p. 226).

The significance of his study thus extends beyond the historical study of the viol's origins; it is of use to both builders and players and an important contribution to the early history of bowed and plucked string instruments. By cutting through traditional classifications of bowed *vs*. plucked, or cornered *vs*. cornerless instruments, the author illustrates that rigid categorisations can be misleading when tracing the early development of an instrument. The wealth of iconographic material he surveys is far from being thoroughly exhausted, and the study of individual representations will undoubtedly yield additional information about all aspects of the early viol. Such future studies will have been made possible by the thoroughness and extensive scope of Woodfield's study.

Mary Cyr
McGill University

Lewis Lockwood, *Music in Renaissance Ferrara 1400–1505: the Creation of a Musical Centre in the Fifteenth Century.* Oxford, Clarendon Press, 1984. xxii + 355 pp.

Reinhard Strohm, *Music in Late Medieval Bruges.* Oxford, Clarendon Press, 1985. xii + 273 pp.

A senior archivist in Bruges recently told me, with amused self-deprecation, of his initial attempt to dissuade Reinhard Strohm from writing a book about the city's music in the fifteenth century. Although Bruges, like many other cities, has mounds of scarcely read archival documents from the Middle Ages, there were two main considerations that led to his judgement. The first was that most of the musically interesting material had been located and published over the past century or so and it would need several years' residence to find enough to forge it into a new, coherent and interesting picture. *Faulx Dangier* waits at the door remarkably often for the historian with an interest in archival studies; and if the Rose thus protected turns out occasionally to be somewhat withered these two books must stand as object-lessons to say that the available material is not only copious but in fact far more substantial than can adequately be covered within a single volume. One leaves both books with an overwhelming impression of how much more could have been said.

The archivist's second consideration was that it makes little sense to separate the musical tradition of one city from that of others in the same area. Fifteenth-century polyphony is an international phenomenon, with works and musicians constantly travelling to and fro. Particular institutions may have their own liturgical traits, and there may be special economic factors that determine developments in each city, but it is difficult to show how the music is therefore necessarily different. How easily can Bruges be distinguished from Ghent or Antwerp? On the other hand, the recent spate of musicological activity based on the archives of institutions and cities arises from an awareness that too much is missed if research is confined to big names and prominent manuscripts. Musical life grows from a complex interaction between innumerable musicians and their employers; the compositions grow not only from the minds of creative geniuses but from a context. To say that both these books can be read as paradigmatic histories of music in the fifteenth century is merely to note how careful study of circumscribed areas can clarify larger patterns.

On the surface they seem similar. The Clarendon Press has packaged them almost as a matching pair. Both take their story from the late fourteenth century through to the death of Obrecht in 1505. Both began life as a search for answers to a musical question: in Strohm's case it was to provide a context for the fragmentary choirbook which he discovered at Lucca twenty years ago;[1] for Lockwood it was curiosity about Josquin's Mass *Hercules Dux Ferrarie*. Both are based on extended archive work and offer astonishing quantities of new information as well as fresh insights into the nature of music-making in the fifteenth century. Both include an appendix full of new biographical detail in highly compressed form. Both show the benefits of their authors' generosity towards other researchers, as a result of which they have received much of the most recent material in return. And, to pre-empt my conclusions, both are magnificent achievements, books that will last.

Yet they are remarkably different from one another in manner, scope and even subject-matter. Strohm's work is largely about independent sacred institutions in one of Europe's richest mercantile towns. Since Bruges was an important source for the Burgundian court's fabulous wealth, the court plays a role in the story, but almost peripherally, as a mere gloss on the surface of the essential Bruges about which he writes with such manifest affection. Lockwood is concerned first and foremost with strategies of patronage adopted by four very different members of a single ruling family, Niccolò III d'Este and three of his sons. Despite his title he concentrates on the d'Este court, merely drawing on the work of others for his comments on music at Ferrara Cathedral and hardly mentioning the other churches or institutions. Ercole I d'Este emerges as the hero of his search, while the city and its geographical or economic situation are scarcely considered. So the books are complementary in that Strohm treats of institutions that provided the musicians in the north whereas Lockwood discusses individual patrons in Italy who sought their services so avidly. It is easy to see why Strohm should describe as 'late medieval' the same time span that for Lockwood and Ferrara is 'Renaissance'.

---

[1]   Lucca, Archivio di Stato, Biblioteca Manoscritti MS 238; see R. Strohm, 'Ein unbekanntes Chorbuch des 15. Jahrhunderts', *Die Musikforschung*, 21 (1968), pp. 40–2.

Strohm adopts a casual style, tends to play down the quantity of archival research involved and concentrates on telling a lively story. His six long chapters are beautifully paced and make compelling reading. Lockwood has a much more serious manner, taking his model consciously from 'straight' historians and weighing each piece of evidence in exemplary fashion. His twenty-seven shortish chapters occasionally impede the flow of the book but are arranged so that each issue is separately and clearly considered and it is easier for the reader to re-trace a particular argument. Strohm has a fifty-six-page appendix of complete musical examples, most of them published for the first time (though sadly a mere one-third of these pieces are from the Lucca choirbook); Lockwood has no complete pieces and very little unpublished music, though what he does print is rather more closely incorporated into the musical argument. On the other hand, Strohm rarely offers a transcription of any document, preferring an English paraphrase, whereas Lockwood is more generous with his *pièces justificatives*. Moreover, Strohm does very little to ease the path for future researchers on the music of Bruges, whereas Lockwood provides beautifully lucid information and tables. (We shall see later that this factor is important and that Lockwood's very clarity makes it easy to build on his information.)

Strohm loves speculation – about atmosphere, biography, attribution, musical intent – and is almost dangerously bizarre in some of his hypotheses; Lockwood by comparison occasionally seems even afraid to look beyond the verifiable facts, as a result of which his book is less enthralling on the surface, less filled with surprises. In fact Strohm's book can be recommended to almost any intelligent reader who wants to grasp some of the fascination of fifteenth-century music (and it is difficult to think what other books could be put into that category); Lockwood's is aimed at a more committed readership. Briefly, they offer two strikingly different approaches to musical historiography despite their superficial similarity. Also, Lockwood is lucky enough to have his documentation and *excursus* printed at the foot of the page whereas poor Strohm has them amid an already confusing body of material at the end of the book. But this is the moment to stop comparing them, because there is considerable danger in playing off the one against the other. To do so can discredit both.

*   *   *

Strohm opens with a racy and imaginative chapter that sketches a vivid backdrop on the basis of pictures and descriptions before he starts on the collegiate church of St Donatian, prominent in the minds of music historians because it had Binchois and Dufay among its canons as well as Obrecht for its choirmaster. From the considerable body of surviving archival material – which unfortunately lacks direct information on the singers – he outlines the history of music in the church.[2] He is particularly fascinating and thoughtful on Dufay's difficult relationship with the chapter, offers some delightfully scurrilous detail about the behaviour of Gilles Joye, shows that the choral foundation of 1421 may have formed the basis for similar foundations established by Philip the Good at Dijon and Lille, and finally argues (pp. 40–1) that the one work of Obrecht demonstrably composed for the church was not the Mass *de Sancto Donatiano* but the Mass *de Sancto Martino*. (One might add, though, that there is an apparently unnoticed feature of the Mass *de Sancto Martino* which somewhat weakens this argument. Its first four beats quote directly and unmistakably from Ockeghem's Mass *Mimi*, though written at a pitch a third higher. Since Ockeghem was, of course, Treasurer of the church of St Martin in Tours, there might be other ways of explaining why Obrecht composed a Mass which is, as Strohm says, 'almost a *historia* of St Martin'. The *prima facie* case must surely be that the work was composed for Tours, and Strohm's evidence for a connection with Pierre Basin is, as it stands, too circumstantial to argue otherwise.)

Here and in the following chapter on 'Other Churches' Strohm is especially careful to observe and evaluate evidence that polyphony was sung in the church services. In view of the regional dispersal of the few surviving polyphonic manuscripts there is every reason for believing that the performance of polyphony was local and unusual before the sixteenth century. Nowadays prudence dictates that any

---

[2]   Two good guides to this material might be added to the literature Strohm cites. Raphael de Keyser's thesis, 'Het St. Donaaskapittel te Brugge (1350–1450): Bijdrage tot de studie van hogere geestelijkheed tijdens de late middeleeuwen' (University of Louvain, 1972), includes in its third volume an extensive listing of the available documentation on all recorded canons of the church. Although Belgian theses are not normally available for consultation, this volume is deposited in the Bisschoppelijk Archief at Bruges for free use. Published since the completion of Strohm's book is B. Janssens de Bisthoven and C. de Backer, *Inventaris van het Bisschoppelijk Archief te Brugge* (Katholiek Documentatie- en Onderzoekscentrum, Mgr Ladeuzeplein 21, B3000 Leuven, 1984), which gives an overview of the archive's holdings.

musical event from the Middle Ages must be assumed to be monophonic until it can be proved polyphonic. Strohm shows a sharp awareness of that problem. Having demonstrated that the church of St Donatian had regular polyphony from the late fourteenth century, he further shows that in the massive church of Our Lady there was polyphony during the Mass well before the middle of the fifteenth century. At St Donatian's the quantity of Mass cycles copied is far in excess of what anybody (or, at least, I) might have expected: at least fifty-two complete cycles were copied there during the last ten years of Dufay's life, for instance;[3] and at the church of St Salvator the copying documents begin with payment for a group of seven Mass cycles in 1482–3. In addition, though with less surviving information to guide him, Strohm demonstrates active musical involvement at the churches of St James, St Giles and St Walburga.

If the temperature falls slightly in his chapter on 'Convents and Confraternities' – they contain much new information but few surprises apart from documentation of a substantial English presence at the Carmelite chapel – there is some astonishing new material in his study of 'The City and the Court'. In particular he discusses a detailed description of Philip the Good's entry into Bruges in 1440 with Charles d'Orléans who had just been released from his twenty-five years' imprisonment in England. This important item seems to have been overlooked by music historians; and in such cases one is inclined to regret Strohm's reluctance to print document transcriptions: here and elsewhere he offers only an English summary.

Here his normally resourceful use of English translation lets him down in his references to the repeated appearance of a 'dulcian' which, if true, would have been its earliest known appearance. This description comes from one of the many unpublished versions of the *Cronicke van Vlaenderen* (a document, or group of documents, with a highly complex transmission history still awaiting full clarification). What would have been clear from a full transcription of the passage is that on each occasion the description of a still-life pageant ends

---

[3] Strohm, pp. 29–31, based largely on the findings of Alfons Dewitte, published in 'Boek- en bibliotheekwezen in de Brugse Sint-Donaaskerk xiiie–xve eeuw', *Sint-Donaas en de voormalige Brugse Katedraal* (Bruges, 1978), pp. 61–95; on pp. 83–95 Dewitte lists payments for copying, binding and repairing books at the church throughout the century.

with a kind of refrain, such as 'ende up de staedge waren drie speleiden, een haerpe, een luitte ende een doulcheyne',[4] or occasionally 'ende up de staedge waren drie speleiden, te wetene, een oorghele, een haerpe ende een luicte'.[5] Thus the instrument concerned is the douçaine, that still mysterious instrument mentioned so often, particularly in the fourteenth century.[6] Moreover, the specified groupings are all of either lute, harp and douçaine or lute, harp and organ. This is important for the history of instrumental ensembles in the early fifteenth century since these are among the few instruments of the time which we can still consider likely to have taken part in performances of written polyphony.[7] On the other hand, the refrain-like nature of those comments at the end of each stage described must cast some doubt on the degree to which it is an eye-witness description.

Another version of the same chronicle adds a telling detail to Strohm's narrative. He mentions that one of the displays was of four singing prophets who were the 'beste zanghers van der kercke';[8] in the Brussels manuscript of the *Cronicke van Vlaenderen* a largely similar description reads: 'Ende alle dese voornemde propheten waren alle de beste zanghers die in Brugghe waren, te wetene kerkelicke persoonen.'[9] In some ways it may seem obvious that the best singers should have been churchmen; but given the lack of information on other singers in Bruges it is good to know that the contemporary chronicler confirms the outstanding position of such musicians.

His last chapter is the longest and gives a detailed survey of music that can be connected with Bruges. It begins with two fourteenth-century motets, one of which Strohm publishes for the first time and discusses at some length (though he might have added that its complete lack of isorhythmic organisation is a detail pointing to English influence). He continues with the music of Thomas Fabri,

---

[4] Bruges, Stadsbibliotheek, MS 436, fol. 210ᵛ.

[5] *Op. cit.*, fol. 211.

[6] Two details could be added to the relevant article by Barra R. Boydell in S. Sadie, ed., *The New Grove Dictionary of Musical Instruments* (London, 1984), s.v. 'Dolzaina'. References to the instrument in fact appear as early as the thirteenth century, in the romance *Cleomadès* by Adenés li Rois. And Herbert W. Myers has recently offered what seems for the first time to be a highly convincing identification of this instrument in 'The *Mary Rose* "Shawm"', *Early Music*, 11 (1983), pp. 358–60.

[7] I have summarised the situation as I now see it in the chapter 'Secular Polyphony: 15th Century' for H. M. Brown and S. Sadie, eds., *Performance Practice* (London, forthcoming).

[8] Strohm, p. 81; the source is Bruges, Stadsbibliotheek, MS 436, fol. 211.

[9] Brussels, Bibliothèque Royale, MS 13073–4, fol. 201ᵛ.

succentor at St Donatian's in 1412–15, and offers compelling arguments to suggest that the composer Egardus in the Padua fragments[10] was Johannes Ecghaert, succentor in 1370, using as evidence the name Buclare, addressed in pieces by both composers.

More tentatively he suggests that the Utrecht fragments 37[1] and conceivably 37[2-3] may have originated in Bruges.[11] Stretching the matter, he discusses elements apparently from Bruges in the Strasbourg, Prague and Reina manuscripts,[12] partly by placing them alongside the Gruuthuse songbook. From there he evaluates (perhaps over-generously) the possible Bruges connections of later sources such as Oxford, Bodleian Library, Can. misc. 213, Paris, Bibliothèque Nationale, n.a.fr. 4917 and n.a.fr. 4379 (parts 2 and 3), British Library, Cotton Titus A xxvi, and the basse-danse manuscript Brussels, Bibliothèque Royale, 9085 (where he helps his argument by confusing Isabelle of Portugal, third wife of Philip the Good, with Isabelle of Bourbon, first wife of Charles the Bold). It is here that one begins to see my archivist's point. Certainly Bruges was an exceptionally important meeting-place for contacts between different parts of Europe, but it seems important to avoid overcompensation; to postulate a major Bruges component in such a large proportion of the surviving sources is to risk loss of credibility.

Strohm finds documentation for the composer Georgius a Brugis, clarifies the connection between Jacobus de Clibano and Binchois, and gives reasons for thinking that the anonymous motet *O sanctissime presul Christi Donaciane* may be by either Power or Forest (though the arithmetic that is crucial to his argument is made to seem wrong by an error in his edition: on p. 216, bar 36, the tenor should read a dotted minim, not a minim plus a crotchet rest).

Then he tackles the fragments that provided the origin of the entire project, remains of a choirbook at Lucca, registered there as a gift to the cathedral from Giovanni Arnolfini – the banker who spent most of his life in Bruges and appears in two famous pictures by Jan van Eyck.[13] The original manuscript was about the size of the

---

[10] See K. von Fischer, 'Egardus', in S. Sadie, ed., *The New Grove Dictionary of Music and Musicians*, 20 vols. (London, 1980), vi, p. 62.

[11] Utrecht, Universiteitsbibliotheek, MS 6 e 37.

[12] Strasbourg, Bibliothèque de la Ville, MS 222 c. 22, burned in 1870 and known primarily from Coussemaker's copy in Brussels, Bibliothèque du Conservatoire Royal de Musique, MS 56.286; Prague, Státní Knihovna ČSSR, Universitní Knihovna, MS xi. e. 9; Paris, Bibliothèque Nationale, MS n.a.fr. 6771.

[13] To this evidence of Arnolfini's interest in painting and music, it is intriguing to be able to

Vatican choirbook San Pietro B 80; and Strohm leaves absolutely no doubt that most of it was copied in Bruges in the late 1460s for presentation to Lucca Cathedral at a time when Hothby was choirmaster there. This portion of the book is brilliantly done, with the background carefully prepared in the preceding chapters. His conclusions carry complete conviction.

He describes most of the manuscript's surviving music in some detail. One conclusion he draws is that the first (Bruges) layer is 'almost an anthology of English music of the period from c.1440 to 1470' (p. 123). And although one of the continuing undercurrents in his book is the extent to which Bruges was a major link in the transference of English music to the continent, somehow that theme is never quite examined. It is as though at a relatively late stage the idea began to seem problematic. It is one thing to argue that Henricus Tik, the composer of the first Mass in the volume, may have been English. But a paradox arises already with the second Mass, Petrus de Domarto's *Spiritus almus*, for while on the one hand asserting that this work is 'in its contrapuntal technique, a virtual twin of the English *Missa "Caput"*' (p. 124, a notion which, like many in the book, one longs to see expanded), Strohm also attempts to identify Domarto with Pierre Maillart, for many years a singer in the Burgundian court chapel. Similarly problematic is the matter of the Mass *O rosa bella*[14] in which he finds English traits but which he has earlier suggested may be the work of Gilles Joye – largely, it seems, for the admittedly attractive reason that Joye had a concubine named Rosabelle. He points to a song by Joye which could have originated as an English ballade, and thereby leaves an even stronger trail of unresolved paradoxes.

Obviously one first way out of the trouble would be to drop the identification of Petrus de Domarto with Pierre Maillart, which has nothing to support it but a vague (and in my view insufficient) similarity of names. Another is to forget the charming theory that the priest Gilles Joye composed Mass cycles in honour of his mistress.

add one further detail: the so-called Rohan poetry manuscript (Berlin, Staatliche Museen der Stiftung Preussischer Kulturbesitz, Kupferstichkabinett, MS 78 B 17) contains, on fols. 115–115ᵛ, a rondeau *Jusque au retour n'aray plaisance* with Arnolfini's wife's name as an acrostic: JEHANNE CENAMI; see M. Löpelmann, *Die Liederhandschrift des Cardinals de Rohan*, Gesellschaft für romanische Literatur 44 (Göttingen, 1923), p. 198.

[14] The first of those published in Denkmäler der Tonkunst in Österreich 22, Jg. XI (Vienna, 1904).

His surviving output of five short songs is hardly enough to support such an attribution (though I must hasten to add that the new details Strohm provides about Joye's life and behaviour make that suggestion by no means outrageous, merely unsupported). And we are left with an original layer in the choirbook where every piece displays English style-characteristics, though in varying strength, and two pieces are ascribed to composers whose biography is unknown – Tik and Domarto.

Given Tinctoris's evidence that English music was a considerable influence on the continent, it would have been easy enough to suggest – as with the English-style Mass cycles attributed to the apparently continental composers Johannes Pulloys[15] and Simon de Insula – that at this stage the 'English' style, sometimes even including Kyrie prosulae and telescoped Credo texts, was often being used by continental composers. But there are two further problems here. Strohm identifies an English presence in the chapel of the Discalced Carmelites at Bruges, and he might have added further details on the way the Flemish fabrics industry was totally reliant on the supply of raw materials from England; but it is difficult to see a sufficient outlet in Bruges for so many extended works in a style so closely bound to English liturgies. And, of course, to accept so many English-style Masses by continental composers is implicitly to open the door for restoring the Mass *Caput* to Dufay. There are perplexing issues here that need to be examined. That Strohm at the crucial point refrains from such examination suggests that he too feels nervous about where the questions lead. Certainly they emphasise that the Mass cycle in the fifteenth century remains a seriously understudied genre.

Moving on from his discussion of the Lucca music, Strohm proposes that the final section of the Mellon chansonnier may have links with Bruges, suggests a Bruges origin for some of the material in Trent (and is the first to point out in print that the Mass cycle in Trent 88, fols. 77ᵛ–84, is based on *Se tu t'en marias*, the tenor of Binchois's song *Files a marier*), and sees a Bruges origin in the earliest section of the Vatican choirbook San Pietro B 80. On the Brussels MS Bibliothèque Royale 5557 he is slightly puzzled to find so much Busnoys, a composer not explicitly represented in the Lucca frag-

---

[15] See G. R. K. Curtis, 'Jean Pullois and the Cyclic Mass – or a Case of Mistaken Identity?', *Music & Letters*, 62 (1981), pp. 41–59.

ments: Paula Higgins's recent information that Busnoys probably did not arrive at the Burgundian court until 1467[16] surely combines with Strohm's proposed dating of the Lucca manuscript to explain that situation. Similarly, he is puzzled to find apparent Bruges connections in the Vatican choirbooks Cappella Sistina 14 and 51: Adalbert Roth's proposal[17] that both manuscripts originate not in the Papal Chapel but in Naples makes this easier to understand, because one of the themes in this part of Strohm's book is the close connection (through trade and, particularly, banking) between Bruges, Florence and Naples.

Finally Strohm enumerates the works of Obrecht that may have been composed in Bruges or for its churches, proposing some hints towards a chronology and offering the hypothesis that the Mass *de Sancto Donatiano* was composed for a Mass in memory of the furrier Donaes de Moor (p. 147). At the end of the book there is a comprehensive list of 'Musicians employed in churches of Bruges until c. 1510', an inventory of the Lucca fragments (with thematic incipits for the unknown music), and his excellent selection of musical transcriptions.

I mentioned earlier that Strohm can occasionally indulge in wild flights of fancy, and perhaps a few examples should be given. He observes, for instance (p. 158):

The [*Missus*] ceremony at St James's in 1519 included a polyphonic mass; prominent chants were *Ne timeas Maria* and *Ecce ancilla domini*. I suggest that the cantus firmus masses by Dufay, Ockeghem, Regis and others, which are based on these chants, originally belonged to *Missus* ceremonies. The same may well be true for motets with the text *Missus est Gabriel angelus* (there are two settings by Josquin), which is the main gospel text of the ceremony itself.

There is a lot wrong in those few lines. First, the description of the *Missus* at St James's painstakingly distinguishes between 'dicitur' and 'canitur';[18] both of the texts Strohm mentions are spoken. Second, those two texts are by no means prominent; they simply appear, as might be expected in any service connected with the

[16] See in particular her preface to the facsimile, *Chansonnier Nivelle de la Chaussée* (Geneva, 1984), pp. iv–v.

[17] A. Roth, 'Zur Datierung der frühen Chorbücher der päpstlichen Kapelle', in L. Finscher, ed., *Quellenstudien zur Music der Renaissance*, II: *Datierung und Filiation von Musikhandschriften der Josquin-Zeit*, Wolfenbütteler Forschungen 26 (Wiesbaden, 1983), pp. 239–68, on p. 268.

[18] W. H. J. Weale, 'Drame liturgique: Le Missus', *Le Beffroi*, 1 (1863), pp. 165–78.

Annunciation. Third, although the Regis Mass indeed uses those chants, Dufay's Mass uses *Ecce ancilla Domini* and *Beata es Maria*. The Ockeghem Mass *Ecce ancilla* uses entirely different material from within another chant. I do not know what further Masses with this title Strohm has in mind. And, of course, although we have a Josquin setting of the text *Missus est Gabriel angelus ad Mariam*, the motet *Missus est angelus Gabriel a Deo* can scarcely any longer be considered the work of anybody but Mouton,[19] even though it appears in the Josquin *Werken*.

Other matters in which the sheer energy and excitement of the writing take Strohm beyond safe hypothesis include: the attempts, already mentioned, to identify Petrus de Domarto with Pierre Maillart and to suggest Gilles Joye as the composer of the anonymous three-voice Masses on *O rosa bella*; the suggestion that the widely dispersed and certainly English *O pulcherrima mulierum* is by Plummer; the speculation (p. 21) that Coutreman's rondeau *Vaylle que vaylle* can be connected with the Burgundian court and the singer Robert Vaille (here given as Pierre) by virtue of its using the verb 's'aseürer' which, he fails to notice, is just Gilbert Reaney's reconstruction of a gap in the metrical pattern; the theory that Cornago's Mass *Ayo visto la mapa mundi* must be based on the lost *mappa mundi* that Jan van Eyck painted for Philip the Good, whereas such maps abound through medieval Europe and the song that forms the basis of the Mass survives with a quatrain of Sicilian origin;[20] the eagerness to suggest Bruges origin for any song concerned with May Day (pp. 100–1 and 166–7); and several others. Similarly, while it is attractive to see Bruges as the connection between England and the Italian chansonniers that contain English songs, the matter might have been expressed more cautiously: Bruges was a major trading centre but not by any means the only one.

I imagine that most of these hypotheses – many of them highly attractive and therefore doubly dangerous – are easily enough identified by the attentive reader, and they add to the colour of the

---

[19] The fullest exposition of the argument is in E. E. Lowinsky, *The Medici Codex of 1518: Historical Introduction and Commentary* (Chicago, 1968), Monuments of Renaissance Music 3, pp. 219–28.

[20] See most recently Rebecca L. Gerber's comments in *Johannes Cornago: Complete Works*, Recent Researches in the Music of the Middle Ages and Early Renaissance 15 (Madison, 1984), pp. viii–x.

book. I dwell on them merely because such hypotheses in the past have tended to become embedded in the literature and have hindered the way towards further insights. But these are mere details. Strohm writes (p. 2) that 'Bruges is not on the map of the leading musical historiographers'. That situation he has brilliantly and conclusively reversed.

Lewis Lockwood's book follows on from a series of at least eleven articles about music in Ferrara that he has published over the past fifteen years. Many of those articles are crammed with documentary detail and extensive transcriptions. Yet in the book towards which they were all leading there is relatively little precise duplication of material already published, and the main drift of his arguments is considerably clarified: not merely the close interrelationship of music and patronage, but more specifically the international political ambition of Niccolò III d'Este, the broad humanistic concerns of Leonello, the changing attitude to music under Borso and the grand cultural aims of Ercole that attained their climax in the appointment of Josquin and of Obrecht.

He opens with a careful consideration of whether the lack of clear evidence for sophisticated musical culture in fourteenth-century Ferrara might conceal any worthwhile activity. And he investigates the considerable French interests of Niccolò. He notes, among other things, the quantity of French books in Niccolò's library, though without comparing this with other courts in an age when French culture was predominant throughout northern Italy. While qualifying the old notion that Guarino's arrival in 1429 led to a sudden burgeoning of humanism in Ferrara, Lockwood emphasises the humanistic interests and talents of Leonello. He weighs the evidence for dating various works with unquestionable Ferrarese associations – Bartolomeo da Bologna's *Arte psalantes* (pp. 19–23), Bertrand Feragut's *Francorum nobilitati* (pp. 34–6), Dufay's *C'est bien raison* and his *Seigneur Leon* (pp. 36–9).[21] In Leonello he finds the first fully cultured Ferrarese patron, stressing not only his patronage of Pisanello and his commission of humanistic texts but also (pp. 44–5

---

[21] While it is gratifying to see Lockwood accept my theory that *Seigneur Leon* concerns Leonello d'Este, it is puzzling that he should suggest dating the work earlier than Leonello's accession in 1441. I would find it extremely difficult to propose a stylistic context for the music much earlier than 1440.

and 50) his active participation in the music at his specially built chapel.

After discussing the relatively sparse documentation on the singers in Leonello's chapel, Lockwood turns to the grandest surviving monument of Leonello's musical patronage, the manuscript known as ModB.[22] As in an earlier article, he connects the manuscript with a binding payment dated 1448 but fails to alert the reader to the important consideration that there is no conclusive evidence to connect this payment with a single manuscript that happens to survive among many that are lost without trace.[23] Certainly the date seems about right (though I would repeat here what I have said elsewhere, that Dufay's motet *Salve flos Tusce gentis* is in a style that suggests a date far later than his known stay at Florence in 1435–6, and that there is a fair *prima facie* case for suggesting 1450 as the date for his *O proles Hispanie*); yet in some ways the most dangerous arguments are the plausible ones based on logic that contains a barely perceptible flaw.

Concerning the manuscript's most surprising feature, the inclusion of over fifty English pieces at the end, he shows that there is no evidence for a major English delegation at the Council of Ferrara.[24] He thereby casts doubt on some of Ann Besser Scott's theories about the source, but then focuses more strongly on her ideas about the English students at the University of Ferrara, expanding them substantially. Even so, it remains curious that the discussion should concentrate so heavily on these students with no known musical connections while at the same time overlooking two English musicians who would surely have been better placed to provide this music. Galfridus de Anglia's two surviving songs set sections from a poem connected with Isotta d'Este, datable to 1444.[25] And 'Johan-

---

[22] Modena, Biblioteca Estense e Universitaria (henceforth *MOe*), MS α x.1.11.

[23] Lockwood mentions (p. 52) the arrival of six Masses brought to Ferrara by two Frenchmen in June 1447. This is remarkably early for polyphonic Mass Ordinary cycles by other than English composers; and it might be worth entertaining the possibility that they were Mass Proper cycles of the kind copied in Cambrai in the year ending June 1447, see J. Houdoy, *Histoire artistique de la Cathédrale de Cambrai* (Paris and Lille, 1880), p. 188. As both Alejandro Planchart and I will shortly be pointing out elsewhere, it is extremely tempting to connect that lost repertory with the large group of Mass Proper cycles near the beginning of the MS Trent 88.

[24] It is slightly disarming that Lockwood cites as his only evidence for this Joseph Gill's *Eugenius IV, Pope of Christian Union* (London, 1961), a book with virtually no documentation, which happens merely to mention the matter in passing.

[25] Lockwood suggests 1444 or 1446 (p. 65); I have argued that 1444 seems by far the more

nes quondam alterius Johannis presbiter Londini' is recorded as a singer at the cathedral in 1448 (p. 80). While it is useful to have so much more information about English students in Ferrara, these two men offer much clearer evidence of the sort of musical connection that would make it easier to obtain so much English music.

Moreover, it seems in this context unwise to ignore the truism that English music was widely available in Italy from the late 1430s onwards. ModB may contain the neatest and largest uninterrupted collection of English pieces; but there are substantial quantities of English music in the earlier Trent codices, and the Aosta manuscript[26] even shares with ModB an important design feature: a first section devoted mainly to continental liturgical music, laid out in approximate liturgical sequence, followed by a large section of English pieces in no discernible order. Within that context (and remembering again that innumerable large sources are lost without trace) there is little point in arguing that Ferrara had a special position in the transmission of English music to Italy. Back to my archivist in Bruges: ModB was certainly in Ferrara, and its later additions show signs of being specifically connected with Ferrara; but for its main contents there is simply not enough evidence to show that it is typical of Ferrara, let alone in any way exclusive to Ferrara.

On 'Secular Music' at Leonello's court Lockwood assembles the relatively little information available on singers, wind players and dancers. Concerning 'Cathedral Music' he briefly describes some fragments now at Cornell University and apparently of Ferrarese provenance, floating the attractive hypothesis that the music may have been English. And by putting the theoretical writings of Ugolino of Orvieto into a Ferrarese context he neatly shows some of the contradictions within mid-fifteenth-century musical and intellectual life, many of them resolved in the early sixteenth century.

Turning to Borso, Lockwood refines much that has been said about his studied disregard for music and substitutes the evidently valid proposal that his interest was more secular than sacred. He may have disbanded his chapel choir, but that is not to say he took no interest in music. Rather he was representative of a general disen-

---

probable date for the poem, see D. Fallows, ed., *Galfridus and Robertus de Anglia: Four Italian Songs* (Newton Abbot, 1977); and Lockwood later (pp. 109–10) reaches the same conclusion.

[26] Aosta, Biblioteca del Seminario Maggiore, MS A¹ᴅ 19.

chantment with what many Italians saw as the 'gothic' polyphony of
the north in favour of something that communicated more directly
and fitted better to the programme of the humanists. In particular
Lockwood dwells on the career of the lutenist Pietrobono de Burzel-
lis, strongly in the ascendant during Borso's reign. He emphasises
the importance of Pietrobono – more widely celebrated in the
writings of his time than any other musician before Josquin even
though not a note of his music survives – and draws the satisfactory
conclusion that a full history of musical culture must take account of
the unwritten traditions which may have been extraordinarily
sophisticated. Certainly there is room for a new extended study of
Pietrobono's career, gathering together the wide variety of information and evaluating it with care.

As the only surviving source of polyphony from Borso's Ferrara,
the Oporto song collection is obviously of some importance in this
section of the book.[27] Lockwood's extended discussion takes issue
with my extremely tentative suggestion that it could date from
1467,[28] but perhaps leans too far backwards in proposing a date in
the late 1450s. Study of this manuscript has been somewhat confused
by the nature of the secondary literature surrounding it: my suggested date of 1467 was based on a document which subsequent
research showed to be at least two years later,[29] and further reflection
makes it clear that I was falling into the common trap of seizing on
the only known documentation of Dufay's music coming to Italy as
an explanation of the manuscript's generous representation of late
songs by Dufay; part of Lockwood's argument had rested on a
document which now seems (p. 118, note 31) to have been misread.
Several confused details in Lockwood's chapter show evidence of its
having seen too many changes and new discoveries between initial
drafting and final publication. I would still maintain the position I
established before so tentatively floating the 1467 hypothesis, that
'in terms of its repertory it belongs firmly in the 1460s'.[30]

Over half of Lockwood's book is then devoted to the reign of

---

[27] Oporto, Biblioteca Pública Municipal, MS 714.
[28] D. Fallows, 'Robertus de Anglia and the Oporto Song Collection', in I. Bent, ed., *Source Materials and the Interpretation of Music: a Memorial Volume to Thurston Dart* (London, 1981), pp. 99–128, on p. 113.
[29] D. Fallows, *Dufay* (London, 1982), pp. 75–6, where I also pointed out that the document concerns not the otherwise unknown Gilles Arpin but the well-known Gilles Crepin.
[30] Fallows, 'Robertus de Anglia', pp. 112–13.

Ercole I (1471–1505) who acceded as duke at the advanced age of forty. Within four months of his succession he had appointed Brebis to lead his chapel choir. He had also written to the Bishop of Constance proclaiming his intention to institute a 'capellam celeberrimam' containing 'cantores musicos praestantissimos' and seeking the services of a singer whom Lockwood convincingly identifies as Johannes Martini.

After sketching the main groups of court musicians and their functions, Lockwood investigates the chapel more closely in terms of its national distribution, various kinds of personnel and individual characters. Perhaps the most interesting discussions are of Cornelio di Lorenzo (pp. 161–5) and Jachetto de Marvilla (pp. 166–7), two members of that important but still insufficiently studied class of singers who were not composers but whose position in the musical life of the time can explain so much about the international traffic of works and styles. An attempt to place the singers' salaries in a larger context – both chronological and within the court structure – leads inevitably to a study of Ercole's handling of benefices, showing the complex workings of this most important tool in the establishment of a fine chapel choir. Then a discussion of Ercole's last years summarises and refines the main issues in his crowning appointments of Josquin and Obrecht.

Lockwood's survey of the music at Ercole's court opens with a discussion of the surviving manuscripts. His datings are perhaps open to future reconsideration, if only because of the need to distinguish between coffee-table books, manuscripts of record and sources that were actually used by performing musicians (of which, some would contend, no examples survive); but the available information is judiciously and clearly laid out. He discusses Martini's contributions to this repertory, making the important point that the manuscript known as ModD[31] often includes versions substantially different from those in other manuscripts.[32] After an all

---

[31] *MOe* MS α м.1.13.

[32] To document this Lockwood refers to the edition of Martini's Mass *Cucu* in Denkmäler der Tonkunst in Österreich 120 (1970), even though its editor did not have access to ModD (which in any case contains only the very opening of the work). A better comparison can be seen from the two versions (ModD and Trent 89) of the anonymous four-voice Mass *O rosa bella* presented in parallel in Denkmäler der Tonkunst in Österreich 22, Jg. xi (1904), pp. 28–69. Laurence Feininger's edition of Dufay's Mass *Ave regina celorum*, in Monumenta Polyphoniae Liturgicae Sanctae Ecclesiae Romanae 1/ii/iii (Rome, 1963), presents the version in Rome in parallel with that in Brussels, suggesting that ModD more or less

too brief discussion of the work that generated the whole project, the Mass *Hercules Dux Ferrarie* (he focuses mainly on the tenor and the fact that its influence on the other voices is formal rather than melodic), and of the double-choir Vespers music in the manuscripts ModC1 and C2,[33] he passes on to 'The Motet in Ferrara', a chapter that comes to its climax with some useful and incisive observations on the style and context of Josquin's *Miserere*. This seems to me the best piece of musical commentary in the book.

His discussion of the secular repertory at court inevitably focuses on the manuscript 2856 in the Biblioteca Casanatense and leads to a more detailed study of two particularly famous pieces: *La Martinella* and *Ile fantazies de Joskin*. Yet his analysis of both pieces is perhaps confused by his view that 'the resemblance to the French rondeau . . . is wholly superficial and probably coincidental' (p. 275). Like many apparently untexted pieces of this generation, both follow the design and many stylistic details of the rondeau stanza as used by Busnoys and Hayne van Ghizeghem. In Lockwood's five-section analysis of *Ile fantazies de Joskin*, I believe that his sections B and C belong together, sharing their initial material and divided only in the sense that many rondeau lines have a caesura after the first four syllables. Seen that way, the piece is a four-line stanza with each line almost exactly twelve bars long. Such pieces also follow the late rondeau in having their main imitation between discantus and tenor. That the contra of *Ile fantazies de Joskin* (here called 'bassus') actually begins by entering second with a canonic imitation of the discantus at the lower octave is a musical 'feint' (endorsed by the subsequent entry of the tenor imitating at the unusual interval of a fourth below the discantus) and should not disguise for the commentator the essential 'contratenor' function of most of this voice; and for Lockwood to see its perfectly commonplace connecting pattern in bars 12–13 as generating the sequential figure at the end of the piece (bars 43–7) is incomprehensible since the two figures have virtually nothing in common. What makes *Ile fantazies de Joskin* confusing is that the four musical sections are melodically and motivically independent of one another. At least, the only possible trace of unification lies in Lockwood's intriguing observation that the leap of a minor third in

equals the Roman version: in fact, as indicated briefly in the preface, the Modena version stands somewhere between the extremes represented by the other two manuscripts.

[33]   *MOe* MSS α м.1.11–12.

bars 19 (tenor) and 20 (discantus) is the first essential non-conjunct gesture in the piece: it could be seen as generating the final point (at bars 36–40) which continues with an allusion to the third phrase (bars 25–9). But in general the motivic material of this piece is loosely contrived and in some ways difficult to align with what we otherwise know of Josquin's music.

On the other hand, *La Martinella* is far more methodically unified than Lockwood suggests. Its broad form is looser than that of *Ile fantazies de Joskin*, though I would still be inclined to read Lockwood's twelve divisions as hiding a simpler rondeau stanza of five or conceivably six lines. But each point of imitation is audibly related to an element in the opening phrase, down to the detail of the inversion that opens the *secunda pars*. To say that 'the number of distinctive contrapuntal . . . points within this piece is impressive' (p. 275) is in my view to miss the essence of *La Martinella*.

Finally Lockwood outlines the little that can be said about music in courtly festivities, and particularly in the important plays presented at court, before presenting a brief essay of synthesis by way of an epilogue. The book's appendices include a useful overview of the Modena archives, six pages of document transcriptions, nine pages listing letters concerned with the conferral of benefices, and fifteen pages of extremely small print listing the musicians documented at court for each year between 1377 and 1505. As with Strohm's book, the index does not take account of this important material. Lockwood may make no claims that Ferrara is the most important centre for fifteenth-century music, but he has made a massive contribution to showing how the musical culture of one such centre developed.

The *Faulx Dangier* I began with may now have taken on a considerably more severe aspect. Two of our most distinguished scholars have thoroughly trawled the archives of two major cities. But *Faulx Dangier* remains *faulx*. The definitive documentary study is a chimera. Impressive though these works are, they should not deter future researchers from re-examining the same ground. A few examples from the archives of the d'Este court can illustrate the point.

Lockwood cites (p. 315) a certain 'Santo trombetta' as appearing in documents for 1434 but not otherwise. In fact he turns up as early as 10 September 1423 and twice in 1424, on 13 and 18 April.[34] Thereafter the relevant documents are missing until 1434, the single occasion when Lockwood cites his existence. But he is still there on 18 August 1435, 30 November 1436 and 25 July 1437.[35] In this last entry he is given his full name in a reference to 'Domino Ludovico Sancti tubicinis', which makes it possible to identify him with the otherwise mysterious 'Ludovico trombeta' whom Lockwood cites (p. 315) as having received a prebend at Ferrara Cathedral in 1432.

For a trumpeter to receive a prebend may seem strange, and Lockwood even states (p. 141) that it could not happen; but the nature of the enterprises for which Ludovico is being paid in the documents just mentioned shows that a trumpeter's function was closer to that of a diplomat or herald, as Lockwood observes in another context (p. 17). The 1437 document records a payment to him for going to Venice where he was to present a gift to the city from Leonello d'Este. In view of this kind of service, as well as the prebend given him in 1432, it seems safe to accept that Ludovico Sancti was in the court service continuously from at least 1423 to 1437. Moreover, it looks very much as though Ludovico, like so many minstrels, passed on his skills to his son. At least, the Filippo trombeta whom Lockwood reports only for 1440 (p. 316) in fact turns up again on 22 January 1442 with the fuller name 'Filippo di Sancto trombetta'; he also appears on 8 August 1446.[36]

And it is as well to remember that the Mandati – which provide our main information from this period – record only special payments. I would therefore be inclined to strengthen considerably Lockwood's comments on p. 48, because salaries, for example, are noted here only in the most exceptional circumstances. They will have been recorded fully in another volume, now lost. Much of the material in the Mandati concerns trumpeters who were often sent individually on diplomatic missions. A group of chapel singers had no such duties, so they do not appear in the Mandati: from that point of view, Lockwood might have given more emphasis to the cathedral payments when the ducal singers sang there.

Some indication of what is missing may be gleaned from a

[34] Modena, Archivio di Stato (henceforth *MOs*), Archivio Segreto Estense, Mandati (henceforth Mand.) 1 (1422–4), fols. 125, 180 and 183ᵛ.

[35] Mand. 3 (1434–5), fol. 138ᵛ; Mand. 4 (1436–8), fols. 77 and 132ᵛ.

[36] Mand. 4, fol. 163ᵛ; Mand. 7 (1445–6), fol. 255.

payment of 10 July 1437 for 'penoni quattro di trombeta' painted by Jacomo Sagromoro showing the arms of France and the d'Este.[37] Evidently there were four trumpeters. And one of them can be named from another exceptional payment in the Mandati, an *ex gratia* paid on 25 July 1437 to the widow of a recently deceased trumpeter: 'pro parte fidelissimis serviciis eiusdem Helene uxoris quondam Passalaque tubicinis'.[38] He is otherwise known only from 1422, but there is every likelihood that his service was likewise uninterrupted.

On the other hand, some trumpeters listed here can safely be excluded from the court lists. Hieronymo trombeta, paid on 1 February 1438 (Lockwood p. 316),[39] received just a gift of 2 ducats, the same as two trumpeters of Francesco Sforza two months later,[40] and comparable with the payments to several visiting musicians. By contrast, in 1437 Gaspare and Clemente d'Alemania were both paid to help them set up home in Ferrara.[41] Plainly they were joining the court; and Lockwood mentions two similar payments in 1441 (p. 47, note 11).

Other entries that might be added to Lockwood's lists include the following. Giorgio 'piferro' was paid on 21 May 1423.[42] Anechino trombetta, listed by Lockwood under 1423, is paid again on 15 July 1424.[43] Pierino trombeta, registered by Lockwood under 1438 and 1440, appears as early as 2 March 1437 when he is specifically and interestingly described as a servant of Borso, not of the Marquis.[44] 'Filippus tubicini', noted by Lockwood for 1440, is also paid on 3 May and 28 May 1437.[45] Antonio piffero is paid on 13 August 1437.[46] And on 3 October 1437 there is a payment for the purchase from Mantua of instruments for the pifferi.[47]

In relation to Lockwood's statement (p. 16) that 'evidence for [Parisina Malatesta's musical interests] is negligible', it is good to be able to cite another entry in the same registers: a payment of 48 soldi on 8 September 1423 for 'quatuor manorum cordarum ab arpa quas prefata domina [Parisina] emi fecit pro arpa sua'.[48] Certainly the

[37] Mand. 4, fol. 150.   [38] Mand. 4, fol. 133^v.
[39] Mand. 4, fol. 187.   [40] Mand. 4, fol. 200^v.
[41] Mand. 4, fol. 151 (9 September) and fol. 158 (10 October) respectively.
[42] Mand. 1 (1422–4), fol. 105.   [43] Mand. 2 (1424), fol. 26^v.
[44] Mand. 4 (1436–8), fol. 99.   [45] Mand. 4, fols. 117 and 122^v.
[46] Mand. 4, fol. 135^v.   [47] Mand. 4, fol. 154^v.
[48] Mand. 1 (1422–4), fol. 124.

documentary items about Parisina and music published by Gandini (1891, cited by Lockwood in documentation of his statement) all concern her sons; but this new item leaves little question that she played the harp herself.

Concerning the most famous dancing master of the fifteenth century, Domenico da Piacenza, Lockwood writes: 'I can add to [the received information] that his name crops up in isolated Ferrarese court registers as late as 1470' (p. 70). In fact Domenico appears three times among the 'salariati' in the accounts for 1472, on 21 April, 7 July and 31 December.[49]

I take no great credit for this haul of material that Lockwood apparently missed. The kind of serendipity involved has nothing to do with the methodical months-long search that produced both these books. But I hope that what may seem a slightly ungraceful display of new material (none of it particularly important apart from that on Domenico da Piacenza) will be enough to show that no subject is closed. I also hope it is clear from this that the d'Este court archives still have much to tell us. If it now seems as though in the case of Mandati Registers 1 and 4 Lockwood missed more than he saw (and the same is true of Register 7), it is likely that he read the documents at an early stage in his researches and simply thought much of the material not particularly interesting. Its interest – as in the case of Ludovico Sancti the trumpeter – is clear now that we can see the broad context in which it belongs. The material was easy to locate because Lockwood offers such a good guide to what is there. And, it will have been noted, I was able to relate most of this new material to broader issues precisely because Lockwood's book is available.

Another feature of archive publications is that the transfer from account-book to historical study is often a subjective matter. The researcher chooses what interests him and presents it accordingly. Lockwood's main interest is the strategy of patronage, and its needs can hide material that might carry hints of something more important to many readers – the sound of the music. A few examples might illustrate this.

---

[49]   *MOs* Libri Camerali Diversi 96 (1472), fols. 24L, 48R and 99L. I use L and R for those registers that are numbered by openings rather than by folios: normally there is a Roman numeral on the left-hand page of the opening and the same number in arabic numerals on the facing right-hand page.

During Ercole's reign the number of musicians (of one kind or another) who turn up in the court is enormous, and Lockwood has sometimes felt the need to omit names from his appendix of documentary material. He somewhat misleadingly heads the list for 1503 with the sub-caption: 'Trumpeters not listed; list of instrumentalists drastically incomplete'. This could easily be construed as concerning the document itself (Memoriale del Soldo, vol. 23), whereas in fact it concerns only Lockwood's listing: in the document the 'trombetti' and 'pifferi' are listed in full each month under those headings; and several of those musicians crop up elsewhere in the account-book.[50] For the history of evolving instrumental ensembles the lists of pifferi are particularly important during these years, since under the heading 'pifferi' we find not only wind instrumentalists but two players of *viola* and occasionally a harpist. This suggests that for some purposes 'pifferi' simply meant 'instrumentalists who are not trumpeters'. That in turn offers room for reconsidering the notion (pp. 225–6 and 268–71) that the chansons in the Casanatense manuscript were copied for performance by shawms and sackbuts.[51]

Lockwood is also potentially misleading when he states (p. 314) that the musicians in the lists 'follow as closely as possible the order in which they are named in the primary archival sources', whereas in most cases he has usefully re-ordered them alphabetically. Many of the registers are confusingly assembled, and it would be a considerable (if eminently worthwhile) task to elucidate precisely what they mean; but occasionally even the most apparently confused register lets through hints as to the nature of the ensembles playing. For instance a list for 13 April 1474 shows the following order (I have added the payments, which seem to clarify the groupings; the names marked with an asterisk are not recorded by Lockwood for that year):[52]

---

[50] The same is the case with the list for 1504, Memoriale del Soldo 25, for which Lockwood gives a similar caption. And although I did not have the opportunity to check, I am inclined to think that it probably applies to all his lists with such captions from 1487 onwards. It would seem that Lockwood misread his own notes, an understandable lapse in a project lasting many years and involving enormous quantities of note-taking. The same appears to have happened with the salary list he discusses at considerable length on pp. 179–82 as Libri Camerali Diversi 114 (and again on p. 320); its correct number is 113.

[51] Howard Mayer Brown seems to have reached the same conclusion, see his *A Florentine Chansonnier from the Time of Lorenzo the Magnificent*, Monuments of Renaissance Music 7 (Chicago, 1983), text volume, p. 45, note 19.

[52] *MOs* Libri Camerali Diversi 103 (1474), fol. 25R.

*	a Jacomo da l'arpa musico	20.–
	a Zanpolo da la viola	8.–
	a Andrea da la viola	8.–
	a Rainaldo dal chitarino	8.–
*	a Cora[do] pifaro	12.–
*	a Ser arista bataino paidiero	6.–
	a Raganeilo tronbetto	12.–
*	a Guaspero tronbetto	10.–
	a Rizo tronbetto	10.–
*	a Luzido tronbetto	10.–
	a Daniele d'Acoli [tromb]	12.–
*	a Zilio de bruselo	12.–
	a Piero antonio di stasi	10.–
*	a Stefano de Savoia pifaro	15.–
	a Joannes de lamagna trombone	—

Particularly when account is taken of the sums paid, this suggests several different groups: four string players; Corado and his assistant; the four trumpeters; and thereafter it is less clear. Plainly Lockwood could not have presented this much detail from every entry he consulted; but all the same the information on this list of April 1474 suggests that there is room for considerably closer scrutiny of many of the documents.

Another matter obscured in the lists, though outlined correctly in chapter 15, concerns the use to which the chapel singers were put. The lists often include thirty singers or more, but they simply record every singer that Lockwood can find in a year's accounts. For instance, in the payment register for 1504 five of the men who are included in Lockwood's alphabetical listing appear separately at the beginning, under the heading 'capelani' and before the section devoted to 'cantori';[53] of the remaining twenty-nine on Lockwood's list there are generally about nineteen present at any one time, going down to twelve in June and up to twenty-four in December. This still falls short of painting a complete picture (though I suspect that patient work on just that question could well prove fruitful), but it gets us a little further.

Earlier, in 1472, there are some lists that appear to sort out the

[53] *MOs* Memoriale del Soldo 25 (1504). Although Lockwood correctly describes the situation on p. 156, his full list (p. 328) organises all the names alphabetically and adds the word 'capelano' to only one of the five.

picture more clearly. In certain respects this payment register seems totally inscrutable, as though each singer simply wandered along to the paymaster for some salary whenever he felt short of cash or had a few minutes to spare. But occasionally it betrays more information. The list for 20 April 1472 reads as follows:[54]

fra Joannes Birabis maestro da capella	5.12.-
don Andrea [de Mantova] tenorista	19. 8.7
don Domenico contrabasista	10. -.-
Jachettes contra alto	13.17.6
Jachetto chiavre soprano	13.17.6
Carlo soprano	13.17.6
Jachetto Nenporto soprano	11. 2.-
don Girolamo soprano	5.11.-
Piedro soprano	5.11.-

This may look strange, implying as it does four-voice polyphony with just one singer on each of the lower voices and five on the top line; but it happens to concord very closely with information from other choirs at the time, particularly the choir of San Pietro in Vaticano.[55]

Separately in the same register there is another group of singers:[56]

Don Joannes maestro di puti che canta	16.13.-
Ulderico tenorista	8. 6.6
Uno famiglio dei puti	2.15.6

Elsewhere this other group (presumably including the 'boys' who were accounted in some other way) appears adjacently with the earlier group. But it is surely true that in Ferrara, just as at Cambrai in the same years, the group with boys was kept for all normal purposes separate from the main polyphonic ensemble. And it is easy enough (not to say at first blush logical) to put this same interpretation on the passage from Sabadino degli Arienti that Lockwood quotes on pp. 157–8.

These reflections on the vocal ensembles at the court of Ferrara

---

[54] *MOs* Libri Camerali Diversi 96 (1472), fol. 23L; the same sequence of names, with generally the same monthly payments, appears also on fols. 15R, 53R and 64L.

[55] F. X. Haberl, 'Die römische "schola cantorum" und die päpstlichen Kapellsänger bis zur Mitte des 16. Jahrhunderts', in his *Bausteine für Musikgeschichte*, III (Leipzig, 1888), pp. 48–52.

[56] fol. 16R.

give some idea of how much still needs doing before we can answer many important musical questions. But then it is among the main virtues of Lockwood's book as well as of Strohm's that they open the mind and the ears. They do so in very different ways, of course. But they both bring the study of fifteenth-century music a considerable distance and thereby establish positions from which many more features begin to look different. The length of this review is intended partly as an indication that I value them both highly; and where it is severe that is because the books are both strong enough to withstand the kind of questioning and challenging under which so many books can disappear from sight. Whether either book entirely answers my archivist's doubts about city-based studies of fifteenth-century music it is difficult to say. But certainly neither book has closed its subject. Rather, each has opened it much wider. And nobody interested in the music of Bruges or Ferrara – let alone other documentary aspects of fifteenth-century music – should be deterred by *Faulx Dangier*.

David Fallows
University of Manchester

HOWARD MAYER BROWN, ed., *A Florentine Chansonnier from the Time of Lorenzo the Magnificent: Florence, Biblioteca Nazionale Centrale MS Banco Rari 229*, Monuments of Renaissance Music 7. 2 vols. Chicago and London, The University of Chicago Press, 1983. ix + 322 pp. xii + 645 pp.

This long-awaited work, which easily upholds the high standards of presentation and scholarship of the distinguished series in which it appears, makes available one of the largest, most musically interesting and visually opulent sources of late fifteenth-century secular music. As befits a subject of such complexity and richness, Brown's study has had a long gestation. Many parts of it were completed at least fifteen years ago and generously made available to scholars in the intervening years. When at last it appeared in published form, this engagingly written and beautifully engraved two-volume opus received the American Musicological Society's Kinkeldey Award as the outstanding book-length study of 1983. Brown's prodigious accomplishment in exploring the manuscript's early history, editing with care its 268 compositions, providing analytical overviews as well as individual examinations of works, and, indeed, pursuing virtually every useful avenue of inquiry, sets a standard that will be difficult for future manuscript studies to emulate. And although, as will soon become obvious, this reviewer will raise questions about certain aspects of Brown's commentary and presentation of the repertory, the achievement that this publication represents cannot be emphasised too strongly.

The visual sumptuousness and musical variety of Florence 229[1] had already attracted scholarly attention decades ago; hence such important aspects of its history as the identification of the illuminators of the manuscript as the brothers Gherardo and Monti Di Giovanni of Florence, and the association of the shield on fol. iv^v with the Braccesi family, also of Florence, have been known for some time. Brown's re-examination and consolidation of the previous work has enabled him to draw existing lines of inquiry still tighter and to progress far beyond them. His investigation of paper, gathering structure and readings has strengthened the Florentine connections. And perhaps most significantly for determining the origin of the manuscript, he has been able to link the shield with a specific member of the Braccesi family, Alessandro, who was 'notary, humanist, poet, secretary of the Chancery of the Florentine Republic, and ambassador during some of the city's most difficult years' (p. 32, col. 1).[2] As one intriguing consequence of this identification, Brown proposes convincingly that the portrait in the upper left-hand quadrant of fol. 1 depicts not the composer Johannes Martini, as was generally believed until now, but the manuscript's owner. Even more important, the association with Alessandro provides the manuscript with a *terminus ante quem*: his shield bears a mark of cadency indicating that he carried these arms only until his father's death, which evidently occurred by January 1493 (p. 25, col. 1). The connection with Alessandro, however, raises what Brown sees as one of two major anomalies about the manuscript. According

---

[1] Manuscript citations follow the convention used by Brown: Florence 176 = Florence, Biblioteca Nazionale Centrale, MS Magl. xix 176; Florence 178 = Florence, Biblioteca Nazionale Centrale, MS Magl. xix 178; Florence 2356 = Florence, Biblioteca Riccardiana, MS 2356; Paris 15123 = Paris, Bibliothèque Nationale, MS fonds français 15123; Rome xiii.27 = Rome, Biblioteca Apostolica Vaticana, C.G.xiii.27; Rome 2856 = Rome, Biblioteca Casanatense, MS 2856.

[2] References to Brown, *A Florentine Chansonnier* – all, unless otherwise noted, to the text volume – appear within parentheses in the main text.

to him, Florence 229 is 'more fit for a king than a commoner' and would almost certainly have been beyond the means of even the most successful civil servant (p. 42, col. 1). He views it as highly improbable, therefore, either that Alessandro himself could have commissioned such a sumptuous book or that some other patron would have had it made in Alessandro's honour. The second of the anomalies that Brown observes derives from the manuscript's opening repertorial gambit, which he characterises as a contest: nineteen pieces alternating regularly between Martini and Heinrich Isaac. Isaac's well-known ties with Florence and the Medici from the mid-1480s make his prominence here unsurprising. Martini's presence in this context, however, appears more puzzling. In the employ of the Este from 1473 until his death in the late 1490s (with a one-year hiatus in 1474), Martini left Ferrara only infrequently, and no surviving evidence connects him with Florence.

The attempt to reconcile these apparent anomalies has led Brown to the ingenious hypothesis that the book was commissioned by King Matthias Corvinus of Hungary, brother-in-law of the Duke and Duchess of Ferrara, Ercole I d'Este and Eleanor of Aragon. Brown argues that Matthias and his queen, Beatrice of Aragon – Eleanor's sister – would have had a particular regard for Martini and his music because of their relationship to the Ferrarese duke. Further, the king himself was a prodigious book collector who ordered extensively from Florentine workshops, including that of the brothers Di Giovanni. At the time of his death, more than 150 of his unfilled orders for manuscripts sat in Florence. In Brown's view, Florence 229 – in which the illumination breaks off after fol. 180 – would most probably have been one of these; and Lorenzo de' Medici, who in fact purchased many of Matthias's commissioned volumes, would have bought it and subsequently given it to Braccesi, perhaps in honour of the latter's appointment as ambassador to Siena.[3]

As Brown himself concedes, this hypothesis has no hard evidence to support it; and while it may well supply explanations for part of the anomalous picture that he draws, it by no means resolves all of it compellingly. One point concerns the Martini connection. Brown notes that the composer visited Buda in 1487, and that in 1489 Matthias's wife wrote to her brother-in-law requesting Martini's

[3] On the approximate but uncertain date of the appointment, see pp. 32, 41 and 44, including n. 16.

help in securing the services of Paul Hofhaimer for her chapel. Brown sees the assumption of a musical tie between Martini and Beatrice further strengthened by what he regards as the probability that she and her sister and brother-in-law would all have had similar musical tastes as a consequence of their shared childhood in Naples. Finally, Brown observes that Florence 229 and the Ferrarese manuscript Rome 2856 resemble each other closely in their cast of composers and in specific works transmitted, a kinship that seems to give the repertory of Florence 229 a Ferrarese stamp, apparently attributable to the musical tastes of the Hungarian queen.

None of these considerations, however, nor even all of them taken together, serves to turn Martini into the favourite composer of the Buda court. The first two, although concrete, are modest, the third is tenuous, and the fourth is underdeveloped: concordances alone – whether of individual compositions or musicians represented or both – do not suffice to determine a repertory's nature unless they are reinforced by relationships in readings and unless it can be demonstrated that the repertory is singularly characteristic of a particular tradition. On this last point, a superficial comparison of the contents of Florence 229 and Rome 2856 reveals that although Martini's dominant presence in both could appear suggestive of a relationship between the two manuscripts – the other composers are accountable as more international figures – the readings of his works common to both sources provide less certain support for this assumption.[4] And other concordant pieces – Agricola's *Dictes moy toutes* (no. 113) and Busnois's *Seule à par moy* (no. 60) provide two striking examples – show unequivocally significant variant readings, indicating that the two manuscripts drew them from different traditions. If there were a more solid basis for assigning Florence 229 to Matthias in the first place, there would be some reason for adducing these factors as possible explanations for his evident knowledge of and preference for

---

[4] Atlas finds that a comparison of the readings of the Martini pieces common to both manuscripts 'turns up a negligible number of variants (except in the widely disseminated "La Martinella")' (see A. Atlas, review of Howard Mayer Brown, ed., *A Florentine Chansonnier from the Time of Lorenzo the Magnificent*, *Journal of the American Musicological Society*, 37 (1985), pp. 153–61, esp. p. 159). Still, the unquestionably significant variants in the readings of the popular *La Martinella*, no. 45, the disjunction between the readings of the opening of *Des biens d'amours* in the two sources (noted by Brown, music volume, p. 41, n. 2), and the lack of correspondence in title between the manuscripts for nos. 5, 7 and, again, 45 (in each case from a garbled French title in Rome 2856 to an Italian one in Florence 229: *Je remerchi Dieu* to *Se mai il [el] cielo e fati fur benigni*, *Per faire tousjours* to *O di prudenza fonte*, and *Vive vive* to *La Martinella*) all seem at least potentially important.

Martini's music. Without that initial basis, however, the rest of the interpretation comes perilously close to circular reasoning.

Most important, the hypothesis founders on considerations dealt with only in passing. Despite the high relief into which the opening 'contest' sets Martini and Isaac, neither of them is, in fact, the best-represented composer. This honour – with the inevitable caution occasioned by pieces with conflicting attributions – seems to go to Alexander Agricola. Agricola, Brown observes, 'might be said to represent Florence's interests in the chansonnier' (p. 47, col. 2). But while the composer is known to have been in Florence in 1474 and was married to a Florentine woman, there are no further traces of him there until September 1491, when he began a tenure as singer that lasted to the end of April 1492. According to Brown's hypothesis, this major period of Agricola's activity in Florence would not have occurred until a year and a half after the proposed terminal date for Florence 229. In principle, of course, the Florentine penchant for Agricola's music need not have been stimulated by his direct presence there; but when one places Florence 229 in the context of the manuscript tradition to which it belongs, that possibility looks unpromising.[5]

The late fifteenth-century Florentine manuscripts of secular music divide into two generations. The earlier of these consists of Florence 176 (*c.* 1475–80), Florence 2356 (*c.* 1485), and Paris 15123 (*c.* 1485); the later consists of Florence 229, Rome XIII.27, and Florence 178. Of these last three, Florence 229, which maintains strong links of repertory and decoration with Paris 15123, is clearly the earliest, and Florence 178, which alone among these books adopts the oblong format that was to become standard for all Florentine secular manuscripts afterwards, presumably the latest; a chronological anchor for all three manuscripts is provided by the middle one, Rome XIII.27, which Atlas has shown to have a *terminus post quem* of April 1492.[6] In the earlier group of manuscripts Agricola is represented by a mere three pieces, all found in Florence 2356, with one of these making a further appearance in Paris 15123. All

---

[5] The following discussion essentially depends upon and elaborates that of J. Rifkin, 'Pietrequin Bonnel and Ms. 2794 of the Biblioteca Riccardiana', *Journal of the American Musicological Society*, 29 (1976), pp. 284–96, esp. p. 289, n. 13.

[6] On the date of this manuscript and the other Florentine sources, see A. Atlas, *The Cappella Giulia Chansonnier (Rome, Biblioteca Apostolica Vaticana, C.G.XIII.27)*, Musicological Studies 27, 2 vols. (Brooklyn, N.Y., 1975–6), I, pp. 246–8, 254–6.

three of the later manuscripts, however – Rome XIII.27 and Florence 178 no less than Florence 229 – accord him a position of overwhelming prominence. Particularly since it is certain that Rome XIII.27 and Florence 178 postdate his arrival at Florence in September 1491, it appears difficult to account for this dramatic increase in Agricola's representation by anything other than his presence on the scene.[7]

At least one other aspect of the repertory argues against a *terminus ante quem* of April 1490: the presence of Pietrequin Bonnel's *Adieu Florens la yolye* (no. 146).[8] Since Pietrequin worked as a singer in Florence between March 1490 and March 1493, there is a considerable temptation to read autobiographical significance into the composition. To be sure, this temptation is kept somewhat in check by the possibility, noted by Brown, that the piece may in fact be a setting of a popular melody. Yet whether the work commemorates one of the composer's own leave-takings from Florence or simply represents a setting of a tune that caught Pietrequin's imagination, the title alone makes it highly improbable that he would have written the composition before he first came to Florence,[9] and other features of the music lend support to this assumption. Unlike the rest of his output, which falls squarely within the genre of the three-voice rondeau commonly practised in the north, *Adieu Florens* appears to be Italian in its affiliations. Apart from two very late German sources, its sole transmission is Florentine. Moreover, its very style – predominantly homophonic writing organised in short, clearly demarcated phrases – is not found in pieces dating from this time that one can securely associate with France, whereas analogous pieces show up among the compositions of Franco-Netherlandish composers working in Italy.

If these aspects of the repertory thus seem to point to a somewhat

---

[7] One might contrast this situation with that of Busnois, who closely approaches Agricola in representation in Florence 229. Busnois is not known to have visited Florence, but his prominence is no novelty in the local repertory. In the most immediate predecessor to Florence 229 among the local manuscripts, Paris 15123, he far outpaces any other composer with at least twenty-three compositions, the second most represented composer with but fourteen.

[8] Caution may be necessary in considering the relationship of this piece to the date of the manuscript in that *Adieu Florens* straddles a gathering (fols. 150ᵛ–151) and could have been copied after the surrounding music. There is, however, no evidence that its entry into the manuscript is later by any measurable gap: the decoration of these pages appears to be the same as that surrounding them, and the script shows no notable distinctions.

[9] That Florence 229 is the earliest source for the composition is at the least congruent with this supposition.

later date, so, at least potentially, does a physical aspect. Brown notes that the main paper in Florence 229 carries an eagle water-mark belonging to a family represented in Briquet as numbers 81–91. He does not, however, mention that a watermark of at least very similar design appears in Rome xiii.27 and Florence 178. Indeed, Atlas indicates that the latter two manuscripts 'bear the identical watermark' and that Florence 229 has 'precisely the same crowned-eagle watermark' that they have.[10] Since Atlas's work predates the currency of truly exacting techniques of paper composition in musicological research, some doubt may still attach to the absolute identity of these watermarks. Nevertheless, the likelihood that the paper thus tightens the chronological relationship between Florence 229 and the other two sources cannot lightly be dispensed with.

In sum, then, the chronological evidence provided by the manu-script itself points to a date whose *terminus post quem* lies after April 1490, the death date of Matthias Corvinus. Indeed, taking together the *terminus post quem* of late 1491 suggested by the repertory and the *terminus ante quem* of January 1493 derived from Brown's heraldic researches, it would seem that one could place virtually the entire manuscript in the year 1492. This dating, however, if it effectively removes Matthias Corvinus from the picture, does not bring us closer to a resolution of the anomalies initially posited by Brown. But are they in fact so anomalous?

Let us consider first Braccesi. His ownership of Florence 229 might remain a puzzle even if we were to take Brown's 'more fit for a king than a commoner' to some extent metaphorically and read 'king' to include such powerful commoners as the book-commission-ing and -collecting Medici. Still, Brown himself draws attention to substantial indications that Alessandro was not quite the modest bourgeois the hypothesis would lead us to expect. He was sufficiently renowned for his portrait to be included in the Uffizi Gallery in the late seventeenth century as one of a series of famous Florentines decorating the west corridor; he was prominent as poet, translator and general man of letters; and, as far as can be determined on the basis of circumstantial evidence, he seems to have had some interest in music – he is the poet of four *canti carnascialeschi*, one of which survives in a musical setting, and all of which, according to Brown,

---

[10] Atlas, *Cappella Giulia*, i, pp. 247–8.

were intended for music. Moreover, while it is certainly the case that many of the most beautiful and sumptuous fifteenth-century manuscripts first belonged to or were commissioned by members of the secular or ecclesiastical aristocracy, others were owned by such civil servants as the secretary to King Ferrante of Naples, and still others by members of families of no higher social rank than the Braccesi.[11] We might also note that the provenance of many lavishly decorated manuscripts bearing coats of arms remains unknown; as the heraldry of the upper nobility is for the most part identifiable, it perhaps does not go too far to suggest that the upper bourgeoisie may account for the ownership of a good share of these volumes.

The problem of Martini, admittedly, remains more refractory. One may even reinforce the case for his anomalousness by the observation that the prominence accorded him in Florence 229 is not reflected in other Florentine sources. Even so, Atlas has already pointed out that there may well have been more connections between Martini and the city of Florence than existing records reveal; and even more crucially, there are good reasons for associating Martini with Isaac.[12] Indeed, seen in a broader context, these connections go beyond the specific relationships of compositions that Atlas notes: Isaac and Martini are the leading masters of the developing polyphonic instrumental music of the time, and it seems appropriate for Florence 229, one of the major sources of the new genre, to open with a series of their works in alternation.

The second part of the commentary deals with the repertory of Florence 229. For the works of known composers as well as those of unknown authorship – the comparative treatment of the anonymi is particularly unusual and welcome – Brown provides detailed discus-

---

[11] See, for example, the descriptions in J. J. G. Alexander and A. C. De La Mare, *The Italian Manuscripts in the Library of Major J. R. Abbey* (New York and Washington, 1969) of MS 13. J. A. 5989 (pp. 44–5 and Plate xvii), prepared in Florence in 1466 for Antonello Petrucci of Aversa, secretary to King Ferrante; MS 14. J. A. 3188 (pp. 46–7 and Plate xviii), written in Florence c. 1460–70, a book originally belonging to Francesco Manno, a member of a family distinguished in Florentine government; and MS 23. J. A. 3236 (pp. 65–6 and Plates xxviiib and xxix), copied in Florence and illuminated by Attavante degli Attavanti c. 1485–1500, for a member of the Pazzi family. Moreover, Brussels, Bibliothèque Royale, MS iv. 922 – a decorated Mass and motet manuscript – was copied in Brussels or Mechlin c. 1526–34 for Pompejus Occo of Amsterdam, a merchant and representative of the Fugger banking firm (cf. H. Kellman and C. Hamm, ed., *Census-Catalogue of Manuscript Sources of Polyphonic Music, 1400–1550*, Renaissance Manuscript Studies 1/1, Neuhausen-Stuttgart, 1979, p. 98).

[12] Atlas, review of *A Florentine Chansonnier*, pp. 158–9.

sions of such elements as formal structure, imitative procedures and melodic style; his insightful handling of these aspects points the way to needed modifications of the more usual, and more limited, analytic approaches. Yet for all their manifest quality, these discussions fall short of achieving one goal for which we might particularly have hoped in a study of a source as complex and multi-faceted as this one, the clarification of the various interweaving strands – generic and geographic – out of which that very complexity emerges. Paradoxically this limitation seems to derive less from the absence of a coherent overview than from the reliance on one.

This viewpoint emerges most essentially in the chapter dealing with the four best-represented composers in the collection – 'Chansons by Busnois, Agricola, Martini, and Isaac' (Chapter x) – which also sets up the points of reference for discussions in subsequent chapters of less well-represented composers and anonymous works. An inferential summary follows. Antoine Busnois, the oldest of the composers, typifies the perfect model of the *forme-fixe*, or so-called Burgundian, chanson. Agricola's chansons resemble Busnois's formally – predominantly rondeaux, the works of the two composers also account for most of the bergerettes in the manuscript – but differ from them in other respects, including their more systematic and more complex use of imitation and their less balanced phraseology. The compositions by Martini distinguish themselves from those of the previously mentioned composers in their lack of formal clarity and absence of clear phrase structure – he 'did not shape the four or five phrases of his rondeaux into a single unit as clearly as Busnois and Agricola' (p. 90, col. 1) – in their preoccupation with contrapuntal manipulation and combination, and in their even more pervasive and structurally crucial use of imitation. Isaac, although unquestionably closer in style to Martini than to Busnois or Agricola, essentially stands alone. The youngest of the four, he wrote

the most modern music, in which the incipient style change from Burgundian chansons $a3$ to structurally imitative chansons $a4$ is most clearly evident. Thus his music stands at the other extreme of a stylistic continuum from that by Busnois. Even the kinds of compositions he wrote demonstrate his differences from the other three composers: in his music the hegemony of the rondeau is finally broken (p. 95, col. 1).

Brown's underlying assumption – developed through his consideration of such aspects as individual use of formal prototypes, phrase

structure, and imitative and motivic procedures in all four composers but revealed explicitly only in the discussion of Isaac – thus
appears to be that of the decline of the *forme-fixe* chanson.

Granted that this overall developmental scheme has a certain
justification if one takes the historical long view – the *forme-fixe*
chanson did stop being composed, and other sorts of pieces did
become more prominent – it leads Brown to define the chanson in
somewhat broad terms, and in so doing to place along a single
evolutionary line musical events that may more profitably be seen as
belonging on different planes. In particular, the resulting teleologi-
cal picture of secular production in the late fifteenth century
measures composers according to a standard of conservativeness
and progressiveness that seems to block the perception of the
differences in production between Franco-Netherlandish composers
working in their native northern territory and those employed in
Italy.

The evaluation of Isaac is a case in point. It is far from certain that
the 'hegemony of the rondeau' ever applied to Italy, or indeed that
composers there ever cultivated the *forme-fixe* chanson at all: there is
scarcely a single piece of music known to have been written in Italy
in the late fifteenth century that can be positively identified as a
setting of a French poem, intended for vocal performance. The
rondeau did nonetheless have a major impact on secular production
in Italy, serving as a resource for a new and uniquely Italian
phenomenon of instrumental composition, either acting as a structural model for freely conceived works, or providing one or two
voices from an existing vocal piece to serve as the scaffolding around
which the rest of a composition was constructed.[13] Most, if not all, of
Isaac's compositions fall within such categories of instrumental
composition. Yet far from constituting a link in a tight evolutionary
chain, this Italian instrumental tradition – for all its internal
richness – seems to represent something of a dead end. On the other
hand, the *forme-fixe* chanson continued to predominate, and to
evolve, in the north, well beyond the time covered by the part of
Isaac's career that Brown is discussing here.[14] The rondeau did

[13] L. Litterick, 'Performing Franco-Netherlandish Secular Music of the Late 15th Century:
     Texted and Untexted Parts in the Sources', *Early Music*, 8 (1980), pp. 474–85.
[14] As Brown himself was one of the first to point out; see H. M. Brown, 'Critical Years in
     European Musical History: 1500–1530', *Report of the Tenth Congress of the International
     Musicological Society: Ljubljana 1967* (Kassel, Basel, Paris and London, 1970), pp. 78–94.

indeed eventually die out there; but especially in view of the almost total absence in French sources of any music by Isaac, it would be risky to assume that he had anything to do with its demise.

The implications of Isaac's involvement in the decline of the *forme-fixe*, or Burgundian, chanson notwithstanding, the discussion of his music for the most part still recognises its fundamentally instrumental character. The discussion of Martini, however – as our earlier summary indicated – treats his music as essentially vocal: although Brown admits to some uncertainties of classification, his breakdown of Martini's works in Florence 229 categorises fourteen pieces as rondeaux and three others as disparate sorts of vocal pieces, only two as instrumental works, and two as unidentified. The main category, rondeaux, is subdivided into two 'with text' and twelve 'without text'. This extreme disproportion alone between allegedly texted and untexted pieces may raise some question about the categorisation of these pieces as rondeaux in the first place, particularly in the light of the remarks (already quoted) on the problem of correlating Martini's phrase structure with that typically implied by rondeau poetry; doubt increases with the realisation that even the compositions 'with text' do not actually survive anywhere in texted form. One of them, in fact, cannot be associated with any text of any kind. That piece, *Des biens d'amours* (no. 19), appears in a dozen sources. As already implied, not one provides any French text beyond its title or incipit. While Brown remains firm in his conviction that the piece is a rondeau *cinquain*, his own admirably thorough search through poetic sources has yielded only one poem that 'resembles Martini's incipit' (p. 67, n. 47). Yet even this poem, it turns out, has obstacles to having served as a basis for Martini's composition, and this piece 'with text' is printed after all without any. Whatever Brown's belief about the validity of the combined evidence of texting practices in music sources and composers' biographies for determining instrumental repertories and typologies, it is puzzling that in the face of the difficulty in finding a suitable text, and for that matter in reconciling the six phrases of Martini's music with any poetic rondeau *cinquain* at all, his conviction about the essentially vocal nature of the composition remains unswerving.

Somewhat different considerations apply to *J'ay pris amours* (no. 179), the other of the 'rondeaux with text'. This composition belongs to the second of the categories identified above as Italian instrumental music: it takes the superius and tenor of a well-known anonymous rondeau and fits beneath them a unison canon at the minim. There is no questioning that the original rondeau itself is a vocal composition: it conforms perfectly to the norms of the type and survives, with text, in many northern manuscripts of the time. But while *it* has text, one cannot be at all certain that its poem should be carried over to Martini's setting.

The disagreement of approach exemplified by the treatment of these pieces relates, clearly, to one of the major issues to be confronted in any discussion of the secular repertory of the late fifteenth century: the distinguishing of vocal from instrumental. The question concerns not the demonstrably genuine, and easily recognised, *forme-fixe* production extant in French manuscripts and written by composers employed in French-speaking regions but the music of Franco-Netherlandish composers who worked in Italy itself (referred to above) and whose compositions cannot be so readily fitted, if at all, into the *forme-fixe* mould. Brown's adoption of the traditional bias towards vocal interpretation for these pieces (which survive in Italian sources with French titles that irresistibly resemble the opening hemistich of a rondeau or bergerette poem) and his reliance on close analysis of each composition as the only means of distinguishing between music written for voices and that written for instruments have serious consequences for our understanding of these individual works and, most important, for our comprehension of the whole period.

The edition of the music itself is, as one would expect, meticulously prepared, and handsome. The provision of footnotes for important variants provides a handy and unobtrusive method for enabling scholars and performers to compare interesting divergences in the transmission. One might, nonetheless, regret the lack of a complete listing of variants or, failing that, a more extensive discussion of the relationships between the sources, something more akin to what Atlas did in connection with Rome XIII.27 or Lowinsky in his edition of the Medici Codex in this very series.[15] As already indicated, for instance, Brown's own suggestion of a relationship between Florence 229 and Rome 2856 highlights the need for such

---

[15] See Atlas, *Cappella Giulia*, and E. E. Lowinsky, ed., *The Medici Codex of 1518, a Choirbook of Motets Dedicated to Lorenzo de' Medici, Duke of Urbino*, 3 vols., Monuments of Renaissance Music 3–5 (Chicago and London, 1968).

material. A short chapter entitled 'Related Sources and Variant Readings' (Chapter XIII, pp. 143–9) gives a brief overview of concordant sources and presents the reasoning behind the editorial policy regarding variants, but it deals with the specific dissemination of only a few compositions; any scholar wishing to know the full picture will have to go back to the sources.

Although the actual manuscript, typically for a source of its place and period, provides text for hardly any of its contents, the transcriptions supply text for all compositions that appear with it in other music sources as well as for pieces that appear nowhere in texted form but for which Brown has identified what he regards as the words belonging to the music. The provision of text in this first instance represents an extremely useful convenience. One might wonder, however, at the particular choice of voices so provided: in three-voice compositions, mostly genuine *formes-fixes* chansons, words are typically underlaid to both superius and tenor. While this procedure in fact reflects the compositional structure of many of the pieces, it finds little support in contemporary sources, which text either the superius alone or all three voices but only most infrequently – after 1480 only one source at all – superius and tenor.

The second category of textual addition comprises a variety of genres: compositions either freely based on or incorporating actual voice parts from previously existing vocal compositions;[16] works possibly or probably based on popular melodies that themselves survive with text;[17] and compositions not based on pre-existent musical material for which Brown has located poems beginning with the same words as their titles or incipits. Here the question is less how many voices should have been texted than whether text should be added at all. It is, to be sure, relatively easy to find words to attach to most of the compositions in the first two sub-categories; but pieces of these sorts typically survive without text and seem to have been intended in the main for instrumental performance.[18] To some

---

[16] See, for example, Isaac's *Helas que devera mon cuer* (no. 6), which takes as its point of departure Caron's rondeau *Helas que poura devenir* (no. 206), and De Planquard's setting of the superius and tenor of Hayne van Ghizeghem's *De tous biens plaine* (no. 178) or Martini's setting, referred to above, of the superius of the anonymous *J'ay pris amours* (no. 179).

[17] See, for example, the severally attributed *J'ay bien nori* (no. 46).

[18] Florence 229 is unique in providing what could, at first glance, be interpreted as evidence supporting the practice of texting such pieces. Three of the arrangements based on voices from *formes-fixes* chansons – two settings of the superius of *J'ay pris amours*, by Isaac (no. 8)

extent this question takes care of itself in connection with the third sub-category: most of the compositions of known authorship that one might wish to include are by composers working in Italy, few in their musical characteristics match the stylistic profile of the northern chanson, and, as our discussion of Martini has already intimated, for only the barest handful can even potential texts be located. Given the Italian predilection for removing text from northern *formes-fixes* chansons, however, there can be little doubt that a number of works of unclear parentage lying textless in Italian sources will in fact have had vocal origins. And, indeed, Brown's efforts have led to the valuable identification of two previously unrecognised and almost certainly authentic rondeaux: *Puis qu'elle est morte* (no. 31) and *Ma perfayte joye* (no. 83), both anonymous.[19] The addition of text in such instances not only reconstructs the presumable original versions of the works, but also helps the reader make stylistic, and generic, distinctions. Even though Brown remarks that 'the presence or absence of text should in no case be taken as a firm commitment about the possibility or advisability of instrumental substitution or doubling' (music volume, p. xi, col. 2) – the very wording discouraging interpretation of pieces as fundamentally instrumental in nature – his suggestions will surely be treated less unreverentially in practice than his disclaimer might imply.

As indicated at the outset, Florence 229 is a source of virtually encyclopaedic scope within its domain, and it demands a similarly encyclopaedic achievement from its editor. In focusing on a few specific issues, this review does not mean to obscure the extent to which Brown has in fact met that requirement. Users of this edition and commentary will find extensive stimulating material that we

and Jannes Japart (no. 152), and one anonymous setting of the superius and tenor of Hayne van Ghizeghem's *De tous biens plaine* (no. 177) – carry in the superius (or what appears to be the superius) the refrain of the poem from the original vocal setting. In at least one of these instances, however, Brown himself recognises that the text had no function for performance and served at best as nothing more than an aid to identification: in writing about Japart's *J'ay pris amours*, he notes that the borrowed voice is 'in fact to be transposed down a twelfth and played in retrograde motion, functioning as the bassus' (p. 269, col. 2; see also music volume, p. 327, n. 1), and that 'since it is not likely that the words would have been sung backwards with the *cantus prius factus*, they have not been added to the music' (music volume, p. 327, n. 1). Moreover, he characterises one of the remaining two compositions, Isaac's *J'ay pris amours*, as 'probably an instrumental arrangement' (p. 210, col. 1).

19 Brown suggests that *Puis qu'elle est morte* is 'by a composer whose style resembles that of Agricola' (p. 218, col. 1) and *Ma perfayte joye* 'by a composer whose style resembles that of Busnois' (p. 246, col. 2).

have barely touched on here – it is a measure of Brown's accomplishment that he has provided far more than any single review could reasonably hope to deal with. Despite the qualifications that we have expressed, there is no doubt Brown has provided a vast fund of information and made available a significant body of music that together cannot help but foster and greatly facilitate future studies of late fifteenth-century secular music and its sources.

Louise Litterick
Mount Holyoke College

R. M. LUMIANSKY and DAVID MILLS, *The Chester Mystery Cycle: Essays and Documents* with an essay 'Music in the Cycle' by Richard Rastall. Chapel Hill, University of North Carolina Press, 1983. viii + 339 pp.

The study of the vernacular drama in late medieval England is in a new and productive phase. The pioneering editions of the Early English Text Society date from the turn of the century; and the 1885 Oxford Press publication of the York Plays (ed. Lucy Toulmin Smith) was replaced only in 1982 by Richard Beadle. Amongst the new editions of the plays is the EETS edition of the Chester Mystery Cycle prepared by R. M. Lumiansky and David Mills (vol. I, 1974). The work involved in that enterprise has provided the material for the richly packed volume under review. It consists of four essays: the first deals with the unusually complex manuscript presentation of the cycle (the only complete texts date from the years 1591–1607); the second reviews 'sources and influences' and also the 'wider issue of the evocation of authorities within the cycle'; the fourth presents new suggestions 'about the development of the cycle from the earliest to the final performances' and is followed by over a hundred pages of documents relating to the plays (charters, expense-list, the Banns etc.).

It is the third essay, contributed by Richard Rastall, which is the subject of the present review, 'Music in the Cycle'. It is not the first study of the music of the Chester plays but it is the most detailed, comprehensive and satisfying. The chapter opens with a generous account of previous scholarship[1] and, further, stresses the import-

---

[1] N. C. Carpenter: 'Music in the Chester Plays', *Papers on English Language and Literature*, 1

ance of the Toronto Records of Early English Drama (REED) in assembling a mass of previously inaccessible information. This information, fascinating and valuable in itself (the York material was the first to be published), has not yet succeeded, however, in substantially altering our view of music in the plays which continues to rest almost entirely on the evidence of the play-texts themselves.

The manuscripts of the Chester cycle are unusual in two respects: there are eight of them and, except for a couple from about 1500 or perhaps earlier which transmit only one play and one fragment of a play between them out of a total of twenty-four, they are very late in date (1591–1607). This means that the evidence of the manuscripts for a Chester drama as evidently 'medieval' in conception as the other great cycles has to be treated with extreme wariness. The editors are certainly right to stress the labile nature of the play-text – there was no fixed cycle-form; and the later revisers were subject to all kinds of religious pressures as old traditions came into conflict with new orthodoxies. The playwrights are concerned to proclaim that their text 'can be defended for its biblical fidelity [a very Protestant emphasis] and general doctrinal soundness'. The problem is not, of course, purely a textual one; it carries over into the style of performance perhaps, and certainly into the interpretation of the musical evidence. Lumiansky and Mills do give some consideration of the general efforts made by the city council to 'offset Protestant antagonism' (which culminated in a condemnatory utterance of 1609 that the plays were 'the abomination of desolation ... [defiling] the sacred scriptures of God') but I should myself have liked to see the problem even more probingly pursued into the text itself.

The first main section of Richard Rastall's essay deals with the functions of music, both representational and structural. In relation to the first he makes a good point when he stresses the music of praise, alongside the music of symbolic order, and suggests most plausibly that the reason God does not sing is that 'the Creator does not praise himself'. But the arguments for denying Herod a salute of trumpets (p. 118) are perhaps over-subtle. As in Shakespeare, the dramatic context tells us how to interpret what we hear. Herod's pomp *is* 'showy and second-rate'; the point does not need a change of

(1965), pp. 195–216; J. Stevens: 'Music in Medieval Drama', *Proceedings of the Royal Musical Association*, 84 (1958), pp. 81–95; and J. Dutka: *Music in the English Mystery Plays* (Kalamazoo, 1980).

instruments to prove it. In the interesting discussion of structural functions (related to Dutka's), there seems to be an underlying assumption, which I find hard to accept, that all dramatic occurrences of music (and there is no music which is not dramatic in the sense of arising from the action 'on-stage') are structural in the proper sense. But characters would move about the 'place' or pageant, would enter and 'exit', and so on, whether music accompanied them or not. In such instances the music is complementary – an accident rather than the essence of form. Even the telescoped passage of time and instantaneous change of location are totally acceptable according to the well-worn conventions of medieval drama and continued to be so in Elizabethan plays. That the music 'marked', i.e. drew extra attention, to some of these moments or happenings is not, of course, in dispute. But the process could be likened to a writer's underlining of a word for emphasis – the underlining itself does not convey the meaning. In this respect the Anglo-Norman *Play of Adam* makes an instructive contrast; there the sung responsories are more genuinely structural, they control the shape of the play.

The next forty pages form the heart of the essay – and a very sound heart it is. 'The Evidence for Music' is considered in the play-text itself, in the Late Banns ('beinge the breeife of the whole playes'), in the guild accounts. Of these sources the most explicit is the play-text: twenty-two out of twenty-five 'vocal' stage-directions name the items; a further eight stage-directions call for instrumental music, unspecified. In addition, a number of marginal directions, having the status perhaps of producer's notes, amplify the information in the directions. This may not seem a great haul from a cycle whose performance typically was spread over three days, but the information gleaned is abundant by comparison with other cycles. Rastall discusses this evidence in detail, and although not everyone will agree with all his conclusions it is very good to have, at last, an up-to-date informed discussion of the issues.

One of the most useful aids to study is the Cue-List, in which all the musical items, including those 'conjectured on the evidence of guild accounts' are given, play by play. This is followed by a valuable discussion some twenty pages long which forms the most original part of Rastall's contribution. The vocal liturgical items are identified with references to their use in the Sarum rite. When a brief incipit in the text makes identification uncertain, all the possibilities are canvassed and an adjudication is made between them on grounds of the suitability of the text, the type of chant (melismatic, neumatic, syllabic), voice-range and dramatic context. There are some interesting puzzles: 'Haec est ara dei caeli', an untraced piece sung by an angel after Christ's birth in the play of the Nativity, is glossed, 'fiat nota secundum arbitrium agentis' (let the music be according to the judgement of the performer). Rastall's suggestion that 'music must be found or composed for this text' seems sensible; improvisation is most unlikely.

Unfortunately only one piece of notated music survives for the whole cycle – the 'Gloria in excelsis' from play 7 (The Adoration of the Shepherds); half the text is given and set. The music is mensurally notated and forms a well-balanced four-measure phrase beginning and ending on the tonic *d*. Rastall argues that it is not related to a chant but is excerpted from a polyphonic setting. Given its shapely self-containedness, I am less convinced than he is that the melody could not have been sung monophonically as it stands and without accompaniment.

However this may be, the existence of this patently un-medieval snatch of melody brings it home how much the musical as well as other aspects of the plays may have varied over the hundred to a hundred and fifty years that they were performed. Rastall is aware of the problem both as one affecting the choice of plainchant or polyphony (p. 155) and in its Catholic/Protestant form (pp. 156 ff: 'Save me, O God', which he thinks probably refers to a metrical psalm version (Ps. 69)). There are assuredly many questions about the music of the Chester cycle which are likely never to be answered. But this thorough, thoughtful and lucid essay marks a genuine advance in understanding.

John Stevens
Magdalene College

Violin Technique and Performance Practice in the Late Eighteenth and Early Nineteenth Centuries

ROBIN STOWELL

The first book to examine in detail the numerous violin treatises of the late eighteenth and early nineteenth centuries, providing a scholarly historical and technical guide to violin pedagogical method, technique and performance practice during the most critical period in the history of the instrument. Topics discussed in detail include the development of the violin and bow, posture, tone production, double and multiple stopping, vibrato, harmonics, scordatura, pitch, tuning, intonation, expression, phrasing and ornamentation.

428 pp.   0 521 23279 1   £45.00 net
Cambridge Musical Texts and Monographs

■ **Cambridge University Press**
—— The Edinburgh Building, Shaftesbury Road,
Cambridge CB2 2RU.